PENGUIN BOOKS
RED SUN

Sudeep Chakravarti attended Mayo College, Ajmer and St. Stephen's College, Delhi. He began his career in journalism at the *Asian Wall Street Journal*, and subsequently worked at *Sunday*, *India Today* and the *Hindustan Times*. Sudeep is also a professional futurist affiliated to the World Future Society. His debut book, *Tin Fish* (Penguin), was published in 2005 to both popular and critical acclaim. His second novel, *Once Upon a Time in Aparanta* (also by Penguin), was published in 2008.

PRAISE FOR THE BOOK

'*Red Sun* is the sombre story of India at war with itself. It describes in vivid detail the explosive situation in vast swathes of rural India, where the Maoists and the state are locked in violent confrontation.'—*Deccan Herald*

'A book that every MP, MLA and minister should read before entering office. Needless to say, sociologists and bureaucrats should treat it as compulsory study material.'—*The Hindu*

'Chakravarti's descriptions are interspersed with reflective comments, but no political theory. That is his strength, for the book raises grievous questions...*Red Sun* should be read widely, especially by those mesmerized by newfound wealth.'—*Outlook*

'Chakravarti travels to the heart of Maoist zones in the country to bring back a story which is as poignant as it is dreadful. Unlike many other armchair "opinion makers"...he tries to understand the phenomenon from a perspective that can only be described as humane.'—*Tribune*

'*Red Sun* is an excellent primer for those who know little of an India where Naxalites live side-by-side with the poor...[and] a prized possession for people who want to work on the subject in future.'—*Down to Earth*

RED SUN

TRAVELS IN NAXALITE COUNTRY

Revised Edition

SUDEEP CHAKRAVARTI

PENGUIN BOOKS

PENGUIN BOOKS
Published by the Penguin Group
Penguin Books India Pvt. Ltd, 11 Community Centre, Panchsheel Park,
New Delhi 110 017, India
Penguin Group (USA) Inc., 375 Hudson Street, New York, New York 10014,
USA
Penguin Group (Canada), 90 Eglinton Avenue East, Suite 700, Toronto,
Ontario, M4P 2Y3, Canada (a division of Pearson Penguin Canada Inc.)
Penguin Books Ltd, 80 Strand, London WC2R 0RL, England
Penguin Ireland, 25 St Stephen's Green, Dublin 2, Ireland (a division of
Penguin Books Ltd)
Penguin Group (Australia), 707 Collins Street, Melbourne, Victoria 3008,
Australia (a division of Pearson Australia Group Pty Ltd)
Penguin Group (NZ), 67 Apollo Drive, Rosedale, Auckland 0632,
New Zealand (a division of Pearson New Zealand Ltd)
Penguin Group (South Africa) (Pty) Ltd, 24 Sturdee Avenue, Rosebank,
Johannesburg 2196, South Africa

Penguin Books Ltd, Registered Offices: 80 Strand, London WC2R 0RL,
England

First published in Viking by Penguin Books India 2008
Published in Penguin Books 2009

Copyright © Sudeep Chakravarti 2008

All rights reserved

12 11 10 9 8 7 6 5

ISBN 9780143066538

Typeset in *Sabon Roman* by SÜRYA, New Delhi
Printed at Repro India Ltd., Navi Mumbai

ALWAYS LEARNING **PEARSON**

For Kalyani and Deepankar

Dear friends,
I am a student.
Former Prime Minister V.P. Singh made a comment,
'What is stopping the youth of our country from
becoming Maoists?'
How does one become a Maoist? Please let me
know.

—From 'Maoist Revolution'
Internet Newsgroup, December 2006

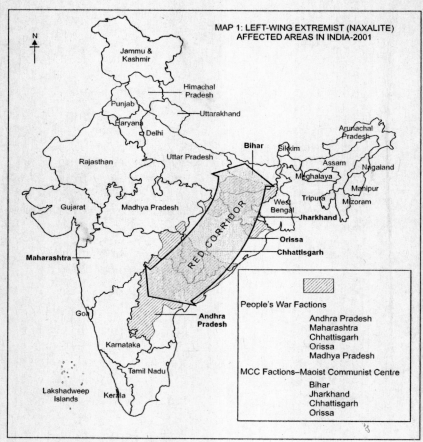

MAP 1: LEFT-WING EXTREMIST (NAXALITE)
AFFECTED AREAS IN INDIA-2001

People's War Factions

Andhra Pradesh
Maharashtra
Chhattisgarh
Orissa
Madhya Pradesh

MCC Factions—Maoist Communist Centre

Bihar
Jharkhand
Chhattisgarh
Orissa

Source for all maps: Institute for Conflict Management

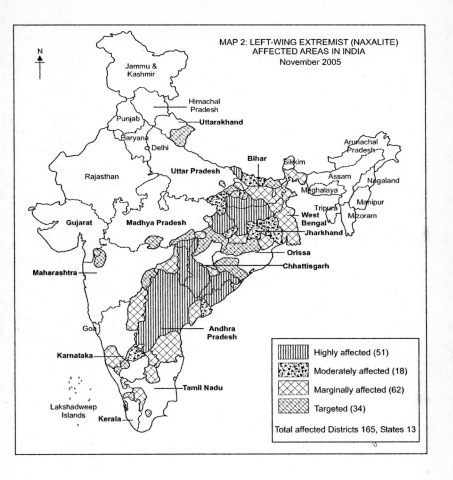

MAP 2: LEFT-WING EXTREMIST (NAXALITE)
AFFECTED AREAS IN INDIA
November 2005

	Highly affected (51)
	Moderately affected (18)
	Marginally affected (62)
	Targeted (34)

Total affected Districts 165, States 13

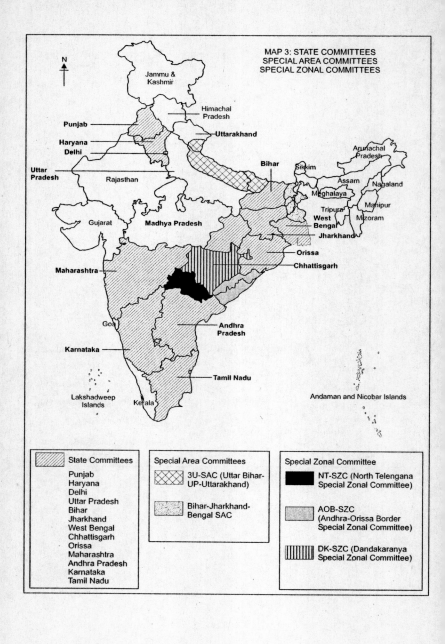

MAP 3: STATE COMMITTEES
SPECIAL AREA COMMITTEES
SPECIAL ZONAL COMMITTEES

N

Jammu & Kashmir

Himachal Pradesh

Punjab

Uttarakhand

Haryana

Delhi

Bihar

Sikkim

Arunachal Pradesh

Uttar Pradesh

Rajasthan

Assam

Nagaland

Meghalaya

Tripura

Manipur

West Bengal

Mizoram

Gujarat

Madhya Pradesh

Jharkhand

Orissa

Maharashtra

Chhattisgarh

Goa

Andhra Pradesh

Karnataka

Tamil Nadu

Lakshadweep Islands

Kerala

Andaman and Nicobar Islands

State Committees

Punjab
Haryana
Delhi
Uttar Pradesh
Bihar
Jharkhand
West Bengal
Chhattisgarh
Orissa
Maharashtra
Andhra Pradesh
Karnataka
Tamil Nadu

Special Area Committees

3U-SAC (Uttar Bihar-UP-Uttarakhand)

Bihar-Jharkhand-Bengal SAC

Special Zonal Committee

NT-SZC (North Telengana Special Zonal Committee)

AOB-SZC (Andhra-Orissa Border Special Zonal Committee)

DK-SZC (Dandakaranya Special Zonal Committee)

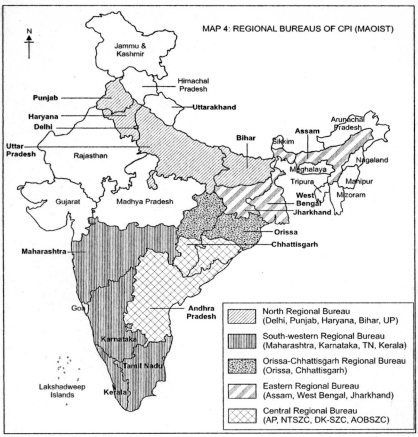

MAP 4: REGIONAL BUREAUS OF CPI (MAOIST)

| | North Regional Bureau (Delhi, Punjab, Haryana, Bihar, UP) |
| South-western Regional Bureau (Maharashtra, Karnataka, TN, Kerala) |
| Orissa-Chhattisgarh Regional Bureau (Orissa, Chhattisgarh) |
| Eastern Regional Bureau (Assam, West Bengal, Jharkhand) |
| Central Regional Bureau (AP, NTSZC, DK-SZC, AOBSZC) |

Source: Central Propaganda Bureau
(SUCOMO, Central Printing Press, People's March)

PREFACE TO THE
PAPERBACK EDITION

Since *Red Sun: Travels in Naxalite Country* was first published, in January 2008, reaction and discourse related to this work has been intense and widespread. It has come from the far-right, the far-left and nearly every persuasion in between these extremes. Book readings and discussions have been attended by a mix of students, academicians, businesspersons, bankers and other executives, bureaucrats, police officers, security and economic analysts, human rights activists, journalists, writers and, I dare say, some Maoists (who continue to be interchangeably referred to as Naxals or Naxalites). In Kolkata, I received the best compliment I could have hoped for when a former chief of army staff told me at a discussion: 'The problem with *Red Sun* is that it's true.'

Such serious and largely positive engagement has shown the urgent need for writing on this grave and most pressing of issues. It also supports the imperative to take the discourse on Maoism beyond learned writing in academic journals, analyses by think-tanks and thinly attended discussions in stuffy conference rooms.

There is a fairly large and excellent body of non-fiction writing in the various Indian languages, including English, on the Naxal movement of the 1960s and early 1970s and the various subsequent extreme-Left incarnations through the 1980s and 1990s. However, besides occasional writing in the media around the time of major skirmishing between rebels and security forces, there still isn't enough accessible literature on the movements of today, such as the one driven by the Communist Party of India (Maoist) [CPI (Maoist)], which is now the country's major extreme left-wing rebel conglomerate. There is also almost no emphasis on the human story. Typically, one comes by pages of statistics and glib sound bites.

The dead and the dispossessed are not numbers. They were—and are—people.

And so, there was every reason to write *Red Sun*.

It helped, of course, that I had an editor and house not averse to going against the grain to publish a questioning book in a blatantly, often nationalistically, good-news environment. (Indeed, this surprised several people I interviewed during the course of my research, both from the establishment and anti-establishment.)

This paperback edition permits me the opportunity to update key developments and add to the narrative with experiences from recent visits to Chhattisgarh and interactions with Maoist sympathizers and security officials. The Introduction and Epilogue have been rewritten for this purpose. However, the nature of left-wing rebellion in India is one of continual morphing, and no book, even frequently updated, can ever hope to keep up. The point, therefore, is not to update the entire narrative or 'story'—which continues to be valid—but to include, without disturbing the tone and structure of the original work, important changes that can help in better understanding this war in the heart of India.

The country is witnessing what could be termed Naxalism Mark IV. This comes after Mark I in the late 1960s and early 1970s across West Bengal, Andhra Pradesh, Bihar and parts of Uttar Pradesh and Orissa; a splintered but stubborn Mark II in the 1980s; a prescient Mark III in the 1990s with the spread into the Dandakaranya region in Central India, which sowed the seed of a formidable guerilla force; and the largely consolidated present-day force of the CPI (Maoist). Surely, there must be serious flaws in a system that boasts repeated annihilation of left-wing movements since the time of India's independence—the Tebhaga movement in rural Bengal, for instance—only to see them rear their heads more emphatically with each cycle of resurgence, through every phase of socio-economic development and growth in the power of the state.

Evidently, putting down is not the same as keeping down, leave alone resolving once and for all.

This past year has seen major strikes and counterstrikes both by the rebels and the security forces, and changes of tactics and strategy on either side. There is also every indication that the state is—finally—following the rebel approach of settling down for the long haul. If anything, this is absolute admission on the part of the state of deep-rooted socio-economic problems that drive India's left-wing movements.

Perhaps it also appropriate to reiterate here what I have said on numerous occasions since the initial publication of *Red Sun*: this book is not meant for left-wing rebels. They are abundantly clear as to why they have taken to arms. It is for the rest of us to be aware of the factors that drive a fellow citizen to pick up a shovel, or an axe, or a spear, or a gun and place his or her life on the line against the undeniable might of India's state apparatus. What drives them to such desperate means to defend their modest positions and aspirations? To kill?

Maoism is not our greatest internal security threat. Poverty, non-governance, bad justice and corruption are. Maoist presence in a third of India merely mirrors our failings as a nation. The Maoist movement comprises people treated poorly, denied livelihood, justice and all the other ideals enshrined in India's constitution. Their leaders see in the country's present realities a certain futility of purpose, and this fuels their belief in violent change.

Red Sun is aimed primarily at the great bulge of middle-class India and its mall-stupor, and at legislators, administrators, policymakers and analysts who live either in wilful or inadvertent denial of the Maoist phenomenon. The book also attempts to offer an understanding of the phenomenon to students of politics and conflict.

This new edition also gives me an opportunity to set right a few small errors. These errors had come about on account of conflicting information and my own oversight. My deepest apologies. And my thanks to all those who took the time and interest to point these out and make valuable suggestions.

While I shall continue to research and write on this subject, I am certain it will only form a small part of an increasing body of 'mainstreamed' work by researchers, writers and journalists. This is as it should be, for left-wing rebellion will be a key aspect of twenty-first-century India.

January 2009   SUDEEP CHAKRAVARTI

INTRODUCTION

Naxalbari has not died and it will never die.

—Charu Mazumdar, 'Long live the heroic peasants
in Naxalbari!', *Liberation*, July 1971–January 1972

Naxalbari lives. It took a chat with B to set me on the road
to find out how deeply. I've known B for some years. He's
been around in the corporate world and in the by-lanes of
some major multilateral agencies. I'd suspected for a while
that he was a closet Maoist, but never realized how plugged
in he was till 2006, when at my request we met one March
evening at his apartment just outside Delhi.

'What brings you to town?' he wanted to know, as we
looked out over high-rise neon suburbia: BPO haven.

Research for a book on left-wing armed movements in
India, I replied.

'Why?' he asked, casually, almost as an afterthought,
reaching for a remote to turn down the Sufi-rock playing in
the background.

Because it's a tragic story of a country at war with itself,
I said, and it can do with all the telling. He didn't seem very
interested, but listened anyway.

—

Since 1985, I have spent my career as a journalist tracking
India's economic development, which has been considerable.

1

And I am a direct beneficiary of the ongoing economic liberalization and expanding freedom of expression that India's urban middle classes now take for granted. But the giddy representation of 'Shining India' in politics and the media that began at the start of the new millennium was making it difficult for me to put aside a glaring public-domain issue. I perceived a grave disconnect between urban and rural India, and, even within urban India, between those with means and those with almost none. To imagine that 'Superstar India' could be 'unstoppable' with its gross poverty and numbing caste issues was to be in lunatic denial. It was insane to believe, as the country was being told to, that a million people employed in the BPO sector would somehow lift 600 million rural folk. It was also dangerous, and there was enough evidence why.

As early as 2002, a top economic advisor to former prime minister Atal Behari Vajpayee claimed to confidants that he lost sleep over the rising Maoist 'problem'. Less than a year later, in October 2003, the then chief minister of Andhra Pradesh N. Chandrababu Naidu, whose security level was only a notch below the prime minister's, was nearly killed when the convoy he was travelling in was wrecked by nine claymore mines between the temple towns of Tirumala and Tirupati, 600 kilometres south of Hyderabad. Naidu's bulletproof car was mangled and flung on its side and he miraculously escaped with some cuts from exploding glass, a broken collarbone and a massively dented ego.

The stunning operation was conducted by the Communist Party of India (Marxist-Leninist) People's War [CPI (ML) People's War], and it happened at the peak of Naidu's hype to turn Andhra Pradesh—specifically the turbulent state's capital, Hyderabad—into 'Cyberabad'. Perhaps he should have paid more attention to his professed friend Bill Gates's premise of danger implicit in the 'digital divide', the software billionaire's way of explaining the gulf between the 'haves' and the 'have-nots'.

In less than a year, Naidu had lost the elections to the

state assembly by a landslide. Besides reasons of politics, it was widely interpreted as a rejection of glib capitalism in favour—or at least the hope—of inclusive development. Naidu's successor, Y.S.R. Reddy, initiated peace talks between his government and CPI (ML) People's War and its regional allies. Only a few months later, by the spring of 2005, talks had broken down; there was no meeting ground.

Meanwhile, the two dominant groups of Maoists in India— CPI (ML) People's War and the Maoist Communist Centre India (MCCI)—had joined to form the agglomerate that now controls the show across the country: the Communist Party of India (Maoist).

From 2004, even before this merger, Maoist strikes have been spectacular. On 6 February 2004, they carried out a mass, synchronized attack, targeting eight buildings at Koraput in Orissa. Several hundred tore into the district headquarters and the armoury, lifting anywhere between 200 and 500 weapons—including .303 and self-loading rifles, light machine guns, sub-machine guns, revolvers and pistols—and a huge stock of ammunition and grenades. For good measure, to create confusion among defending forces and to make a point, they also attacked the district jail, the Koraput police station, the office of the district superintendent of police, a camp of the Orissa Special Armed Police Centre and the district treasury.

In Jehanabad, Bihar, just an hour's drive south of Patna, over 200 active Maoist men and women armed with semi-automatic and automatic weapons, and some 800 sympathizers armed with everything from crude machetes to ancient rifles, stormed a prison on 13 November 2005. They freed 341 jailed colleagues and took away with them twenty sworn enemies— also jailed—of the Ranvir Sena, the upper-caste vigilante army that has for decades fought pitched battles with Maoists in Bihar. It was part of a concerted effort that drew reluctant admiration even from army officers amazed at the planning behind synchronized strikes at the district court, the judge's residence, the main police lines, a paramilitary camp and the district armoury.

On 9 February 2006, Maoists raided the main store of the National Mineral Development Corporation at Hirauli in Chhattisgarh's Dantewada district. They bumped off the guards and made off with a massive haul of explosives and other material. The 20 tonnes of loot was reportedly spirited away by several hundred militia in bundles slung from bamboo poles.

When I began work on this book in early 2006, nearly every other week brought news of strikes and counterstrikes by the Maoists and security forces. And little has changed since. What stand out are the precisely planned and focussed Maoist attacks—on the security forces, on vigilante groups like the Ranvir Sena and Salwa Judum, and on state property. In Maoist parlance this is known as Tactical Counter Offensive Campaign, or TCOC. An unlikely, dispersed army of 10,000 'hardcore underground cadre'—to use a phrase of the central Ministry of Home Affairs—largely secreted in forests and remote villages is taking on the might of the state, flatly disproving current notions of democracy and its most visible symbol, an elected parliament. They carry, according to intelligence estimates, between 6,000 and 7,000 regular weapons—AK series automatic rifles, INSAS rifles used by the army, ancient .303 Enfields, and a range of revolvers and pistols—some bought, but mostly grabbed from police and paramilitary personnel or guards at railway stations in snatch-and-run or kill-and-take strikes. In addition, they carry an entirely incalculable arsenal in country-made handguns, choppers, knives, bows and arrows. They build rudimentary but devastatingly effective mines from robbed explosives using know-how initially learnt from the Liberation Tigers of Tamil Eelam (LTTE). They have also developed basic designs for rocket launchers, made through fronts in small foundries across India.

As my research gathered momentum and I planned my travel and interviews, vast swathes of the country were already given up to armed revolutionaries and militia: local guerilla squads—called *dalam* in southern and central India—and groups of active sympathizers, or the militia, called *sangham*. Maoist militia was estimated by several intelligence analysts at over 50,000; and sympathizers, on account of many being underground in urban India, as well as in several front organizations, was described as a shadowy army of as yet inestimable numbers. In July 2006 former Home Minister of Karnataka M. Mallikarjun Kharge announced in the state assembly that members of 5,000 families in Bengaluru alone were in one way or another involved in Naxal activities, as fronts, for active propaganda or in providing shelter and logistics. A Maoist intellectual in Hyderabad told me smilingly, 'You would be surprised to know where all we have friends.'

A 2006 report by the Ministry of Home Affairs, with a clarity not typically associated with this ministry, noted that 'Naxalites typically operate in a vacuum created by inadequacy of administrative and political institutions...[they] espouse local demands and take advantage of the prevalent disaffection and perceived injustice among the underprivileged and remote segments of the population.' Yet, I encountered little mainstream debate that the spread of Maoist influence was at its core the consequence of bad governance—or plain non-governance—and crushing exploitation in a country that so many saw as an emerging superpower. There have been instances in Bihar and Jharkhand where illiterate tribals have been told that they own just six inches of their land; what lay below the six inches belonged to others, namely, the state, the local trader, the local moneylender—established via-media for mining interests.

The world was sitting up and taking notice of India because the good news stories were coming at a faster clip than before. Finally, India was in a position it had long pined for: from being known as a country of little hope and few jobs, it was now known as a country with a future and one that took away First World jobs. From being a geopolitical minnow, it was badgering the world for a permanent seat in the Security Council of the United Nations. And by playing host to the World Social Forum in January 2004 and other major forums since, in strident celebration for the 'have-nots' and 'been-slighteds' of the world, India also appeared to have arrived at a neat balance of victor and victim.

This is what 'India Shining' was built around. But the slogan, among other things, broke the back of the Bharatiya Janata Party (BJP) in the 2004 national elections. It entirely missed the plot in rural India, where three-quarters of the country's 1.12 billion still live, and where about 280 million comprise landless agricultural labour, traditionally trod upon. It also missed the point by trumpeting the achievements and aspirations of the middle class—which even the most optimistic estimates put at 250 million. According to a recent National Sample Survey Organization report, a similar number, which constitutes a third of the rural population, live on less than Rs 12 a day (the lowest 10 per cent, or 25 million, live on less than Rs 9 a day). In Orissa and Chhattisgarh, the proportion of rural people living on less than Rs 12 a day is between 55 and 57 per cent; in Bihar, Jharkhand and Madhya Pradesh, it is between 46 and 47 per cent; even in relatively wealthy and hyped Maharashtra and Karnataka, it is 30 and 32 per cent, respectively. All these states, in their rural entirety or in vast rural pockets, count left-wing extremism as severe manifestation.

The United Nations Development Programme (UNDP), Unicef and the World Food Programme have other depressing statistics: close to half the children in India are malnourished or stunted, and a fifth of the total population of the country go hungry. Nearly three-quarters of Indians still don't have access to safe drinking water or sanitation. Reports by Transparency International regularly list India as among the most corrupt nations in the world.

These are numbing clichés that, tragically, lead to blindness, as if the numbers are too large and, therefore, meaningless.

The country's policymakers, however, continue to be mesmerized by the promise held out by the so-called BRIC Report of 2003 that made headlines around the world, and in India made a star of Roopa Purushothaman, a co-author of Indian origin of the report issued by the global investment firm

Goldman Sachs. *Dreaming with BRICs: The Path to 2050* predicted that Brazil, Russia, India and China (BRIC) would over the next four decades overtake the economies of UK, Italy, France, Germany and Japan. Between 2015 and 2025, India would move past Italy, France and Germany. Around 2032 or so, it would bid sayonara to Japan. By 2050, it would emerge as the third largest economy after China and the US. (A 2007 edition of the BRIC report speeded up India's goals, spurred by impressive economic growth rates of 9 per cent a year. Even post the recent global recession, when India's growth rate may drop to below 7 per cent, the talk is self-congratulatory—that India and China are much better placed than the rest of the world.)

If the BRIC report were published in 1991, the year India's fits-and-starts economic liberalization programme took root, derisive laughter would have sounded across the world. In 2003, there was grudging acceptance abroad, and euphoria at home. As ever, though, the caveats were there: greater macroeconomic stability is required, along with more transparent institutions and smoother functioning, more openness to investment and trade, and much better education, social care and healthcare. The report stayed away from issues such as corruption, social inequity and grinding poverty—after all, it was a 'good news' document.

In 2020, roughly a decade from now, around the time my daughter would have graduated from university and would be looking for a job, and around the time, going by the BRIC report, that India's economy would be readying to zip past Germany's, our urban population would have gone up from around 23 per cent of the total now to 40 per cent. In absolute numbers, this would mean shooting up from 285 million to 540 million, an immense challenge, even with a rapidly growing economy. Alongside, while the proportion of rural population would lessen, it would still be in the range of 820 million. The same area, 350 million more people, and around the same number of new jobs to be created, with the average growth in wages expected to remain below the rate of inflation through much of this century. As for feeding them: food grain production would have to increase to 260 million tonnes a year, up from the 191 million of 2005. Between 1990 and 2005, food grain production went up by 29 million tonnes; in the next fifteen, it would need to increase by more than double that.

Meanwhile, the squeeze on India's creaky cities and largely unorganized, only-good-for-votes rural India would be massive, and so, too, the chances of anger and resentment at being bypassed by growth.

'Sorry, India is not a superpower,' Fortune magazine, usually upbeat about India this past decade, would scathingly reflect in an article by a top editor, Cait Murphy, quoting numbers of destitution to show that the country wasn't much better off than some down and out African nations. Indeed, Murphy suggested that given how much India needed to fix before it could assume the pretension of a world power 'that is probably the wrong ambition for it anyway.'

The spokesperson for CPI (Maoist), who goes by the name of Azad—Free—says strikingly similar things: 'Our beloved country, so rich in natural wealth, human power and ingenuity, has been reduced to a condition that is, in some respects, worse than that of countries of sub-Saharan Africa.'

Both the exuberant and the cautious signal a set of truths. But both are agreed on one point: With extreme inequity, the two Indias will irrevocably remain two.

And often at war with each other.

—

'Yeah,' B watched me, unblinking, after I had laid out some basic observations. 'So?'

So I am not really surprised, I said, that the essence of Naxalbari, the movement that began in 1967 with farmers fighting landlords in a tiny patch of rural Bengal abutting the tea gardens, still lives as a reality check. It lives more than thirty years after the government killed off several thousand idealistic, often naïve armed activists—mostly students towards

8

the end—and tortured and scared the rest into submission and assimilation. So much so, that while present-day armed revolutionaries call themselves Maoists, in public discourse they continue to be interchangeably known as Naxals, or Naxalites.

'Oh, they're much more organized now,' B intervened. 'Compared to the Naxalbari folks, these people are far more disciplined, closer to the book.'

B meant the Red Book, a popular name for the writings and revolutionary philosophy of Mao Zedong, with its cornerstone phrase: 'To rebel is justified.' Mao once described himself as 'a lonely monk walking the world with a leaky umbrella'. In 1945, as World War II was winding down, he wrote, 'Without a People's Army, the people have nothing.' By 1949, the people, and the people's army, had an entire country, driven by a ruthless, determined man who united a trodden, split and dispirited nation.

Of course, in China today, Mao, 'The Great Helmsman', exists mainly as a watermark on currency notes, as a portrait at T'ian An'men Square and as chic memento, an unlikely witness to the country's runaway economic growth. (Mao's policies are now diplomatically labelled by the leadership as '70 per cent good, 30 per cent bad'). And, disturbingly, in a parallel that commentators who thrive on 'the Dragon versus the Elephant' comparisons of China's and India's economies often choose to ignore, China is a country where three-fourths of the population is forcefully kept away from the urban magic of the eastern seaboard. In January 2006, the Ministry of Public Security admitted that 'mass incidents'—riots and protests, in simpler language—related to poverty, corruption and loss of land and livelihood in the previous year totalled 87,000. This was nearly 7 per cent more over 2004. And this was what the communist government admitted to publicly. Tellingly, the Chinese appointed a senior minister just to deal with poverty.

India's Maoists have taken general guidelines from Mao:

broad strategic imperatives like 'protracted people's war', and extensive use of guerilla tactics to build 'guerilla zones' in rural areas, then 'liberated zones', before finally 'encircling' the city—or the 'Citadel' of Maoist lore. India's Maoists have also, chillingly, gone lateral, moving with the times: they believe that while rural action remains the core, ground must simultaneously be prepared from the inside out; from the heart of urban, industrialized, consumerist India.

A document titled *Urban Perspective: Our Plan in Urban Areas* from 2004 by CPI (Maoist) declares: '...we will have to concentrate on the organization of the working class, which being the leadership of our revolution has to directly participate [in] and lead the agrarian revolution and the people's war...On the basis of the revolutionary workers movement we will be able to mobilize millions of urban oppressed masses and build struggles against imperialism and feudalism...The urban movement is one of the main sources which provides cadres and leadership, having various types of capabilities essential for the people's war and for the establishment of liberated areas.'

This involves creating legal fronts to agitate on a wide range of issues from dowry to WTO, harnessing the fear and anger of India's workers and of India's slums, and recruiting tech-savvy people to enrich the movement's arsenal and communications.

The stealthy spread of Maoist practice and intent in India has been stunning.

Yet, till very recently the Ministry of Home Affairs in its reports mildly termed left extremism as 'another area of concern'—itself an admission of the riven state of the nation that also counts the arterial bleeding in Jammu and Kashmir, terrorism and insurgencies in the North-East as 'areas of concern'. Till the spring of 2006, Naxalism had typically clocked in at number three in the ministry's reports, after the premier spot held by separatism in Jammu and Kashmir, followed by the North-East insurgencies. Evidently, ceding from India holds greater primacy as an internal security threat than left extremism, which doesn't seek to cede from anything or assert regional identity but to violently change the political system altogether by discounting the present constitution and dismissing electoral politics. However, the ministry did acknowledge that Naxalism 'is not merely a law and order problem but has deep socio-economic dimensions', an admission that has, ironically, been paid little serious attention.

In its annual report for the year ended March 2004, the ministry admitted that '55 districts in 9 states, namely Andhra Pradesh, Bihar, Maharashtra, Orissa, Madhya Pradesh, Chhattisgarh, Jharkhand, West Bengal and Uttar Pradesh are afflicted with Naxalism.' This, even the ministry now acknowledges, was in pursuit of the rebels' aim of creating a Compact Revolutionary Zone extending, to begin with, from the borders of Nepal to the depths of Andhra Pradesh— sometimes luridly referred to by politicians and the media as the Red Corridor. By the next annual report, for 2004–05, the states 'afflicted with Naxalism' remained the same but the district count had climbed to seventy-six. By the time the new-look, multiple-colour-photograph report for 2005–06 came in, the ministry had blatantly begun to finesse data, sometimes in the same paragraph. In this report, the same nine states are listed in the opening section on left extremism, but with the heading 'Naxal Violence' changed to 'Naxalism', and the phrase 'afflicted with Naxalism' changed to 'badly affected, though in varying degrees'. After a sentence, the report admits that 'Naxal violence has been reported from 509 police stations in 11 States including these 9 States,' but qualifies this by reminding us that the total number of police stations in the country is 12,476. I would hear from caustic intelligence officials and security analysts that the home ministry might as well begin counting the number of households affected by Naxalism, as that approach would present an even rosier picture. (Home Minister Shivraj Patil, who lost his job after the Mumbai terror strikes in November 2008, publicly aired this 'police station view', as it has come to be known in some quarters, only a few days before he left office.)

This somewhat unreal and confused presentation continues in the same report, with a chart listing a twelfth state—Kerala. It also includes some mention of Karnataka and Tamil Nadu. By the time Prime Minister Manmohan Singh termed Naxalism as India's 'greatest internal security threat' in April 2006 at a meeting of chief ministers and senior officials of states 'critically, moderately and marginally affected' by Naxal violence, the count of 'affected' states had climbed to fourteen, to include Uttarakhand—bordering Nepal—and Haryana, bordering Delhi.

Punjab, well represented in the late 1960s and early 1970s during the Naxalite movement, is next in line. Here, too, it is the anger of the alienated and insulted: failed crops, high debt, humiliation of lower castes, a feeling of being trapped without a voice in one of India's most prosperous regions. Bant Singh, a Sikh—member of an avowedly progressive faith that broke from caste-bound Hinduism—is today a quadruple amputee because in January 2006 'upper caste' Sikhs whom he helped to put in jail for raping his daughter took brutal revenge and hacked off his arms and legs. He has emerged as a beacon for the lower castes and budding Naxals of Punjab. He sings songs from his hospital bed about how the days of the 'oppressors' are numbered. Broken and angry men, women and children gather around him.

By the Indian government's own admission, the number of Naxalism-affected districts is 165—that's nearly 30 per cent of the country's total of 602 districts. It isn't surprising, then, that the home ministry's reports for public consumption do not carry maps of this reach. Maoist links have grown, and despite the government's ruse, it's becoming a gradually recognized truth, occasionally seen in the maps that appear in the print and electronic media at times of a spike in Maoist violence.

When I met the revolutionary poet and Maoist ideologue P. Varavara Rao—popularly known as VV—in Hyderabad, he gave me an interesting perspective on statistics. The movement began around one village, West Bengal's Naxalbari, he said, and was crushed in six months. Yes, it had by then hyper-jumped into several areas of Bengal, Bihar, Andhra Pradesh, Punjab and Orissa, but the original uprising in Naxalbari was crushed in six months. 'Likewise, in Andhra, our revolutionary movement was inspired by the Srikakulam struggle, in the areas of Vatapatra, Parvathipuram and Palakonda. Even Srikakulam ended soon.' Charu Mazumdar—Naxalbari icon—had said that the Indian army would not be able to do anything to Srikakulam, which had been declared a 'liberated zone', and that by 1975 the whole of India would be liberated. But it was all mostly over by 1972. 'Even the Telengana armed struggle of 1946 to 1951 was essentially in two districts, Warangal and Nalagonda,' VV pointed out. 'And [now] see where it has gone,' he gloated. 'Two districts. One village. Three areas. And today, the government itself acknowledges that revolutionary movement exists in fourteen states and is increasing all over the country.'

People tasked with combating the Maoists on the ground are aware of the true import of this spread. They are not taken in too much by the number and nature of 'skirmishes'. I heard Chhattisgarh's former director general of police O.P. Rathor, for one, dramatically caution a room full of senior policemen and intelligence hands from across the country in Raipur in February 2007, at a time when the Maoists were clearly on the defensive in Andhra, but not elsewhere. 'Statistics of incidents never give a real picture on the ground,' he warned. 'Whatever is visible is only the tip of the iceberg. Whatever numbers [of Maoist cadre strength] are coming up, there are ten times more underground. Unless caution is exercised, volcanoes can erupt...Instead of going by statistics we should grapple with the problem.'

For much of India's middle-class, Maoism is still something vaguely alarming, to do with shifting lines on the country's map that they see every once in a while in the mainstream media. To me, these lines are as much Lines of Control as the ones on India's borders with Pakistan and China. These lines within India mark ideologies of the 'oppressor' and the 'oppressed'; they mark lives lost to landmines, crude bombs, gun battles and 'encounters'—a euphemism for killings during staged escape attempts—both real and fake. They are the connected Lines of Actual Conflict across which police and paramilitary forces battle daily against bands of the desperately disaffected.

The danger lies in increasing the degree of denial. By all accounts, half a billion people will remain a long way away from the country's high-growth party in the foreseeable future. They won't like it one bit, and many—even a modest one per cent of this amounts to 5 million people—could do anything to crash the party, to destroy the framework, if they cannot join in the merrymaking. There is already enough ill will and resentment for generations. Here's just one example: by the government's own reports, of the 40 million people displaced since Independence by various projects like dams and big industries, less than a quarter have been rehabilitated. For the rest, policy is as you go, or none at all. There was the incident of the chief engineer for a dam on the Narmada river in Madhya Pradesh simply painting '162' over the approved figure of '101' when the number of villages submerged by the dam project exceeded the latter number. According to a report by Amrita Patwardhan, 'Dams and Tribal People in India', prepared for the World Commission on Dams, more than 1.7 million people have been displaced by major dam projects— the higher numbers and proportions of displaced tribals match the major Maoism-affected states: Orissa, Bihar, West Bengal, Andhra Pradesh, Madhya Pradesh, Maharashtra and Uttarakhand.

Spikes in statistics of caste-violence and crimes against tribals are also the highest in Maoism-affected states, and in 'new' areas like Haryana.

Meanwhile, there is a steady growth in urban influx from rural areas, bringing with it a fallout of development that few planned for. The story isn't at all pretty in urban India. Mumbai is 60 per cent slum. In Delhi, there is a continuing political battle to 'regularize' vast illegal colonies of migrants, little more than tin shack and exposed brick laced with open sewer—many of which, in typical Delhi acronymic, are called JJ Colonies. Nothing to do with Jawaharlal Nehru, the country's first prime minister, as I had erroneously assumed in my university days. JJ is simply *jhuggi-jhonpri*. Hovel-hovel. Bare shack-bare shack. It's how an estimated 50 million Indians in large cities live. Tinder for the taking: always the first choice in politico-religious pogroms, and according to Maoist documents a major component of their blueprint.

It is increasingly being accepted in top security and policymaking circles that India carries the potential to explode in socio-economic cataclysm. Wars fought on account of standards of living and opportunity will continue to have increasingly greater purchase. The Maoists, their sympathizers, or any emergent left-wing movement, will be present to leverage this.

The Maoists are patriots, by their own admission. India's Maoists do not want a separate country. They already have one. It's just not the way they would like it—yet.

—

I want to find out more, I told B that March evening. Put faces and thought to statistics, obfuscation and denial.

Finally, B reacted. 'Revolution is a no-brainer in this place!' he exploded. Then he unleashed a string of curses that included several of the present-day cabinet of the Government of India—including the prime minister himself—and high-profile policymakers like the deputy chairman of the Planning Commission, Montek Singh Ahluwalia.

'The ingredients are all there,' B ticked them off. In India life continues to be cheap, the system corrupt, governance patchy, and basic facilities and human dignity a matter of daily struggle. He rattled off numbers, using the universal million and billion instead of the traditional Indian units of lakh and crore. 'You approve 150 billion rupees for fresh paramilitary forces, you can write off 1,000 billion rupees in non-performing assets of companies, but you can't write off the 75 billion in agricultural indebtedness that will immediately raise the lives of the 700 million who depend on agriculture! Farmers are dying by the hundreds and they're following the World Bank prescription of reducing subsidy to agriculture, to food, and handing over land to companies for what is nothing more than contract labour for cash crops. But sure, you have no problem allocating a billion dollars to promote Indo-US partnership. How can these guys ignore more than half the country and then expect those who have little or nothing to roll over and play dead?'

It's how angry people talk, in suppositions and throwaway figures to make general points. But B wasn't far off the mark. In India, numbers are in danger of losing all meaning, remaining just numbers when they ought to tell a story to shake the country out of slumber. Agriculture these days may account for only a fifth of India's gross domestic product (GDP), ceding space to booming services and resurgent manufacturing sectors, but over two-thirds depend, in one way or another, on agriculture to make a living.

As B and I spoke—early March 2006—more than 300 farmers had already committed suicide in Andhra Pradesh, Maharashtra and Punjab in the first three months of the year primarily over indebtedness arising from increased input costs, crushing interest rates charged by private moneylenders, and unsold produce on account of oversupply and low prices.

To be fair to B, he is in good company, though more from Civil Row than Angst Avenue.

'...Yet even a hundred Bangalores and Hyderabads will not, on their own, solve India's tenacious poverty and deep-seated inequality. The very poor in India get a small—and basically indirect—share of the cake that information technology and related developments generate,' Nobel Prize-winning economist Amartya Sen writes in *The Argumentative Indian: Writings on Indian History, Culture and Identity*, a collection of essays that hasn't moved from bestseller lists in India since its publication in 2005 and is a well-regarded gift among the upper-middle classes. 'The removal of poverty, particularly extreme poverty, calls for more participatory growth on a wide basis, which is not easy to achieve across the barriers of illiteracy, ill health, uncompleted land reforms and other sources of severe societal inequality.'

In November 2006, I heard another person say this, and as politely, to an auditorium full of students, activists and a smattering of leaders from business and politics. Anu Agha, chairperson of the Pune-based heavy engineering company Thermax Limited, widely respected as both a successful businessperson and also one with a conscience, crumbled India's delusional ideas of progress. 'The state has to uphold ethical values,' she said, and beseeched both state and business to guard against 'unjust development that excludes and alienates the poor'. She urged more spending on education and healthcare, mentioned that the largest single cause of deaths in India is diarrhoea, and how a rank of 126 out of 176 in the global Human Development Index is a matter of great shame, an indicator of the distance India has yet to travel. She quoted a newspaper article to call for a second independence, 'independence from hunger, ignorance and marginalization'.

Two months later, in January 2007, at the high-powered World Economic Forum meet at Davos, an Indian co-chair of the summit, Bharati Telecommunications chairman Sunil Mittal, among the wealthiest people in the world, said more or less the same thing: 'At the upper end, it is a very small pyramid of high growth. People outside have to be brought in. If the world does not harness this restless pool, we could be looking at trouble.'

In India the call of the market through helter-skelter capitalism and that of Mao are both proving to be seductive and immensely dangerous.

—

'Are you going to help me?' I asked B.

'No problem,' he said smoothly. 'I'll make some calls. You never know who might agree to meet you.' He turned sombre at the door, as I got up after thanking him for the drinks and conversation. 'I suggest you be careful. It's very messy out there. Both the government and the Maoists are on edge. Things are really escalating now. The government may be confused but there's factionalism and paranoia among the Maoists as well, with the state turning on the heat.'

To go anywhere alone without telling those who might help you is to be silly, he said. 'Try not to get caught in the middle. Neither the government nor the Maoists like to be told they are wrong. If you're seen to be playing games, you're marked.'

I would soon come to realize it. As an independent researcher-writer, I was welcome, as it signalled no ties to any media organization, the establishment—or the anti-establishment. But independence was an irony that cut both ways. If I wasn't affiliated to any media, university or identifiable organization, who was I really with and what kind of story would I tell? Could I be trusted? Was I playing both sides? If I wasn't 'one of us', was I then 'against us'? While numerous doors were opened, this uncertainty cost me some closed doors. This is particularly true of my interaction with the Maoists; on the defensive in Andhra Pradesh, and acutely aware of enhanced state security in several other key states where they dominate and operate, they were deeply suspicious, and stopped the kind of easy access—which some journalists call Maoist Travel Service—that they had provided the media through much of 2005 and the early part of 2006. (It was far easier to gain access in Nepal, where the Maoists have for long had the run of the country.)

From the beginning I was clear that I would not attempt a history of Maoism in India; I'm not qualified, and I believe the best histories of the movement have been and will be written by those within it.

Equally, I was determined to not call left-wing rebels a 'menace' or 'curse' and their presence an 'infestation'. If I did so, I would also have to similarly address several agencies of the state and several officials of the state—both elected and appointed.

This is a very complicated business. Perhaps that is why representatives of the Indian army as well as a serving minister of defence have stated publicly that they wish to have nothing to do directly with militarily engaging Maoist rebels. From what I gather, the army is quite willing to engage enemies of India, those that come from outside, those that wish to, in one way or another, break from the Union of India and the idea of India. The country's defence forces are as yet unwilling, beyond indirectly providing training and reconnaissance facilities to paramilitary and police, to combat folk whose rise and spread is entirely on account of the abasement of fundamental rights.

This book is mainly a travelogue. Essentially, I wanted to adopt the role of storyteller, to attempt to tear the veil of denial that urban, middle-class-and-up, policymaking India lives behind without realizing there's a poison pill inside the nation—of the nation's own making. I wanted to portray the everydayness of Maoism and reactions to it. It seemed important to me to expose the thinking of both the Maoists and the state; get a sense of how people, subject and victim on both sides, play the game, or are caught in the middle. What I found is both revealing and disturbing.

—

As a child in Kolkata—then Calcutta—in the late 1960s and early 1970s, Naxals for me were young men in jeans and batik kurtas who threw Molotov cocktails and soda bottles at police, fought battles with knives and handguns. My family and I had been caught at the sidelines of pitched battles between groups of Naxals and the police while shopping for someone's wedding or visiting family, or while out to Sunday lunch. Shielded by our parents, my sister and I looked out at an urban jungle we couldn't understand, with boys falling to their face on the street, and sometimes, policemen. It was like the movies. Screaming, sirens, explosions, blood.

Walls, especially near colleges and university campuses, were covered in graffiti; in angry letters and exhortations against 'oppressors'; in red flags; in depictions of police firing and torture in lurid blood-red. Studies would be blanked for days, even after the Bangladesh war of 1971, the euphoria of victory forgotten as violence peaked in the streets.

For me, personally, the climax came with an overnight operation by the Indian army against a university residence right across our apartment that housed students of the Jadavpur University, established, ironically, with American money. Using a work-in-progress drainage ditch that had eaten up the road, late one night the army massed attack with automatic weapons trained on windows that during the evenings would be full of students. My sister and I saw soldiers marching in through the gates. Seeing our open window, some of them shouted at us to shut it. We did, and discreetly opened another one further along. Then we heard automatic weapons firing, what sounded like pistol shots, and what sounded like bombs. Then we heard screams. This went on through the night.

It was quiet the next morning. Even the crows and sparrows seemed to have flown away somewhere safer. We watched students being marched, hands above their heads, like prisoners and several being kicked and beaten with sticks and rifle-butts. Some were taken into the adjacent police station, others were herded into trucks. For close to a week, we heard the frequent sound of screaming from the police station. It confused and frightened us. The Government of India and Indira Gandhi—depicted in West Bengal as the goddess Durga after the 1971 war—whom we were taught to revere by the family and at school, appeared to us to do a lot of killing. My father, a mild-mannered businessman more comfortable with theatre and languages, was shocked at the extent of it. He had no answer when I innocently asked him why some people were picking up guns and why they were being killed when there wasn't any colonial power ruling us any more. Why were they fighting? To gain freedom from what?

20

I would ask these questions even today. This book has taken me across several states in India, from air-conditioned offices and homes in places like Delhi, Mumbai and Kolkata to lesser cities, dirt-poor villages and mosquito-infested forests in Chhattisgarh, West Bengal, Andhra Pradesh, Bihar and Jharkhand to get a sense of India's little understood, most misunderstood war.

If I have focussed on Chhattisgarh, it is for the same reason that the Maoists and the government have focussed on it. For the former, it is both a sanctuary from the establishment and a laboratory of sorts, well-meaning and savage in turn, for its rural government and the development of a base area; for the latter, it is a laboratory, too—and seldom less than savage—for state crackdown camouflaged as a people's 'counter movement', the riotously controversial Salwa Judum. In the local Gondi dialect, Salwa Judum means 'purification hunt'. The government's translation of it is 'peace march', another card in the game of counter-insurgency which essentially pits groups of state-sponsored vigilante tribals—those frightened by the Maoists as well as those forced by police and paramilitary to herd into special camps—against Maoist-indoctrinated and controlled tribals.

Chhattisgarh, and the region known as Dandakaranya, is where the current stage of left revolution will meet its glory or death. Either way, I believe the movement will morph into something unrecognizable by today's yardsticks, in much the same way that today's state of revolutionary play would have been incomprehensible forty years ago in Naxalbari or the streets of Calcutta.

In 2006 India's economy touched a growth rate of 8 per cent a year. The World Economic Forum in Davos heralded India as a showcase country. Outsourcing *became* India.

In neighbouring Nepal, Maoism won, and the revolution, after getting rid of the king's absolute power, engaged in co-writing a new constitution, cooperating in a new interim parliament, showing—disturbingly—what armed revolution triggered by decades of neglect, nepotism and corruption can achieve. It was a classic case of privileging violence: Nobody listens in this part of the world until a fire is lit.

The same year, in India, nearly 750 people died in Maoist-related violence across fourteen states, second only to Jammu and Kashmir and ahead of the body count in the North-East.

Through the first half of 2007, as *Red Sun* neared completion, nearly every week there was news of Maoists, mostly in ones and twos, being apprehended or killed in Andhra, Chhattisgarh, Maharashtra, Orissa, West Bengal, Bihar and Karnataka. A squeeze, if you will, on the Maoists.

But there was also news of how the Maoists were shedding skin even as they licked their wounds. In spite of some spectacular, brutal strikes, such as the one on Rani Bodli police post in Dantewada, in which fifty-five policemen and conscripted 'Special Police Officers' of the Salwa Judum were killed in mid-march 2007, the relative Maoist lull into the new year was to lie low, regroup and devise new strategies. For the time they moved away from directly taking on the might of the state, and focussed, instead, on selecting targets to attack through propaganda and precisely planned armed strikes. I was reminded of what BJP legislator and columnist Arun Shourie had said that February in Raipur, about the futility of talking peace with the Maoists. 'Talk is the strategy of Maoists,' he said as a roomful of policemen and security analysts smiled in appreciation. 'Talk-talk, fight-fight.'

The truth of Shourie's comments—though made from the scathing perspective of right-wing politics that, ironically, much like the Maoists', permits little room for dissent—rang true through the latter part of 2007 and all of 2008. In India, unlike Nepal, the stage was hardly yet set for peace talks—indeed, talks of any sort.

The clearest indication came in Andhra Pradesh, on 8 September 2007, when Maoists exploded a landmine at Vakadu in Nellore district, as former Andhra chief minister N. Janardhan Reddy passed in a motorcade. Reddy was on his way to receive an honorary doctorate from a university in Tirupati. He had cracked down on left-wing extremism in the early1990s; the Maoists hold him responsible for killing 400 rebels. Reddy and his wife survived, but some security personnel and his party workers did not. A wire and a flash gun—used to trigger the massive landmine blast—were later found near by.

In October, *People's March* crowed about the incident, saying the early morning attack in 'plain terrain', more daring than at night, had to be carefully and precisely planned around Reddy's movements. 'The Vakadu incident has shown how the Maoists, even if they had become weaker due to the continuous attacks by the Greyhounds [Andhra Pradesh's elite anti-Naxal force], central paramilitary forces and other special police forces, can still deliver effective blows on the parasitic ruling class by adopting guerilla methods of warfare and executing plans with courage and determination...It also shattered the myth floated by YSR government that [the] Maoist movement is finished in Andhra Pradesh.'

The report warned: 'Maoists can strike anywhere, anytime.'

And they did. The incident of 29 June 2008 still has the security establishment staggered: thirty-six Greyhound personnel along with some policemen from Orissa lost their lives when Maoists fired on a boat carrying them in Balimela reservoir along the Andhra-Orissa border. The force was on its way to track Maoist strongholds in Orissa's Malkangiri district. I would later hear security officials engaged in combating Maoists admit to crucial mistakes made by the Greyhounds and their presumptuous guides: cramming into a single boat instead of several to minimize risk; opting to go along the course of the reservoir overseen by high points on either side—perfect ambush territory—instead of crossing a narrow stretch of water and marching the rest of the distance; abysmal failure of intelligence, and so on. That security forces as well-trained as the Greyhounds, and as familiar with Maoist tactics and capabilities, would behave so foolishly was in sharp contrast to the clear planning, pin-point action—and single-mindedness—of the Maoists.

Among other things, the incident speeded up the deployment of the COBRA force, raised specifically to combat

Maoist rebels. With typical bureaucratic overstatement it is an acronym—Combat Battalion for Resolute Action—and is a specially conscripted paramilitary entity under the control of the Central Reserve Police Force (CRPF). In its full ambit COBRA will have a thousand personnel to each of its ten battalions. The first COBRA personnel were introduced into the Dantewada area of Chhattisgarh in the first week of October 2008, in time to test the waters, as it were, in the run-up to assembly elections in the state a month later.

Meanwhile, even as the cycle of violence looks set for an upswing, more stealthy play is at work elsewhere.

Documents, including the ones mentioned and excerpted in this book [the 'Urban Perspective Plan 2004' of the CPI (Maoist) is placed as Appendix], suggest that the Maoists now have basic command and control centres across two-thirds of the country, even in seemingly unlikely places like Gujarat, Himachal Pradesh and Rajasthan. Also, getting squeezed in Andhra Pradesh simply meant spreading further and wider into Chhattisgarh and the surrounding forest areas of Dandakaranya, Orissa and Jharkhand. And, according to doctrine, merging with NGOs, labour unions and other front organizations to carry on, to continually spread the message of revolution with any available means in India's urban spaces. As Union Home Minister of the time Shivraj Patil had acknowledged in Parliament as early as 5 December 2006: '...Like forests provide safe hideouts to Naxalites in tribal areas, the cities also provide them cover. Taking advantage of this, they plan to target major installations in cities.'

There is no indication of Maoism wrapping up, because the key triggers for Maoism—massively skewed development, massive corruption, and great social and ethnic discrimination—show no signs of wrapping up either.

Of course, it doesn't have to be this way—if the central and state governments do as they should, if India's prejudiced millions do as they should, and do the right thing. If they don't, if a country desperately seeking superpower status is blinded by unrealistic ambition and social apathy, the Maoists and others like them will be there to show the way.

BOOK I

1

Dawn comes reluctantly to Dantewada. It's a quarter after five in the morning, and this one-street town is waking up under the fading light of a half moon. Along with the vestige of night, there's a lingering chill. The town, district headquarters for an eponymous district, is at the edge of the forest. For some, this is the edge of civilization.

It's been a long night. The 7 p.m. service from Raipur the previous evening on Payal Air Lines—a bus—was the typical Other India special: take it or leave it. My sleeper berth, on top of a tier of two diagonally across from the driver, was a bed of musty rug stiffened with dirt and decorated with rat droppings. Sitting up meant hitting my head against the ceiling. Scant air came from tiny cracks in the grime that jammed the windows shut, and from exhalations of breath.

As it turned out, this was the luxury option for the ten-hour ride south from the capital of Chhattisgarh. Those of us on the top tiers were spared the crush. The lower berths on either side, the twin aisles and the single row of straight-backed seats were all packed with people by the dead of night, as we crossed a range of low hills that divide Chhattisgarh into Relatively Safe and Torn. Dantewada, also known as South Bastar, the southernmost district of the tamarind-shaped state in the heart of India, lies in Torn.

People stood two-deep in the aisles. Tribal men, women and children who had scraped together a few rupees for the bone-rattling ride from somewhere that few care about to somewhere else that few care about; patient, vacant expressions, barely able clothes, impervious to the sudden cold that shook me to the bone as we crossed the hills. My fare—Rs 260—is worth ten days' earnings in good times in these parts. In bad times—well, bad times are bad times, anything more than the absolute brutality of zero is a blessing. It's how a third of the country lives, and half of Chhattisgarh.

In these parts, if you don't have your own car or two-wheeler, you ride broken buses or broken jeeps on broken roads. There is one major railway that cuts the state in half, at Raipur, running from Mumbai to Kolkata. Another mega city line goes north to Delhi, and runs east to end in urban Orissa, close to that state's own death lands seething with stories of deprivation and turmoil. The National Highway system largely follows a similar pattern, leaving the rest of Chhattisgarh to be ribboned with minor secondary roads, dirt tracks and most often nothing but impressions made by the directional instinct of generations. A slim, occasionally mined highway does run west from Dantewada into the northern cleft of Andhra Pradesh, but only rebels, police and the truly desperate use it.

There is now irony in the non-development in this tribal heartland. It is hard to get here, and harder to move around, except on foot. When Maoist revolutionaries scouted the region over 25 years ago in preparation for a major staging area, they found sanctuary to regroup after being nearly annihilated twice: in the naïve uprising of the 1960s and 1970s over issues of food, land and notions of class; and later, in the early 1980s, when caste anger and tribal disaffection boiled over. They found in these ancient jungles a place to breathe, to hone tactics, to plan social experiments to elevate the lot of India's ignored and trampled populations and recruit them into the Maoist fold. A true-blue 'guerilla base' to upgrade to a 'guerilla zone'. GB to GZ, in Maoist-speak.

In this play of anger and arms, it was logical to assume that a place so remote and forsaken would also deter the police and paramilitary forces. No longer. 'You'll see a lot of road-building work in the villages there,' professor of sociology at the Delhi School of Economics and human rights activist

Nandini Sundar, a long-time observer of Bastar, had told me in Delhi several weeks earlier. 'Even near villages that have been forcibly emptied by Salwa Judum,' she added, referring to the belligerent, often violent state-sponsored programme of resettling tribals and denying Maoist rebels their greatest assets: food, shelter and sympathizers. 'Nobody bothered with roads for decades. They're now building roads to carry troops and supplies. It's a war out there.'

Nandini had also told me of other things. Of how the administration, to inspire terror, spreads rumours about the paramilitary Naga battalion stationed in Bastar to combat the Maoists—rumours that these hardy soldiers from Nagaland 'are not above cutting off heads and eating human flesh'. The otherwise genial Naga troops, mostly boys in their early twenties transported 2,000 kilometres from home to fight someone else's war, have sometimes fuelled the rumours with their actions. Nandini told me of an experience while on a fact-finding mission as part of Delhi-based People's Union for Civil Liberties in December 2005. 'I saw them slaughtering confiscated cattle in front of us. There have been many other instances of grabbing.' It's a war, and alienation and thoughtlessness come with it.

It's a war of propaganda as well, often fought outside the jungle. Invitations from Maoist front organizations arranging meetings to protest displacement of tribal villagers often add on 'sayings', like one that purports to be 'A popular saying of the Muria Adivasis of Bastar, Chhattisgarh' and uses the image of the mahua tree, the fragrant flower of which is a key source of livelihood:

Heaven is a feast of miles and miles of mahua trees.
And hell is a feast of miles and miles of mahua trees
    with a forest guard in it.

Politicians too routinely exaggerate things. Former BJP minister and member of parliament Arun Shourie would claim to delegates at a February 2007 security conference in Raipur that all civil rights groups were to be treated with the deepest suspicion, and that he had severed links with the People's Union for Civil Liberties—active, among other places, in Chhattisgarh—several years ago when he realized that it was 'populated with Naxals'.

The climate is poisoned in Bastar, and the times vicious. For deterrence and revenge, people have been raped, beaten, murdered by the state, their homes reduced to ruin, footstock destroyed for even a tiny hint of collaboration—ready or forced—with Maoist rebels. The Maoists too have done their dance, hacking to death suspected informants, blowing up both police personnel and members of Salwa Judum, as well as innocents who happen to be at the wrong place at the wrong time.

On 25 October 2005, near the small town of Bhairamgarh in west Dantewada, the Nagas and Salwa Judum toughs ran through a tribal village called Mukavelli. They burnt down some huts, demolished others, and shot dead two women, wives of a suspected Maoist sympathizer. One of the ladies was pregnant. A stray bullet grazed a child's head—he lived. A few days earlier, near Usoor, further west, police and toughs had smashed through Pangodi village. They burnt the place down, though not any people, as the inhabitants had escaped into the surrounding jungle.

In Mankeli, a village in the nearby Bijapur area, Nagas and Salwa Judum randomly smashed and burnt huts, and descended upon a suspected Maoist sympathizer and his pre-teen son, who were farming at the time. They first beat the man, then axed and knifed him, gouged out his eyes, cut open his chest, cut off his limbs and, for good measure, smashed his head. His wife and two smaller children were made to stand and watch. Of the older boy there's been no news since that day. This happened on Gandhi Jayanti, 2005.

The police and Salwa Judum have cut a swathe through over a hundred villages and hamlets in the region. And in almost every case, retribution has followed. On 28 February 2006, a truckload of Salwa Judum activists met a landmine planted by the Maoists on a hard-packed dirt road in southern

Dantewada, at Eklagoda, near Errabore. They were returning from a rally to mobilize support against the Maoists. Twenty-six died; over forty were wounded.

On 25 April 2006, villagers of Manikonta were ambushed by some Maoists as they returned from a relief camp to collect utensils and such from homes that the Salwa Judum had forced them to abandon in order to enforce a scorched earth policy. Two hundred Maoists—some cadre in olive green uniforms and armed with guns, and the rest militia carrying a range of household weapons from axes to bamboo staves—attacked the villagers. It was to be a lesson to turncoats. Two villagers were lynched. Nearly fifty were abducted and beaten. Thirteen of them were executed before the rest were released.

On at least one occasion, revenge went horribly wrong. A little to the north in Kanker district on 24 March 2006, just a month before I took the bus to Dantewada, elements of PLGA or People's Liberation Guerilla Army of the CPI (Maoist) blew up a jeep full of traders and tribals returning from a weekly market in neighbouring Kanker district. It was meant to be a warning against extending Salwa Judum beyond Dantewada district. Fifteen died, torn apart in the landmine explosion, and five were injured. The CPI (Maoist) was forced to issue an apology, faxed to several media organizations: 'We publicly apologize and are keen to help the families of those killed in whatever way we can...The incident was a total failure of our intelligence network in which we mistook a private vehicle for a police jeep.'

In this, the Maoists are one up on the state, such as it is—Chhattisgarh has offered no apology for any police, Central Reserve Police Force (CRPF) or Salwa Judum action beyond the bounds of operation, passing off excesses as 'it happens'. It happens for the Maoists, too. In the collateral damage of retribution, terror and terrible justice, infants have been burnt alive, people blinded or their limbs hacked off. In one instance, a dead body was booby-trapped, so those who came to search, rescue and investigate would be blown up. It happened near Bhairamgarh, where Maoist militia killed a Salwa Judum member. They placed a bomb under his body. As a group of Special Police Officers (SPOs)—Salwa Judum cohorts paid and armed by the Chhattisgarh government—accompanied a team of police to remove the body, the bomb exploded. Two SPOs were killed and several others injured. In another incident, two Salwa Judum members picked up a radio that sat innocuously in their path to a meeting. It blew up in their faces.

Rebels match the state of Chhattisgarh in guile and brutality. It's a dirty little war.

—

Punjab Provision Store, a collection and drop-off point for Payal Air Lines in Dantewada town, is shut. I have to wait an hour to use the phone it advertises, as the mobile network I subscribe to and all other private networks are useless here. Only state-run BSNL works this far into Chhattisgarh, and that, too, patchily.

New Suruchi Store, a tiny shop across the street, is open; the owner is pumping a primus stove to get tea going. I ask him for a glass of it, and settle down on a bench to wait. He occasionally leaves what he is doing to try and kick awake the helper, asleep foetus-like on the floor on a piece of packing board. The dusty glass cabinets hide garishly coloured sweets, already flyblown this early in the morning. On the wall shelves are half-litre bottles of Sprite lemonade and Thums Up cola. And smaller bottles of the mysterious Max Cola, which, the label proclaims, 'Confirms International Standard and good taste'. It costs Rs 8 a bottle. The owner tells me it's a hit with some villagers on occasional splurge.

Nearby, the Bright Institute of Technology & Education in a decrepit two-storey building encourages prospective computer operators with the slogan 'Step Into the Brightness'. Sweepers, all women from Andhra across the border—several key Maoist leaders and combatants in Dandakaranya are also from Andhra—come by, raising clouds of dust as they clear the debris of the previous day into neat piles: pulped tomatoes,

32

banana peels, bottles of Zingaro beer and plastic trash. A man, a co-passenger from Payal Air Lines, stands outside the run-down Amber Lodge yelling to be let in. The Nagar Panchayat office, the record-keeping and administrative power centre of the town, has two spanking new Samsung split air conditioners perched outside, bits of plastic packing still stuck to them. (I will see none anywhere else, except in the offices of a senior bureaucrat of the district and the police chief.)

Two pigeons become four, then six, then dozens, breakfasting on the dirt of the broken sidewalk. A few tribal boys cycle past on rusted machines, slim fishing rods tucked under carriers. A sturdy tribal boy wearing faded track pants and a worn T-shirt that proclaims 'L.A. Gigolo Business'— cheap rejects from India's booming garment export trade that unites students on pocket money with the urban and rural poor—walks past balancing two huge loads of chopped wood on a pole. His name is Lakhan, and he tells me he'll sell the entire load, up to two days' work, to eateries and households for anything between Rs 20 and Rs 45, depending on negotiating capacity.

Just then, Punjab Provision Store opens with a rattle of iron shutters and proffers from a dangling sign the acronymic triumvirate that links modernizing India more than any amount of state propaganda: STD-ISD-PCO: Subscriber Trunk Dialling; International Subscriber Dialling; Public Call Office. My hosts at the Vanvasi Chetna Ashram, a local NGO, are only 12 kilometres away. The call goes through at first attempt. I'm early, Himanshu Kumar tells me. He'll send someone to collect me in a half-hour.

Remarkably, someone turns up in just twenty minutes. It's a taciturn man on a motorbike. 'Namaste,' he introduces himself. 'I'm Lingu.' And we're off, scattering the pigeons.

Just 200 metres behind Dantewada's main street lies idyllic watercolour country: Some farmland; meandering streams, red from iron ore and mud, that feed the Shankani and Dankani rivers; clusters of people and buffaloes bathing in large ponds;

tall, proud tribals walking in ant-like line; carpets of sal trees and patches of palm; the cry of birds and cicadas. The green ore-rich range of Bailadila—Ox-hump Hill—stretches away to the horizon to the left. It's a glorious cliché of natural beauty, as with that other faraway conflict zone, Kashmir.

Of course, all isn't as it seems. The Chhattisgarh Human Development Report of 2005, prepared with the blessings of the UNDP, which initiated the practice of what is now universally called HDR, put things plainly enough. 'The role of forests in people's lives and their livelihoods is the defining characteristic of Chhattisgarh state...It is apparent that for many people, forests are not just a supplementary source of livelihood but are central to their lives.

'This high dependence is found mainly in the three southern districts [Maoist-heavy Dantewada, Bastar and Kanker] as well as in Surguja, Korea and the forested belts of Kabirdham, Janjgir-Champa and Raigarh. Access is however increasingly regulated and governed by policy and unsympathetic policymakers. The control of the state is all-pervasive and is operationalized through the forest guards and their administrative hierarchy.' The root of harassment of tribals: corruption, which is ammunition for the Maoists

Nearly a third of Chhattisgarh's population is tribal, the report says. Twelve per cent more are low-caste, spread in the periphery of forests, rural areas, and at the bottom of the urban heap. Eighty per cent of the rural population, including tribals, depends on primitive mono-crop agriculture, and in a bad year this group has little recourse except to scrounge in the forests—if possible—or migrate, or shut up and put up.

Perversely, the region is actually extremely rich in mineral and coal deposits, and the Chhattisgarh government has signed a series of deals worth over Rs 130 billion (13,000 crores) for companies to manufacture steel and generate power. The designated areas are all within Maoist territorial ambit. The root rationale of Maoist presence in the state has thus escalated from protecting tribals from the petty thievery of traders and moneylenders to what rebel propaganda labels as grand larceny perpetrated by business houses, in compact with the state, by taking over land that belongs to tribals. If the Maoists don't protect them, nobody else will.

Lingu drives fast and efficiently over the ribbon of tar. A turn left before Faraspal village, and we have arrived. He switches off the engine. We're in the middle of a forest, the only sign of habitation, two low buildings and a hut. There's absolute silence. For all practical purposes, we've disappeared in Dandakaranya.

In the *Ramayana*, Dandakaranya, the forest of Dandaka, is where Prince Ram settled down for his fourteen years in exile before reclaiming the throne of Ayodhya. It was a cursed wilderness; full of demons and pestilence, and it was to remain so cursed till Ram set foot in it, accompanied by his wife Sita and brother Lakshman. Peace was fleeting. Sita was abducted from their forest home by the demon king Ravan, and in Ram's lofty chase to recover his bride, men, animals, gods and demons, all displaying various shades of good and various shades of evil, joined the battle. True to epic form, good and evil are often interwoven in the *Ramayana*, and perception holds the key.

Today's Dandakaranya covers an area of nearly 92,000 square kilometres and spans impressive chunks of the states of Andhra Pradesh, Orissa, Maharashtra and Chhattisgarh—mostly Chhattisgarh. The area is nearly twice the size of Kerala. It is quite hilly, and thickly forested, easily seen as a dark green deciduous vastness on Google Earth or any proficient school atlas. Patches and strips of similar dark green link it all the way north to Nepal and all the way south to Kerala. The forces of establishment and the police, the assumed forces of good, simply call it DK. The forces of anti-establishment, the hardcore of left-wing revolutionaries who comprise the CPI (Maoist) also call it DK, but they have an additional acronym for the area: DKSZ, or Dandakaranya Special Zone. It's been their home for over a quarter century, since the early 1980s, when armed action began against landlords and moneylenders.

The Maoists too insist they are the forces of good. A post at the popular web log 'Naxalrevolution' says: 'The notion that a Naxal is someone who hates his country is naïve and idiotic. He is, more likely, one who likes his country more than the rest of us, and is more disturbed than the rest of us when he sees it debauched. He is not a bad citizen turning to crime; he is a good citizen driven to despair.'

And to radically break the law, for which he is hunted and killed.

Good versus good. As ever, reality can be deceptive.

Well inside Dandakaranya, I'm in the four-room cottage Himanshu calls home. It's more sprawling hut. I'm refreshed after bathing in chilled well-water, and the simple lunch of roti, dal, and potato curry tastes heavenly after greasy eggs and glasses of sickly sweet tea at a Payal Air Lines pit stop in the middle of the night. Himanshu's wife Veena is feeding their daughter Haripriya lunch in an adjacent room, from which Mallika the mongrel has been banished for the duration. She sits and whines outside the mosquito-screen door. Sampatti the maid brings us fresh rotis.

'Tell me about Salwa Judum,' I ask Himanshu after lunch as we stroll towards his office, a low air-cooled building powered by solar energy. Workers and volunteers—young men and women, a mix of tribal and non-tribal—are feeding in data into several desktop computers, data on literacy programmes, water use and sanitation. 'There must be some root for Salwa Judum to take hold. It can't happen out of nothing.'

'The Naxalis did get a little overconfident,' he admits. 'And some cadre were clearly pushing villagers. They would say, Don't do this and don't do that. Don't collect tendu leaves [used to roll bidis] if you don't get a better price. But what will villagers eat if they don't work? They would decide on projects and sometimes even marriages. In some places this became a problem.

'Equally, I believe Salwa Judum is wrong. It's not a

spontaneous Jan Jagran [People's Awakening] as the government claims, but a government-sponsored movement. The government pays for everything. I tell them, you can't fight violence with violence.'

Himanshu claims to be a believer in the Sarvodaya movement, a manner of post-Gandhian simple-living, do-gooder philosophy propounded by Vinoba Bhave, whose framed photograph finds pride of place in the homestead. It's also what prompted Veena to give up the middle-class dream of an American Green Card and join her activist husband in these jungles thirteen years earlier.

'This Pisda, the collector, he's a tribal himself,' Himanshu refers to Dantewada district collector K.R. Pisda, the seniormost civil administration official of the region. 'I told him, You are giving away bows and arrows in the name of Salwa Judum. As a collector you should be giving away pens.' Pisda is in good martial company. Just days into Salwa Judum, the local paper *Haribhumi*—the Land of Krishna—of 10 July 2005 carried a photograph of Pisda's counterpart in Kanker, S.K. Raju, posing with a standard military-issue INSAS rifle. 'They say, Listen to us, or we'll send the Nagas,' Himanshu says. 'It's like asking children to shut up or a nasty dog will bite them. This is how the administration scares villagers.'

A young man drops by Himanshu's desk to take a draft of a letter to Pisda, mentioning that a Dutch doctor has volunteered to work in Salwa Judum camps in the area, so could he be given permission. I raise my eyebrows. Himanshu is grinning. I ask if the administration has ever put pressure on him, a do-what-we-say-or-else sort of thing.

'The collector has said to me more than once, and so have the police—You must be giving information to the Naxalis because you travel from one place to another. I tell them I live in the forest, I can give information to them anytime, I don't need to travel for that. You see, we empower people, teach them to read and write, tell them about basic rights, and this goes against local landlords, politicians, moneylenders and traders. So they call me a Naxali...Let us just say the administration and I maintain our peace.'

But this qualifier is evidently too much for Himanshu. 'I mean, look at the mentality of the administration,' he says with more frustration than anger. 'Some days ago I wrote a letter pointing out that there are no facilities in Salwa Judum camps, and yesterday the concerned minister announces flamboyantly, "*Kaun kahta hai nahin ho sakta*? We will have ten lakh toilets in Dantewada." A million toilets for 2,00,000 families in the area. These people say whatever comes into their heads.'

A sturdy local, Sukhdev, drops by to say Salwa Judum have called a meeting towards the end of April and that they have requested use of the ashram's computers and printer to design posters for it. Himanshu folds his hands and raises them to his forehead in a classic gesture of exasperation. 'Please thank them and tell them to let us be.'

'We're caught in the middle in this civil war,' he says, turning to face me. 'The Naxalis think I'm with the government as I don't openly support them, and the government thinks I'm with the Naxalis because I live in the forest and I criticize Salwa Judum. Both think if you're not with us, you're against us.'

We sip some tea and lapse into silence.

'*Hum to buri maut marengey*,' Himanshu says suddenly.

He then escalates from how he will die a 'terrible death' to 'a dog's death': '*Hum kuttey ki maut marengey*.'

2

The news was pouring in as I prepared to travel to Chhattisgarh on 20 April 2006. Nepal was exploding with popular protest. CNN-IBN had a story about the secretary to Nepal's home minister being arrested for participating in an anti-king rally— if it had come to this, the monarchy's autocratic rule was all but over. Aaj Tak, the Hindi news channel, showed visuals of street battles in Kathmandu between riot-police and protestors, including women. A boy screamed: 'We have fought for 14 days, we will fight for 14 weeks, 14 months and 14 years, but we want the king to go. Gyanendra *chor*!' Times NOW zoomed in on Karan Singh, special envoy of Prime Minister Manmohan Singh to Nepal, as he settled into his business-class seat on the Jet Airways' Delhi–Kathmandu flight. 'Yes, it's a delicate mission,' minced the son of the former maharaja of Kashmir, related by marriage to King Gyanendra, as many Indian royals are. 'But I'm not awed...overawed by it.'

The channel then cut to a story titled 'Cradle of Death', about a staggering 180 infant deaths in two months at a government-run hospital in Agartala, capital of Communist Party of India (Marxist)-led Tripura. But expectant mothers keep going there, said the reporter, as the poor don't have an option. India's health secretary came on camera for a convoluted retreat: '...We will look into it. It shouldn't happen, and if anything had happened we would have known, but still...' Sitaram Yechury, Communist Party of India (Marxist) [CPI (M)] spokesperson and dear friend to Nepal's Maoist chief Pushp Kamal Dahal, better known as Prachanda, or Fierce One, looked every which way but at the camera: '...In such places disease can pick up...increase before the rains...and...we are asking the state government to look into it...'

In this part of the world excuses are used by the left, right and centre.

Seat 10A on the flight to Raipur from Mumbai was a bit cramped, but there was enough elbowroom for me to open a recent issue of *Businessworld* magazine that I found tucked into the reading material and barf-bag flap in front of me. Blunt-talking economist Omkar Goswami, a longtime acquaintance who runs the New Delhi-based CERG Advisory, had a column in it. He explained how former columnist and current minister of state for commerce Jairam Ramesh (who would in June 2006 incense Andhra Pradesh's political leadership by wise-cracking that the state had created a Special Economic Zone to export Naxalites) had told him years back about an 'East of Kanpur characterization of India'. Jairam's point: the regions west of Kanpur, marked by the longitude 80°24' (East), were doing better, while those to the east of it were 'withering away'. Omkar wrote that he decided to go and check Jairam's hypothesis by collecting detailed data on India's districts, development blocks and villages. His colleagues and he pored over this data for two years and, alongside, used data from the Census of India 2001—the most recent such exercise—to map an India based on ownership of or access to 11 assets and amenities: whether the household had a bank or post-office account; a *pucca* house; electricity connection; owned a TV set; owned a scooter or motorcycle; used cooking gas; had an in-house drinking water source or one within 500 metres; had a separate kitchen area; a separate toilet; a separate and enclosed bathing space; a telephone. CERG then took the results of these indicators of necessity and basic aspiration, what it termed Rural India District Score, and put it on a map. The districts were ranked in six grades, with accompanying colours: Best (dark green), Good (light green), Better than Average (very light green), Average (white), Worse than Average (orange) and Very Poor (red).

All of central India showed as great patches of white and orange, with a couple of splotches of red. Moving east into Jharkhand, Chhattisgarh, eastern Andhra Pradesh, eastern Maharashtra, Bihar, Orissa, West Bengal and most of northeastern India, it's a sea of red and orange with peripheral white and ten islands of varying shades of green—one of these in the region of Kolkata. The white bank of 'average' spreads into peninsular India, with some orange penetrations of 'worse than average' in Karnataka and Tamil Nadu.

'These "east of Kanpur" districts are dropping off the development map,' Omkar concluded. Anyone going through the 'red' and 'orange' districts of the east, he wrote, 'can easily trace the hotbeds of Maoist insurgency. Getting the benefits of growth to these districts is the greatest challenge of development and political economy.'

If police and intelligence officials were to open statistical tables of socio-economic growth and demographic spreads of the marginalized and the dispossessed, and look at maps of attacks by the Maoists, they would easily see the future course of the 'red enemy'. Across much of rural India. And much of urban India.

We had taken off for Raipur as I read Omkar's column. Bits of conversation came from my companions, 10B and 10C. I stole a glance. 10C had her manicured forefinger on a multicoloured price/earnings (P/E) graphic in 10B's magazine— The Week, with CPI (M) general secretary Prakash Karat on the cover. ('Is the left going right?' a blurb on the contents page asked when I later read the magazine. 'A new Left is emerging in India. One that loves American capital and loves beating the imperialists at their own game.')

'When P is more than E, it's not very nice,' 10C was telling 10B, a quiet gentleman. 'The P/E of tech stocks are very high, generally the P/E of Indian shares are higher than, say, China's. You should look at funds, mutual funds.' She reeled off some names: Franklin Templeton, SBI Mutual...

I leaned forward. 'Ah, the gentleman is getting disturbed,' she said. No, I told her, just surprised to hear this conversation on a flight to Raipur, the capital of India's premier Maoist-embattled state. They smiled politely.

10C, as it turned out, was Ritu Jain, a graduate of Hyderabad's Indian School of Business, and employed at American Express in New Delhi as an investment specialist. She was visiting hometown Raipur after 15 years for a family get-together. 10B was S.D. Karmalkar, manager, human resources and administration with the cement company ACC Limited and recently posted to Raipur. He would be travelling onwards to an ACC plant in Jamul, near the industrial township of Durg, a militant labour hub, to carry on negotiations with recalcitrant union workers there. His father had worked at the same plant for several years, but this was one homecoming he wasn't looking forward to.

Karmalkar's main worry was restive contract workers.

'Anoop Singh?' I asked. Singh is a well-known labour

leader in the area, and a leader of Chhattisgarh Mukti Morcha, an organization that, among other things, had pressed for the state's breakaway from Madhya Pradesh. Police accuse him of Maoist links.

'How do you know?' Karmalkar was surprised.

'I heard somewhere. What does he want?'

'Permanency. Permanent positions for contract labour.'

'Will you do it?'

'No. We'll take some, make some permanent, but we can't afford to do it with all. It's the contractor's responsibility, too...it's also the responsibility of the state.' It's political at any rate, we agreed.

'Have Naxals hassled you?' I asked. 'Here and elsewhere?'

'Yes, but not now.'

'For what? Better terms for labour?'

He nodded.

It turned out Ritu had a Naxal connection too. Her policeman husband, a management graduate, away in the US to attend a programme at the John F. Kennedy School of Government, had been head of the anti-Naxal cell in Madhya Pradesh till four years back. These days he is posted on deputation to Sashastra Seema Bal, armed paramilitary that patrols the India-Nepal border. 'Every morning we would talk about the Maoist problem in India, Nepal...about how it's spreading. He told me, "If you spend some time in that area, you begin to empathize with the Naxals. We see it as a law and order issue, but it's a development issue. You should see what happens—the levels of exploitation are so high."'

I showed her Omkar's column, and the adjacent article on indebtedness driving farmers to suicide in Andhra Pradesh. That article mentioned how several micro finance institutions in rural areas funded by major private-sector banks like ICICI and HDFC were hitting farmers with sky-high interest rates. Rates 'as much as 40 to 50 per cent per annum', according to the Krishna district collector Navin Mittal. (That's more than double the rate at which I repay ICICI for my car loan.) In addition, Mittal alleged, they were taking collateral like blank cheques and home ownership documents—unethical practices according to current banking law on micro finance.

The plane wobbled. 'Bad landing,' Ritu warned. 'It's going to be a bad landing. I know it.' It was a hard landing on Raipur's short runway. Bang. Screech to a crawl. Hard left at the apron turnoff, and 180-degree turn to park. It felt like riding an auto rickshaw fitted with jet engines.

'Where are you going?' Ritu asked in farewell. Both Karmalkar and she were smiling.

'Dantewada,' I replied. The smiles disappeared.

A small twin-engine B200 King Air, white with blue-striped livery, was readying for departure as I walked towards Raipur's modest terminal. It's a plane owned by the Chhattisgarh government, inherited along with Maoists when the state was carved from Madhya Pradesh in November 2000.

As I entered the terminal, it became clear whom the plane was being readied for: K.P.S. Gill, former director general of police of Punjab, the hard-driving man credited with annihilating Sikh militancy in a run from the late 1980s to 1995. He'd also had an emphatic stint earlier in Assam. The retired policeman, and now controversial president of the Indian Hockey Federation was only a day old in his job as security advisor to the government of Chhattisgarh.

A day before Gill took office, thousands of Maoists surrounded Usoor village in Bijapur, near the border with Andhra Pradesh, and basically cut off the village of 2,000-odd inhabitants from the rest of the state. The *Times of India* quoted Chhattisgarh's chief minister Raman Singh as saying that 3,000 Naxalites—soldiers and militia—had taken part in the operation. As there was a threat of landmines, the CM said, police from an outpost 22 kilometres away in Awapalli wouldn't reach the place before evening. As it turned out, the Maoists merely roughed up some villagers, threatened all to keep away from Salwa Judum cohorts and, point made, melted into the jungle.

Two days prior to that, on 16 April, the Maoists attacked

a post of the Special Armed Forces at Murkinar, about 30 kilometres from Bijapur, with AK-47s leading the charge. They killed 11 policemen, injured five more, and cleaned out the armoury.

As it stood, then, the score since Gill's appointment read Mao Zedong: 2, Kanwar Pal Singh Gill: 0. On account of fair play, I hadn't counted the strike of 19 April. That day Maoists blew up an armoured landmine-proof vehicle in Gadhchiroli district of neighbouring Maharashtra—part of DKSZ, but out of Gill's jurisdiction—killing two policemen and badly injuring a dozen others.

Given the tag of 'super cop' by the media, Gill is known to be a stubborn but crafty man. 'He won't simply employ old strategies,' D, with Chhattisgarh intelligence, would tell me later. 'He's a very practical man. So far, he listens more than he talks. He will *not* do what he did in Punjab and Assam. [Here] he will engage.' I said I'd believe it when I saw it. The super cop's philosophy, articulated by a former minister in the Union government, is known to be quite simple: 'Out-gun them, out-communicate them, outrun them'. Old habits.

Gill, past 70 now, walked slowly, sharply dressed in perfect turban, full-sleeved shirt and iron-crease trousers, and was accompanied by a senior officer in camouflage gear. A couple of state police commandos with Heckler & Koch sub-machine guns shielded him, accompanied by a dozen or so less emphatically armed policemen and some officers and men of the Central Industrial Security Force (CISF) tasked, among other things, with protecting India's airports. Even stooped, Gill towered over everyone. They didn't waste time; as soon as he was in the plane, along with the camouflage-gear officer and the commandos, it turned propellers and rolled for take-off.

'Where's he going?' I asked a CISF guard.

'*Mujhe kya malum?*' he snapped. How should I know? He hefted his rifle. 'Why do you want to know? Who are you?'

—

The office of Chhattisgarh's Directorate of Public Relations, Jan Sampark, is a 15-minute rickshaw ride from Stambh Chowk, Raipur's choked centre, a mess of pedestrians, rickshaws, savagely honking auto rickshaws, buses, cars and all manner of two-wheeled transport. All around are decrepit buildings. In this, Raipur is reflective of the subcontinent's planned urban poverty and vehement, up-by-the-bootstraps prosperity. Advertisements for the latest mobile phones, DVDs and home loans front open sewers, uncollected garbage and destitute dogs and humans.

At Jan Sampark, in the relatively quieter enclave of government offices, additional director Alok Awasthi was holding court with a group of media persons. They were settled in rows of chairs arranged in front of his desk and on settees around the room. One or two left every 15 minutes or so and more arrived. Afternoon was the time for the story, a 'tip', a 'briefing', or just plain chitchat, tea on the house, newspapers and magazines on the house, web browsing on the house. In Raipur, local media rarely moved out of the city, generally on account of the Maoists and particularly on account of the Chhattisgarh Vishesh Jan Suraksha Adhiniyam, or Special Public Safety Bill, enacted into law, by the President of India's consent, just weeks earlier. It is little more than a gag law to prevent media and human rights groups from presenting the Maoist point of view.

I waited for the crowd to thin. Awasthi received a phone call. '*Achcha*? Three blasts?'

'*What*? Where? When?' the bureau chief of Press Trust of India, a major wire service, put down a magazine to ask.

'*Batayengey, batayengey*,' Awasthi imperiously pacified everyone. 'Let me get more information first.' He replaced the phone.

A wag took a break from checking email. 'Super cop *aya hai, na*. This is his welcome.'

'*Achcha? Achcha?* Where is he?' Awasthi was blasted with queries.

Wire service had the answer. 'He's off on a helicopter tour of Bastar.'

'No, he is not,' Awasthi reclaimed territory. 'He has taken a *plane*.'

'*Achcha*, plane, is it?' The notebooks came out. 'Where to?'

Awasthi reeled off the destinations, all in the Zone: 'Narainpur, Bijapur, Dantewada, Jagdalpur and back. *Bas*!' Some were furiously scribbling, others made calls on mobile phones. Gill was always news.

I looked around. A TV anchor was exulting over the Sensex, the benchmark index of the Bombay Stock Exchange, reaching 12,000. 'It could reach 13,000 in another *week*,' she shrieked. 'And punters say 14,000 is not out of the *question*.'

Finally, the journalists went away to file stories with promises of updates from Awasthi.

'So tell me,' he turned to me. 'What can I do for you-*ji*?'

Not much, just some numbers, and Chhattisgarh's latest budget papers. Also, a copy of the Jan Suraksha Adhiniyam, 2005.

'Why?'

'For my research. These are all public documents, aren't they?'

He flung a mauve Rexene-bound 2006 diary at me, standard Chhattisgarh government issue. 'All the numbers you need are there. Call and ask them what you want.'

Budget papers?

'I don't have them. They're available in the government press in Rajnandgaon.'

But that was several hours away, I protested. I'd checked in several bookshops that stock government documents in Raipur; none had it. If he had one spare, I'd be happy to buy it.

'Go to the Chhattisgarh government website on the net.'

I had. The link for the budget papers didn't work.

'So what can I do? Ask National Informatics Centre. *They* maintain the website, I don't.'

Could I at least have the full text of the Adhiniyam?

'I don't have it. Go to the law ministry website. It's there.'

I'd searched, but hadn't found it.

'Why do you keep asking about the Act? What is it to you?'

Nothing, except that it seemed like a gag law to me. 'Why do you need it?' I asked. 'Aren't existing laws enough?'

The Act allows imprisonment for up to three years if anyone is caught making contributions to 'unlawful' organizations, even if the contributor is not a member of such an organization. A district magistrate has the right to seize any building or area where 'unlawful activities' take place, and evict occupants. This includes even a meeting, a conversation, let alone writing and preparing visual material such as posters— anything that the authorities feel can 'create risk' or 'endanger public order, peace and tranquility' or 'impede the administration of law'. If Chhattisgarh wants to push it, anyone criticizing the government's handling of the Maoist issue would be prosecuted. So would I, if I wrote about it, and any journalist, writer, anybody. Front organizations of the Maoists would certainly come under the ambit of this Act, but so would human rights organizations that legitimately function as watchdogs.

In response to my observation, I got a stream of gutterspeak laced with sarcasm. '*Bhainchod un logon ki fati pari hai* (Those sisterfuckers are shit scared). *Sab chaley deshpremi banney* (they're all lining up to be patriots). They meet Naxalis, they take their interviews, they print them, they attend their press conferences. *Gandu hain sab* (They're all assfuckers). Now there is a law, *sabki fati pari hai*. But why are they scared? *Chubha kya* (Has it poked them)?'

We smiled at each other, drily. The invective was directed as much at me as everyone else. He knew he could stomp on local media—official 'access' and 'advertisements' were as ever the magic words. Media from outside Chhattisgarh either didn't know about the gag law or didn't care. Or the government was shrewd enough to realize it would trigger off a PR nightmare should anything happen to well-known, well-connected journalists and human rights activists from New

Delhi or Mumbai. BBC's David Loyn, the network's developing world correspondent, was over in Dantewada recently, videographing Salwa Judum relief camps and trekking to see villages destroyed by 'SJ'. South Asia bureau chief of *The New York Times*, Somini Sengupta, had zipped in and out less than two weeks back. In a 13 April story she wrote about this 'deadliest theatre of the war', where 'government-aided village defence forces have lately taken to hunting Maoists in the forests. Hand in hand with the insurgency, the militias have dragged the region into ever more deadly conflict.'

If Awasthi and his ilk ambushed Loyn or Sengupta with the gag law, a hard rap on the knuckles would descend from Delhi, no matter that Chhattisgarh was run by the BJP, and the country by a Congress-led coalition. No matter that Chief Minister Raman Singh and his rival Mahendra Karma, the leader of the opposition (Congress), 'are together', as a top Chhattisgarh police official told me. 'They have a joint strategy against Naxals.'

Still smiling a 'fuck-you' smile, Awasthi rolled his eyes at the diary. 'What you need to ask, you ask *them*, okay?'

'Yes boss,' I promised.

3

The British have long gone, but Authority of Empire is maintained in these parts with small, potent symbols. Like the bearer wearing a red sash over white native uniform who waits outside the office of K.R. Pisda, IAS, the collector of Dantewada. The bearer takes in my business card, and is back quickly. '*Sa'ab* will see you,' he says with a short bow. 'Please come.'

A scruffy guard carrying an AK rifle with a large 'banana' ammunition clip won't let me take my small backpack in. Used to Delhi's security paranoia, I open the zipper and show him notebooks, tape recorder, camera, useless mobile phone.

I press various buttons to demonstrate that the gadgets aren't bombs or triggers for one. Satisfied, he nods an okay. I notice he's nursing an ugly cut on one foot, he winces when it scrapes against the sandal-strap. I give him a couple of strips of adhesive gauze I always carry on trips, and our compact of trust is complete.

I enter a large, air-conditioned room decorated with other touches of empire: a regulation photograph of the head of state—now the President of India—and a wooden honour-board that lists in perfectly lettered white the names of the previous collectors of Dantewada. Pisda's name is halfway down the board, with a blank for when his tenure ends. He's a wiry, polite man, and offers me *laal-chai*, black tea with a dollop of sugar.

He speaks eloquently, mostly in formal Hindi, with a few words of English thrown in. He begins by outlining a superstructure; a bureaucrat stepping on hot coals in a very hot zone. 'This problem of Naxal-*badi*, it's not just a law and order problem, but also a social and economic problem. If I look at it from an administrator's perspective then along with law and order we have to bring total development and progress to this region. And this we need to do with maximum effort.'

That's been known for years. So?

'There are several reasons for Naxalism growing in this area, but the main one is there is no connectivity. This is the largest district in Chhattisgarh and there are just a few main roads, that is all. People from outside find it difficult to go in. Those inside find it difficult to come out. Fifty per cent of the people of Dantewada have not seen this district headquarter. They don't know what a train is and many don't know what it is like to ride in a bus. There's no electricity, so there's no radio or TV. Their life is about their village and a radius of 20–25 kilometres around the village. Whoever gets to the interior—whether Naxals or the administration—the people accept them. If they see more Naxals, they think of Naxals as their own.'

Pisda calmly continues, without pause: 'Law and order and police will take care of exactly 50 per cent of the problem...if we use police strength to suppress them, shake them, force them to run, or kill them, we can only solve 50 per cent of the problem. You cannot solve this problem as long as the public is not with you.'

I wonder aloud if his bosses in Raipur listen to good advice from their tribal officer. Pisda ignores me. He still has the preamble to complete, and he won't be denied. 'So the problem is not going to disappear. It is going to escalate if there is no development. In this region, hamlets and villages are really spread out, and this makes it very difficult for us to bring electricity, water, health facilities and *anganwadi* [community crèches] close to individual houses. It's easier to do it in a cluster of houses.'

'Like in resettlement camps?' I venture.

Pisda rushes on: 'If we move rapidly, link villages, educate people—of course, all this can't happen in a day or two, but with good planning, change can come about in five, ten, twelve years.'

So the best insurance for development that an undeveloped region has is to trigger a Naxal problem, I joke. No development for decades, and when Naxalism begins to peak: Boom! Development. Therefore, Naxalism is in the long run good for India.

It's a cynical snare, and Pisda doesn't even put a toe in it. He fixes me with an unblinking stare.

I try another approach. 'Do you watch TV? Read the national papers? These days the media is full of news about rampant Naxalism in Chhattisgarh. And about Salwa Judum—it's one thing for the state to send in police and paramilitary; it's another thing altogether to set tribal against tribal with a state-sponsored force of vigilantes. Isn't this escalating the situation? Do you know what the international press is saying about it?' I wave a copy of *The New York Times* article by Somini Sengupta at him.

He pulls a copy out as well, like mine a printout from

www.nytimes.com. There's a yellow highlight over a part that reads, 'Villagers, caught in between, have seen their hamlets burned. Nearly 50,000 are now displaced, living in flimsy tent camps, as the counter-insurgency tries to cleanse the countryside of Maoist support.' I put my finger on it, and he admits smoothly, 'Yes, we are aware of what people are saying, and we need to do something about it.'

'Do you know how Jan Jagaran began?' he asks, studiously avoiding the term Salwa Judum, instead using the state-endorsed term: People's Awakening.

He picks up a pen and starts sketching on his notepad. 'See, this is Talwandi.' Dot. 'I'm talking about eight to ten hamlets near Kutru village.' Dot. Dot. Dot. 'This is in June 2005. People of the hamlet were discussing how they no longer wanted to put up with the Naxals. They decided that they would ask all sangham members in their hamlet and nearby hamlets to surrender and nobody would help the Naxals. Some sangham members didn't agree, so the villagers and these people started to fight. Not to the death, just simple *maar-peet*.'

While this was happening, a sangham fellow [active Maoist sympathizer] slipped away to tell the Naxals, Pisda says. The Naxals arrived and fired in the air to scare the villagers. About 80 ran away, though all came back within four days or so. There was uproar in Chhattisgarh about villagers getting the wrong end of the stick as police stood by doing nothing.

Then, a couple of days later, according to Pisda, people in Jangla village held a meeting and managed to convince sangham members there to no longer cooperate with the Naxals. Jangla folk also decided to go to nearby Kotrapal village 'and make them understand', too. But the Naxals got wind of this. When they attacked Kotrapal on 20 June 2005, about 5,000 villagers were gathered there. One person died on the spot, another on the way to a health centre, and a dozen were kidnapped. The villagers were upset, says Pisda, 'that there was no trace of government in Dantewada...'

'So something had to be done?' I prod.

'Something had to be done. There were rumours that the Naxals were entering villages to loot, beat and kill. Anger began to spread, and a huge crowd of 20,000–25,000 people gathered and started to move towards Bijapur one afternoon. We got the news but were able to leave only the following morning, and on arriving, found 15,000 or so in clusters of a couple of thousand around Bijapur. We established camps and organized food, in Bijapur, Kutru and Jangla. Then we asked around, checked, and discovered there was no looting or intimidation as rumours had it. So in four to five days, people began to return home.

'Then Mahendra Karma arrived there. He toured the area, talked to people, held meetings with important people, with elders.' Pisda speeds it up here, once he has named the architect of Salwa Judum. Karma, a Congressman and leader of the opposition in Chhattisgarh's assembly—the BJP and Congress are officially united over Naxals in these parts—decided to brazen his way to Kotrapal. Bijapur's superintendent of police Dasrath Lal Manhar accompanied him even as Naxals were engaged in fighting with police on a nearby hill. Karma held frequent meetings in the area, on 1, 3, 7 and 11 July, whipping up anti-Naxal sentiment till poorly attended meetings became mass gatherings. 'Then in the middle of all this we appointed Special Police Officers, created village defence committees. Naxals started to attack these people—that continues.'

Naxals are hitting out, I counter, but Salwa Judum too appears to have gone out of control, with rampaging SPOs—tribal boys and girls—forcibly clearing entire villages. I draw the Collector's attention to a report by a group of prominent civil and human rights activists—dismissed by most security officials as a bunch of Maoist sympathizers—presented at a press conference in Raipur on 2 December 2005. The report, which first blew the lid on Salwa Judum, claimed:

1. The Salwa Judum is...an organized, state-managed enterprise that has precedents in the Jan Jagaran Abhiyans

that have occurred earlier under the leadership of the current Dantewada MLA, Mahendra Karma. The Collector himself has been part of 75% of the Salwa Judum meetings and security forces have been backing the Judum's meetings. The main cadre of Salwa Judum are comprised of Special Police Officers who are being paid and armed by the state, at a rate that is standard in counter-insurgency operations across the country.

2. The Salwa Judum has led to the forcible displacement of people throughout Bhairamgarh, Geedam and Bijapur areas, under police and administrative supervision...People have left behind their cattle and most of their household goods. The entire area is being cleared of inhabitants even as new roads are being built and more police and paramilitary stations are being set up. The region is being turned into one large cantonment...

3. When Salwa Judum meetings are called, people from neighbouring villages are asked to be present. Heavy security forces accompany the meetings. Villages that refuse to participate face repeated attacks by the combined forces of Salwa Judum, the district force and the paramilitary Naga battalion, which is stationed in the area...These raids result in looting, arson and killings in many instances. In some villages, the raids continue till the entire village is cleared and people have moved to camps, while in other cases only old people, women and children are left. Many villages are coming to camps to avoid these attacks in the first place.

4. Once in camps, people have no choice but to support the Salwa Judum. Some of them are forced to work as informers against members of their own and neighbouring villages and participate in attacks against them, leading to permanent divisions within villages. Individual families are sometimes being split between Judum supporters and those who wish to remain in their villages. We also came across instances where the Salwa Judum took young people away from the village and their families were unaware of their whereabouts.

5. Salwa Judum members man checkpoints on roads, search people's belongings and control the flow of transport. They enforce an economic blockade on villages that resist coming to camps. They also try to force civil officials to follow their dictat.

6. FIRs registering the looting, burning, beatings/torture by Salwa Judum mobs and the security forces are not recorded. We were told of specific instances where security forces threw dead bodies inside or near villages. The intention seems to be to terrorize people into leaving their villages. These killings are not reported, and therefore hard to corroborate. Some reports suggest that 96 people from 34 villages have been killed. However, the only killings that are officially recorded are those by Maoists. In the period since Salwa Judum started, it is true that the killings by Maoists have gone up substantially and the official figure today stands at 70. Rather than being a 'peace mission', as is claimed, the Salwa Judum has created a situation where violence has escalated.

7. Salwa Judum has strong support among certain sections of local society. This section comprises some non-adivasi immigrant settlers from other parts of India, sarpanches and traditional leaders whose power has been threatened by the Maoists...Both the local Congress and the BJP are supporting the Salwa Judum together.

8. We have heard from several high-ranking officials that there is an undeclared war on in Bastar, and we fear that the worst is yet to come...In addition, people are being encouraged to carry arms. Village defence committees are being created, SPOs are being trained and armed, and the entire society is becoming more militaristic...

And so on.

Pisda is agitated. The play in the national media, and a subsequent report by these activists in April 2006, *Where the State Makes War on Its Own People*—being widely circulated as we speak—has hit hard.

'These things can happen in a *griha*...' Pisda stops. I suspect he was about to use the Hindi word that translates as 'war at home', the first time I might have heard a serving official use the word 'civil war' on record in this context. Pisda resumes, 'Sometimes excesses can happen, by police or SPOs...in moments of anger...some wrong things may have happened...these things happen. We try to keep these in check. But it's wrong to say it's out of control. It's fully controlled.'

He misses the irony of admission. 'Then what about this?' I point to two other places in the *NYT* article on his desk. One reads: 'Salwa Judum leaders say they have waged their campaign with a singular goal in mind: to clear the villages, one by one, and break the Maoists' web of support. "Unless you cut off the source of the disease, the disease will remain," is how the group's most prominent backer, and influential adivasi politician named Mahendra Karma, put it. "The source is the people, the villagers."'

I point to another place, a few paragraphs up. It relates the story of an adivasi named Baman from Kotrapal. 'Last September the Salwa Judum, backed by the local police, swept through Kotrapal with a clear message: Move to the camps or face the Salwa Judum's wrath. "We finished off the village," said Ajay Singh, the Salwa Judum's leader in a nearby town, Bhairamgarh. Then he clarified: "People were excited. Of course they destroyed the houses."' Ajay Singh is a key associate of Mahendra Karma, and local Congress tough.

Pisda looks at his watch, and presses a buzzer concealed on his side of the desk. My time is up.

—

I can understand why. It is difficult to pass Salwa Judum off as a spontaneous mass movement, though nobody denies increasing resentment in many villages with Maoist pressure tactics. Neither is it the first time official thought has been put into play. In its report for 2003–4, the Home Ministry picked on an incident in Lango, a village in East Singhbhum district of Jharkhand that got its back up against Maoist intimidation which includes kangaroo courts, infamous for passing summary judgement for a variety of 'crimes' from exploitation to collaboration with the police. 'This feeling needs to be harnessed and channelized [into] making peoples' resistance groups to counter the atrocities committed by the Naxalite outfits.' The ministry further suggested, 'States have been requested to explore the possibility of appointing SPOs, Nagrik Suraksha Samitis (NSSs) [or civil defence groups] and Village Defence Committees (VDCs) in the villages affected by Naxalism. These local groups are required to be encouraged to come out against Jan Adalats and also to expose other misdeeds of the Naxal outfits and their leaders. This will help reduce the overground support to the Naxalites.'

Soon, manipulated by local leaders like Karma and supported by the administration, including the chief minister (Raman Singh of the BJP in this case), the battle is corrupted as tribal is set against tribal. And those in the crossfire, too, are tribals.

It may have begun innocently enough, as a document, generated in mid-2005 by Pisda's office—and filched by the Maoists—corroborates: '...it is imperative that the campaign receive administrative support...Firstly the campaign needs a common leader who can direct the campaign in a planned way. Secondly, adequate security must be provided to the participants so that they can overcome pressure from Naxalites. And thirdly, during the campaign villagers must be provided transport as and when needed, as well as food and a place to stay at government expense.'

Further, 'It is proposed that young men and women from the villages be made Special Police Officers. Depending upon the size of the village 5–10 SPOs would be needed. These SPOs will receive Rs 1500 per month as honorarium.

'Apart from imparting training to the villagers, providing them with traditional weapons such as bow and arrow, *farsa*, axe, stick, *ballam* etc. is extremely important...While villagers are asking for guns or licence to use them this is not advisable. Even if licenced guns are provided, [these] can be looted by Naxalites or the licencee could be killed to get his gun...Besides, an armed person can later on join the Naxalite organization which will enhance the strength of the Naxalites. Therefore, villagers' request is not worth accepting and they should only be provided traditional weapons.' (This suggestion was over-ruled. Many SPOs in Chhattisgarh are now armed with rifles.)

And here's the clincher: 'If we look minutely at police work in Naxalite affected areas it is more defensive and less aggressive. Now the time has come when the police have to change their style of work. Police have to become more aggressive. Although sometimes because of reasons beyond one's control some excesses do take place and some innocents do get affected. But keeping in mind the overall context of major operations it is important that the higher ups remain silent...only when people see Naxalites fleeing or getting killed will they side with the administration. Therefore, this policy must be pursued strictly. And for this police officers should be given a target.'

The Plan incisively suggests including unarmed sangham members in the ambit of surrender and government rehabilitation schemes: while armed cadre of the dalam are obvious targets, sangham members provide grassroots support to the Maoists, and are provided for by their mentors; therefore 'to end the problem of Naxalites it is not enough to kill Naxalites but more important to crush and destroy their system operating at the village level.'

Finally, to get it all going ship-shape with appropriate spin, errant media needs to be handled, as '...Media coverage of Naxalite attacks makes it look as if they are gaining the upper hand'. The way out—and this is the root of Chhattisgarh's gag law—is to reach out to all media with meetings and requests, and suggest that state business and business of the people have greater currency than what the Maoists or their sympathizers do and say. It's a tactical stick of state control. The carrot of media freedom implicit in India's constitution can, basically, be chucked out of a convenient window.

People like Kamlesh Paikra learned this the hard way, away from the relative glamour and immunity of big-city, big-name journalism. Till earlier in the year, he used to write for *Hindsat*, published from Jagdalpur, the headquarters of the neighbouring district of Bastar, and lived in Bijapur, deep inside Dantewada. Now he runs for his life, and scratches around for a livelihood—Himanshu has place at the ashram for Kamlesh's brother Nagesh but Kamlesh is too much of a political hot potato even for the belligerent Himanshu. The Paikras live in a one-room tenement in Dantewada town.

'I used to write what the administration did, and I used to attend press briefings called by the Naxals,' he tells me, this tiny, soft-spoken man, as we share tea at the ashram. 'I did not take sides, but believed that what the Naxals said was as important as what the administration said. The administration did not like it.' Kamlesh says he was asked many times to stop writing about the Maoists, but he didn't. 'Bijapur SP Manhar spoke to me in the worst possible way with the worst possible curses. He threatened me and told me I would be responsible for my actions. They would follow me around. I was scared I would be killed off in an encounter.'

The administration, according to Kamlesh, leaned on distributors to stop selling *Hindsat* at key outlets, like the local bus and train stations. It got to the point when the family—his parents, pregnant wife and brother—decided it was too dangerous for them to continue in their village, Chernapal, near Bijapur, so they left one night after arranging for transport with the help of a friend. They haven't been back since.

'I have these new clothes now,' Kamlesh says, 'because friends helped me. We used to sleep on newspapers on the floor. Now we have mattresses, again because friends helped us.' But he says he leads the life of the walking dead.

4

Salwa Judum
Rape Two,
Murder one for free!
Hurry!
Offer open till Tribals last!

—Message at naxalrevolution.blogspot.com

Salwa Judum is never too far in images or reality. In the summer of 2005, when the 'purification hunt' was in full flow, Maoists tapped into a conversation in Hindi between the person they claimed was the superintendent of police of Bijapur, a man called D.L. Manhar, and his subordinates. Officials publicly dismissed the recording as fake—though few believed them—but were in private stunned at this coup. Among other things, the authenticity was endorsed by bureaucratese in the conversation. The police never took up the Maoist offer of voice print analysis to establish the truth.

It's quite a story. Listen.

[SP Bijapur]: You will have to take out a party and you should go to every village in your police station area...the villages that are awakened—message us separately about them. Two lakh rupees have been sanctioned for each awakened village.

And for villagers who will help retrieve arms there is three lakh rupees for LMG, two lakh for AK-47, and one lakh for SLR. You will have to inform the villagers. If anybody helps recover a small pistol, 500 rupees, and for a big pistol 1000 rupees should be given immediately...

And if anyone kills a Naxali he will get awards from the central and state governments...you need to tell them all these things.

[Voice]: Roger, sir. Roger.

[SP]: Call Reynold and ask him to talk to me and call the steno and ask him to talk to me...steno *ko bulao*.

In Bhairamgarh, there is a function of Jan Jagaran in the Keshputul area today and there is a chance of an encounter. So there will be large-scale attacks on Naxalis and their supporters, the sangham members. For that reason, put Mirtur and Gangalur on high alert...If they run away we will inform them—from 9 a.m. onwards every wireless will be on listening mode. Nobody should engage; these should be on listening watch. Did you understand? This is a permanent order for you. Whenever there is a function like this on any day everyone should remain on high alert.

In Kotrapal nine [Naxals] were killed. Had a [police] party come from the other side they would all have died...So this is the situation, ask everyone to be on high alert, and don't keep the button pressed in your machine—so that if any message needs to be passed on to you, it can be done. Everyone should inform each other of what they are doing...Did you understand the point?

[Voice]: Point noted, sir. Point noted, sir.

[SP]: Steno *ko bulao*.

[Voice]: Sir, the sentry has gone to call him.

[SP]: All officers and forces should be well distributed. And be on high alert. If any journalists come to report on Naxalis—get them killed. Did you understand?

[Voice]: Roger, sir.

[SP]: Put one person on 24-hour work to note down the vehicle numbers for all the people going to that side. And put one person to make a list of how many villages there are, how many have joined Jan Jagaran, how many sangham members there are. Your records should be up to date.

[Voice]: Yes, sir, point noted. I'll do it.

[SP]: ...And act accordingly, today's message is that it is very tense. They [Naxals] have challenged villagers and villagers have also said that they will go for a direct fight. They will also come with sangham members today...so if you get any message, check with Alpha *saheb*...The telephone line here is dead so you need to do hard work; spend maximum time in the control room.

[Voice]: Yes, sir, all points clear, sir.

[SP]: You should send just one message: all work will be done...The other point is—all this is keeping in mind the situation here and in your area—as soon as this area is covered they will enter your area. So don't shout at any workers. There is enough rice, pulses; there is no problem...What is the view of people in your area?

[Voice]: Three encounters happened, nine people died, and Jan Jagaran people have burned all the grain storage.

[SP]: Today Kotrapal sangham members will surrender...They are saying people are dying on the other side, no development is happening, so they will surrender today...The Jan Jagaran people are telling villagers very clearly, 'You come with us...If you do not come [after being told for the] third time, we will burn your village.' Their challenge is direct— understood? That's why there is no need to worry...So Kotrapal sangham members will surrender today. After that, we will make a team including them and send it to your area...These Jan Jagaran people are telling us, 'You don't need to do anything. We will go with our bows and arrows and bring them back on our shoulders after killing them...today everything will be done as organized. Understood? It is possible that Kotrapal people may kill Nirmalakka today. So that is the situation in Kotrapal. Some [Naxals] will try to escape and they will kill Nirmalakka.

[Voice]: Okay, sir.

Radio jockeys of Dandakaranya, proposing counter-revolution, ethnic cleansing of tribal by tribal, scorched earth—all rolled into one.

Chhattisgarh's police chief O.P. Rathor has the grace to term it 'public movement with police support'. His political bosses, however, live in a world of their own making.

In February 2007, at a great remove in time and space from the circa-day of this recorded intercept in Dandakaranya, I would hear Chhattisgarh's chief minister Raman Singh make a boast. 'Salwa Judum cannot be defeated. Salwa Judum is a turning point in the Naxal history of the world,' he would tell senior police and intelligence officials engaged in anti-Maoist operations from Chhattisgarh and several other states. 'It will be written a hundred years from now. Salwa Judum is showing Gandhi is alive, showing non-violence is alive.' The senior police officer seated next to me choked, and hastily reached for a glass of water to cover his discomfort. The roomful of people heard Raman Singh glibly add, 'Salwa Judum is like the fragrance of the forest in summer.'

—

Resettlement in times of conflict is not a fresh idea in independent India. Nor are the ideas of village defence committees and SPOs. For instance, village defence committees were used extensively, and with remarkable effectiveness, during the Punjab secessionist insurgency of the 1980s and 1990s, and continue to be used in Jammu & Kashmir with patchy success. SPOs in Jammu & Kashmir are trained in basic handling of arms and ammunition as a wing-and-a-prayer holding strategy against heavily armed, well-trained and ultra-zealous Islamist terrorists and fidayeen or suicide squads.

As far back as 1966, the Republic of India contemplated a deliberate resettlement strategy in Mizoram, when in March that year Mizoram National Front 'President' Laldenga declared the region's independence from India and the Mizo National

Army launched a withering guerilla insurrection. It led to thousands of ethnic Mizos fleeing the region to other parts of India and many more being squeezed between demands of the ethnic rebel army and Indian troops. 'The years 1967–9 saw the entire rural population of Mizoram (roughly 80 per cent of the total) uprooted from their homes, to be relocated miles away in what were euphemistically called "Protected and Progressive Villages",' writes Vijendra Singh Jafa in 'Counterinsurgency Warfare: Use and Abuse of Military Force', an essay in a volume of *Faultlines*, a publication by the Institute of Conflict Management. It was among the most brutal military campaigns independent India has engaged in: open season for the brutality of peace.

Jafa, a former IAS officer and chief secretary of Assam state was clinical in his observations made in 1999: 'The army argued that the segregation and control of the population by this method was necessary for a successful counter-insurgency campaign. The general humiliation, loss of freedom, of property, and, very often, injury and death involved in this process of so-called "grouping of villages" were incidental to the military operations in Mizoram, as perhaps they are to internal wars anywhere. But it appeared to many then, as it would appear to many more acutely now, that the policy of "grouping" was tantamount to annihilation of reason and sensibility and certainly not the best policy to follow against our own ethnic minorities.'

Towards the end of the essay Jafa comes to two conclusions, both chillingly mirrored in Salwa Judum. First, that such resettlement is incalculably destructive. And second, that there is a code for it, in the best tradition of masking a hostile takeover: alibi at any cost.

'Darzo was one of the richest villages I have ever seen in this part of the world,' Jafa quotes an army officer who was involved in relocation in Mizoram that included destroying anything that couldn't be carried away—food, belongings and shelter—so that the enemy would be denied all such resources. '...Night fell and I had to persuade the villagers to come out and set fire to their homes. Nobody came out. Then I had to order my soldiers to enter every house and force the people out. Every man, woman and child who could walk came out with as much of his or her belongings and food as they could. But they wouldn't set fire to their homes. Ultimately, I lit a torch myself and set fire to one of the houses...

'...I called the Darzo village council president and his village elders and ordered them to sign a document saying they had voluntarily asked to be resettled...as they were being harassed by insurgents...Another document stated they had burned down their own village, and that no force or coercion was used by security forces. They refused to sign. So I sent them out and after one hour called them in again, this time one man at a time. On my table was a loaded revolver, and in the corner stood two NCOs with loaded sten-guns. This frightened them, and one by one they signed both the documents. I had to do it, as I had no choice in the matter. If those chaps had gone to the civil administration or the courts with complaints, there would have been all kinds of criminal cases against us...All individual officers were expected to carry out their tasks in such a manner that it left no scope for embarrassment to our higher formations.'

In turn, India bought peace. Mizoram has the highest ratio of government servants to the population of any Indian state— one in every nine people. If that is narrowed to the working-age population, then it is one in every four.

Alibi at any cost.

In Dantewada, the alibi came in the form of letters signed by villagers. Pisda himself had shown me a dozen, and then generously provided photocopies for me to keep as record.

Each is addressed in formal Hindi to '*Shriman* Collector *Mahoday*' and has as subject line: 'With reference to being protected from Naxalites.' In these, between four and thirteen inhabitants of a dozen hamlets—among them Nugur, Kodepalli, Hinjmeta, Aramarka, Musli, Chhotebodli—have put their names down and affixed thumbprint signatures to identical applications in a style that suggests these either being recorded by the police or the administration. In rough translation, they submit, 'In our area Naxal terror is so pervasive that we are unable to protect our lives and property. They torture us and forcibly take away our belongings after scaring and threatening us and insist that we send our mothers and daughters, young men and women with them or we would be punished.

'Therefore, we request the Government of Chhattisgarh and the Collector to either save us from Naxalites or give us leave to die and kill as we see fit.'

There is no date of writing these letters, but all are shown as received on 14 June 2005, several days before the incident at Kotrapal that Pisda claims started the buzz of a people's movement, and several weeks before the series of meetings Mahendra Karma held in the first fortnight of July that year. By mid-June, the administration already had its alibi for tribals of Chhattisgarh versus tribals of Chhattisgarh, signed, sealed and delivered.

—

By August 2005, Salwa Judum had made it to discussion in India's Parliament, in the Lok Sabha, and was endorsed by the Government of India—naturally, with none of the fire, brimstone and death contained in dry, parliamentary language used for affairs of the state:

GOVERNMENT OF INDIA
MINISTRY OF HOME AFFAIRS

LOK SABHA

UNSTARRED QUESTION NO 2337, TO BE ANSWERED ON 09.08.2005

FIGHT AGAINST MAOISTS

2337. SHRI JUAL ORAM

Will the Minister of HOME AFFAIRS be pleased to state:

(a) whether the tribals in Orissa and Chhattisgarh have joined hands with police to fight against the Maoists/Naxalites;

(b) if so, the details in this regard along with the steps taken by the Government to encourage and assist them in this mission;

(c) the success achieved by such move of tribals in affected areas;

(d) whether any action plan has been prepared by the Government to promote such groupings against Naxalites/Maoists; and

(e) if so, the details thereof?

ANSWER
MINISTER OF STATE IN THE MINISTRY OF HOME AFFAIRS (SHRI SRIPRAKASH JAISWAL)

(a) to (e): Available reports indicate that villagers including tribals in Bijapur and Dantewada Police districts in Chhattisgarh are holding anti-naxalite rallies against the atrocities being committed by the naxalites despite threats from the latter. Anti-naxalite rallies are picking up momentum in Bastar region and the villagers have vowed to resist the naxalite activities. Keeping in view the retaliatory action of the naxalites, the State Government has been asked to provide to the villagers and encourage formation of 'Village Defence Committees'. The Central Govt. has assured all possible help to the State Govt. in this regard.

5

Sukhdev takes me for a spin. He sticks to the blacktop only as far as a turn-off just beyond Mahendra Karma's village home at Faraspal—he isn't there—past a nearby CRPF camp. We're tracked by two sentries positioned at the gates and a half dozen more from the veranda of the camp commander's office. We then go off-road, on treacherous dirt tracks in a wilderness, expertly manoeuvring through loose earth and scree. We're heading for the looming range in the horizon, the Bailadila hills, on to a winding cut and then through them, into a dense forest of shrub and sal.

The government never bothered with this route, which saves nearly 40 kilometres on a journey to Bhairamgarh, where we're headed, bypassing the much longer route by Geedam. But there are signs of awakening. Small road crews here and there are engaged in patching up sunken portions of track near where we cross the hills. The slash and burn remains of trees and bushes are 10 to 15 metres from the verge; Sukhdev says paramilitary forces did it several weeks earlier to ensure that Maoists can't easily sneak up on foot patrols and convoys, spraying bullets or triggering IEDs—improvised explosive devices: material crammed into crude boxes of iron sheeting and set off with timers. Even with this shrubbery insurance, trees and shadows are everywhere.

A tiny hamlet flashes past, Sukhdev not bothering with it except to point out a gathering of tribal folk near a small trader's truck, here to collect mahua and tamarind, the so-called 'minor forest produce' listed in innumerable reports, classification by which 90 per cent of tribals in these regions subsist. Or used to, till Salwa Judum came their way. People warily turn to us as we pass, women with carved faces and men on their haunches, already at mid-morning *salti*, drink made from the sap of an eponymous palm look-alike, with narrower, longer leaves than the palm. They drink from leaf cups stitched together with twig, holding the sides with ginger fingertips, and reach out for more from a container of hollowed gourd.

We hit the slim dusty-black ribbon to Bhairamgarh—designated National Highway Number 16, the much-bombed road that snakes southwest to Andhra Pradesh—after half an hour, a little distance from Kodoli village. 'The Nagas were here two months ago,' Sukhdev growls. This is also the first place I see with Salwa Judum signage—in Hindi, bright white on blue: 'The core mantra for freedom from Naxalism—Salwa Judum. Get rid of Naxalis and save Bastar. Get rid of Naxalis and save the country.'

With typical bureaucratic flourish, all Salwa Judum boards are white on blue. This differentiates them from the yellow boards of Sarva Shiksha Abhiyan (the national Literacy for All mission), the blue on white boards of the Rajiv Gandhi Watershed Management Mission, the plain black on white of the Prime Minister's Rural Roads Programme, and the rust on rust of long forgotten 'missions'. These markers litter the highway as well as dirt tracks. They are often the only indication to a visitor that a habitation exists—and suggest that being a contractor for government signage is a lucrative practice.

The signs follow us all the way to hell.

—

There are two Bhairamgarhs. Type One is the typical in-the-middle-of-remoteness Indian village that has come of age as nucleus, market town and administrative centre to other nearby villages. It has brick units for traders, leaders and the police and mud hovels for the rest.

Type Two is the Salwa Judum camp. Past a barbed-wire-enclosed, well-tended but basic den of CRPF is a large field, about half the size of a football pitch, covered with 'sheeting-blue'—often, roofing for India's teeming slum dwellers, and victims of natural disasters, riots and those displaced by projects. Other kinds of roofing are evident as well: tattered canvas, holed tin, scrap wood, straw and plain air. The camp is unguarded. Nobody bothers to ask Sukhdev and me our business, though eyes follow us everywhere.

Pits in and around the camp have become open sewers. The smell of garbage, urine and faeces overpowers the aroma of cooking fires and boiled rice. Children with distended bellies walk around. Women cook, sit or lie listlessly. A lady feeds her child and herself a tiny meal of rice and dal from small leaf bowls. Men sit in knots; here the pleasures of salti are denied. Some sleep. There is little to do.

The camp has been in existence since July 2005, nine months as I visit. Through torrential rain, heat, bone-chilling winter and, now, baking heat. There will be more rain on the way in five to six months. Collector Pisda had told me of two kinds of people in camps. The sort that want to remain in camps out of fear of the Maoists, and those who would like to return once there is peace. To me, both seem indefinitely consigned to the cesspit of the camp.

Budhram Apka, an 18-year-old from Pondum village, an eight-kilometre walk from Bhairamgarh, isn't sure which category he belongs to. Sukhdev translates from Hindi to Gondi and back as Budhram mumbles in desultory conversation, not once looking at us, as if that one act would absolve him of guilt if prying SJ informers came calling—or perhaps so that we, who can do little, will not probe too much and leave him to privacy.

'How long have you been in this camp?'

'Since the rains.' Last July, Sukhdev clarifies.

'Why did you come here?'

'I was afraid of Naxalis.'

'Did they threaten you directly?'

'No, but I was frightened.'

'What do you do?'

'Sometimes, I get daily wage work. Most of the time there is no work.'

'How do you eat?'

'Salwa Judum people give us some rice, some rations. Two days ago they gave us pots.' He points behind him. There are two by a dead clay oven, blackened from wood smoke, badly dented. They were to be new.

'Do you want to go back to your village?'

'When there is *shanti*.' He tears. Sukhdev and I give him a couple of minutes to calm down as he stands, gripping the slim wooden-pole support of his riddled-plastic home.

'Do you have to ask Salwa Judum for permission to leave camp or go back to your village?'

'Yes.'

'Have they allowed you to go back to your village?'

'No.'

'Where is your family?'

'In the village. Mother, father, sister.'

'So why did you come, all by yourself?'

'They told me to.'

'Who?'

Budhram jerks his head, and looks around nervously.

'Salwa Judum.' Sukhdev adds in aside: 'Maybe they thought he would join Naxalis.'

I press on. 'When will you go back?'

'I don't know.' Budhram replies savagely and walks away.

We walk a few metres and come to the tin-roofed, open-sided home of Somaru, formerly of Alvoor, further on from Pondum. A year older than Budhram, his responses are nearly identical, with one difference: his family moved with him.

'We were afraid of both Naxalis and Salwa Judum,' he says, as a small, naked girl with distended belly and fly-encrusted nose and mouth stands by his side and stares at us; by her side is a snot-nosed boy, a little older, also naked, identically adorned with protruding belly and flies. Two women watch us warily. A third lies on a reed mat, covered by torn cloth, eyes open and glazed, unmoving. Pots and pans lie around her, some plastic bags, and a plastic pot of water. I am transfixed. Finally, she blinks. I exhale.

'Is that why you moved? Because you were afraid?' I ask Somaru.

'No.'

'Then?'

'Salwa Judum said we had to leave the village.'

'Did they force you?'

No response. Somaru looks away.

'What do you want him to say?' Sukhdev snaps at me. 'Can he say more than he already has?'

Few can, by many accounts. 'There is complete collapse of civil administration,' Nandini Sundar had told me what seems like a lifetime away in New Delhi. 'SJ can stop vehicles, check them and people, ask questions. The state has abdicated to SJ.' (Sukhdev and I were spared the honours at the barrier before Bhairamgarh. 'They wouldn't dare stop me,' he had growled when I enquired as to why we were let off.)

You make it sound like 1970s' Cambodia or Vietnam, I had told Nandini.

'It's exactly like that,' she agreed. 'Nagas and SJ visit villages and ask people, even those not part of the sangham or even *seen* as Maoist sympathizers, to attend meetings and come into camps. If they refuse, they are attacked for no reason. And once they've been herded into the camps, they are completely under the control of SJ.'

The Salwa Judum is evidently a strange and compelling animal: part imagination, part administration, part intimidation, and part corruption.

Sukhdev and I move on. Normality comes in the shape of a crèche school—anganwadi—in progress on a raised concrete platform, under the shelter of sheeting-blue. It's the only visible saving grace of SJ—such as it is. A ten-year-old girl, Kumari, cares for younger children, combing their hair after a *dai*, ayah-cum-helper, in bright yellow sari rubs a thrifty finger-dab of mustard oil into their scalps. Another dab is used to rub gloss into the chapped arms, legs, faces. They bathed the previous day; they will bathe again a day later. Water is in short supply at the camp. Readied, they head on to school, right there.

This is clearly the high point of the day, as parents and hangers-on in the camp come to life and crowd around to see children spout alphabets. Prem Kumari Nishant, formerly of nearby Dhuma Ghotpal and now headmistress of the haunted, takes care they get their sentiment's worth—even though she hasn't been paid her Rs 1,000 a month salary for two months, the same as the two dais haven't been paid half that for as long. The money for SJ is routed through Karma's henchmen in the area, powerful local Congress functionaries whose word is law. It's a long way from Raipur's treasury to the destitute in Bhairamgarh and elsewhere. As with many conflict situations in Jammu & Kashmir and almost the whole of India's northeast, nobody counts development funds, just as they don't the 'collateral damage' of both protest and administration by force. Pisda says he has asked the Chhattisgarh government for immediate infusion of 300 crore—three billion—rupees to spread around Dantewada district and keep the Maoists at bay. It will be an impressive gravy train.

Prem Kumari turns to a paper chart of Hindi alphabets and pictorial cues nailed to a dead tree that is part roof support, part classroom wall. The children loudly intone the lesson on vowels in chorus: '*A se Angur, Aa se Aam, Ee se Imli...*' Then, onto consonants, '*Ka se Kabootar, Kha se Khargosh...*'

Grape, mango, tamarind, pigeon, rabbit. Such exotica. It's the first time I see smiles and hear laughter in the camp.

6

The sun is merciless as we walk back towards Bhairamgarh's market and the thread of highway. The CRPF camp is to our left, fenced with three strands of barbed wire. A few trucks, a jeep. And one olive green personnel carrier strengthened to withstand mines—a recent export to Chhattisgarh and already a casualty; the Maoists simply pack in more explosives into IEDs and rain bullets on whoever emerges from the 'mine-proof' vehicle. The previous year, in September 2005, Maoists blew one up, killing 26 policemen. There's a sandbagged gun emplacement near the entrance to the camp. A few unarmed khaki-clad police and paramilitary stroll about. Apart from these, a few boys in faded olive green—resident SPOs.

'*Bas?*' I'm astounded. 'If the Maoists mount a massed attack...'

'Anytime,' Sukhdev cuts me off. 'They can do it anytime,

and nobody can do anything about it. Where all will the police keep watch?'

Jai Bhairam General Store and Gift Corner is to our right. Sukhdev and I are both parched and he eagerly nods to my suggestion that we stop for water or soft drink. We settle for 7Up. Sukhdev is tense. There are three SPO boys at the shop, armed with .303 rifles and bandoliers stuffed with magazines, the elite tier of a band of 5,000 created by the state that is permitted to carry guns, more privileged than those left to the device of bows and arrows, axes and spears. They're hanging around; it's why I suggested the pit stop to Sukhdev. They track us as we approach.

Are you SPOs, I ask politely. One of them, in rubber slippers, jeans, full-sleeve T-shirt and knitwear skullcap, nods. The other two keep staring. Why don't you sit beside me, I suggest, patting the rickety bench by empty cases of soft drink. He comes by. His two companions don't. They remain at the store counter, looking at us.

That's how I meet Lachinder Kondh, 18, formerly of Patarpara village, now stationed as PSO at Bhairamgarh. He rests the rifle butt-first on the ground. I opt for shameless PR as icebreaker and offer him a fizzy drink. He declines with a shake of his head and holds up a plastic tube of something cola-like. It's iced cola. Popsi Cola. The boy-men of SJ are all nibbling on it. They seem relaxed. Maybe it's because the Salwa Judum is in a lull of sorts, ostensibly as a reaction to media and public outcry after the last major drive, in the second week of April 2006, where Mahendra Karma personally led Salwa Judum teams to ten villages; human rights activists spoke of 800 houses burnt. (The lull would last all of a month; on 8 May SJ cadre along with police would storm villages near Konta and burn an estimated 50 houses.)

Must feel good, I try, to be in a town, to carry a gun, to be able to pay for things with money earned. Lachinder nods. Then he tells me he has been here since the previous July. The boy speaks broken Hindi, so Sukhdev takes a break from translating.

'Why did you join?'

'To stop Naxalites.'

'Are you afraid of them?'

He straightens up, takes a huge pull of Popsi Cola and tells me matter-of-factly: 'With a gun in your hand you feel less afraid...you don't feel afraid.'

'How much do you get?'

'Rs 1500 a month.'

'Is that why you're here?'

No answer. Then in a torrent, 'In Bhairamgarh it is better, we get rations. In other SPO camps, you don't get rations, you have to buy what you eat.' Another method of finessing the distribution of 'development' funds.

'You stay in that CRPF camp?'

He nods, smiling. I would, too. It's a step up from the broken, catatonic life in the state-sponsored sewer behind us, and relatively safe from Maoist attack. I turn to look at his companions, and adopting his body language, stick my chin out and raise my eyebrows in query.

'He's my senior.'

'Senior?' I burst out laughing. Senior is laughing, too. 'How old is he?'

'Seventeen. Raju. He's from my village, He's my senior. He became SPO a month before me.' That would be June, when SJ took wing. When Raju was 16 and Lachinder nearabout 17. Even if they wanted, they wouldn't be able to vote 'No' to what was happening to them—or be made part of the state's police force, or the country's army.

Over in Maoist areas, attitudes towards engaging the young are only marginally better. Pre-teen tribal children—part of what is known as *bal sangham*, a children's 'army' of indoctrinated sympathizers—are not given guns. But they are prepared for the time when they will: the cadre encourage them to play a specially devised game, a variation of cops-and-robbers. In Hindi, it's *chor–police*. Here, it's Maoist–police.

A group of children walk in single file holding sticks like

guns, the same way police patrol the jungles. Another group, the preferred group—some with the Maoist-red scarf tied round their heads—stay behind bushes and trees, crouching, on their bellies, silent. At a word, they attack with their own stick-guns. Most 'police' drop 'dead', as they must, being on the wrong side of the system, the wrong side of propaganda. Those who don't die are taken—'arrested'. The Maoists always win.

In Dantewada, democracy is quite dead, on both sides of the battle line.

'They have not paid me for two months,' Lachinder whines. 'Money always comes late, sometimes many months behind. Sometimes they ask us to make our own arrangements.' I look to Sukhdev for translation. He discreetly rubs a thumb and forefinger in universal language. Bribes. 'Cuts' from passing buses and trucks, individual travellers. Sometimes, cuts for someone to stay alive.

'Can you do something about it?' With his free hand, Lachinder shakes my arm.

'I'll see,' I reply, with what I hope is sufficient authority. I take his rifle and inspect it. There's neat etching near the butt: *1945. No 1 Mark III. No 522.* Then with white paint, Chhattisgarh's inventory is added to 60-year-old factory markings: *No 28.* 'Must weigh 20 kilos,' I joke, handing the .303 back to him.

'No, four and half,' he corrects me. 'Fifty rounds. Forty-two in the belt and eight in the *banduk*. Seven in the magazine,' he fine-tunes, looking around, 'one in the chamber.' There's a small knot of people. We're entertainment.

'*Chaalu hai*?' I ask, using speak-easy for 'Is it on?'

'*Haan, chalu hai*.' He shows me.

'Have you ever fired it?'

'Many times. We go to the hills to practice.'

'What about action? Have you seen action?'

'Yes, just last week. We were out late at night. We were in a truck. I fired three times.'

'Did you hit them?'

'No, but they were shooting back.'

'Were you afraid?'

'A little, but there is no time to think. You just fire.' He turns to look at me. 'You become a brave man with a gun in your hand.'

Do you know how to clean the rifle, I prod. Dismantle it? Put it back together again? Yes, he replies, as others crowd around. 'See, this part comes away,' he shows the trigger housing. 'All this comes off.'

He slides open the chamber to show me how it works. A round pops up from the magazine and he slams it into the breech and locks it in one smooth motion. Then he aims the rifle at a nearby wall. A woman and child are passing by. I hold the barrel and force the weapon down. Lachinder rests it on the ground, and then, demonstration over, puts a hand over the barrel in repose. I quickly snatch it away, saying he might blow a hole in his hand. The small gathering laughs.

It then quickly descends to dangerous farce. To compensate for loss of face, Lachinder angrily opens the breech to eject the round. It flies off and lands at my feet. I pick it up, rub the dust off the sleek brass bullet against my jeans and hand it back. He presses the bullet back into the magazine, ensures the chamber is empty, and again, to regain face, aims the gun at the wall of people near us and presses the trigger. Click.

Lachinder finally smiles. Senior smiles, too, pats down the camouflage cap on his head and fiercely pulls on his Popsi Cola.

I get up and salute Lachinder. He is grinning, soaking up another round of laughter. 'Hope to see you again,' I tell him. 'Remember my face. If you're on patrol and come across me...' The smiles freeze. Game over. Sukhdev takes my arm and pulls me away.

As we drive off to Matwara, further down the highway towards Bijapur, to see more relief camp hell, I notice a small shop festooned with clothes: khaki tunics and pants, camouflage caps, T-shirts—liberally displayed among export-surplus garments, clothes for a mix of work and play, war and peace.

The shop has a sign for male innerwear as well. It's called Macro Man.

And it reminds me of my meeting in Delhi with B, my closet-Maoist friend, from whom I hoped to get some contacts as I planned my travels in Naxalite country. We had found ourselves talking a lot about Monty that evening. In the Delhi manner of assuming familiar diminutives for the powerful, this was how B referred to Montek Singh Ahluwalia, deputy chairman of India's Planning Commission. B doesn't at all like Monty.

B doesn't care much for Prime Minister Singh either. 'Bloody Monty and Manmohan,' he had railed at me. 'Like other policy chaps, they will kill the half of India that is weakest and *that* will kill India.' The Prime Minister and Ahluwalia had formed a team in 1991 when Singh was appointed India's kick-start finance minister and Ahluwalia— an alumnus of the World Bank and former Prime Minister Rajiv Gandhi's 1980s' think tank—his crack finance secretary. B accused them of 'selling India's agriculture to multinationals by corporatizing the farm sector and weakening it to the point of starvation and death. Their big-picture crap is killing the small man. Macro is killing micro.'

B's views are extreme, but he's right about one thing: development has become an internal security issue, and lack of development a self-inflicted, festering wound. To calm B down, I had attempted Americana, and jokingly referred to Ahluwalia as 'Macro Man.'

B had dissolved in laughter. And I had my contacts.

I laughed at the memory. But how could I explain it to Sukhdev, who slowed the motorbike to ask me if all was well?

7

There is hardly any sign of life at Patarpara. Some cattle roam barren fields. A couple of children watch the world from a hut under the shade of a large banyan.

We are travelling on a broad packed-earth road raised a couple of feet from surrounding fields. The road wasn't there two months ago, Sukhdev says. It's new, to transport troops. The road has been laid with the help of the Border Roads Organization (BRO), which is in itself an admission that there's a war raging in the heart of India: the BRO usually works way to the north, along India's bitterly contested border with Pakistan and China, and in the death zones of Jammu & Kashmir and the North East. Few civil contractors will risk death and destruction from the Maoists. It's got too tense in these parts for traditional permission—a percentage of the contract, between ten and twelve. It can amount to crores of rupees a year, as rebel armies, a parallel administration, need to be clothed, fed and armed, and families of the cadre taken care of. Bihar's chief minister Nitish Kumar is among a few to actually put a figure to it; he estimates the Maoists in his state pull in Rs 150 crore a year—not counting the cost of outright looting of money and snatching of arms and ammunition from security forces—from contractors, traders and big business engaged in a range of activities from forest produce and timber trade to mining and construction. Raman Singh, Kumar's counterpart in Chhattisgarh, says he estimates the Maoists pull in Rs 100 crore a year from Bastar, the Dandakaranya zone within his state.

We are in Patarpara because Sukhdev decided it was too dangerous to move beyond Matwara; SPOs were on hair-trigger further towards Bijapur—two of us were too few for the journey—and he was also getting restless. After we had tramped through yet another SJ refugee-holding pen in Matwara, he had irritably asked me: 'How much more of this do you need to see?'

'Fine,' I had shot back. 'We'll do as you say.' He had turned around, scorching rubber on the road, and roared back along the highway, past dozens of special forces emplacements and SJ pickets, not caring what they thought of us, doing 80 kilometres an hour on a road on which I wouldn't go beyond forty.

'An IED went off here a few days ago,' he shouted as we hurtled over a culvert, Bhairamgarh behind us. Then, brief revenge over, he cooled to a more sedate speed. By the time we reached the turn-off for Patarpara and Pondum several minutes later, Sukhdev was again his affable self.

Two men had waved us down some distance past the turn off. I feared they were SJ thugs. But they were unarmed, and turned out to be dressed in torn, soiled vests and lungi, not quite SJ chic. They rattled off a stream of dialect. They wanted money, Sukhdev said, disgusted. Money to drink. 'Drink is the downfall of us adivasis.'

But it wasn't quite like that. At my insistence, Sukhdev probed further. It turned out that they were complaining about not being paid for work. For some days of roadwork done in October 2005, they had been paid only two days earlier—the 'food for work' programme at Rs 58.89 a day, the rate fixed by the Chhattisgarh government. They said they hadn't been paid for any work since.

'Who is supposed to pay you?'

'The *sachiv*.' The local panchayat secretary.

'Why hasn't he?'

'Maybe he has drunk it all up.' They bent over laughing.

'Where does the sachiv get the money from?'

'Block sahib.' In Bhairamgarh, under which this patch falls, the power of dispensing belonged to Ajay Singh, a crony of Mahendra Karma. He wasn't in during our trip into Bhairamgarh, but I knew the name from conversations with Nandini and Himanshu, and the *NYT* article that had Pisda in such foul temper. (Ajay Singh would be killed a month later, on 22 May. The Maoists snared him as he moved out from Bhairamgarh, confident it was now relatively Maoist-free. Ajay and his colleagues found a tree across a track. When they stopped, the Maoists blew them up with a hidden pressure bomb. Ajay and three others died, on home turf. Police officials later told me several villages are strewn with such booby traps, the exact locations of which are known to villagers.)

'Where does all the money go?' I asked Sukhdev. In reply, he looked at the sky.

One of the adivasis was more forthcoming. 'He keeps it,' he said. 'When there is "imgency" he gives it.' Emergency was when he couldn't any longer deny payment.

'Sachiv, sachiv,' the two adivasis started shouting as a motorcycle came closer. We moved to the middle of the road to stop him. The sachiv was nattily dressed in full-sleeve shirt, trousers, new sandals and large sunshades. His moustache was neatly trimmed.

'These two say they haven't been paid for their work,' I said in Hindi. 'When will they get the money?'

The two adivasis stopped their chatter in Gondi and took up a chorus in Hindi to demand money, putting on a show. '*Paisa do, paisa do. Dey do.*' They looked at Sukhdev and me for approval. Sukhdev seemed to be an inch away from clouting the sachiv. The man gunned his motorcycle and scythed a path through us, covering us in dust.

'These people even steal relief money,' Sukhdev said, and spat on the track.

I was reminded of an article by Debal K. Singharoy I'd read recently in the *Economic and Political Weekly*, entitled 'Peasant Movements in Contemporary India: Emerging Forms of Domination and Resistance'. In it, there was mention of an incensed tribal lady in West Bengal's Khanpur village, and her refrain:

Hamra mathot karong kam
Thaakong bhanga ghorot
Porong fata sari, charong gorur gari
Hamar babur hol sada dhoti, Paichen fotfoti
Pakka hol ore bari

(We work in the fields, stay in broken huts
Wear torn clothes, and ride on bullock carts,
While our 'babu' wears a clean white dhoti,
Has a motorcycle and lives in a pucca house.)

I was reminded, too, of a story that D, an intelligence officer, had told me about former Chhattisgarh chief minister Ajit Jogi, himself without the reputation of a saint. According to D, Jogi used to say that if all the funds spent in Bastar since 1947 were added up and totalled with interest, there would be one crore, that's ten million rupees, for each family. 'Where did all that money go?' the officer asked me rhetorically. 'There is still nothing. You move around and there's nothing anywhere. So it is to their advantage, *na*?' he said, meaning to the advantage of the Maoists. 'For years nobody checked how money was being utilized. Corrupt administration and politicians were so sure nobody would bother to check. It's a fact. Everybody knows it. But there's nothing we can do about it.'

Good money continues to be poured after good. Dantewada and 54 other Naxal-affected districts tagged by the Home Ministry for special treatment in 2003 were each provided an additional Rs 15 crores a year of central government funding for three years under what is called Backward Districts Initiative 'so as to fill in the critical gaps in physical and social infrastructure'. More jam.

—

We stop under the banyan for a break. The massive tree is at a crossroad. The children we'd seen in the hut, a boy and girl, approach us, as I move towards a nearby building. It's the local anganwadi, now empty. Sukhdev says there's no teacher for the remaining children. There's a sign, painted on the walls of the locked anganwadi that the SJ hordes have overlooked: '*Hathiyarband sangharsh se hi adhikaar mileyga.*' Armed struggle is the only way to empowerment. The message urges people to boycott elections in 'April'—probably a reference to the national elections of 2004. It's signed off with '*Marxbad, Leninbad, Maobad Zindabad. Navjanvadi kranti zindabad*,' wishing long life to M-L-M ideology and also to the revolution to create 'new people'.

Where's Pondum, Sukhdev asks the little girl. '*Idikey*,' she replies, pointing at a narrower track winding south past the tiny school building. After a kilometre through forest, we come across a large clearing with work-in-progress clusters of houses of a SJ-mandated rehab. It's actually two hamlets, as we soon discover. To the right of the track is the new hamlet of Pondum. To the left is the new hamlet of Polliwaya. Sukhdev gestures to a young man casting mud bricks from a pile of clay scooped from the roadside. Where's Pondum?

'*Idikey*,' the man says, in now familiar bisyllable, pointing up the track, into the forest.

'Then what is this?'

'This is now the new Pondum. And that,' he points across, 'is now Polliwaya. Salwa Judum gathered everyone and brought us here under Patarpara panchayat.' The young man, who's called Chaitu, gives us some details of the resettlement. A hundred families from Pondum and 71 from Polliwaya resettled in adjacent fields with no shelter from trees, two newly dug wells between them, and no help to make the houses beyond Rs 12,000 per family from the Chhattisgarh government.

Rs 12,000 for the house, and a supply of asbestos roofing sheets on purchase that replaces local thatch, wood and palm leaf with a dangerous composite that will bake anyone inside. The mud bricks are Rs 2 per brick, and the tiny two-room cheek-by-jowl houses take about 2,000 bricks to build. Those able to make bricks save money. They anyway have to make their own house.

It was the same story, I'd seen, in the refugee village up the road from the sewer of Bhairamgarh. And in Matwara. People enmeshed in the drag and drop of instant SJ resettlement that takes inhabitants from open habitat that often sees a kilometre separate one homestead from another to clusters of instant slum. From a livelihood, however basic, some farming, tending cattle, and gathering forest produce, to nothing at all. SJ can better keep its eyes on its herd so the Maoists cannot poach. As always, broken people are collateral damage.

We move along the track to vociferous protest from

Chaitu—SJ has expressly forbidden anyone from going to Pondum—the real Pondum. Sukhdev and I choose to ignore him; there aren't many people around in the blazing sun and those who remain are busy setting up home.

It would have been better if we had stayed. It is heartbreaking to see an empty home, a dead village. Huts large and small are silent, peeling, broken. Even those resettled down the road aren't allowed to return to undertake repair. And so their former homes and farms waste away in the shade of sal and gum trees, the green-brown-red of leaf, tree and earth dusted with the brilliant white fluff from giant simal trees. Still life.

We walk into a home at the edge of Pondum—I coerce a reluctant Sukhdev. That is how we meet the beautiful Bhagwati.

It's difficult to say who is more surprised. But there is fellow feeling once Sukhdev assures her we're not from SJ. Her young daughter, a wisp of six or seven, comes out from behind the hut to sit by her mother, who uses a twig to keep flies off drying mahua flowers.

Bhagwati speaks with great intakes of breath, her answers incomprehensible to me except for sighs that wrack her slight frame. Her husband isn't around, she tells Sukhdev, but does not say where he is. She knows how and why the troubles began but has no idea when it will all end—in that the Prime Minister of India and the wretched of India are one. Her clan is helping build a hut in New Pondum, and maybe she will request them to help dismantle the roof of the old hut and crown the new one with it.

What will she do when the money the government has given runs out? How will they live? What will they eat? Bhagwati answers in sighs and silent tears. Her daughter reaches out to cradle her.

Sukhdev, crouched, lowers his face. These are his people, and there is little he can do to help beyond empty words and gestures.

I leave quietly, taking care to not disturb the tableau of grief, shame and desperate longing.

8

'These guys came in quietly,' says Prabir Kumar Das. 'The dalam would move in. Eight to ten people. Flags, Mao bands and slogans. Eighty per cent were these bloody guys, these Telugu fellows. They would go to villages and just do "Hello, hello, how are you?" That's all. What would they offer them? Nothing. Just the arms they carried. They would say, "We have opposed them, we have chased them away."'

He lights a cigarette, taking a break in the telling of a short history of Maoism in Chhattisgarh, from the time it was nothing but an administrative backwater of Madhya Pradesh, before 2000. He is describing how the Maoists begin claiming territory, show they care, by chasing away forest guards, moneylenders, petty traders, even police, the traditional scourge of tribals and other forest dwellers.

'Then they reach a level where they can be brazen. If you read Mao's philosophy, there are various stages—you know, the struggle stage, then the guerilla stage, and then the liberated stage...they follow Mao's book page by page.'

'Have you studied it?' I ask Prabir, the superintendent of police of Dantewada.

'No, just read it here and there. So here, these guys continue in the struggle stage and guerilla stage. When they found they had enough influence, they introduced weapons, started creating local dalams. Then they created sanghams in villages. These villagers don't know what Maoism is, what democracy is, they know nothing—it's like four per cent of the people control 96 per cent of the population. They would hammer down the whole village into submission.' I swallow a comeback: SJ is now the reversed hammer, and people caught in between are pulp.

The atmosphere is as relaxed as it can be with a man who always travels in armed convoy, the way to whose office has four barricades. Armed guards at the entrance to the compound; then a sandbagged gun emplacement with a machine gun and carbine crew; a thick mud and brick wall with firing slits fronting the main door; and personal security detail outside the door to his office.

'Then, they became so powerful they thought they could challenge the police. It was a bit of a bad scene,' he uses boarding school slang, 'there were some blasts in the south...they killed 17-18 policemen. This was 1988 or so. We never expected it. Things didn't really register then. They suddenly reached the guerilla stage. The government of India was hardly there. It was purely a police thing. It became police versus these guys, or Naxals as they were then called.'

Prabir lights another cigarette. He is tense and speaks in bursts, not with the practiced smoothness of Pisda. His edgy urbanity, courtesy of elite education, makes him seem a little raw compared to Pisda with his slick politician-talk. Policing these parts isn't easy for a man like him.

'See, Andhra had been suffering from this problem from a little earlier,' he resumes. 'There, they created their counter-insurgency force, the Greyhounds, in 1985. But Chhattisgarh at that time was part of Madhya Pradesh and too far away for those in the capital, Bhopal, so nobody bothered. Till they were hit systematically, and very hard—'89, '90, '92, '93. A lot of people died. A time came when Dantewada, the southern part of Dantewada at least, was overrun.'

'You mean the Konta region?' I refer to an area deep to the south, near the state's border with Andhra Pradesh, near the Andhra town of Bhadrachalam. It's where Chhattisgarh police took critically injured survivors of a landmine blast in Konta that shredded a truck carrying SJ supporters on 28 February 2006.

'Yes, Konta. You go now and see; most of the roads are *kutcha* type. Where the kutcha starts, I wouldn't like to drive on it. It sends shivers, you know.'

There's a good reason. Unlike Kashmir, where most roads are blacktop, attacking security forces is a matter of ambush or planting IEDs and mines on the verge, on embankments, under bridges. I've seen ROPs—road-opening patrols—

painstakingly make their way in pre-dawn, and only when they signal all-clear is traffic allowed to pass. In Maoist zones, packed or loose earth roads and tracks can hide a pressure mine or remotely activated mine with no telltale. D, the intelligence official in Raipur, had called the 80-kilometre stretch from Sukma to Konta 'a mess, extremely dangerous for us; all tracks are full of IEDs'. The Maoists, he had said, use pressure mines triggered by explosive caps and even hypodermic syringes; other IEDs are set off remotely, using wires as well as wireless signals. 'This is LTTE-inspired,' he had told me. 'It's a kind of favour returned. During the blockade of Jaffna in the late 1980s, People's War helped to get arms across to Jaffna. We believe that the LTTE are still providing training and also arms.' These arms are easily available to anyone with money and contacts, he had continued. If they want to supplement the grassroots method, as it were, of looting armouries or snatching weapons from guards, landlords or police-kill, the Maoists can easily shop around in India's northeast and Nepal with the LTTE—or go even further afield courtesy of 'friendly' networks in Pakistan and Bangladesh.

'So naturally we walk,' Prabir is saying, 'and you can't walk hundreds and hundreds of kilometres. You roam around one village and you have walked seven kilometres on average. It suits the Maoists very well—and they don't allow roads to be constructed. Why? Because once roads come in, it's a threat to them.'

'You can see it here,' he gets up and paces in front of a large map of Chhattisgarh to the left of his desk. It's marked with red and green crosses and stars—signs of Maoist and state strongholds, huge patches of green marking dense forest. He moves a forefinger up from the bottom, travels east tracing the state border with Orissa right along to the north. 'This entire region. Then here...' He travels back down to the lower third of the map and cuts across the state west to Kanker district, which is separated from Dantewada by a thick slice of Bastar district. The forefinger moves west into Maharashtra across the blue line of Indravati River, slashes north and south, and then arcs back east to end at Konta. 'They dominate in all this area. This is bad. You could call it a sort of "liberated area".'

I'm too stunned to react. An official who speaks the truth.

The Maoists do call it 'liberated zone'. It is one step up from the concept of 'guerilla zone'—at one time practically all of northern and eastern Andhra Pradesh—in which the state and rebels are matched for domination and governance, a stage that allows flat out offensive. A 'liberated zone' is arrived at when the rebels' level of domination exceeds that of the state. Which, it would appear from what the Dantewada SP is showing me on an official state map, includes large parts of southern Chhattisgarh and parts of Gadhchiroli, along with a few heavily forested border districts along the Orissa–Andhra border.

Prabir is on a roll.

'Smoke? No? Okay. I joined in February 2004 and in April you had Lok Sabha elections. The situation was quite bad.' There was no voting in this area simply because it was too dangerous and the Maoists wouldn't allow it. 'A lot of these guys came in, from Gadhchiroli, south, east—there were more than 120 encounters during the elections.'

It didn't let up afterwards either, as Andhra Pradesh, which had held elections to its state assembly along with parliamentary elections, had a new government, led by the Congress, and the new chief minister Y.S.R. Reddy initiated peace talks with the Maoists in October that year. This temporary détente had the effect of the Maoist cadre regrouping. When peace talks broke down in a matter of months—with both sides trading charges of peace being used as an excuse for greater infiltration and arming—increased pressure from the Greyhounds led to many Maoists spreading outwards from Andhra, mainly into Chhattisgarh.

The way Prabir and his fellow officers—and of course the state—see it, the Salwa Judum was just waiting to happen in Chhattisgarh; the Maoists were on a high and they basically went ahead and asked for it with ideological extremism, browbeating tribals into their cause. It's a logical reaction of a people pushed into a corner. The same as when the state went right ahead and invited Maoism decades earlier with extreme callousness, and continues to, by usurping traditional tribal lands and condoning all manner of malpractices that are so inherent in India.

'I believe that even if you were to give the adivasi a car, telephone, a pucca house, a road to each house, they would still have revolted against the Maoists—Mahendra Karma just gave it a shape, and we gave it a name.'

The Maoists, says Prabir, echoing the words of his colleague Pisda, and numerous others across the spectrum, let loose their own reign of oppression, imposing barriers on a people who were used to nothing beyond living with nature. He mentions the control of tendu leaves that Himanshu had also talked about. 'When we entered an area 50 kilometres from here, deep inside, we found they had broken hand pumps. Initially, we thought it was to deny police water. Later, when we went to areas we hadn't been to before, there too the pumps were broken. Villagers told us that they were asked by the Maoists to drink only from wells and other natural water sources.' Hand pumps were provided by the state or by NGOs with state funding; they were a sign of oppression, and therefore taboo.

'If villagers had to go to the weekly market, [the Maoists] would say, "All of you can't go, only such and such people can go." If a group of villagers were talking, these sangham guys would appear like the KGB and listen in.

'So we realized something was happening. A year ago we would not get a single villager to help us, not a single guide. Today, I get so many volunteers. And these People's War guys [Prabir uses the old name out of habit] must also have realized it, so they went about hacking and killing people. They are doing it even now.'

So, if the Maoists are bunch of nasties and SJ a bunch of angels, why does the world know about SJ brutality more than Maoist excesses?

'We just like to do our work and to hell with it. Propaganda is a very, very weak aspect of this operation. We have just not been able to project.' Prabir pushes back his chair, agitated, rocking back on spring. 'If you ask me, I get fed up talking to press people. And then, secondly, a lot of the local press—from here—a lot of them are involved.'

'Can you prove it?'

'Involved in the sense...you look at press people here, they are not really staffers of big media. Some of them run shops, small factories, most have some business or the other. The local press had no guts to write against the Naxals. Today, this has changed a bit.'

Well, you guys took care of that with your gag law, I intervene. He ignores me.

'The Maoists, of course, are very good at this.' No contest. I can vouch for it. 'They have a legal set-up, they have a propaganda set-up,' Prabir says. 'The Naga forces have done a damn good job here. They talk about how Naga forces here are doing nothing but headhunting. There's not a single case...there may have been an excess here and there, but when you're talking about operations in an area of 30,000 square kilometres, you can't avoid a few cases.'

'Collateral damage?'

Prabir nods. 'If you compare it with Kashmir and other places, we haven't done anything.'

Ah, Kashmir, beautiful Kashmir, where militants slit the throats of innocent men, women and children as retribution. They toss grenades at security posts in crowded market areas in Srinagar that often bounce off barricades and explode among innocents—mostly Kashmiri. And hair-trigger forces that detain at will, make people disappear, and have sometimes killed gruesomely to make a point.

I will never forget a conversation I had with an officer of military intelligence at Delhi airport at the turn of the millennium. Dressed in mufti—bearded, in scruffy Kashmiri *firan*, the voluminous poncho that can conceal a tiny brazier and sub-machine gun with equal ease, his real ID now flashed by the tiny brass Military Intelligence symbol worn on a beret—he was on his way to Srinagar and active duty after a few days with the family. His colleagues were scattered across the lounge. My family and I were heading to Goa, our eventual home. After giving the gentlest of hugs to my little daughter with a tearful 'she's just like my daughter', he told me some tales. Of how he came to have a bullet wound in his right palm—still healing. Of how one time he and his team hacked off the heads of six militants deep inside a forest, to petrify their Islamist colleagues, of course, but also as spiritual insult—to ensure that their journey to paradise would be confused, with headless torsos not knowing which way to go.

'Then we heard these human rights chaps were coming,' the military man told me in flawless, clipped English. 'So we put the heads back on somehow, crudely stitched them up. We didn't bother with matching head and body.'

Cynical laughter. 'Don't know if we'll meet again,' he said. 'Have a nice holiday.'

'Something wrong?' Prabir asks, puzzled by my silence. No, I tell him, and relate the military officer's story, and few others, seen and heard over the years.

'You see?' he says in self-vindication. 'And we haven't resorted to any false encounters as such. We even know where the family members of many of these guys stay in Andhra—in Khammam, in Bhadrachalam, but we have never picked them up. We've never played any dirty games like that.'

'But if you did, wouldn't the Maoists target the families of your people? Wouldn't the whole thing escalate?'

'Yes. In fact, when one of my sub-inspectors was abducted by these People's War fellows, in August-September 2004, there was a big *hungama*. The press went in, interviewed the sub-inspector. I even talked to Gadar,' he says, referring to the openly pro-Naxal balladeer from Andhra Pradesh, a cult in his own right, who is always dressed in short dhoti and wrapped in a black shepherd's shawl, and known for singing popular lines like, Grease *leni bandi eppudu nadaraledhura/ Thyagam leni viplavamu mundhukku podhura*. Without grease a cart cannot move forward; without sacrifice revolution cannot move forward. 'I took the name of their fellow whom a TV channel had interviewed, who said all sorts of nasty things about us,' Prabir continues. 'I told Gadar, "Give me one instance when we have troubled anybody's family in Andhra. If I was playing a dirty game, I could have killed 150 of them by now." So he said, "I assure you no bodily harm will come to your sub-inspector." He sent a letter to me on my fax. And then I secured a release.'

'All you guys are in a funny business. Overground, underground, overt, covert,' I say.

'The overt [among the Maoists] are the legal set-up, people who advertise openly because they are not banned. The propaganda set-up is overground. A lot of journalists are with them...But something has gone wrong for them here in Bastar, Dantewada—I have crosschecked this with my colleagues in Andhra. It's spreading. Why are they prepared to crush the Salwa Judum at all costs in Konta? Why? Because it can spread into Andhra. Then it will spread into Orissa, into Jharkhand. So right now, their major cadre is in my area. They have inducted their real firepower in my area—to divert us, to engage us and, somehow, to defeat this thing called Salwa Judum.'

'And together you will create a deathscape.' I whisper, holding back before I say anything more indiscreet. 'Do you consider what will happen in the future?'

Prabir waves that away like batting a pesky fly. Then he gathers his hands together, steeples his fingers and rests his arms on the table. His voice has lost all agitation, and he speaks calmly. 'I like to stay in the present, you know. I have to crush it. I can't keep thinking about what's going to happen. Professionally, it's not my job to think all that. Focus. Crush it. At face value. Crush it.'

9

I say my farewell to little Haripriya and her faithful companion Mallika. Himanshu and Veena have gone to Dantewada town to do some chores, check email. Sukhdev tells me I will probably meet them on the way. It's getting dark, he warns, I should be off or I'll miss the bus. He will remain in the forest. Lingu will reach me to Dantewada. After a warm handshake and embrace Sukhdev turns and disappears into a postcard dusk.

Kamlesh and two friends, both journalists, are waiting for me at Punjab Provision Stores. I have a berth on the 7.30 p.m. Payal Air Lines back to Raipur, and there's an hour to kill. Kamlesh makes the introductions. One works for ETV, a big Andhra Pradesh-based news and entertainment channel, the other for *Dainik Bhaskar*, a major national daily in Hindi. We retire to Tip Top Ice Cream Palace. It is opening day, the garlands of marigold are fresh over the door, but there's no ice cream. We settle for sweet, milky tea, with diesel fumes and the smell of fresh paint as accompaniment.

'How was your trip?' ETV asks. Interesting, I reply. Between journalists, there's sometimes a bit of trying to out-cool the other as part of initial wordplay.

'Ah. Interesting meetings, haan?'

Not bad, I allow, and say I wish I could have met Mahendra Karma and D.L. Manhar. Neither was around.

'Karma is these days between Jagdalpur and Raipur. It's difficult to talk to him, especially for journalists. He's keeping a low profile. And you won't find Manhar. He's now posted to Raipur to the *Manavadhikar Aayog*.' They laugh as I choke on tea. The heavy-handed SP of Bijapur, now posted to the Chhattisgarh State Human Rights Commission!

'I saw his people molest two good-looking tribal girls of the sangham about two months ago,' ETV says. 'They had surrendered. I can't say they raped them, but I can definitely say they molested them. Their father was outside, crying and asking for help.'

'*Shoshankariyon ka raja*,' *Dainik Bhaskar* adds. The king of exploiters.

'They are all in it. The police, administration, politicians,' it's ETV again. 'They eat up funds. Then there's smuggling. A lot of smuggling goes on here. Sagun trees find their way from Bastar to Bangalore, Bhopal, Mumbai, Delhi, Kolkata. Everyone is involved. There is hardly anyone in government who is not involved in everything from smuggling to the liquor business to the Salwa Judum. I've been here for four months; it took me not more than two to understand the level of exploitation and corruption. Why won't the Maoists succeed?'

'Aren't you scared of the law?' I ask all three.

Kamlesh answers for them. 'I am out because of PUCL and PUDR.' People's Union for Civil Liberties and People's Union for Democratic Rights. 'But with the new law [Chhattisgarh's Special Public Security Act, 2005], they can put me or anyone inside for three years without producing any charge or evidence.'

'You know, I think often I'm pushing the government line,' ETV says, 'because there is no other line these days. Independent reporting has become dangerous.'

Kamlesh nods, tea forgotten.

'*Arrey*, did you hear about the killing?' *Dainik Bhaskar* intervenes in the silence. He turns to me. 'The former block president of this area was beheaded by Naxalis this morning at three.'

'That's what the administration says,' ETV cuts in. 'It's actually not a beheading. They hit his jaw, face. Then he is supposed to have got up and run for 500 metres with Naxalis chasing him, and then he fell onto the rocks by the river. They say Naxalis asked him for Rs 1300. Naxalis don't take such small amounts—would they kill him for that? It's something else: who or why is unclear.'

I spot Himanshu's car, a white, worn Maruti sedan with Delhi plates. Himanshu is cheerful as he gets down from it, accompanied by Veena.

'So, your yatra is over, is it?'

'Only for now.'

'Did you hear?' he asks as we shake hands. 'The Naxals have killed a former president of the block, just a few kilometres from here, near the river. Said he was a police informer. Ran after him with choppers.'

Payal Air Lines arrives. The driver has cranked up the volume on the scratchy stereo. It's a perennial pan-India favourite from the iconic movie *Shree 420*: '*Mera joota hai Japaani/ Yeh patloon Inglistaani/ Sar pe lal topi Roosi/ Phir bhi dil hai Hindustani.*' My shoes are from Japan, trousers from England, a red hat from Russia, and yet, a heart that is all Indian.

An up-tempo globalization song.

'*Achcha*? Choppers?' I deadpan to Himanshu's telling of another version of the story. Truth is only what you see, what you hear, and different people see and hear different things. But if indeed the man was killed by the Maoists, it would have been Police Informer Execution No. 36 in the past two years in these parts.

'We cannot defeat Naxalism with force,' D's telling rings a bell. 'That has been tried and we have failed. We have to try other approaches. Development, for instance. There has been so little of it in Bastar, from the British times. Even Noronha, a well-known officer who later became chief secretary [Ronald 'Ron' C.V.P. Noronha of the colonial Indian Civil Service, and later well-regarded chief secretary of undivided Madhya Pradesh] did nothing. People would come, live well, go hunting, write about half-naked people and their dances, their jewellery and their way of living. They would write books on anthropology and culture and go away. No development.'

'Bad business,' I shake my head at Himanshu.

Himanshu smiles. 'Go in peace.'

BOOK II

*We have tried to develop the army in some areas
without class struggle and have failed. Without class
struggle—the battle of annihilation—the initiative of
the poor peasant masses cannot be released, the political
consciousness of the fighters cannot be raised, the new
man cannot emerge, the people's army cannot be
created. Only by waging class struggle—the battle of
annihilation—the new man will be created, the new
man who will defy death and will be free from all
thoughts of self-interest. And with this death defying
spirit he will go close to the enemy, snatch his rifle,
avenge the martyrs and the peoples army will emerge.
To go close to the enemy it is neccessary to conquer
all thought of self. And this can be achieved only by
the blood of martyrs. That inspires and creates new
men out of the fighters, fills them with class hatred
and makes them go close to the enemy and snatch his
rifle with bare hands.*

—Charu Mazumdar, at the First Congress of the
CPI (ML), Calcutta, May 1970

10

The grammar of left-wing extremism in India is quite simple if you accept the fluid nature of things.

'Naxal', in singular and plural, derives from a movement that sparked off as an anti-landlord campaign in the Naxalbari area of Darjeeling district in West Bengal, in May 1967. It was fuelled by fiery handling of the issue by an extreme-Left faction of the CPI (M). CPI (M) had split from the Communist Party of India in 1964, but was itself riven with divisions soon after. This extreme faction, led by Charu Mazumdar and other disenchanted party members from across India—West Bengal, Andhra Pradesh, Orissa, Punjab, Kerala, Uttar Pradesh, Bihar—formed the All India Coordination Committee of Communist Revolutionaries after the initial Naxalbari incident of farmers' protest and police retaliation in May 1967. This faction would formally break away from CPI (M) in 1969 and call itself the Communist Party of India (Marxist-Leninist)—the source of all 'ML' parties—and adopt annihilation of 'class enemies' as a key plank to achieving revolutionary success.

The 1967 movement grew beyond everybody's expectations, mainly because of the reaction to massive crackdown by the state. Interestingly, Jyoti Basu of CPI (M), who was later to become West Bengal's longest serving chief minister, was then the home minister of the coalition government. The often brutal government crackdown resulted in the movement spreading to other areas of Bengal and Bihar, and into cities, primarily Calcutta, where it became a straightforward 'state versus the revolutionaries' battle. Soon it crossed the class barrier and consumed intellectuals and students, even those with no background or interest in communist principles. It grew into the now legendary Naxalbari movement, which emptied an impressive fraction of several universities in Calcutta and Delhi, among other cities, and in Andhra Pradesh, which was on the boil with a similar movement of its own.

The phase in Andhra—the 'Srikakulam phase'—began in 1968, when, inspired by the peasant uprising in Naxalbari, a group of dissident CPI (M) leaders from Orissa and Andhra Pradesh, among them the iconic Nagabhushan Patnaik, Tarimala Nagi Reddy and Chandra Pulla Reddy, decided to initiate two nuclei of armed revolution in Andhra Pradesh: Srikakulam in the east and the Telengana region—the entire northwest of the state which already had a history of peasant revolt. Some of its leaders met Charu Mazumdar in Calcutta the same year. When they returned, a decision was taken to immediately launch an armed struggle; that happened on 25 November 1968, when Patnaik and others, along with about 250 tribals, attacked the house of a landlord in Parvatipuram, took away food grain and destroyed documents that formally indentured labour. The following year, the movement spilled across to the border regions of Orissa, strikingly similar to current areas of Maoist activity.

The movement was more taken with the principles of Mao than of Marx or Lenin. Mao was alive then, while the others were history; he offered a combination of punchier ideology, clever strategy, and greater romanticism: a well-meaning young man from an impoverished corner of China who undertook the epic Long March, rose to dominate China, and was making it a power to match the Soviet Union, and challenge America. Mao's Red Book offered tactical and strategic solutions along with rhetoric—the notion of 'protracted' guerilla war, 'People's War', to capture first the countryside and then encircle urban areas before taking them over. Along with agrarian revolution, he said, it was crucial never to lose sight of the ultimate goal of capturing political power.

But in India it would prove to be asking for too much, too soon.

When the relatively naïve, relatively disorganized movement was shattered by state action in 1972, and squeezed almost completely by the time Indira Gandhi imposed Emergency in 1975, blanking out civil rights and mandating brutality of the state, the cycle was ended. Over the remainder of the 1970s and early 1980s the movement broke into several dozen 'ML' factions, mainly nitpicking over personalities, doctrine and whether the 'objective conditions' for revolution were right. (It is a trend that continues among the subcontinent's left-wing revolutionaries; there are a bewildering number of groups, often with similar sounding names, who have broken away—and continue to—from larger parties.)

Several Naxalite leaders went underground. Some reinvented themselves, primarily in Andhra Pradesh, Bihar and West Bengal. This reorganization of sorts was further aided when the Janata Party-led coalition assumed power in 1977 after the landslide defeat of Indira Gandhi's Congress. Many jailed Naxal leaders were released after public pressure and petitions by national and international human rights groups and activists.

In Andhra Pradesh, the state committee of the CPI (ML) regrouped and started a discussion about what had gone wrong with the Naxalbari movement. Among other things, this introspection led to the conclusion that, while CPI (ML) was 'basically correct', it had made serious mistakes. For example, it was wrong to have expected a quick victory; annihilation could not be the only form of struggle; it was wrong to have discouraged the building of a mass organization by terming it 'revisionism'; it was a mistake not to have focussed on building the party organization. This line of thought gradually led to the formation of CPI (ML) People's War and another faction, CPI (ML) Party Unity, which took root in Bihar. (The latter faction would merge with People's War in 1998.)

Another major group, the Maoist Communist Centre, or MCC, dug deep into Bihar by the early 1980s, including areas of present-day Jharkhand, reflecting the increasing trend of consolidation for better operational stability. (In 2003, MCC and a Punjab-based group, the Revolutionary Communist Centre of India-Maoist, would merge to form the Maoist Communist Centre of India, or MCCI.)

These groups were openly 'Maoist', rejecting parliamentary democracy, believers in organized, steadily evolving armed action leading to revolution. They set themselves apart from several other Marxist-Leninist breakaways, most notably, CPI (ML) Liberation, that were—and are—open to contesting elections and conducting overground propaganda even as they don't entirely write off the possibility of selective action if a situation demands it.

This is where the real beginning of present-day Maoists can be located, and they eventually evolved far beyond their Naxalbari roots. Even as they continued to revere Naxalbari icon Charu Mazumdar, they dispensed with his primary notion of immediate military mobilization to push along the uprising of the people—a sort of people-are-ready-and-they-will-join-us-if-they-see-us-rebel approach. That had been tried, and it had failed. Today's rebels are more focussed. They believe in, and work for, the long haul of armed revolution, using armed cadres and unarmed cadres to work in tandem, staying true to Mao's doctrine of People's War. And so a second M has been added to ML, to form the ideology of M-L-M: Marxist-Leninist-Maoist. (It was first expressed as 'Mao Thought', and later, after a major meeting of rebel minds in 2001, was smoothened to 'Maoism'.)

CPI (ML) People's War emerged as the most powerful group in Andhra with its northern ally, CPI (ML) Party Unity. The group began to escalate its activities after 1980, kidnapping state legislators, bureaucrats, killing police, triggering landmines. The party leadership had already taken a call to establish guerilla zones in Andhra Pradesh—Karimnagar, Adilabad, Warangal and Khammam in the Telengana region—Bihar, Madhya Pradesh (including present-day Chhattisgarh), Orissa, and eastern Maharashtra. The latter part comprises the area that is Dandakaranya. 'Base areas' were to be established. To achieve that, armed squads were formed—a result of focussed village-level propaganda incursions from 1978 onwards. These ingressed deep into the Telengana region of northern Andhra Pradesh, to begin with. This region was in many ways the ideal choice—among the least developed areas in the country, it had already seen a communist-led peasant revolt in the late 1940s. Later, in 1969–70, there had also been violent student protests demanding a separate Telengana state. (Robust demand for a separate Telengana state continues.)

From Telengana, armed squads were sent into Dandakaranya. In Bihar, a decision was taken to develop and base squads in the Palamau forest area—in present-day Jharkhand. Everywhere, the primary goal, besides ingress, was to focus on a 'land-to-the-tiller' approach, by encouraging and inciting tens of thousands of landless peasants to take over land; in numerous cases, the Maoists themselves redistributed land. In large parts of central Bihar, horrific skirmishes between upper-caste landlord armies like the Ranvir Sena and the Maoists would become routine. News of massacres committed by either side, with the state playing expedient participant, filled the pages of newspapers and magazines. Turf war would also break out intermittently between People's War and MCCI.

By 2000, in several areas controlled by People's War, guerilla squads had been stitched together and upgraded to the People's Local Guerilla Army, which doctrine and pratice calls to be ultimately scaled up to the People's Liberation Army, when the numbers are big enough and the time is ripe enough for all out revolution.

The day of the deliberate, systematic left-wing revolutionary had arrived.

—

Over the years, both People's War and MCCI cleaned up several smaller ML factions along the way. In October 2004, these two groupings publicly announced a merger, after two years of talks, to form the Communist Party of India (Maoist).

They had attempted merger several times earlier, to end major skirmishing over territory as People's War and its ally, Party Unity—by now merged into People's War—moved into MCCI strongholds, but nothing had come of it. CPI (Maoist) is today the unquestioned extreme-Left conglomerate, and accounts for over 90 per cent of Left revolutionary violence in India.

Its intention was made clear on 14 October 2004, in a joint press statement by Muppala Laxman Rao, or 'Ganapathy'—People's Leader or People's benefactor—the general secretary of People's War and now chief of the unified CPI (Maoist), and 'Kishan', the general secretary of the central committee of MCCI. The two mapped their 'immediate aim and programme'. It could be Mao talking: 'This revolution will be carried out and completed through armed agrarian revolutionary war, i.e. protracted people's war with the armed seizure of power remaining as its central and principal task, encircling the cities from the countryside and thereby finally capturing them. Hence the countryside as well as the Protracted People's War will remain as the "centre of gravity" of the party's work, while urban work will be complementary to it.'

Small ML groups still remain, such as the CPI (ML) Janashakti, with an estimated 300 armed and active cadre in Telengana and small areas of Maharashtra and Chhattisgarh. This group, formed in 1992 by coalescing seven fractured factions out of the chaos of the 1980s, when the detritus of the Naxalbari movement manifested itself in several 'leaders', is now allied to CPI (Maoist).

Then there are a few ML groups that practice revolutionary thought, such as CPI (ML) Kanu Sanyal, led by a Naxalbari leader who even then emerged as a critic of Charu Mazumdar, which is now renamed, like the original, as CPI (ML), and is engaged in organizing labour in several tea gardens in the Naxalbari area. Another such group is CPI (ML) Liberation, prevalent in Bihar, Jharkhand, Orissa, Punjab and West Bengal, that uses a mix of overground and underground activism in the twilight zone between hard Left and extreme Left. It's a tricky business. For example, in Bihar, Jharkhand and Punjab, this group has contested elections to the state assembly and won. While in some parts of Bihar members of this group have been hunted not only by the state and upper-caste vigilante groups but also by CPI (Maoist), with whom it has a running turf battle, occasionally resulting in deaths but mostly limited to sniping in party journals. Only towards the end of 2006 was an uneasy, unwritten truce worked out.

As a result of these seemingly chaotic splits and mergers and alignments, over the past decade radical leftists in India, including the 'softer' ML parties, have all come to be called both Maoists and Naxalites or Naxals. In vernacular, for instance, they could be 'Naxali' or 'Maobadi'—or 'Maovadi', depending on the language. The terms have come to be interchangeable, freely used by revolutionary intellectuals, academics, media, government, the public, and sometimes the Maoists/Naxals themselves. India's Ministry of Home Affairs refers to all extreme-Left attacks as 'Naxal Violence'.

This is where the relatively simple matter of naming ends—the tortuous journey from Marxism-Leninism to Marxism-Leninism-Maoism—and the more complex matter of what the nomenclature actually portends comes into the picture.

11

The central Ministry of Home Affairs prefers not to release much of the data on Maoist activity and planning that its own intelligence agencies, in collaboration with the police apparatus of the affected states, have gathered. What the ministry must know, but chooses to conceal, is occasionally revealed through intercepted Maoist documents and in *People's March*, the exhaustive CPI (Maoist) journal. These show very precise plans, worked out in astonishing detail, to drape India, as it were, in red. The Maoist plans have gone into high churn in the past five or six years, with minimum fuss relative to grand affairs of state: a burst of Hindu nationalism; the spectacle of elections; the high drama of coalition politics; the high tide-low tide of the India–Pakistan relationship; and, of course, the noisy, much-feted growth of the economy.

In 2001, the visible picture was relatively simple (*Map 1* in the opening pages of the book). People's War was spread out in Andhra Pradesh—barring a few districts in the south—and in eastern Maharashtra, southern Chhattisgarh, the southern tip of Madhya Pradesh and remote southwestern Orissa. Its compatriots in MCCI held operational sway over northern Chhattisgarh, northeastern Orissa bordering West Bengal and Jharkhand, nearly all of Jharkhand barring the industrial belt in and around Jamshedpur, and southern Bihar. The emerging, near-contiguous 'Red Corridor' from Andhra Pradesh through five states into Bihar was already evident.

By 2005, after integration, the scene had dramatically changed (*Map 2*). In the 'Highly Affected' category were 51 districts, essentially the area of influence recorded in 2001, with a notable new blip in northern Bihar, near a tri-junction of its borders with Uttar Pradesh to the west and Nepal to the north. The 'Moderately Affected' (18 districts) and 'Marginally Affected' (62 districts) areas pretty much filled the blanks in Andhra Pradesh, nearly all of West Bengal, the northern reaches of Orissa, the remainder of Jharkhand, most of Bihar, the eastern part of Uttar Pradesh and a little more of Madhya Pradesh. There were also large pockets of moderately affected areas in northeastern Karnataka, bordering Andhra, and the southwestern regions on the thickly forested hills of the Western Ghats, and in small parts of Kerala and the hills of Tamil Nadu.

If 'Targeted' areas in 34 districts were to be included, it would mean more chunks of Madhya Pradesh, Orissa, Chhattisgarh and Bihar—these last three to near-total spread; the entire eastern half of Uttarakhand that borders the Maoist haven, Nepal; and the tribal-dominated forests just north of Maharashtra's industrial hub of Nashik that extend across the border into Gujarat. According to Naxal specialists, there is evidence that operations have been extended to new areas, such as Gujarat, Rajasthan, Himachal Pradesh, Jammu & Kashmir and Meghalaya.

To grow, and to manage operational revolutionary areas, Maoist planners have already carved out various categories of zones, according to degrees of 'people's war', both armed and unarmed (*Map 3*). State Committees are either recently appointed or operational in 13 states and union territories, apart from the currently critical nine to include Delhi, Haryana, Punjab, Karnataka and Tamil Nadu.

Besides these, two Special Area Committees (SACs) are earmarked. One comprises eastern Uttaranchal, the entire northern portion of Uttar Pradesh, and the contiguous part of north Bihar—all bordering Nepal. The second SAC includes eastern Bihar, northeastern Jharkhand, and entire chunks of the West Bengal districts of West Dinajpur, Malda and more. This could provide a stranglehold on the so-called chicken's neck portion of West Bengal, a crucial road and rail link between northeast India and the rest of the country.

The elite tier comprises three Special Zonal Committees (SZCs). These, for all practical purposes, are the maximum impact—and maximum conflict—North Telengana, Dandakaranya, and Andhra-Orissa.

The level of planning gets even more complex and thorough at this stage. To ensure perpetuity in all these areas, CPI (Maoist) has established five Regional Bureaus (*Map 4*). The Northern Regional Bureau includes Delhi, Punjab, Haryana, Uttar Pradesh and Bihar. The Eastern Bureau comprises West Bengal, Jharkhand and Assam. The northern halves of Chhattisgarh and Orissa make up the Orissa-Chhattisgarh Regional Bureau. The Southwestern Regional Bureau has with it enormous territory: Maharashtra outside the Dandakaranya Zone, Karnataka, Tamil Nadu and Kerala. And all of Andhra Pradesh plus the three Special Zonal Committees comprise the heart: the Central Regional Bureau.

The Central Military Commission oversees planning, training and operations in all the divisional and zonal military groupings. This is the operative, underground core. A technology committee oversees R&D and procurement—it would be in charge, for instance, of getting the best communication devices and working out how to fabricate rocket launchers and other weapons. There is a sub-committee on military assessment. 'Agit-prop', also increasingly in play, is looked after by the Agitational Propaganda Committee. A network of underground and overground political workers and sympathizers look after recruitment, besides acting as couriers and fronts. An elaborate network of cells ensures both interplay of functions and watertight functions, depending on perception of security risk.

All these are manned at the very least by 10,000 armed Maoists, with sympathizers in rural and urban India—including both willing converts and those caught between a rock and a hard place—who are altogether beyond count. The specialists also suggest that Maoist recruitment exceeds death, arrest and surrender. In Chhattisgarh, for instance, the director general of police, O.P. Rathor, speaks of 500 Maoist armed cadres, including the militia, being killed in the past three years—the Maoists see this as exaggeration. In the same breath, the officials say Maoist recruitments number 10,000 in three years, and put the total strength in Chhattisgarh at 7,000 hardcore Maoists and 40,000 militia.

In Orissa, former director general of police of the state, N.C. Padhi, speaks of two districts in the state, Malkangiri and Rayagada, being akin to 'liberated zones'—where Maoist writ runs. He also mentions that both the frequency and intensity of Maoist attacks have gone up; the Maoists are 'not afraid to go in for frontal attacks'. 'There are open [Maoist] front activists in Bhubaneshwar,' he says. 'Training camps are being held in the jungles. Cadre strength is fast increasing.'

G.S. Rath, a senior official involved in anti-Naxal operations in Jharkhand, simply terms the situation in his state as 'alarming'. Nearly the entire state is vulnerable.

What is happening now is of little surprise to those who track revolutionary intent, amazing as it may seem as to how rapidly the anti-establishment keeps pace with changes in the establishment. For instance, to underscore a sense of solidarity, and trumpet spreading Marxism-Leninism-Maoism, the Second Annual Conference of the Coordination Committee of Maoist Parties and Organizations of South Asia, or CCOMPOSA, declared in August 2002:

> ...People's Wars waged by the oppressed masses and led by the Maoist Parties of Peru, Nepal, India, Turkey, Bangladesh and Philippines and armed struggles in other countries provide living testimony to this truth. Not only the oppressed countries of Asia, Africa and Latin America, but also the people of imperialist countries are fighting against 'globalization' and 'privatization', which has plunged the working class and sections of the people of the imperialist countries into crisis and despair never felt before.

The Declaration then listed out a ten-point agenda, which later provided the cause for officials and the media describing the South Asian Maoist swathe as the 'Red Corridor'—the Maoists were content to simply call it 'Compact Revolutionary Zone'. The agenda was:

- Our unity will be based on the scientific ideology of our class, which is Marxism-Leninism-Maoism. The Great Proletarian Cultural Revolution is the pinnacle of this development, a path through which we march ahead.
- Our common goal is to achieve Socialism and Communism on a world scale by accomplishing the New Democratic Revolution and continuing the revolution under the dictatorship of the proletariat.
- We are committed to opposing all shades of revisionism including armed revisionism and parliamentary cretinism.
- We must propagate M-L-M widely, particularly in the subcontinent and also worldwide, to counter-revisionism in all its forms.
- We must build solidarity with anti-imperialist struggles throughout the world.

- Build a strong anti-imperialist resistance movement, particularly against US imperialism and Indian expansionism.
- Build a broad front with the ongoing armed struggles of the various nationality movements in the subcontinent.
- Lend mutual assistance and exchange experiences and deepen bilateral and multilateral relations amongst Maoist forces in the subcontinent.
- Coordinate and consolidate the unity of Maoist Parties and Organizations in South Asia.
- Bring out journals and periodicals as instruments of ideological and political propaganda.

The agenda ended with trademark exclamatory flourish: 'Hold high the red banner of Marxism-Leninism-Maoism! Spread the flames of revolution from the high Himalayas to the seas! Develop South Asia as the storm center of world revolution and as a base area for marching towards world communism!'

CCOMPOSA and the Red Zone are all about the geography of demand, justice, perversion or disregard of law, and bloodshed. The dream is to have a red sunrise.

12

'Parliamentary cretinism,' I tell Ajai Sahni. 'I love the sound of that.'

'Oh, these guys are full off interesting phrases.'

We sip green tea at his cosy office on Talkatora Road in New Delhi, in the heavily guarded residential campus of K.P.S. Gill. Ajai runs the Institute of Conflict Management and the South Asia Terrorism Portal, a think tank and information service where Gill serves as president. In the universe of denial that India lives in, Ajai is among a handful of people who closely observe and study Naxalism/Maoism and comment on it. He calls this a 'relatively tiny pool' that tracks the country's greatest internal security threat.

It would take the Home Ministry till October 2006 to establish an exclusive Naxal 'desk'—the quirkily titled Naxal Management Division. And then, too, a pure-bred bureaucrat, of the rank of additional secretary, was appointed to head it. The desk would take even longer to become operational. A police officer, with the rank of joint secretary, would assume office only in February 2007, with the scantiest of support staff.

'Is that all?' I ask Ajai. 'Interesting phrases? They must have more than that.'

Ajai is professorially deadpan as he pours tea into tiny, delicate cups. He could have been discussing the weather—a gathering of cumulonimbus, but weather nevertheless. 'I'd like to suggest that Maoism is, in fact, *the* ideology of the future. Not only in terms of the preaching in the Red Book. There is an enormous content of strategic and tactical material that goes with the ideological. And at times it is very difficult to differentiate between ideological and instrumental—in the sense that the ideology comes with a method of realization, which makes the two inseparable. It makes it one of the most coherent systems available—whether valid or invalid is not a judgement I would care to make.'

'Are you talking of its application in matters of war?'

'As an ideology of rebellion. Of course you can learn a great deal about matters of war and strategy from Mao...this ideology provides one of the first organizational structures for revolution. And that is going to kick us in the face.'

He sips some tea, taps a few keys in a sleek notebook computer perched precariously by the side of the tea tray and scrolls up data and maps. It is a blur of action-plan.

He sees my dumbfounded expression and smiles. 'When you see the degree of detail with which Maoist enterprise has been planned in India...' he waves his hand at the computer screen. 'Why do I say this? Very crudely, you have small pools of great prosperity emerging in vast seas of poverty.' This marginalized population has been attracted—this is the principal population attracted to these mass movements. Leadership, of course, comes from a different category. If you see any of the major movements of violence in this region, whether it's Islamism, ethnic fundamentalism, the left-wing insurgency, the leadership always comes from the region's elite.' He says these are, in part, people who have fallen out with their backgrounds, well-to-do, educated, upper caste (in the Indian context), and angry enough with the world to take up violence on others' behalf. These leaders feed on the process of marginalization. This process of marginalization can only become more and more widespread, more menacing, he says, echoing the thought of some economists.

What prevents policymakers from seeing poverty as an internal security threat, I ask. Why are they more amenable to intelligence with regard to Pakistan or jihadis or separatists and not to intelligence about on-the-ground, destroying-your-heart India?

'Because we don't like it. There is no foreign hand; we'll have to face our own failures in this particular case.' After the thumb, he ticks off with forefinger: 'Then, more than the failure of governance, there is the near-complete absence of governance. You go into the villages, and you try to make an assessment of how much is the individual consciously aware of the government's presence as the dispenser of good health, clean water, education...'

'Not to speak of justice,' I offer, meaning 'government' in the traditional, inclusive sense of *mai-baap*—literally, mother-father; the state as parent, as benevolent dictator.

Ajai laughs. 'Not to speak of justice. You don't have to move out of Delhi and Mumbai to know the government has little role in the dispensation of justice.'

There is now a growing sense of urgency about the Maoist issue in New Delhi, especially since late-2005, but not nearly enough, he explains. In great part, it has to do with how the bureaucracy works. The bureaucrat tends to focus on the file brought to him. 'And in that file, only what concerns *me*...When you're looking at internal security, files are being thrown up to you every day. One of which, possibly every third day, is connected with Naxalism. And then he [the bureaucrat] says, "I've allocated a battalion to deal with the problem," which is basically what they do in the Home Ministry, or approve funding for modernization of police forces.

'"I've done it," he will say, "now things will sort themselves out." And he's the only person who knew what was going on, because the rest of the Home Ministry, which is not connected with Naxalism is not even looking at the issues.'

Given this, the only people who really know what is going on are the people in intelligence, says Ajai, but that even here there is a 'reigning philosophy' imposed on everyone, which is then internalized.

'I've been told at the highest level, at the level of certain DIGs, whose wisdom I otherwise greatly respected, that "no, this is internal, we can handle it, we can sort it out anytime. The main problem is Islamism, Pakistan..." So I said if it's so easy to sort out, why don't you? Where is the premium in keeping the monkeys alive if we can neutralize this thing in days, weeks and months? And *then* let's focus on this Kashmir that you're so worried about.

'"No, no, there are other priorities," they would tell me. "You don't know how government works."' Ajai shakes his head disgustedly. 'They are beginning to shift now.'

'Meaning what?'

'They have to decide on things. For example, is policing a non-development, and consequently, in some sense a wasteful expenditure? Just as you have to build infrastructure, you have to build police stations, arm and upgrade them. Look at the police–population ratios in Maoist-affected states.' Ajai says Andhra Pradesh, among the best equipped at this juncture, has a police to population ratio of 99, lower than the Indian average of 123 per 1,00,000. In Bihar it's 66; Jharkhand, 74; and 92 in Chhattisgarh and Orissa. All are way below. Compare this with 702 for Sikkim and 620-odd for Mizoram. 'Obviously you're creating jobs, nothing else. So how can you *have* a response?'

Most government responses are in the form of slogans, Ajai insists. Development versus Maoism. 'But how will you develop these areas? You have no penetration into these areas any more. The only people who can go into these places are cops—central or state. People with guns. Government teachers, health workers, Block Development Officers are all absent. Or they are present in arrangement with the Maoists: '*bhai, itna paisa ayega*'—this much money will come—'we will spend it according to your directions, and you will get a cut'. It is the Maoists who define the projects. It doesn't matter if the money comes from the Government of India or the state government. What matters is that the local dalam commander says, "Put the money into a track here or a pond there or into waterworks."'

I let him go on. 'You know, we can be as patriotic about these things as we like. The point is if you don't govern an area, it is not yours. Except on the maps, it is not part of India. At least half of India today is not being governed. It is not in your control...you have to create a complete society in which local people have very significant stakes. We're not doing that.'

'And that is giving the Maoists space to move in and claim...'

'Precisely,' Ajai snarls. 'And then, there is a crucial asymmetry that you must recognize in people's expectations. It's not as if the government is not doing anything. Even with leakage and corruption, roads are being constructed, wells are dug. But with the amount of work that needs to be done in India, even if government builds thousands of kilometres of roads and irrigation there are people who will be left out, and are going to say, there is nothing for us. Conversely, if the Maoists go into a new area and do a bucket and pail operation people will say, "See, these people are fighting, sacrificing their lives, they are concerned about our development." Nobody expects anything from a Naxalite, so everything they do is a bonus.' By default, the perception that the Maoists care more than the government is married to the reality of inequity.

Ajai stops abruptly, then adds, 'But leakage—I'm sorry, actually there is *only* leakage of funds. The delivery mechanisms don't exist.'

He's angry, but I want his feedback on another point, one on which I'm getting mixed signals. CPI (Maoist) claims unity in the ranks; however, many police and intelligence folk I talk to claim cracks are beginning to appear. 'What's your take? Is there a sense of unity among CPI (Maoists)?'

'Absolutely,' Ajai has calmed a bit. 'Anyone telling you differently is doing wishful thinking.' He sees my disbelieving look. I tell him I've heard too many things to the contrary; if there is unity, it is enforced in some part.

He steps in. 'It is an ideological unity, a unity imposed by a plan. And if you study their plan documents...And it's also not unity imposed by a direct command and control system where a person from Andhra is ordering a person from Bihar to do something. They have common goals. They have a Central Military Commission in which the Bihari sits, the Andhraite sits, the Oriya sits. After gathering data they define vulnerabilities: caste problems, declining wage rates, problems with religion.'

'I've heard they are moving in on Punjab in a big way,' I say, to take the discussion away from unity; I am not as convinced as Ajai on this score.

'Yeah. And they've brought in this guy called Lanka Papi Babu Reddy. He was initially secretary of the Telengana Special Zonal Committee—North Telengana SZC. NT was the critical base area for the PWG.' In 1996, People's War declared North Telengana as a 'Guerilla Zone', when they deemed themselves as powerful as the government. 'He later became secretary of Dandakaranya SZC. So you can understand the criticality of their now attributing to him Delhi, Haryana and Punjab Special Zone.'

'They seem pretty confident.'

'Oh yes! You see, people don't seem to understand the coherence of their plans—and the state's apparent lack of coherence...Whatever plan [the Maoists] implement, it's life and death for them. For the government, it's just a bureaucratic job. That's a very crucial difference in the psychology of the Maoists and the psychology of the state.'

'Till then the Maoists have a free run, I guess.' I shake my head.

Ajai isn't done scare-mongering. 'You've seen the Urban Perspective document these chaps put out in 2004? It involves mobilization of students and the urban unemployed, and they've targeted two principal industrial belts to begin with: Ahmedabad-Surat-Pune-Mumbai and Bhilai-Ranchi-Dhanbad-Kolkata.'

One side of the tape ends just then, so it doesn't record my 'Bloody hell!' as I scramble to flip it.

13

The path to revolution is occasionally paved with capital letters, and nearly always with exclamation marks. Posters at Ganga Dhaba, the bustling chai-and-chitchat heart of Delhi's Jawaharlal Nehru University (JNU), are full of them.

75 YEARS OF MARTYRDOM OF BHAGAT SINGH, RAJGURU AND SUKHDEV!

AGAINST UNITED PROGRESSIVE ALLIANCE'S ABJECT SURRENDER BEFORE US DIKTATS!

FOR NATIONAL SOVEREIGNTY, EDUCATION, EMPLOYMENT!

It isn't as incongruous as it can seem at first glance, this celebration of Bhagat Singh and company by the 'revolutionaries' of one of the country's premier universities with perhaps its largest concentration of radical or Left-leaning students and intellectuals. Bhagat Singh was hanged by the British for terrorism and treason against the state in 1931.

He is today a symbol of Indian resistance to imperial rule, eulogized in song and cinema, acknowledged by politicians from left to right, enshrined in India's Parliament and at countless crossroads across much of the country. But he was something more than popular history usually lets on: an anti-imperialist, yes, but also a communist—trained, armed and emphatically Left, as evidenced by a statement of his from an often-quoted Draft Revolutionary Programme: 'We don't wish to suffer by inviting a black evil to replace the white evil. Indian workers must come forward—overthrowing imperialists as well as their Indian agents who wish to perpetuate the same economic system rooted in exploitation.'

The poster I see at Ganga Dhaba is signed by AISA, or All India Students Association, the student wing of the CPI (ML) Liberation. The party is in the twilight zone of India's often bizarre political scene. It's both openly overt and openly covert, with some underground cadre in Bihar, Jharkhand and Orissa, and the bosses and ideologues headquartered in Delhi with strong chapters in these states as well as in West Bengal and Punjab, where they attend rallies, publish magazines, plot, fight for—and occasionally win—elections to state assemblies.

The immediate reason for vitriol in the poster appears to be the visit to India at the beginning of March 2006 by George W. Bush, President of the United States, and a nuclear deal he's pushing with the UPA government of the day. Below the slogans, the poster carries a programme for the week beginning 23 March 2006, packed with shows and speeches. That day, a series of speeches at ten in the morning at the Gandhi Peace Foundation, based on all the exclamatory points. On 27 March, screening of a short film on Myanmar's student movement, and another short on Bant Singh, the low-caste farm labourer from Punjab whose limbs were hacked off by upper-caste Sikhs after he demanded justice for the rape of his daughter. After these, a screening of *Damul*, a movie from 1985 that is well known in the art house circuit here and abroad. It details the brutalization and eventual massacre of low-caste labour in a Bihar village by a Brahmin landlord with political connections. Also listed as a highlight of the film schedule is *Omar Mukhtar, Lion of the Desert*, in which an ageing Anthony Quinn stars as the hero who sets 'Arab nationalism against Mussolini's army in WW II'.

Listed for 30 March is the 'Chandrashekhar Memorial Lecture' to commemorate the 1997 killing of the eponymous party leader, popularly known as Chandu, by thugs of a rival political party in Siwan, Bihar. 31 March would cap the week of commemorative protest with a torchlight procession at night.

—

I'm to meet AISA's leader in a students' residence across the street. I drop the paper cup into an overflowing waste bin and make my way past young men and women just hanging around, under scrub trees, on boulders, on rickety benches. The scene at Ganga Dhaba has been this way ever since my university days in the early 1980s, give or take fashion, mobile phones, the cost of a cup of tea and cigarettes. It's also pretty much similar to the time of Baburam Bhattarai, deputy to Nepal's Maoist supremo Prachanda, and now star alumnus of JNU.

The way to the interview is past a temporal battle zone. A right-wing poster at the entrance to the hostel decries the 'perversion of secularism' and curses the 'Lef-shits of JNU' for it. Overlaying the words 'Red Flag' at the end of a torn poster are the words 'Brown Shit'. A narrow, dank passage past a men's toilet reeks of urine and weak disinfectant. Motorcycles and scooters are parked at the centre of a hallway with rooms lined on either side. Peeling, faded paint, cracked floors. To the left of the door to 11B are two large self-explanatory stickers. 'No Escapé from corporatization?' says one, quite cleverly. 'Resist Corporate Take-over of Campus Spaces! 24/7 Dhaba, Yes! Nestlé outlet, No!' The second one is worded simply, with no attempt at humour: 'Bush the Butcher GET LOST! SHAME on Manmohan For Playing Host!!'

The room is tiny, seven gentle paces by four. There are two cots. One is piled high with leaflets, pamphlets. Rolled-up flags on bamboo staves are stacked to its side. On the other cot, a young man is trying to catch some sleep under a faded quilt, in the glare of a neon lamp. In one corner, three people are hunched over a personal computer that makes a racket, loud disk drive plus very loud fan in the CPU. A wallboard is tacked with colour photos of Yasser Arafat and postcard-sized leaflets that scream 'Go back Bush'. Another wall has a large, lurid-red poster of Bush with fangs, and the legend, 'Gimme Bloood'.

The knot at the computer are loudly criticizing an editorial in the day's *Indian Express* that sarcastically talks about 'a horde of exceedingly photogenic protestors'. It's a blatant reference to author-protestor Arundhati Roy, among others, who lends her face, voice and words to a great variety of protests—against large dams that displace thousands of people, against judges of India's Supreme Court who muzzle protest, against George Bush and big business. The editorial urges India's minister for water resources Saifuddin Soz and his bureaucrats to not give in to such inducements, to 'resist the temptation to perform to their chants' and just go ahead and raise the height of the Sardar Sarovar Dam on the Narmada river in central India.

The stale air crackles with invective. 'Bourgeois bastards,' sneers a lady. 'Of all the papers, never thought the *Express* would...' They notice me.

The lady straightens up from the knot at the computer. Regulation activist: unkempt hair, slightly crumpled ethnic block-printed churidar-kurta, zero make-up, tired eyes.

'Hi,' she says. 'Yes? Ah, okay, we spoke. I'm Kavita. Sorry for the mess in the room. This is Tapas, my husband.' We shake hands. Tapas is dressed in regulation left-wing academic: plain half-sleeved shirt worn over trousers, frayed at the bottom. Simple flip-flops. Several days' growth of beard.

Kavita is impatient. 'It's too crowded here. Shall we go get some tea?'

Are you sure, I ask, can the movement spare you?

She glares at me and then figures I'm joking. 'Don't worry. There will always be someone else.'

We get ourselves some sickly sweet tea at Ganga Dhaba and settle down on some rock surrounded by cigarette butts, away from the crowd. We're below the approach path of aircraft landing at Delhi's Indira Gandhi International airport. There's a steady stream of international carriers and home-grown ones, the novelty of overhead aircraft two decades ago turned to nuisance with India's burgeoning civil aviation sector. There will be more; India is now among the top five purchasers of passenger aircraft in the world, with orders in the pipleline in the region of $15 billion. It's an oddly appropriate setting.

'So tell me. What do you want to know?' Kavita asks. Tell me about your movement, I say. Tell me about yourself.

I get a stream of the need to 'build social hegemony', and that is enough. Not this book talk, I tell her bluntly. Please talk to me.

For someone I've met for the first time, and have just been rude with, she is remarkably calm. 'I'm 33,' she says softly. 'I'm the general secretary of All India Students Association and on the board of *Liberation*, our party journal.' She is also associated with an extension of the party, the All India Progressive Women's Association.

The girl from Tamil Nadu grew up in Bhilai in the heart of Chhattisgarh, where her father worked at a major steel plant. He is retired there. Her mother teaches English at a local college. 'My father is not at all interested in politics. He calls up his daughters to ask whom he should vote for,' she laughs. 'But my mother is keener, and she would have joined us, you know, but for commitments, like looking after my father.' Her younger sister works with an environment magazine in Delhi. 'I call her a "caderized Gandhian".' Kavita is grinning now. 'She's very spiritually driven.'

Her graduate year at Mumbai's elite St Xavier's College, where she read English Literature, was the turning point.

There she came into contact with the All India Revolutionary Students Federation, the students' wing of People's War. 'They would not even bother with most people, saying they are all consumerist bastards—they didn't club me with this lot. They would keep to themselves. But I was deeply affected with the post-Babri riots and bomb blasts in Bombay. I went to the affected areas, and I saw the work students were doing. I got really upset and berated them for not letting me know they were working to help people in riot-hit areas. I was quite drawn to them, the organization was how they recruited students into People's War.'

She was drawn to Left ideology, not the irrevocably extreme Left of People's War, but the softer extreme Left of CPI (ML) Liberation, especially its work related to caste and gender issues. This happened after she had moved to JNU. The crunch shift came during her PhD programme. 'My instructor asked me to choose between the party and PhD,' she says, swatting at mosquitoes. 'So I dropped out of the programme. I chose this.'

'This' is a strange business for her party, a bizarre halfway house between a partial acceptance of parliamentary democracy and a sometimes violent rejection of it through armed action. 'See,' Kavita says, 'we were told by the SP of Jehanabad [Bihar] that we can't be both—overground and underground. "You choose. Either you become CPM,"' she uses the common reference for Communist Party of India (Marxist), "or you become PW or Maoist. I won't let you be both. You can't be one thing in the day and another at night." Another SP in eastern UP told us the same thing. But of course we need to be both. We *have* to be both.'

'So you do believe in armed action,' I find myself whispering, almost relieved with her admission, and look around to see if anyone is within earshot.

'It's okay,' Kavita says. 'Nobody except those I know will drop in. Look, armed action and political action both have to be used. Armed action is to be used for tactical purposes, but not indiscriminately, not for revenge and retribution, but for a specific purpose, for a political end.'

'Do you folks have a chance? Besides the state getting after you, you have other revolutionary organizations after you.' I tell her I was discussing her group with someone, who said her party—usually referred to as ML—has scaled back underground activities in Bihar to the advantage of the Maoists. A lot of ML cadre left in the lurch went bag and baggage to People's War—now CPI (Maoist). And they have now taken to attacking and killing ML cadre and activists, their erstwhile partners in revolution.

On 13 November 2005, Maoists looted an armoury in Giridih, Jharkhand. Afterwards, the Maoists' Bihar-Jharkhand Military Commission issued a sarcastic public statement slamming into ML: 'The seizure of the armoury of Giridih is a victory song of the armed struggle...This action is also a slap in the face of the official Naxalites of the CPI (ML) Liberation who indefinitely postpone the armed struggle.' I remind Kavita of this.

'We haven't scaled back.' She is angry now. 'We have killed...but targets are not individuals in that sense. They represent something. You can't just kill. State retribution and retaliation by groups like the Ranvir Sena can make life very difficult for a villager. A political situation must be created to spread awareness. People must be educated about issues, politics. If you kill innocents, it goes against you.'

'Maoists will tell you we've been killing their people,' she says. 'The fact is, *they* have killed ML cadre. Our office was attacked in Paliganj in the dead of night. Five people were killed...there was a lot of demand for retaliation. But our leader, Dipankar Bhattacharya, kept requesting our cadre to not retaliate but work politically to isolate these people. We raised such a hue and cry—'

'So your revolution is right and others' are wrong.'

'Look, there have been instances in Jharkhand where tendu contractors, in collaboration with Maoists, have got a truck partially filled with tendu leaves blown up. Then the contractor claims Maoists have blown up several trucks, gets compensation, and that is divided between him, Maoists and the administration.'

120

'Armed squads can be tricky,' she adds, as her mobile phone beeps. '*Ek* minute,' she talks into it and looks up to finish. 'It can happen that the leader of an armed squad feels a sense of power and is corrupted. A poor man or woman has a terrible life and then they get a gun...'

She returns to the call. It's an update on the party-organized visit to mark Chandu's death anniversary in Siwan, they'll take along some friendly activists and journalists. I hear her say the local administration in Siwan has given permission to take out a procession but trouble is expected from 'the MLA's thugs'.

A friend of B's, A, more radical than he, had been quite dismissive about the commemoration when I had dropped in to see him one morning. 'It's ten years after Chandu's death,' A had fumed in dismissive anger as we sat cross-legged on a modest Kashmiri carpet in his den in south Delhi with a grand view of the Qutab Minar, 'and all they are doing is putting up a statue of his in Siwan for birds to shit on. Where is the next logical step for the movement? Where is the structure?' ML is all '*phoos*', he had said, using the Hindi colloquialism that suggests air escaping from a punctured balloon. '*Inmay abhi dum nahin hai.*' They have run out of steam. Only Maoist formations, whatever their state of preparation, had any, he claimed, keeping pace with changes in society, neatly moving from classical Maoist exhortations of 'land to the tiller' to more contemporary hooks of displacement on account of projects, privatization, globalization, and the danger of worker redundancy and unemployment.

I relate A's rant to Kavita as she ends the call. She blazes her eyes at me, then takes a deep breath, calms down, and says in a quiet voice: 'Find out how many of those who helped kill Chandu are still alive.'

B drops by just then, jauntily twirling his car keys. 'Ah, the capitalist-pig communist,' I joke, to thaw frost.

—

The area around Ganga Dhaba is filling up with the evening crowd and loud drone of conversation. It's amazing to see India gathered in this small patch of open space, all manner of racial and ethnic representation, a riot of gender, skin colour and language in this melting pot of a university; in JNU there is no overt shame in being of a lower caste, backward caste or tribe, unlike in many vaunted universities and colleges where the economic and academic order have not quite managed to replace ancient social order even with all manner of voluntary and state-imposed affirmative action. The state's propaganda balm for all ills ranging from caste and ethnicity to religious turmoil has always been 'Unity in Diversity'. And at Ganga Dhaba, it seemingly is. But in its presumption of greatness and assured success, the Indian state never figured what to do about the opposite: Diversity of equity. That failure has a bigger bite than ever before.

As I leave, B and Kavita are in animated conversation. 'Fucking media,' B is railing. 'Forty thousand farmers show up for a protest rally in Delhi and the media completely ignores it. We need to make news...anyway, Pascal Lamy is in Delhi at the invitation of ICRIER.' B is talking about the director general of the World Trade Organization, and former trade commissioner of the European Commission. WTO is a pet hate with B. And ICRIER is the Indian Council for Research in International Economic Relations, sometimes a seminar-and-perks way station for superannuated bureaucrats.

'Why don't you picket Pascal Lamy?' B animatedly tells Kavita. 'His big meeting is to be held in Pragati Maidan. The idiots have deemed it "safe". Just sneak in as many people as possible on the 15-rupee entry tickets and *gherao* him. Make him miss his bloody flight—*that* will make news.'

As it would turn out, Pascal Lamy would make the flight, though not before receiving a memorandum from farmer activists. Kavita, and much of activist Delhi and activist India were busy elsewhere, rallying around Medha Patkar, convener of the Narmada Bachao Andolan. She was on a hunger strike along with her colleagues, at Jantar Mantar, down the road from Parliament, hoping to pressure the government into abandoning plans to raise the height of the Narmada Dam and prevent several thousand more people being displaced, to be 'rehabilitated', if at all, in tin-and-asbestos slums on barren land.

14

'You see that?' my brother-in-law Pradip asks a few minutes after we cross the stunning oriental-fan cable suspension sweep of Vidyasagar Setu from Kolkata into Howrah district. He is pointing at paddy fields to the right as we move along at close to 120 kilometres an hour on a new expressway, more than double the maximum pre-expressway speed. Like the 'Second Howrah Bridge' over a muddy, filthy tributary of the Ganga, the expressway is a symbol of resurgent West Bengal. 'That's going to be called International City. World class. As good or better than anything in India.'

Fields of paddy have already given way to scattered 'model' apartments. A slew of bulldozers are parked here and there on levelled land. A few minutes later, Pradip points to a huge stretch of paddy. 'Tata Motors want to set up a plant here.'

The plan is to make low-cost cars, enable hundreds of thousands of Indians to upgrade from motor scooters and motorcycles to four wheels. But by December 2006, too far away for us now in April, the deceptively peaceful patch would be roiled in confrontation: Chief Minister Buddhadeb Bhattacharjee had offered two massive chunks of land to Tata Motors, a flagship of the Tata Group, India's biggest privately run business house, for the plant to manufacture the 'people's car'. Only, by choosing Singur over the other, the company and the government would walk headfirst into controversy over buying fertile agricultural land at knock-down prices. There would follow allegations that cadres of CPI (M), the party in power in West Bengal and a crucial ally of the UPA government in Delhi, were using strong-arm tactics to bend those unwilling to sell their land.

Protestors, shepherded by the Singur Krishijami Raksha Committee—committee to protect farmland—would be beaten up by police. Seventeen-year-old Tapasi Mallick would be found in a field, her body charred. All hell would break loose with accusations that guards protecting the site had first molested and then killed Tapasi. The chief minister of the state would be red-faced; officials of the company in charge of the proposed Rs 10,000 crore, or 100 billion, project, would insist on going ahead and, with technical correctness, suggest that land procurement was the state government's problem. By January 2007, it would become a major political issue. Life and business in Kolkata would be shut down several times by members of the Trinamool Congress, the opposition party led by the fiery woman leader Mamata Banerjee. Homes of CPI (M) activists would be attacked by villagers—and, as police and intelligence would allege, by front organizations of CPI (Maoist). By then a loose confederacy called the People's Democratic Front of India would have emerged, stage-managed mainly by the gentle-voiced Professor Darshan Pal—seen by intelligence analysts as a core front player for the Maoists in Punjab, Professor Pal is co-convenor of the Revolutionary Democratic Front. An alliance of convenience, the People's Democractic Front would count among its members people like Medha Patkar and CPI (ML) Liberation's secretary general Dipankar Bhattacharya. They would make trips to Singur, protesting a raw deal to 6,000 villagers, and the bigger trend of turning India's farmlands into factories that would ultimately put a squeeze on food production.

Bhattacharya's 'class enemy', the chief minister of West Bengal, would publicly announce that the state needed to rethink its land procurement strategy. Debate would rage as to whether the state should procure land on behalf of prospective business using all manner of legal and political muscle power, or should the business negotiate directly with those whose land they would like to buy.

Singur would become, like Kalinganagar in Orissa's Jajpur district—the proposed site of the Tata Group's steel plant in the Kalinganagar industrial complex—a leitmotif of urban versus rural, big business versus small people, development versus displacement struggle. (Police firing killed 13 tribal protestors at Kalinganagar in January 2006. Exactly a year later, 10,000 people, mosly tribals, would gather at the site to mark the day, about half with their heads tonsured in ritual mourning.)

By mid-March 2007, Singur would be overshadowed by Nandigram, also in West Bengal. Police would fire into a crowd, killing dozens, for the sin of protesting possible displacement by a Special Economic Zone (SEZ) to be run by Salim Group, an Indonesian business house.

Yet another leitmotif.

The churn would surprise few who track Naxalism, as with the comparatively smaller incident at Gurgaon's Honda factory in early 2006. It would surprise few in the know of the mechanics of organized protest related to the several hundred suicides by cotton farmers on account of indebtedness in Maharashtra's Vidarbha region. Four districts of the region are deeply Naxal-affected. Of these, Gadhchiroli, part of which marks the western extremity of Dandakaranya, is only a slow overnight bus journey south from the industrial hub of Nagpur, where Boeing and Airbus plan to establish major airplance maintenance centres.

It would also come as no surprise to those who had tracked an incident of caste atrocity in Khairlanji village in Naxal-affected Bhandara district of Maharashtra, just 150 kilometres from Nagpur. On 29 September 2006 four members of a Dalit family, the Bhotmanges, were killed by upper-caste farmers of the village of 700, because they were witness to an earlier beating of a relative who mediated on their behalf and on whose account the upper-caste folk were arrested. Upper-caste people wanted to cut a track through the Bhotmange farm to reduce commute time to their own farms. The

Bhotmanges refused. So that evening, with patriarch Bhayyalal out in his fields, a mob descended on the Bhotmange household. His wife Surekha, sons Sudhir, 21, and Roshan, 19, and daughter Priyanka, 17, were all stripped, paraded naked through the village and beaten. Then the boys were forced to have sex with the ladies, who were then gang-raped in public view. With little left to do after this, the upper-caste men killed all four and threw the bodies into a nearby canal.

It took more than a fortnight for Maharashtra's social justice minister to drop by, offer Bhayyalal money, shelter and police protection, and suspend the local police inspector who ignored both the threat and the incident.

The brutalities of the caste system and the callous response of the authorities to caste violence and discrimination are routine in the country. There are over 2,00,000 pending cases of atrocities against lower castes across India, and the conviction rate is just a little over two per cent. A book, *Untouchability in Rural India*, records numerous instances of continued humiliation, old and new, by so-called upper and intermediate castes that can daily be supplemented by media reports. It mentions the killing of Dalits in Chundru, Andhra Pradesh, because a Dalit youngster accidentally touched with his feet an upper-caste man while watching a movie at the local cinema hall. It mentions a judge of the Allahabad High Court using holy Ganga water to have his chambers purified because his predecessor was a Dalit. It records the public humiliation and beating of the Dalit panchayat president of Chottahatti village, in Tamil Nadu's Sivaganga district, who dared to do his duty by unfurling the national flag at the panchayat's official function during Independence Day celebrations in 2003.

Each such incident—and there are many every single day—provides justification to the revolutionary. Maoist literature was found among civil rights protestors in Nagpur who whipped up public sentiment against government inaction over Khairlanji. Letters were sent to major newspapers by the party's North Gadhchiroli-Gondiya Divisional Committee, bluntly stating: '*Khairlanji Dalit hatyakand ke doshiyon ko sazaye-maut dengey! Sashastra sangharsh ke siva Dalit mukti nahin.*' Death to the perpetrators of the Khairlanji killings! Dalits have no alternative but armed struggle to break free. The Maoists and others like them who think of extreme solutions—an emerging brand of militant Dalit leaders, for instance—have enough of a pool to pick from. There are an estimated 162 million untouchables in rural India, according to the National Federation for Dalit Land Rights Movement. Seventy per cent of them don't own land.

Public reaction to Khairlanji began as a slow burn, and then, seemingly out of nowhere, exploded into protest in the urban areas of the region, especially in Nagpur. For the Maoists and those in the security establishment who track them, it was a perfect operation: take anger from rural areas, merge it with disaffection in urban areas, and then give it a highly visible platform. The show of force in Vidarbha is an example. The management of protest in Singur, Nandigram and Kalinganagar, too, are examples.

All this gelled with the plan outlined in *Urban Perspective— Our Work in Urban Areas*, a 2004 document. It's a long-term plan of the Maoists to prepare the ground for greater Maoist influence in India's towns and cities. 'The urban areas are the centres for struggle by various classes, under the leadership of several organizations representing them,' the Plan suggests. 'It is essential that we unite with such struggling organizations and build up broad struggles against the ruling classes. Thus a significant part of the party's work in the urban areas concerns joint front activity. This includes the formation of various tactical united fronts, as well as building the worker peasant alliance, which is the basis of the strategic united front. This extends from the task of building basic working class unity, to solidarity with the peasantry, to unity with the other revolutionary classes like the semi-proletariat and petty bourgeoisie, right up to maintaining relations and even joint activity with national bourgeois and even ruling class organizations.'

This 'Urban Perspective Plan' is, in several ways, a distillate

127

of thoughts that resulted from a major 19-day gathering for introspection and show of strength that CPI (ML) People's War held in 2001, at the end of which it identified several tasks. Among these, to develop a strong underground party structure, and increase recruitment from what it called 'basic classes'—workers, lower classes and castes, students, intellectuals—to broadbase the movement. It sought to upgrade the fledgling People's Guerilla Army in numbers and quality—the very corporate phrases 'quantitatively and qualitatively' were used to signal it. And build 'united fronts' with all manner of organizations to take on the 'fascists' of Hinduism, economic repression and globalization. By the end of 2006, this action plan, underscored by the Urban Perspective Plan, would be in full flow. The tempo of urban recruitment would be speeded up. The buzz in intelligence circles would be about militant Dalit groups tying in with the Maoists. Other, more overt, alliances such as with farmers' groups, would emerge as key propaganda platforms. The Ministry of Home Affairs would acknowledge this in dry language in its annual report for 2006–7: 'The CPI (Maoist) have also been attempting to intensify their efforts at social mobilization. The Revolutionary Democratic Front (RDF) set up in May 2005 for this purpose has been enlarged into the People's Democratic Front of India (PDFI).'

Morph, morph, morph. It's happening in Nepal. It's happening here.

But as we drive through the Bengal countryside sliced by the impressive expressway, all these events are of the near future. Right now, the paddies are a soothing green blur.

'You've seen the Wipro Campus in Salt Lake, haven't you?' Pradip asks. I nod. The previous day, we had cut through a new development in eastern Kolkata, where towers of steel and glass were blindingly shining, even as much of the metropolis lay decrepit and in disrepair. Pradip turns to me. 'Cal is rocking!'

Rocking with a communist government. Led by the CPI (M) for an uninterrupted run since 1977, riding primarily on massive development of cadre, land redistribution in rural areas and providing cultivation rights to *bargadar*, or sharecroppers, West Bengal has, in general public relations estimation, gone from scourge of capitalism and centre for rampant industrial and civic disruption to poster boy of the 'reformed' Left in 'new' India. If the Left wants business in its bastion state, then India must indeed be shining. And so Kolkata is today a hyped destination for real estate deals, sprawling suburban townships, and billions of dollars of actualized and promised investment in business and industry. After Mumbai, Delhi, Bangalore, Chennai and Hyderabad, it's now Kolkata's turn to play megapolis with its hinterland.

The thing is, the Brotherhood of Mao lives here, too.

—

We speed on towards Santiniketan. We are to meet my parents-in-law. My father-in-law is a former revolutionary who lapsed into the corporate world and later into aeronautical engineering, and I am eager to talk to him about the old times, learn his ideas about what's going on now. Are the objective conditions ripe for revolution?

We pass endless fields of paddy. Place names flash past. Shaktigarh, Bardhaman, Panagarh. Between Bardhaman and Panagarh, the paddies have an accompaniment—brick kilns, or *bhatta*s. This eastern edge of the Gangetic plains is well known for it. The soil is rich, and has provided food and shelter for millennia. It's from where Kolkata's growth comes, a brick at a time. This region and others like it in a ring around Kolkata will help build International City.

Brick kilns like these are also symbols of some of the greatest exploitation in the area and other parts of the country, where profits are made on the back of cheap labour from dirt-poor tribal men and women trucked in by brokers—or *sardar*s, often tribals themselves, hardened by their own ordeal and survival—for reduced pay and maximum work to lead lives of bonded labour. What they get at home is often less, their traditional rights over forest land lost to legislation that allowed land-grab by the state—revenue land—and to local and migrant traders, petty businessmen, landlords and moneylenders.

'The sardars prefer young unmarried girls. They are better workers and good for sale,' activist and writer Mahasweta Devi elaborates in a recent collection of her work, *Dust on the Road*. The brokers, she writes, force the girls to sleep with the owners, the supervising staff, the truck drivers, '*khalasi*s and local *mastan*s'. To ensure cooperation and minimum trouble, a girl is made to drink heavily before she is sent to pleasure the men. Any girl who refuses is locked up in a room, beaten and seared with a hot iron.

'In politically conscious West Bengal these [people] are denied a minimum wage, medical facilities, maternity leave or any kind of leave, and, of course, the right to form a union. There is no attendance or pay register, identity card or employment card...

'These unfortunate beings live in *jhopri*s worse than pig-holes. There are no sanitary arrangements, nor drinking water where they work through the summer days. The kiln is closed with the onset of the monsoons and [they are] sent home.'

Mahasweta Devi wrote this in 1981, in the fourth year of CPI (M) rule. Till 2006, the government of West Bengal refused to even acknowledge bonded labour existed in the state.

This habit of denial continues. Chief Minister Buddhadeb Bhattacharjee, in a fit of pique against card carriers of the extreme Left who use his cadre as target practice and pick them off at will, claimed in 2006 that West Bengal didn't really have a Maoist problem of its own. Jharkhand, Orissa and Bihar, the states that share borders with West Bengal, were to blame for it.

R.K. Majumder, self-professed Naxal-hunter, and director general of West Bengal Armed Police, had claimed to me in an interview that Bhattacharjee is partly right. That West Bengal's Maoist problem 'is a two on a scale of ten, compared to states like Chhattisgarh, Jharkhand and Andhra', which he said were close to the top of the scale. 'We don't have much of a problem,' he told me, 'an average of a couple of murders a month. That's hardly...'

On seeing my raised eyebrows, he had stopped.

'Tribals are fighting back, aren't they?' I queried. 'How many armed Maoists are there in West Bengal?'

'The core strength would not be more than 200. Hardcore. People who have been trained in tactics, weapons and so on. When they go to a village, the entire village is theirs.'

'So there *is* a Maoist problem in West Bengal.'

'Well, they have armed squads. In Belpahari there is one. There's one in Bandwan, one in Lalgarh, one in Gopiballabhpur.' All these are in the three districts of West Bengal flagged extreme red—West Medinipur, Purulia and Bankura—where land reforms on the scale effected by CPI (M) in other parts of the state haven't taken place. 'Then the Dalma Squad comes in from Jharkhand'—this, among other things, is the basis of the chief minister's statement; the squad is named after the Dalma forest near the industrial city of Jamshedpur in Jharkhand; the Dalma Hills overlook the city. 'When the squads go in for a big operation, all of them combine.'

That was more like it. 'Like the Jehanabad jail break?'

'Jehanabad, yes,' Majumder allowed. 'With the platoon drills we found in some camps [we know] they definitely have some people from the army or paramilitary forces who teach them army movements, battle plans, field craft, weaponry techniques. Many people join the army or some other force from rural areas. Even a driver in the army is a combatant, they have basic knowledge. They are 40–45 years old when they retire and come back to the village. They have to survive in the village; they have to cooperate with them.'

Them, the Maoists. But with just 200 cadres in West Bengal? I voiced the thought, but Majumder had batted it away.

'If you have ten people underground in a rural area, they

can walk down at night and annihilate any person they want. Police can't be on every inch of territory.' He then offered a variation of a timeworn, universal saying, but it sounded weirdly, aptly, like something from Mao's Red Book. 'If you throw a pebble into a pond, the waves will travel.'

'You're saying 200 hardcore Maoists with some technical expertise can control vast areas across three districts?' I persist, despite having heard similar assertions from other security officials. One of them, from Andhra Pradesh, had waxed about the Maoist philosophy of 'destroy to build' and 'kill one to terrorize 10,000'—pretty much the standard doctrine of political violence. It took only 19 radically converted young Islamist men to bring down the twin towers of the World Trade Centre, attack the Pentagon and trigger the still unwinable global war against terror.

So numbers, I've been told by many, as I was by Majumder, don't need to be large. They merely need to be effective for the purpose at hand.

'I mean, they wouldn't know how to fly an F-16,' Majumder said, 'but they know the basics of infantry weapons, other techniques. They have engineers helping them.' Majumder had said impatiently, sitting forward on the settee of his living room in central Kolkata, crowded with rallying memorabilia; formerly an avid motor sport rallyist, he is today a fan and organizer. 'These explosions that are happening, these IEDs— I have actually physically measured in five cases the length of the wire leading from the IED over ground, and it was never more than 100 metres.'

He was describing an Improvised Explosive Device set off with something as basic—and as powerful—as depressing the plunger in a flashlight. School physics. 'It has four batteries,' Majumder explained. 'Four into 1.5 volts. Six volts. That goes to an oscillator circuit, DC current is converted into AC, and that is stored in a capacitor. When you press the switch the capacitor discharges, but the current passes through a small transformer and as a result you get very high current of one kilovolt as a pulse. But if the length of the cable is more than 100 metres it won't be able to send a pulse of that magnitude.'

'Where would the person be?'

'Hundred metres away, in the jungle with a flashlight. A basic plunger.' Used to deadly effect in the mud-tracks of villages and jungles, it has decimated trucks, jeeps and even armour-plated 'mine-proof' vehicles, in addition to security foot-patrols. While this relatively old technology still continues—a basic mine can be put together for as little as Rs 500—these days Maoists in key areas of Andhra Pradesh, Chhattisgarh and Jharkhand are also known to use wireless sets for detonation, such as the American-made Icom IC-V8 hand-held transceiver that can trigger explosions from five kilometres away.

And stealthily, a recruit at a time, the Maoists are building up strength, finding some more to depress that plunger, press the button on the remote, and fire the rifle when police and paramilitary scatter from the blast. In the old days, the late 1960s and 1970s, there wasn't such sophistication, more blind anger against socio-economic injustice and the romance of being part of something path-breaking—what Majumder without a trace of irony called '*Shokher Naxal*', Bengali for 'hobby-Naxal'.

How did it work in these parts now?

'I have spoken to a lot of people in this area,' Majumder had explained after taking a call to discuss logistics for an upcoming rally. 'A lot of the poor people have been told: Your father is not well, you don't earn anything, you'll never get married. We will organize food for your family, we will find a good wife or husband for you.'

'That's better than their lot now,' I said.

'Well...money for the family, two square meals a day, some pocket money—and power. One person we captured said, "Sir, I am from a lower caste. In my village high-caste people would not even permit"'—here Majumder used the Bengali '*Amader chhaya maratey deeto na*', they wouldn't even allow us to walk on their shadows. '"But now I sit on a charpoy above them, and they sit on the ground. Because I am a Maobadi. When I am not there people go and ask my parents how they are. This would never have happened otherwise."' Majumder spread his hands: 'Seeing this, other people have also joined, become part of armed squads and militias.'

One recruit at a time.

In July 2005, a gentleman calling himself 'Dhruba', a member of the Central Committee of CPI (Maoist), announced through the media, with little fanfare, the state of play in West Bengal. He said that work was going on in several districts: in North and South 24 Parganas and Howrah, the three districts that ring Kolkata; in the west, in Bardhaman; in the north, from Baharampur, Murshidabad and Malda districts along the border with Bangladesh to Krishnanagar and Nadia to their south. All this is very far from the chief minister's glib alibi.

'Our mass base in Murshidabad, Malda, Bardhaman and Nadia is ready,' Dhruba announced. 'After five years, we will launch our strikes.'

Going by CPI (Maoist) doctrine, he was planning to consolidate, get comfortable, and then hit. He knew that when the state hit back, it wouldn't at first know what to hit. And the more the state hit, the more people would go against it. The strategy was largely copy-pasted from elsewhere in India, and then tactically fine-tuned to suit the situation in Bengal's wretched rural poverty and urban tension. In Andhra Pradesh it sparked off with caste and domination by landlords, as was the case in Bihar. In Chhattisgarh the leverage was provided by tribal destitution and exploitation and has recently shifted to displacement on account of large mining and metals projects, the same as in Orissa. Eastern Maharashtra provided leverage with tribal exploitation, but the planned expansion expects to capitalize on the resentment against caste exploitation, massive farmer indebtedness and seething unrest. In Karnataka it's a combination of both; in Punjab, agrarian crisis and caste issues; and in Haryana, mainly caste issues—building on incidents like the burning of Dalit houses by upper-caste Jats in the village of Gohana in August 2005. Security officials in

Haryana point to militant farmers and youth organizations like the Krantikaari Mazdoor Kisan Union (a 'revolutionary' union of workers and farmers), Jaagruk Chhatra Morcha (a students' front), Shahid Bhagat Singh Mazdoor Morcha (a workers' front), Naujawan Dasta (a youth organization) and Disha Sanskritik Manch (a cultural organization) as being bridgeheads to Maoism. The television channel CNN-IBN ran a news report in January 2006 mentioning such groups are 'active in the Jind, Kaithal, Kurukshetra, Yamunagar, Hisar, Rohtak and Sonepat areas of Haryana'.

Any toehold, anywhere.

And there are new issues to exploit almost every year. Take for example the rant of 'Comrade Sujan' of CPI (Maoist) on GM—genetically modified—crops and seeds, which constitutes an already developing line of battle in India, especially in the cotton-growing states of Maharashtra, Andhra and Karnataka. It builds on the ongoing, raging controversy in India and elsewhere that GM seeds force dependency on corporations that manufacture these, as seeds cannot then be gathered from the crop.

'...There is evidence that these inventions of Dr Frankenstein damage the health of the soil and reduce national sovereignty,' claims Sujan. '...Aren't we now trapped in the cage of Monsanto and other giant companies whose seeds, herbicides and pesticides we have become dependent on? The vast expanses destined for GM...razing native forests and forcing out poor farmers. The highly mechanized form of farming creates very few jobs; instead it exterminates small farm plots and orchards with the poison it spreads. The exodus accelerates to the big cities...'

Sujan then rubbishes India's leadership, dismissing them as 'shameless', saying that none have sovereignty 'in their hearts'. 'What they have in their mind is how promptly they can follow the projects dictated by the imperialists, more particularly, at present, the US imperialist. Mr Manmohan and Mr Pawar (the agriculture minister), with great enthusiasm, have been peddling the UN Millennium Development Goal of reducing hunger by half by 2015. So under the cover of suitable slogans, as dictated, they are introducing biotechnology to meet imperialist hunger for more exploitation and plunder.'

Going back to Dhruba, if he and his cohorts hit, he will depopulate his chosen region of all civil governance. Bureaucrats will pick up their bags and run to the district headquarters. Schoolteachers and health workers employed by the state will run. And it will happen long before someone finally wakes up and declares, 'This is a Naxalite area.' About Maoist plans for Kolkata, Dhruba had calmly said: 'We do not plan violence in Kolkata because we know when we establish our base there, people will be forced to obey us.'

A handful of incisive security analysts well-versed with Mao's doctrine and the progression of Indian revolutionary intent have for years warned that the way to assess Naxalite activity or threat is not only by killings. It's by the degree to which they have created an infrastructure, and the degree to which they have succeeded in mobilizing their institutions and front organizations and sympathizers.

Moreover, as far as armed cadres go, these analysts maintain, there is a need to clarify what exactly is an armed cadre. It is important to cut through the fog of obfuscation floated by the Ministry of Home Affairs. The numbers don't matter—small, sophisticated ten-person operations or a thousand people armed with just bows and arrows and pipe guns. The point is that all of them would have gone though Maoist military training. The day a person is given even a bow and arrow he or she is an armed cadre. He/she has made the psychological transition already and is waiting: when will I be upgraded from bow and arrow to pipe gun? From pipe gun to .303 rifle? From .303 to a self-loading rifle, to an AK-47 or AK-56?

'Revolution is not a dinner party, or writing an essay, or painting a· picture or doing embroidery,' Mao wrote in *A Report on an Investigation of the Peasant Movement in Hunan* (1927). 'It cannot be so refined, so leisurely and gentle, so temperate, kind, courteous, restrained and magnanimous. A revolution is an insurrection, an act of violence by which one class overthrows another.' Using any available tactic. While Mao binds India's Maoists in ideological bear hug, he also preaches adaptation, fine-tuning.

I hadn't had the heart to remind Majumder about Dhruba. It might have ruined his rally. And now, as we breathe fresh, glorious air scented by the paddies and damp earth, buffeted by speeding, overtaking cars, I haven't the heart to tell Pradip about Dhruba either. It will ruin his jolly we're-on-the-highway mood, enhanced by Chicago-blues at great volume on the car stereo.

—

There's a sudden downpour. We stop at Baba Hotel at the crossing after Panagarh, called Darjeeling Mor, where a right turn pulls off the expressway that heads on towards Delhi, and into potholed chaos. We drink sweet tea and munch on Frito-Lay potato wafers. I go to wash my hands and look up to see a poster: 'Happiness is the Everyday Sunshine of Your Life', printed on a picture of a sunset, palm trees and breaking surf. Near the exit is another: 'Where there is a Will, There is a Way'. This will come in handy for the 40 kilometres through early dark, blinding rain and bad roads, especially as I have offered to drive on this stretch.

Outside, plastered on the wall, is a tacky mural of Ganga descending from the Himalaya, her force dammed by a benevolent Shiva before she finds her way to earth, a lot gentler, and brings succour to parched land. The land in the mural is lush green. Ganga pours into a vast lake. There are a few swans about, some trees, a few elephants, some deer, and a tribal lady painted ash-gray, carrying wood on her head. A meeting of heaven and earth. The picture-perfect idyll of wishful thinking.

It's a bit like the Republic Day parade each year in Delhi that sweeps down the grand expanse of Rajpath—literally, the Avenue of Kings. After the long line of dashing soldiers in perfect marching order and the long line of state of the art weaponry that can get patriotism brewing in the most sceptical Indian, comes a long line of farm and tribal folk from across the country. It's a singing, dancing showcase of colourful, choreographed Other India that completes the picture of a wholesome nation.

Of course it's a misrepresentation, as all such things are—more dream than reality, and a morale booster for a tortured country at the halfway house. Naxalism, or Maoism, is only the newest star-scourge in official documents, along with the Al Qaida. On a visit to the Ministry of Home Affairs website in September 2006 I found listed 34 active, violent, and potentially violent organizations—several times that number if all factions and front organizations were to be counted.

In this order, neither alphabetical nor based on perception of threat, it includes United Liberation Front of Asom (ULFA), and another, the National Democratic Front of Bodoland (NDFB), that seeks a smaller portion of Assam, banned despite pretension of peace talks with the first, and partial assimilation of the second through negotiation, surrender and electoral participation in the state elections of 2005. Neighbouring Manipur lists seven such organizations: People's Liberation Army (PLA), United National Liberation Front (UNLF), People's Revolutionary Party of Kangleipak (PREPAK), Kangleipak Communist Party (KCP), Kanglei Yol Kanba Lup (KYKL), Manipur People's Liberation Front (MPLF) and Revolutionary People's Front (RPF). Nearby Tripura has two: All Tripura Tiger Force (ATTF) and National Liberation Front of Tripura. Meghalaya rounds off northeastern India with Hynniewtrep National Liberation Council (HNLC) and Achik National Volunteer Council (ANVC). Major militant organizations from Nagaland are off the list, as the central government engages them in regular talks, and this uneasy peace has limped from one six-month ceasefire to another for the past several years.

More than a decade since active religious and ethnic foment that took many lives, including Indira Gandhi's, Punjab lists three: Babbar Khalsa International, Khalistan Commando Force (KCF) and International Sikh Youth Federation.

Then there is a flurry of Islamist outfits, a mix of those

concerned with Islamist domination and liberation of Jammu & Kashmir to Islamist domination and consequent liberation of the world. The list has Lashkar-e-Taiba/Pasban-e-Ahle Hadis, Jaish-e-Mohammed/Tahrik-e-Furqan, Harkat-ul-Mujahideen/ Harkat-ul-Ansar/Harkat-ul-Jehad-e-Islami, Hizb-ul-Mujahideen/ Hizb-ul-Mujahideen Pir Panjal Regiment, Al-umar Mujahideen, Jammu & Kashmir Islamic Front, Students Islamic Movement of India (SIMI), Deendar Anjuman, Al Badr, Jamiat-ul-Mujahideen, and towards the end, Al Qaida, and Dukhtaran-e-Millat, a radical women's organization in Jammu & Kashmir. These form the A-list of extemist threat, the potential to recruit from even a tiny fraction of India's 120 million Muslim population perceived as grave danger by the state.

The LTTE occupies solus space, even as the ruling Congress party toys with its historical aversion to the organization since it assassinated Rajiv Gandhi, former Prime Minister and husband of current party president Sonia.

Then come the CPI (ML)—People's War, all its formations and front organizations; and Maoist Communist Centre (MCC), all its formations and front organizations. It's either a sign of vagueness or being out of touch with the times that the list does not include ultra-radical ML groupings, or even acknowledge that since September 2004 People's War and MCC have combined in new nomenclature: CPI (Maoist).

The little-known, somnolent Tamil Nadu Liberation Army and Tamil National Retrieval Troops taper off the list.

And the end is reserved for Akhil Bharat Nepali Ekta Samaj, a pan-India organization that forms arguably the most significant catchment for Nepal's Maoists, should the Maoists ever require a topping up.

—

There's a patch of dense forest after Islampur. The headlights of our air-conditioned Tata Motors sedan suddenly illuminate Santhal tribals making their way through the pitch dark, walking in a long line, or on cycles. We take our light with us. We leave them behind. How they see in this dark is a mystery.

139

15

Deepankar, my father-in-law, snorts when I tell him about my intention to visit Naxalbari, the once intended 'liberated zone' where it all began. 'Nowadays they talk about liberated zones, but there was one way back, much before even Srikakulam. Around the time of Telengana.' He is referring to the peasant uprising against the landlords and agents of the Nizam of Hyderabad, the *jagirdar* and *deshmukh*, between 1946 and 1951. It was controlled by the undivided, outlawed Communist Party of India—established in 1925—in conjunction with Andhra Mahasabha, and led to the death of several thousand activists and protestors. The Telengana movement was formally withdrawn after the accession of Hyderabad State to the Union of India, and just before free India's first general elections in 1952. But life in democratic India wasn't terribly different for farmers and lower castes, and for some intellectuals. This later provided the spark for the next cycle in Andhra, in Srikakulam.

'That was the Tebhaga movement,' Deepankar says. Literally, three parts; to share by thirds. Sharecroppers in undivided Bengal demanded that two-thirds of the crop belonged to them, not zamindars and other landlords—they should receive no more than one-third—as they tilled it, and received less than subsistence in return. It coalesced into an organized movement from 1945, helped along by the Kisan Sabha, Communist Party of India's farmer-front, and became very active in Jalpaiguri district, not far from Naxalbari, in the 24 Parganas area to the north and south of Kolkata, and in several areas of present-day Bangladesh. A law enacted by the provincial administration of the time, the Bargadar Act, to lower temperatures, wasn't effective, owing to pressure from the powerful landlords' lobby.

After the division of the province of Bengal in 1946 and more so after India's independence a year later, protests turned belligerent. The administration and police waded into protestors, beatings and torture were commonplace. Several dozen protestors were shot in 1947, and another short-lived movement had the legitimacy of revenge: 'We will give our lives but not our crop'.

We're both sipping a light Portuguese wine I've carried as a gift from Goa, an import now made easier and cheaper by Indian law.

'In 1948, the area around Kakdwip [an estuarine area south of Kolkata] used to be called Lal Ganj—the Red Borough. People used to quake.'

I draw closer. It's story time. The rain has eased. There is no electricity, a common feature. Hurricane lamps and candles complete the mood in Santiniketan, Place of Peace, created as an ideal community for learning and the arts by Rabindranath Tagore in the early twentieth century in the middle of western Bengal's tribal zone. Nouveau riche sahibs from Kolkata have now bought up land around the campus, building brash bungalows where earlier stood understated homes. An intellectual, spiritual getaway is today a weekend getaway. Little has changed for the area's tribals, though. They still drink, squabble and work as maids, gardeners and rickshaw-walas. They see Kolkata sahibs buy their land and relocate them into slums; see well-meaning culture tsars of the university celebrate their simplicity in art, sculpture and song, while they sell trinkets at village fairs and lead a life made simple by design.

'A group of us went to the house of a *jotedar* called Akrur Das,' Deepankar begins—the simplicity of his tale is chilling. 'We killed the guards and went in, and found nearly 100 *tola* of gold ornaments stuffed inside pillows, and about 1.5 lakh rupees in cash. Can you imagine the value of it those days?'

After looting the landlord, Deepankar and his associates escaped and went in different directions. He was soon doing a steady, shambling semi-trot through the clayey soil of the paddies. '*Kadam-chaal*,' he says, in Bengali. 'That way, you don't sink into the mud. The momentum keeps you going.'

Then he heard someone calling out to him. What is it, he

141

asked, without stopping. The man, a villager, pointed out four armed policemen in the distance. 'They were after me in the same half-trot.' They went on like that through the night. He says he 'had the edge on them' and made his way to the station, just in time to catch a train to Ballygunje—part of then, as now, plush Calcutta. But the policemen had made it as well; he saw when he looked out. He jumped off on the other side, made his way to a vendor's coach and hid himself among the sacks of vegetables and baskets of fish. 'They couldn't imagine someone would hide there, in all the muck and the smell.' He got off at Ballygunje station and in broad daylight walked down Rashbehari Avenue to the upper-middle-class repository of Hindustan Park where the family then lived.

'When I walked into the living room, my mother and uncle and some house guests jumped up screaming!' He guffaws and sips more wine. '"Relax," I told them, it's me, Deepankar—Khokon.' He was sunburnt, had a beard, and was wearing a dhoti in the way farmers still do, wrapped tight about the body and hiked above the knee; and his hands and feet were caked with mud.

My mother-in-law, Kalyani, calls out to us for dinner. It's her priceless chicken curry, accompanied by healthy unpolished rice, fried eggplant, lemon and green chillies freshly plucked from the modest garden outside.

Later, he lights up a cigarette and we move aside from family chitchat to carry on with his past. 'You know, it's difficult to explain the romance of the times, for a just cause. There was a famine. People were eating roots.'

I've heard worse of the Bengal famine. My mother had told me stories of how on the streets of Kolkata she saw starving people pick the grains of undigested rice from the vomit of others and eat it. A sordid chapter in history subsumed by the greater immediate histories of India's freedom struggle and Partition.

Deepankar tells me another story, from 1949, two years into India's independence, a brave new world. 'People were starving in these three villages in Sandeshkhali. We led a raid.' The jotedar there, like all wealthy landlords, lived off tenant farming and squeezed the tenants. He had thirteen large stores of paddy. 'There was a stream around his property, and barbed-wire fencing. There was a Muslim fellow in the group. He went ahead, a short sword clasped between his teeth, crawled under the fencing and got rid of the guard by slashing his throat.' Deepankar is matter of fact. 'Then we went in and opened the doors to others. There were thirty *maund*s of paddy.' Well over a tonne. 'A group of starving villagers were with us, about 200, but many more were waiting. We formed a chain gang and managed to roughly distribute the paddy.'

The police caught him while he trying to make his escape, and beat him badly. His eyes never quite got all right and his head, at 76, still aches blindingly every few days, the legacy of an angry life he left behind to return to a widowed mother and younger brother. And eventually, a career first with blue-chip Burmah Shell and later as a top engineer with Hindustan Aeronautics Limited—a compromise he still finds difficult to accept. Deepankar was first taken to the nearby Bashirhat Jail, he says, where he was tied to a tree and beaten for eight to nine hours with a thick rope. 'After a while, I lost consciousness. When I awoke, I had lost all sense of time and place. I don't know how long I was there. The jail was filthy. I got eczema. But one day, when they found out that I was a "student comrade", not a local villager, the threat perception went up. They immediately moved me to Alipur Jail in Calcutta.' He says the judge threw his case out because he simply wouldn't believe the police version that a bunch of *bhadralok*—genteel— revolutionaries and scrawny villagers would have the strength to spirit away so much grain in a few hours of night. Fortunately for Deepankar, the judge didn't know of the logistics support provided by hunger and anger.

Do you think it was justified, I ask him, this scion of the elite tier of Calcutta society, a graduate of St Xavier's School, holder of an engineering degree from Jadavpur University, who spurned the legacy of a father who went to Cambridge.

'It was absolutely justified,' he roars, waving away Pradip who sticks his neck out from the dining room to see what the ruckus is all about. 'Even now, I think it was absolutely justified. We were determined to bring justice to the poor—at any cost. And for that we were willing to give up our families, wealth, our lives, everything.'

'Would you do it all over again?'

'Yes.'

Several months later I would find the same quiet conviction and dignity in an ill Ram Naresh Ram, in his seventies, like Deepankar, a legend in Bhojpur, Naxalism's fertile breeding ground in Bihar. Bhojpur is home to Ekwari, Bihar's Naxalbari, and a bloody battle zone in which left-wing rebels fighting for low-caste peasantry took on the Ranvir Sena, the vigilante army of the upper castes. The five-time MLA with CPI (ML) Liberation, and a member of the party's Politburo, was seated on a wooden bench, dressed in lungi and tattered sweater, soaking up a weak February sun in 2007 by a tiny outhouse at the back of the party office in Patna.

Ram, still better known as Paras, his name from days underground, gently dismissed my talk of his adopted party being both underground and overground—with five elected MLAs in Bihar's assembly, and one in Punjab. 'You can be underground from your *dushman* [enemies],' he told me with a tired smile, 'but you can't be underground from the people, can you?'

'I find that a similar sense of justice is prevalent now,' Deepankar continues. 'Though conditions are quite different in many parts of India. And also, compared to Nepal, where the objective conditions are very different to India's. Here, there is growth, a sense of movement, not the complete lack of diversity of wealth as in Nepal. So, what is your sense of what is going on?'

The sudden question throws me off balance. He smiles, the clever so-and-so. It's always easier to ask questions than provide answers. Journalists—and revolutionaries, I assume—know it only too well.

—

I first started thinking about modern-day Maoism in 1997, I tell Deepankar, when I worked at *India Today* magazine. As editor of a special issue to commemorate 50 years of India's Independence, I also had to handle two projects, one an opinion poll with ORG-MARG, among India's top polling organizations, and the other a futuristic study to map India in 2047 by New Delhi-based Centre for Policy Research, a major think tank that was already into the process of its own documentation in this regard. Both threw up a few startling assertions that have stayed with me.

The opinion poll covered a fairly large sample of 12,651 respondents, and cut across age, income, education, caste, religion and rural-urban barriers. Thirty-four per cent felt corruption was the number one evil; unemployment followed with a number one ranking by 20 per cent; and rising prices were at 18 per cent. This is a pretty standard mix of admission and concern: *India Today*'s semi-annual 'State of the Nation' polls usually see these three parameters move around the top three slots.

The finding for me was the answer to the question 'Do you think India will stay united in the next 50 years, or disintegrate into independent nations?' In a year of both propaganda-led and spontaneous burst of patriotic celebration, only 41 per cent answered 'Yes'. A stunning 36 per cent answered 'Yes' to 'Disintegrate', and an equally stunning 23 per cent belonged to the category termed DK/CS—Don't Know/Can't Say.

The India 2047 projection by the Centre for Policy Research threw up some grave concerns, at the other end of the spectrum of what most people even then took for granted, that if India were to keep even a semblance of order, the sheer momentum of economic growth, greater public accountability and geopolitical progression would propel it into some sort of reckoning in the global pecking order. To begin with, the report said, India's count of 25 states would double to 50 or more to satisfy continuing inequities in development, and regional aspiration; three have already been carved out since the poll, the present-day Maoist strongholds of Chhattisgarh (carved out of Madhya Pradesh) and Jharkhand (from Bihar), and Uttarakhand (from Uttar Pradesh), where the Naxals have begun to make inroads and which Nepal's Maoists freely use as sanctuary. The formation of Telengana in the near future, from the volatile north-central chunk of Andhra Pradesh, is a near certainty.

The report added: 'The challenge of providing basic services like adequate food, clothing, housing and water will be enormous. For instance, we will need about 400 million tonnes of grain by 2047, or more than double the current production, on more or less the same arable area. Productivity must therefore double, which means huge investments in irrigation and on improved land and water management.

'A demographic explosion over the next 50 years will create any number of political, economic, social and environmental tensions. The different growth rates of different communities, castes, and regions could become a political time bomb...Above all, the consumption standards of the poor will be eroded by rising numbers.'

The study remarked that while insurgency in the north and northeast would recede on account of various political solutions, there was likely to be great churning of society. 'There will be more empowerment of submerged or suppressed social classes. The tribal awakening will quicken, especially in the Northeast and Middle India. The larger Dalit assertion will seek equality, identity and self-determination within the Indian state. There will probably be a major political upheaval around 2005-10 on the issue of agrarian and social relations, particularly in Bihar and Andhra Pradesh, as "stability" finally gives way to change.'

There wasn't a word on Naxalism as a political movement

or threat to internal security. In 1997, Nepal's armed rebellion was only a year old, dismissed by many as a romantic notion. In India, already in the throes of chest-beating economic liberalization, Naxal formations were either a thing of the past, or splintered movements concentrated in parts of Andhra Pradesh, and undivided Bihar, Madhya Pradesh and Uttar Pradesh. Generally out of sight and, therefore, out of mind.

Yet, the very concerns as expressed in the projection are being leveraged by the Maosists and others.

I never got around to asking the experts at the Centre for Policy Research—out of politeness, I guess—whether the tone they used was so subdued because they wanted to appear balanced and credible. Or because they saw a future that scared the hell out of them and they didn't want to make it any scarier than it already was.

—

'There was this chap who recruited me,' Deepankar gently intervenes. 'Ashish Bose. I guess he understood I was extreme Left in my thoughts.'

As a student Deepankar would sell *Swadhinata*—Independence—the journal of the undivided Communist Party of India. The police would beat him up, and he would go right back and sell the paper. 'He drew me in. He said, "Go teach at Kakdwip. You don't have to do anything else." That's it. And I did it. The young and old came to learn the alphabet from "engineer-*dada*". And I was in, just like that, without even fully realizing it. When the police later caught me, I heard they wanted to hold a condolence meeting for me—they assumed I would die. My providing just a little bit of education had that effect on these people.'

In 1992, he heard again about Ashish Bose. He had gone underground for 44 years in Chhattisgarh under an assumed name. 'He was involved in organizing villagers to assert their rights and ask for their constitutional dues. The police shot him dead. His wife came over to gather his documents and later handed them over to *Kalantar*, the successor to *Swadhinata*.'

'We were dedicated. But we made mistakes then,' Deepankar continues. 'We were not well organized. Now things are much better organized.'

He looks at me for a while before speaking. 'The objective conditions for revolution exist in many more ways than ever before.'

16

It's quiet as I ride a rickshaw into Bolpur, the station for Santiniketan, a little after 10 p.m. More than two hours still for the Darjeeling Mail to arrive from Kolkata's Sealdah station on its overnight run to New Jalpaiguri, the gateway to northeast India. In the old days, it would carry sahibs of the tea gardens, children of the elite from schools in Darjeeling, Kurseong and Kalimpong, and holidaymakers to Calcutta and back. Then, as now, it was difficult to obtain a reservation. Better roads, better cars and cheaper flights haven't reduced the popularity of the train. Only one place is available from Bolpur tonight and I have it, in what the railways cryptically term 1AC—air-conditioned first class sleeper, the 'burra-sahib' class.

The usual flotsam of poor and dirt-poor is milling near the entrance, around the nuclei of a late-night chai shop and a ramshackle cart selling boiled eggs and greasy omelette sandwich. Villagers squat, waiting out the dark, covered with light, tattered shawls. A lady with matted hair is loudly demanding money from a sheepish man. She could be his wife, or a comforter of the poor; I don't wait to find out. Inside the station, the scene is more cosmopolitan-destitute. There is no place to wait, so deformed beggars, homeless humans and homeless dogs and the middle-class share benches and platform space near eddies of air created by noisy fans.

As I find out, to move away is to be feasted upon by

Godzilla mosquitoes. A ragged boy has found a solution. He sleeps kneeling, face turned sideways on the floor of the platform, collar pulled up, presenting the minimum possible profile to mosquitoes. A loader has found another solution; he naps on his cart by a small pile of burning rag-and-paper egg trays.

The notice board past the stationmaster's office is plastered with fantastic promises and blunt demands. UBR Productions is hosting the All Bengal Solo Dance Talent Hunt, organized by an 'Eminent Nritya Guru & Eminent Personalities of India, entry Fee Rs 10/- only'.

An undated notice exhorts dancing to a different tune. 'Fight for our Legitimate Rights', it emphatically announces. 'Join O.B.C. Railway Employees Federation', it reads, announcing solidarity for 'Other Backward Castes', political-administrative finessing to describe reservation in government jobs and state-funded education for a clutch of low- and intermediate-caste groups. 'Joining OBC Association is our birth right and can not be criticised...opportunity was given by the Grate Union of India...' It lists some demands: clear up anomalies in pay scales, fill up the backlog of reserved seats in jobs with the railways, form 'OBC cells' in various railway zones and divisions, 'check against excess harassment' and provide 'promotion facilities to OBCs'. It is signed 'Yours Fraternally' by R.P. Singh, Zonal President, and J.P. Ray, Zonal General Secretary.

Take out a few words here and there, especially the reference to the greatness of the Indian Union, add bourgeois-comprador-imperialist-state repression, and you might have a Maoist leaflet.

At midnight, the Howrah–Jamalpur Express arrives on Platform No. 1. Railway Protection Force (RPF) personnel with decades-old .303 rifles and sub-machine guns are located in every coach. The previous day, 8 April, a section of track between Gaya and Dhanbad was blown up by the Maoists— not the section this train will go on, but any train heading to Bihar, Jharkhand and Uttar Pradesh, or through the Maoist borderlands of West Bengal, has armed guards.

Not that it always works. On the evening of 13 March 2006, an estimated 50 Maoists hijacked a train going from Barwadih in Jharkhand to Mughalsarai in Uttar Pradesh. They stopped the train in a patch of jungle in Jharkhand—a few onboard Maoists made the task easier by uncoupling the vacuum link between coaches. Several hundred passengers and railway security men were held hostage till after daybreak, when the rebels simply melted away. The area's senior police officer would later claim that the Maoists had pulled off the trick for two possible reasons. The first was retaliation for the death of an 'area commander', Jagannath Koiri, in nearby Palamau ten days previously. The second reason was a corollary: The Maoists had actually waited to ambush security forces who they knew would inevitably arrive. Suspecting this, the police had deliberately delayed their arrival, and the Maoists, not having planned for an extended siege, let the train go. Either way, a point was made by both sides.

Several months later, on 10 December 2006, about 25 Maoists would board a train from Tatanagar to Kharagpur. Near the border of Jharkhand and West Bengal they would emerge in true colours, snatch a couple of rifles from railway guards, stop the train, take away the engine driver's walkie-talkie, inform the stationmaster of Chakulia of what they had done and, before disappearing in a couple of hours, past noon, take along Rs 1,00,000 from the salary being carried for railway staff. One result of this would be that railway policemen in outposts at Manoharpur and Donguaposi in southern Jharkhand would insist they were better off being unarmed. At least the Maoists wouldn't then attack their posts to loot their weapons and, in all probability, kill them.

Less than half an hour after the Howrah–Jamalpur Express, the Sealdah–Varanasi Express checks in. A group of vendors get off from a coach near where I'm standing, with vegetables for the morning indulgence of traders and babus of Bolpur and Santiniketan, huge sacks of onions, spring onions, potatoes, spinach, okra and capsicum. An argument breaks out. One of two RPF personnel steps down from the coach as the train begins to move and snatches a bag of capsicum with a curse snarled in Hindi: '*Bhainchod, ek paisa nahin diya.*' Sisterfucker, didn't give us a single paisa.

I notice a railway official next to me. I start shouting for him to do something, but the train moves on with the evidence, and he calmly returns to the depths of the station after flagging off the train.

Now the cursing is in Bengali, from the vendors. '*Khankir bachcha, gandu saala, banchot.*' Son of a whore, assfuck, sisterfucker.

One of the group of five turns to me. 'We have to give money to these station-walas also. You started shouting so he didn't take it. But tomorrow? Will you be there tomorrow?'

The now awake loader helps them pile on the sacks on his trolley and they move out, cursing each other—the vendors because the loader had asked for too much money, and the loader because the vendors had beaten him down to too little.

My train arrives soon after. The coach is a little way away from where I am, so I walk towards it, my small backpack weighed down with a motley selection of books I purchased at Subarnarekha, a bookstore that has become an institution in once-gentle Santiniketan. *The Blue Mutiny, The Indigo Disturbances in Bengal 1859–1862* by Blair King; a book in Bengali on Mughal-era agrarian economy and farmer revolts, by Gautam Bhadra; *The Naxalites and their Ideology* by Rabindra Ray; and *Truth Unites*, a collection of essays edited by Ashok Mitra on a range of subjects from feudalism and resistance to food-grain prices to realism in Marxist cultural movements. Over-the-counter records of anger and violence against the state.

There are some poems, too, in *Truth Unites*. There's one in a chapter on revolutionary poetry—'Cannons Buried in Flowers'—written by Sumanta Banerjee, a long-time observer of the Naxalite movement. The poem is by Murari Mukhopadhyay, and it is as much unfinished agenda as unashamed romanticism:

When in love,
Do not become the moon.
If you can,
Come as the sun.
I'll take its heat
And light up the dark forest.
When in love,
Do not become a flower,
If you can,
Come as the thunder.
I'll lift its sound
And pass the message of battles to every corner.

The moon, the river, the flowers, the stars, the birds—
They can be watched at leisure
Sometime later.
But today
In this darkness,
The last battle is yet to be fought.
What we need now is
The fire in our hovel.

—

Abhijit Mazumdar meets me at the gates of Siliguri College, where I arrive from the station, a bone-jarring 70-rupee ride in an auto rickshaw through a long street of slums and tenements. Siliguri, West Bengal's second largest urban sprawl after Kolkata, is today a crowded, polluted, stupendously noisy and filthy trade-and-transit hub that, with New Jalpaiguri, straddles the routes from the southern plains to the hills of Bengal, the state of Sikkim, Bhutan, and onwards to China; and from the Gangetic plains to India's roiled northeast.

Abhijit's ancestral home, a structure of wood and tile, is being repaired. So while his family occupies part of it, Abhijit rents a one-bedroom apartment near the college. I had a false notion that the weight of being Charu Mazumdar's son might make for a sombre life. As I will discover, Abhi—the name is soon shortened—doesn't need forced sobriety. Nor does he feel any need to dress the part of the son of a revolutionary, or the Darjeeling district head of CPI (ML) Liberation. In his full-sleeve striped shirt, faded Lee jeans, Velcro strap-on sandals, and with curly hair, trimmed beard and trendy spectacle frame he could be an academic anywhere, or a painter, a poet, the creative director of an advertising agency.

It's a compact, walk-up apartment on the first floor where he lives. A cot in the living area is to be my bed. Pride of place on the wall belongs to a black-and-white photograph of his father. It shows a handsome, delicate-featured bhadralok in western clothing, circa 1953. Very different from the emaciated, grimacing man in the iconic photograph taken at Lalbazar Police Station in Kolkata, of the revolutionary surrounded by policemen, before his incarceration between 16 and 28 July 1972 during which he died. It isn't yet clear if he died from ill-health or rough prison therapy that became the hallmark of West Bengal's anti-Naxal operations. It was when custodial beatings and torture and faked 'encounter' killings were popularized by the police as an important secondary method of dealing with extremism—the primary method being shootouts during real encounters.

Charu Mazumdar had written about the rapid transformation, to his mind, that the Naxalbari movement had undergone from peasant uprising to something more ambitious. I had also read about it earlier this morning on the train, in Rabindra Ray's book. Ray had quoted Mazumdar from the June 1968 issue of *Liberation*, a journal he founded (a journal of the same name is now published by ML) in an article titled 'One Year of Naxalbari Struggle':

'This is the first time that peasants have struggled not for their partial demands but the seizure of state power. If the Naxalbari peasant struggle has any lesson for us, it is this: militant struggles must be carried on not for land, crops, etc., but for the seizure of state power. It is precisely this that gives the Naxalbari struggle its uniqueness.'

No ambiguity whatsoever about intention. Today's

revolutionaries have also taken a leaf out of another of Mazumdar's writings, the call to formally break away from CPI (M) and form a revolutionary party, what led to the formation of CPI (ML). Ray, a scholar, sneeringly terms this call to revolution a 'utopian one, rhetorical and plaintive', a write-off. He had researched the book in 1983, and it was first published in 1988. The movement has adapted and spread, in bizarre yet inevitable fashion, from a small cluster of villages to an ideological and operational playground across half of India's landmass.

'...Revolution can never succeed without a revolutionary party,' Ray quotes Mazumdar, 'a party which is firmly rooted in the thought of Chairman Mao Tse Tung, a party composed of millions of workers, peasants and middle-class youths inspired by the ideal of self-sacrifice...a party whose members put into practice the Marxist-Leninist ideal in their own lives and, by practicing the ideas themselves, inspire the masses to make greater self-sacrifices and to take greater initiative in revolutionary activities; a party whose members never despair under any circumstances and are not cowed by any predicament but resolutely march forward to overcome it. Only a party like this can build a united front of people of different classes holding different views in this country. Only a revolutionary party like this can lead the Indian revolution to success.'

The other visuals in Abhijeet's room are a photograph of Abhi's wife, who teaches history at Purdue University in the United States, and a crowded black-and-white calendar for 2006 from the local chapter of the Association for Protection of Democratic Rights (APDR) that is more poster of protest. Interspersed between the dates are photographs of protest icons and occasionally, points.

I scan it while wolfing down a breakfast of chapatti, stir-fired vegetables and black tea. There is Irom Sharmila from Manipur, calendar girl for January, February and March, at the time into the sixth year of her hunger strike demanding the revocation of the Armed Forces (Special Powers) Act which allows security forces in the North-East and in Jammu &

Kashmir—all 'disturbed areas'—to 'enter and search without warrant any premises to arrest' anyone they suspect of doing anything remotely construed as anti-state, and be immune from prosecution without 'previous sanction of the Central Government'. The act has often meant abduct-at-will and shoot-to-kill. Irom's is a classic case of the state 'privileging violence', to use Arundhati Roy's phrase, by ignoring non-violent protest.

The next few months of the calendar change through a rush of photos, sayings and slayings: Martin Luther King Jr, nuked Hiroshima, Aung San Suu Kyi. And Thangjam Manorama Devi, tortured, raped and killed allegedly by troops of the Seventeenth Assam Rifles in Manipur on 11 July 2004 on suspicion of her association with the insurgency outfit People's Liberation Army.

The UN Charter of 1945 and the UN Declaration of Human Rights, 1948, flow into September and October, with photos of Bob Dylan, Paul Robeson and Pete Seeger. Some photos from the Buchenwald concentration camp, circa 1945, bring in November and December.

'It's time to go,' says Abhi. He has taken the day off to take me on a tour of Naxalbari, to meet some of his father's old comrades.

—

There really is a place called Naxalbari. It's a small town with its own tiny railway station and state highway, straddling the route that links northern Bihar to northern Bengal, through forest, farmland and tea gardens. But the Naxalbari of revolutionary grammar is really a cluster of villages and hamlets with quirky names from nature and history: Hatighisa, after elephants; Phansideoa, literally, hanged; Bagdogra, derived from *bagh* or tiger. These are places on the way to Naxalbari from Siliguri.

Abhi and I get on to a small bus at Hospital Mor. We're off to a place just shy of Naxalbari. From Hospital Mor all buses lead through a slice of the region known as Dooars to Panitanki—literally, water tank—at Nepal's eastern border. A sliver meanders on to Khoribari for a dip south towards Katihar in Bihar.

It takes an age to negotiate Siliguri's former pride and joy, Hill Cart Road, the sedate avenue of my childhood, now a smoking, honking mayhem of pedestrians, rickshaws, auto rickshaws, buses, scooters and motorcycles, and all manner of cars, sub-compact to luxury sedan.

'What's so surprising?' Abhi snorts, when I point out expensive cars. 'Siliguri was always a centre for timber, tea and smuggling. Now you have new businessmen in old businesses, and there are new millionaires in construction.' After crossing the sewer of Mahananda river that marks the boundary of Siliguri, we take a left at Tenzing Mor—to the right is the road to Darjeeling. There is a sprawling development just outside town, work in progress, neat, clean, a clone of suburban bungalows and condominiums in scores of cities across India. 'Uttarayan,' a board says. 'Heaven on earth in Siliguri.'

'The babus find the city too noisy and unclean,' Abhi notices my curiosity. 'These used to be tea gardens, the land now converted for commercial use with government help. All the labourers of the garden lost their jobs and went away.' He laughs. 'The communist government of West Bengal has done this. You know, for us here in Bengal, the greatest enemy of the Left is the Left.'

Soon, there is unbroken expanse of tea gardens, old and new, on either side. Matigara Tea Estate, Pahargoomiah Tea Estate—where that other Naxalite icon Kanu Sanyal controls the union—Atal Tea Estate...

Then it's time to get off.

We walk into a hut a few yards off the road. It's broken, a patchwork of mud, straw and tile that covers an open veranda-like area, a couple of rooms and a tiny kitchen. A few hens and a rooster strut around, small potatoes are laid out on a coir-strung cot. The wall facing the open area is in disrepair, basic woodwork cracked and peeling. There is a poster on the wall of the Hindi movie star John Abraham on a humongous Yamaha motorbike. There's another poster washed with the saffron, white and green of India's flag. The pitch is simply worded: 'Love your Country'.

Punjab-da and I shake hands as Abhi introduces us. He's an old man in his seventies with stubble and epileptic shake, eyes awash with cataract. I sit beside him on another cot; Abhi pulls up a rickety chair. 'Someone here likes motorcycles,' I offer. Punjab-da grins. 'I love my country, my two sons love motorcycles.'

The door leading to the interior is open, and I can see some framed photographs on the wall. From left to right, Marx, Frederick Engels, Lenin, Stalin, and dirt marks left by a removed frame. 'The police come now and then to ask me questions. The police came a few months ago and broke it,' Punjab-da is still grinning. 'It was a photograph of Mao Tse Tung.' A young boy, whom we had seen at a tiny bicycle repair shop by the road comes and stands near Punjab-da.

'Why only Mao?'

'Everyone talks of Maoists. They are scared of Maoists.'

'Oh, they are really scared of Maoists,' Abhi chips in. 'The border [with Nepal] being so close and porous.'

Punjab-da's wife walks in then. Abhi and she greet each other with raised fist and 'Lal salaam'. There is an offer of the inevitable laal-cha from Boudi, as Abhi calls her, elder brother's wife.

After she leaves, Punjab-da gets a little pensive, and after a little verbal nudging from me that his name, Punjab Rao, seems a little 'foreign' for Naxalbari, he says he's originally from Amravati in the Vidarbha region of Maharashtra. A posting in the army brought him to these parts in the 1960s, and he married a Nepali girl and settled here after being decommissioned. They are all dead now, he tells me, his Nepali wife and the three sons they had together. 'She is my second wife,' he says of Boudi, 'and this is one of my two sons. They run a cycle repair shop and worship this,' he nods at the poster of John. 'I still farm, do a little party work. That is not for them. Each to his own. But they have never held me back. I have been fortunate. They said, "You go and do what you have to, we are with you."'

Respectfully, the boy brings a plaque wrapped in plastic from a shelf to our right that has some broken farm implements, a plate, a few stainless steel glasses. The plaque reads: '2nd All India Conference of All India Kisan Mazdoor Sabha, On 9th to 11th Sep 2005, Jallandhar. Presented to Com. Punjab Rao, In Honour of His Glorious Services to Revolutionary Peasant Movement. Presented by AIKMS.'

'Did you feel proud when they gave you this?'

'No, not proud. People like us should have no place for pride. We are workers. We should work.'

The same year he travelled across the country to receive this honour, he approached a landlord near home and told him that as he had five acres of land, but really needed only four, could he spare one and settle landless peasants on that land? Amazingly, the landlord agreed. 'But the panchayat, which is CPM controlled, stopped it. They were upset that they weren't seen to be doing it. It is a strange world in this state. Left versus Left.'

Abhi and he laugh. It's clear Punjab-da is very fond of Abhi, and seems to treat him like a son. I mention Charu Mazumdar's name, and he places his hand to his heart. There's a pacemaker there, Abhi tells me later, courtesy of donations from friends that cut across all ML factions, and party colleagues in CPI-ML (New Democracy). This faction is relatively safe here—for now. In Andhra Pradesh's Khammam district, CPI (Maoist) cadres would in a few days visit Bironimadava village and beat up residents, threaten them to keep away from ML (New Democracy) folks. Extremely radical Left versus radical Left.

'Do you remember what happened on that day?' I ask Punjab-da.

He knows what I mean. 'Twenty-fourth of May, 1967. Just up the lane from this house,' he points behind him, eyes alight, voice sharper. 'Landless peasants had had enough.' Anger had been brewing over scarcity of food, issues of landlessness and bonded labour for a year. 'There was talk of revolution, but they just wanted to assert their rights,' he recalls. 'They had taken over land. Then the police came, called by the jotedar. As soon as we heard about it, we set off with whatever we had—swords, bows and arrows, spears, farming implements. The people with us, as soon as they saw the group of police and landlords, they let the arrows fly. One hit the landlord, another hit someone on the leg. The police ran away. That was the beginning.'

The police came back in large numbers the next day, though, Punjab-da recalls, and destroyed houses, broke what they could, mixed rice and lentils with dirt, destroyed all other food. By then the spark had spread to Bengaijote, just beyond Naxalbari; eleven protestors died by police firing that day.

'Naxalbari had its first martyrs,' says Punjab-da, looking at Abhi, tea forgotten. 'And the Naxalbari movement was born. *Bas.*' Revolutionaries spoke of it in glowing terms: 'Spring thunder struck all over India.' It spread to Ekwari and Mushahary in Bihar, Lakhimpur Kheri in Uttar Pradesh, parts of Punjab, and Srikakulam in Andhra Pradesh, areas of pressure-cooker rural poverty and caste discrimination. In two years, in April 1969, the CPI (ML), newly formed and energized, would be powerful enough to hold a massive public rally at Shahid Minar—Martyr's Column, renamed from the earlier, colonial Ochterlony Monument—in Calcutta. In a matter of weeks, most leaders were underground, several were jailed, some killed.

By 1972, this edition of revolution would be pretty much over in Bengal and elsewhere, utterly steamrolled by the state. One of the worst massacres took place in August of that year in Kashipur and Baranagar areas near Calcutta, when police literally dragged out and killed known and suspected Naxals. There is no credible estimate of the numbers killed, beyond 'hundreds'. Dozens disappeared, including some well-known Naxal leaders like Saroj Dutta and Sushital Roychoudhary, suave well-to-do intellectuals who looked like kindly uncles or indulgent grandfathers—as ever, revolutionaries are difficult to discern till they speak, act, or wear battle garb. Skirmishes continued well into 1973, a year when the number of Naxals in jails across India exceeded 30,000. Little remained thereafter, barring sentimental outpourings by urbane remnants before they were killed or had revolution squeezed out of them. Journalist and Naxal chronicler Sumanta Banerjee recorded such a moment:

'On 3 May 1975 five Naxalite prisoners were killed by the police in Howrah Jail, West Bengal. One among them was a 22-year-old student—Prabir Roy Choudhury, whose pet name was "Pakhi" or bird. When they heard about the killing, Prabir's comrades in Presidency Jail, Calcutta, inscribed the following lines on the wall of their cell with a piece of stone (they were not allowed the use of paper and pens):

Silence!
Here sleeps my brother.
Don't stand by him
With a pale face and a sad heart.
For, he is laughter!
Don't cover his body with flowers.
What's the use of adding flowers to a flower?
If you can,
Bury him in your heart.
You will find
At the twitterings of the bird of the heart
Your sleeping soul has woken up.
If you can,
Shed some tears,
And—
All the blood of your body.'

Banerjee writes that 300 academics and writers from across the world, including Noam Chomsky and Simone de Beauvoir, wrote to the Indian government on 15 August 1974, Independence Day, asking it to take a compassionate view of matters. It was ignored. So was a call later that year from Amnesty International, when it listed in its annual report several cases of illegal detention and torture of Naxals in jails across India. The imposition of Emergency in June 1975, which led to massive censoring of news and banning of any form of public protest, brought the curtain down on Naxalbari—Maoism in India Mark I.

As Abhi and I leave, I try a lal-salaam in farewell, to see how it feels. I do it like a nervous novice—hesitant voice, heavy hand. I feel like a bad actor, but it's oddly satisfying when Punjab-da bellows his response. Thirty-four years since his guru's death, and this man still has religion.

As we wait for another bus to take us to Naxalbari town, I see the old movement's alternate guru zip past riding pillion on a motorcycle, hunched against the wind, firmly gripping the back of the seat, broad pyjamas flapping in the wind.

'Kanu Sanyal,' Abhi says, pointing out the man who broke with his father, a development that many believe proved the death-knell for a faltering Naxalbari Mark I. 'He's out campaigning for elections, or could be that he's heading on to a tea estate. He's organizing tea garden labour these days. You know that.'

Yes, I say. I hope to meet him.

—

But that is for tomorrow. Meanwhile, there is Khokon-da. Khokon Majumdar wasn't part of the first uprising, but after that he claims he was there all the way with Charu-da, as he calls Charu Mazumdar. Now 78, and member of another ML faction, the militant CPI (ML) Janashakti. Materially he seems only a little better off than Punjab Rao. The low wooden house with a tin roof on the lane to Naxalbari Hindi High School is ramshackle, but more solid than his former comrade's. Another old, but not tired, man, dressed in regulation lungi, vest.

In the beginning he doesn't look me in the eye, but at Abhi, as if for clearance to talk, for trust. That gradually changes as I tell him about my chat with Punjab-da, about how he persists with the revolutionary movement.

'*Kissu nai.*' He viciously spits it out, speaking in a dialect commonly spoken in Bangladesh. There is nothing. 'Movement *kothai*?' There is nothing as in Andhra, in Nepal. In Bengal there are only factions, he says. 'In Nepal they are organized. I went to Nepal. They are not forcing people to do anything—the Royalists are spreading propaganda. When I was there, I saw that those who joined the movement went voluntarily.'

The part about royalist propaganda is true, as is much of the part about volunteering, but recruitment by the Maoists in Nepal is not always voluntary and that fact is well-documented by local human rights groups. Rights groups in India have recorded similar trespasses by India's Maoists. I look to Abhi. He senses what I'm about to do and shakes his head. Khokon-da misses our sideshow and carries on. He has travelled back to the past, talking to himself as much as to us.

'When I went to southern Bengal once, I referred to him—his father,' he jerks his head at Abhi, 'as "Charu-da". They were most upset and reacted violently. They said you should say "respected comrade Charu Mazumdar. *Shraddheya* comrade Charu Mazumdar."' His eyes blaze. 'For us he was "Charu-da". All these "Shraddheya" types created all the trouble—they were more loyal than the king. How would he get caught otherwise? Traitors!'

There was reason for it, according to CPI (ML) lore. It says Mazumdar was arrested in mid-July of 1972 in Calcutta only because police arrested a courier, then squeezed the information about Mazumdar's hideout from him. Those like Khokon-da believe the leak had to have come from higher-ups no longer interested in instant revolution. Mazumdar's 12-day incarceration in the lock-up of Lalbazar Police Station, which had gained quite a reputation for strong-arm tactics, and his eventual death in custody, have only added to the resentment of those who still care. The police ensured he was cremated with minimum fuss, with only immediate family in attendance as the police watched over: ensuring the 'martyr' lost the leverage of emotion with the cadre. But whispers and rumours still abound among old-timers, as they inevitably will: the only reason he wasn't released to greater public adulation is that after days in the care of police, he was gruesomely marked.

This blind belief in Charu Mazumdar isn't uncommon. Punjab-da hinted at a similar thing during our conversation. The core Charu Mazumdar acolytes on ground zero still consider the actions of other leader-intellectuals such as Kanu Sanyal who publicly dismissed readiness for armed revolution as nothing short of treason.

'There are so many factions today,' Khokon-da carries on, almost reading my thoughts.

'Why don't you unite? You say if all groups unite you will have a force larger than all the insurgency groups in India put together. What's stopping you?'

'Yes, we should,' he replies, looking out of the window. 'Ideally, we should. But people say different things. They feel differently.'

Battle now or battle later? Overground or underground or both? Forego armed revolution and instead adopt militant confrontation with the state and business? Kill as policy or kill as last resort? Factionalism is the greatest weakness of the extreme Left movement in India. And among the greatest points of leverage for the Indian state—apart, of course, from the violence unleashed by the Maoists themselves on people they suspect of being informers, or of defying their diktats, or simply being at the wrong end of law as they see it—the dreaded Jan Adalat, or People's Court, which is little more than kangaroo court. These acts are as gruesome, and gratuitous, as what the Maoists accuse state security of.

And they would peak as I worked on the final draft of the book, a period during which the Maoists would claim they were scaling back 'needless' violence, in a bid to reclaim public confidence.

Towards the end of 2006, Rajkumar Perchelwar, a forest

guard in Gadhchiroli, in the DK zone, had his throat slit by the Maoists on suspicion of being a police informer. In April 2007, two brothers from Tamba village near Ranchi were first tied to a tree and beaten on suspicion of being police informers, and then beheaded. In August 2007, Arjun Dehuri, a shopkeeper from Talab village in Sambalpur, Orissa, was beheaded—again on suspicion of being a police informer. But on slim evidence: Orissa State Armed Force personnel from a nearby camp had shopped at his establishment.

Also in August 2007, Maoists in Jharkhard at a Jan Adalat in Arki, near Ranchi, held two men, Hero Singh Munda and Rajesh Singh, guilty of rape and extortion. They were picked up from their homes, beheaded, and their bodies dumped on the highway, where police patrols found them.

Sometimes, folks are penalized for aspiration. On 30 September 2007, Bandu Narote, a tribal youngster, was killed in Etapalli tehsil of Gadhchiroli for daring to appear for recruitment in the police force. In the same month, schoolchildren in Aurangabad, a Maoist-riven area of Bihar, took out a procession requesting the Maoists to let them study. Schools in the area suffer from attacks if school authorities don't pay up money demanded by Maoists.

This is the other side of justice. The other side of a 'just' war.

—

We're on a decrepit 'minibus' again, our third of the day. In these parts as elsewhere in Other India, it's rattletrap or nothing for most. Abhi looks tense. I wonder if it's all the talk about the past, his father hauled out repeatedly in reference. We're quiet as we go through Naxalbari town. It's run-down, dusty, a blur: sweetmeat shops with fly-blown offerings, some temples, ubiquitous chai shops. A couple of tin-roofed movie theatres with curtained entrances advertise with posters of buxom women; their enticement has drawn large knots of youngsters. Past tiny Naxalbari station the bus crosses the metre-gauge line, and we again breathe fresh air.

We reach Bengaijote and get off. Tukuria forest looms to our left, with great tall trees, mixed with the shorter eucalyptus. It's beautiful. It's a little after three in the afternoon, and the sun is gentle. There's a cooling breeze from the direction of the hills. Paddy fields shine liquid green. Some huts peer through coconut trees and clumps of plantain.

'Tukuria was really dense once,' Abhi says as we cross the road on to a bund between fields. 'A good hiding place. There are so many stories from that time—legends, really. There was talk that Charu Mazumdar would walk about on stilts.' He uses here the Bengali *ron-pa*, literally, battle legs, used to cover great distances at speed. 'That Kanu Sanyal would ride a horse with a sword in each hand, cutting down enemies.' He laughs. The imagery is absurd. The two were never known to be more than frail. Fiercely determined, but frail.

The hamlet of Bengaijote is mostly a scattering of mud huts, a handful of brick houses. Inhabitants are a mix. Some Rajbongshi tribals, indigenous to this area, some ladies in traditional sarong, snot-nosed children in rubber chappals; a half day's ride to the east, this trodden and forgotten group are fighting for their independent homeland of Kamtapur. There are some Santhal tribals, shipped generations earlier from parts of present-day West Bengal, Bihar and Jharkhand as labour for tea gardens. A radio somewhere behind us on the narrow winding lane crackles with Nepali pop music.

A turn of the lane to the right, and we come to a small school. It's closed. On the wall facing the clearing is a sign: 'Sarva Shiksha Abhiyan'. Mission to Educate All. And below that, in English, a language that few here can read: 'Education for all means progress for all.' No side in the country's wars is short of slogans.

The wall-sign overlooks a small clearing that has a great expanse of paddy as backdrop. At the far end is a makeshift flagstaff with a small red flag, and four pedestals painted blood red with busts on each. Marx, Lenin, Mao, and Charu Mazumdar. The Naxalbari pantheon.

To the right, appreciably away from the pantheon, is

another memorial, to the 11 killed on 'Historic 25th May 1967', all unarmed protestors, men and women, all now co-opted as 'Comrades'. Dhaneshwari Devi, Seemaswari Mallick, Nayaneswari Mallick, Surubala Burman, Sonamati Singh, Phoolmati Devi, Samsari Saibani, Gaudrau Saibani, Kharsingh Mallick, 'and two children'.

Abhi is quiet.

I'm taken aback yet again with the realization that places associated with historical events of great significance can be so ordinary. Plassey, 'Palashi' in Bengali, where Warren Hastings defeated Nawab Siraj-ud-daulah of Bengal and established the core of the East India Company, is today some mango trees, a modest museum and an abandoned airstrip from the Second World War. Jallianwala Bagh in Amritsar, where hundreds of innocents died under the orders of paranoid British, is today overly done concrete and emotionally worded plaque. The site of Gandhi's assassination in Delhi is little more than a facsimile of his last footsteps in concrete, sometimes walked over by teenagers.

'So this is it,' I say.

'Yes, this is it.'

'How do you feel being here? Do you think of your father?'

'Yes.' Abhi is looking everywhere but at me.

'Do you hate the state for what happened? Why it all began?' I ask after several minutes, as we begin walking back.

'Yes, of course I hate the state.' We could be discussing the weather. 'I hate the state a lot.'

'The state? Or the state of affairs?'

'The state is responsible for the state of affairs.'

We stop at a hole-in-the-wall shop and buy a small packet of biscuits for five rupees and five tiny packets of peanuts at a rupee each. It's lunch—my treat.

'We were very young, my sister and I,' Abhi says between bites of orange cream biscuit. 'We idolized our father, as any child would. But we knew something big was happening around him. People were coming and going. People would talk about him—we were very proud. Then one day, he was gone.' Abhi was twelve.

We walk on in silence, sidestep a few ducklings, find a new way back to the road.

'We need to *do* something,' he suddenly bursts out. 'If you do not see with your own eyes how people are being ill-treated and discriminated against...There is a situation building up in the tea gardens. People are starving. A thousand people have died in the gardens since '99 and the government hasn't acknowledged a single starvation death.'

Your outrage isn't news to me, I tell him. The chief minister of Orissa, Naveen Patnaik, when he was told people were eating roots and berries in drought-stricken Kalahandi, had said that's what they eat. In prosperous Maharashtra, of which Mumbai—the self-professed Shanghai of tomorrow—is the capital, over a thousand farmers had committed suicide from indebtedness and crop failure before a minister thought of visiting the area and offering relief.

'Just *listen*,' Abhi is insistent. 'When the going was good from the 1980s to about '95, with good international and domestic prices and new markets, tea gardens made money hand over fist. In many ways, the industry even made up for the loss of captive markets in the former Soviet Union.' But when prices dropped, he says, tea gardens just moved away from everything, all responsibility. 'You have to look after the gardens, upgrade plants, that sort of thing. Very few estates did that. The boom brought to the tea business a speculative breed; they made a killing, and were the first to ditch the gardens and their labour when markets crashed. They just walked away, leaving tens of thousands destitute. This region survives on tea. If there is no tea, there is nothing.'

We're back at the road across Tukuria forest. 'Three and a half lakh people labour in gardens in Darjeeling district,' he says as we wait for our bus back to Siliguri. 'They don't pay; workers get three days' pay for working six. They've done away with health benefits, subsidized rations and minimum wage. The last agreement was on thirty-first March 2003.

Nothing has moved since. It's a huge, huge crisis. The Left Front government in this state backs the owners. There's a lot of anger in the tea gardens...and the government is now really scared of Maoists in this area and the hills because of the situation in Nepal.'

People in this region have an affinity for Nepal because of their ethnic majority—Nepali—and, consequently, language. In the mid-1980s, the Gorkha National Liberation Front (GNLF) rode on unemployment, frustration and ethnicity to light an emotional fire in the nearby Darjeeling hills that is estimated to have killed more than 1,200 and ruined and displaced many thousands in a sweep of terror. It brought for ethnic Nepalis of the region, mostly unemployed youngsters, a sense of power and, ultimately, devolutionary governance: the Darjeeling Gorkha Hill Council. Its once righteously indignant leader, Subhash Ghising, a fiery speaker, a former writer of racy pulp novels, is today a local fat cat—as ever, a revealing story—peaceably a part of the administration he once fought, through political compact with the West Bengal government.

Evidently, the fire today is more about survival, less ethnic pride. Abhi maintains it has created 'objective conditions' for protest beyond the Nepali community—welcome tinder for the most simple-minded movement, revolutionary or otherwise. Maoist leaders are anything but simple-minded.

And they may have found just the martyr to work the minds and hearts of potential constituents in this volatile clavicle of India.

—

On 25 February 2006, a month-and-a-half after the management of Chongtong Tea Estate closed the gardens, B.R. Dewan, a 64-year-old tea employee, hung himself in one of the workers' sheds. Co-workers found a letter written in learned Nepali tucked inside the pocket of his sleeveless coat.

It savaged the well-connected owner of Chongtong, Siliguri-resident Ajit Agarwal, accusing him of '*anyay ra atyachar*', wrongdoing and oppression. It talked about how for years workers had been underpaid, but things had got so bad lately, especially since closure without any benefit, that workers had started selling whatever they could to eat. During earlier troubles, they sold whatever jewellery they had at home, saved for the marriage of children and for bad days. They sold 'hanra-bhanra', utensils. They are doing it again, and also selling goats, hens, whatever they own. 'Now sarvahara'—literally, those who have lost everything—'five of us have taken an oath to commit suicide as a protest against the garden's owner Ajit Agarwal.'

A few days earlier, he had written in another letter that if he donated his eyes and body, it would help four people. If he killed himself, it would help the 6,500 workers of Chongtong.

The incident created a brief media furore, but largely in the local universe of Siliguri, the Dooars and Darjeeling hills. Then it faded from the media, but the underground moved purposefully and swiftly—at any rate, faster than the administration that had not intervened in any way. Within days, copies of Dewan's correspondence with a covering note had circulated among the region's media, tea garden workers and students, helped along by a few civil rights groups. The covering note that I see calls 25 February a 'historic day'. It raves about how the elderly Dewan had displayed 'youth' with his act, and shown he wasn't afraid of death for the just cause of his colleagues' future. At the end, it expresses 'heartfelt sympathy' and 'intimate respect' for Dewan. It is signed by 'Parimal', within apostrophes, a standard underground practice of adopting loaded aliases. Parimal means 'fragrance'.

Equally interesting is another note circulated as 'an approach paper on human rights' at a meeting called by Tika 'Bhai', or Brother Tika, on 9 April, under the aegis of the Darjeeling Terai Dooars Sanjukta Vidyarthi Manch, a student organization. Titled 'Plight of Human Right in Present Darjeeling', the eight-page note is in eager English. It's a direct attack on GNLF chief Ghising and Bengal's Left Front government.

'Darjeeling is known as the Queen of Hills from the day

she became a refuge for the British against the sweltering heat of the plains of Bengal,' it begins sedately enough. 'The socio-politico peace and communal harmony was the basic characteristic and culture of Darjeeling. But the peace, tranquillity, harmony and calmness of Darjeeling got stirred in the eighties of the twentieth century. As in the period a violent and devastating agitation was started by a political party named as Gorkha National Liberation Front [GNLF] under the leadership of Subhash Ghising. The years of sufferings of the people on account of administrative lapses, lacunae, negligence etc were used as fuel to the agitation led by GNLF.'

Then, the twist that claims GNLF's angst-ridden origin as its own by damning—correctly, in this case—a rampaging GNLF's excesses that are well-documented by police, media and human rights organizations. 'The people not subscribing and supporting the line of GNLF were subjected to torture, intimidation, abduction and murder on the one hand. And on the other hand taking a plea of containing the agitation and in the name of maintaining peace and security...awful measures and method was employed by the administration with help and support of Communist Party of Marxists [CPM] and its workers. Thus, during that agitation period the Human Right was crushed by the two steam rollers...'

The note claims 'political therapy' was then done to clear the ills by forming the Hill Council under Ghising's chairmanship. 'But the party and the leader being on the chair by taking mandate through political manoeuvring and coercion but presently by the benign grace and blessing of the govt of West Bengal has...been carrying activities which has made the people bereft of human right for several times.' It lists misdemeanours such as executing development schemes funded by the central and state governments by giving 'top priority' to benefit 'GNLF and its members', and focusing on villages with relatively strong GNLF cadre-strength.

And finally, the reference to revolutionary Marxism, as far back as 1998—two years into Nepal's armed movement, and during a presumably somnolent phase in India. For parliamentary elections that year, the note claims, a candidate of 'Communist Party of Revolutionary Marxists'—a breakaway from CPI (M)—was to contest from Darjeeling Parliamentary Constituency. The candidate had 'successfully enlisted the unconditional support' of Akhil Bharatiya Gorkha League, CPI (ML) New Democracy, CPI (ML) Liberation, CPI (ML) Janashakti, Socialist Unity Centre of India, Sanjukta Krisak Manch, Samajbadi Jana Parishad, Uttar Bangla Janjati Adivasi Sangh, Terai United Forum, Ambedkar Vichar Manch—a collection of radical Left organizations, farmers' groups, regional groups, tribal groups, Dalit groups. A coalition of the angry, the disaffected, the wretched.

Running scared in the face of reality that 'conspicuously showed the tilting of the balance in favour of' revolutionaries, GNLF called a three-day strike from 20 February 1998 to 22 February—polling day—and a 'reign of terror was let loose'. The impact: ten per cent of the electorate voted. The candidate supported by CPI (M) and GNLF won.

Ever since, the note claims, it's been a case of intimidation, deliberate neglect and corruption, and only a 'loose conglomeration' of different political parties calling itself the People's Democratic Front has dared stand up to Ghising and his state-supported cohorts against all manner of intimidation.

'...It is crystal clear,' the note concludes, 'the general people of Darjeeling and Dooars has had been robbed and plundered of their human right. Hence in terms of human right the region is seriously ill. The nature of the illness shows the urgent administrative therapy. The procrastination of therapy might lead to catching of conflagration of great intensity. Hence it is fervently requested and appealed to all concerned for the protection of individual liberty and human right of the helpless and forlorn citizen of India living in the region at the earliest.'

The media ignored this and similar pleas which are all classic revolutionary background work.

Several months later, on 18 September 2006, *Hindustan Times* would run an article quoting 'intelligence sources' that a new organization calling itself Darjeeling Gorkha Maobadi Sangathan had begun to operate in the 'hills of West Bengal', its leader Ajay Dahal a former trooper of the CISF and former GNLF functionary. 'A new Maoist movement in the Darjeeling hills can be dangerous for India,' the 'sources' said, even as a Maoist leader from Nepal strenuously denied any link at a press conference in Kathmandu.

Sure enough, major media now picked up the story. In news, as elsewhere, it is usually easier to handle developments as fait accompli, hardly ever as work in progress.

In Febraury 2007, just a year after B.R. Dewan became a 'martyr', Gautam Chatterjee, chairman, Tea Association of India, North Bengal, would worry at the chapter's thirty-sixth annual general meeting in Siliguri about 30,000 people without jobs in the area's gardens and the trouble this disenchanted multitude could bring. He would also fret: 'I am equally worried at the disruptive acts by various extremist forces...They are taking shelter in the gardens and instigating...workers.'

17

Debashis Chakrobarty arrives at Abhi's place around 7 p.m. with a belligerent '...if you hadn't insisted I wouldn't have come'. He says this to Abhi, but it is aimed at me, seated on the floor by the divan. His handshake is perfunctory. He takes off stylish square-toed black shoes, places his laptop-tote by the door, rolls up the sleeves of his pinstriped shirt, hitches up perfectly pressed cotton trousers and settles his stocky shape on the divan, right under the photograph of Charu Mazumdar. Then he turns to me and glares. Ah, well. He has been angry for a while.

Debashis was released in October 2005 after 90 days in jail on charges of being a Maoist. Siliguri police applied broad-spectrum antibiotics from India's Penal Code, largely unchanged since its inception in 1860, when the East India Company ran the subcontinent. Like Debashis, thousands have had sections 121 to 124A thrown at them, with sentences that can include fines, jail terms up to life imprisonment, and in the case of offences under Section 121, death.

Section 121 censures against 'Waging, or attempting to wage war, or abetting waging of war, against the Government of India.' Section 121A makes it tighter: 'Conspiracy to commit offences punishable by Section 121.' Section 122 covers 'Collecting arms, etc., with intention of waging war against the Government of India,' and Section 123, 'Concealing with intent to facilitate design to wage war.' Section 124 takes care of 'Assaulting President, Governor, etc., with intent to compel or restrain the exercise of any lawful power.' And Section 124A covers 'Sedition', plain and simple: 'Whoever, by words, either spoken or written, or by signs, or by visible representation, or otherwise, brings or attempts to bring into hatred or contempt, or excites or attempts to excite disaffection towards...the Government established by law...'

Debashis was released after a very public and sustained campaign by CPI (ML) Liberation, APDR and a clutch of human rights groups. He's lucky. People charged under these IPC sections aren't released for years together. Each time the 90-day period for producing formal charges expires, the person is slapped with accusations under another IPC section. Debashis is quite the hero in the region's left-wing space.

'So, you're the hero,' I tease him.

'I'm not a hero. I never *wanted* to be a hero. They *needed* a hero, so they *made* me into one.' He glares at Abhi.

'Yes, we made you into a hero,' Abhi calmly replies. 'We needed one. Politically, it was necessary.'

'I disagree with you,' he barks back. 'But leave that aside for now. Let's talk. I can't stay too long.'

I take the cue. Do you see yourself as a revolutionary?

'I'm just a human rights activist,' he tells me. They all do. By this yardstick, Medha Patkar, Right to Information combatant Aruna Roy, and activist-writer Arundhati Roy would all be doing the rounds of jails. But they are too public, too well known for the government to openly take them on. People like Debashis are generally easier to snag, less messy. But Siliguri's Left decided to make a go of it with him to make a point. I tease Debashis some more, tell him he doesn't look like an activist, but some sort of yuppie.

He ignores me, and whips out a sleek Nokia mobile phone to show Abhi digitial images of a recent meeting of tea garden workers. Abhi passes the phone to me. I scroll down image after image of scrawny, seemingly tense people squatting on the floor; a few stand. Some officious people are at a table, speaking into microphones.

'Who're they?'

'Leaders,' Debhashis says. 'Activists.'

'See, this is a hi-tech Maoist,' Abhi jokes, as I hand the phone back to Debashis.

Finally, he smiles, and begins to talk about himself in staccato bursts. He came back to Siliguri the previous year from Bangalore after a two-year stint with Japanese office equipment manufacturer Ricoh. Earlier, he was with Gestetner, till it was taken over by Ricoh. He came back to start a business of selling copiers and accessories. After the stay in jail, he's back at his business—the day job, as it were.

Short introduction over, he gets into what I will soon begin to think of as 'justification mode'.

'I've come up the hard way. I earned for the family, for my mother, sister and brothers. I know what not eating means. I know what not having money means. So I do this during the day and my activism by night—and whenever I can.'

Were you beaten or otherwise pressured in jail, I ask. Any third degree?

'No,' Debashis is emphatic. 'They didn't treat me badly in jail. But they kept me with convicts.' This isn't an unusual complaint; the Maoists, like the Naxals before them, and separatist militants and others, wish more than anything to be treated as political prisoners, not a more garden variety of criminal—thieves, rapists, murderers.

'They would have shunted me around to other jails on other charges, but they let me go on account of popular pressure, there were many demonstrations'—he jerks his head at Abhi. 'These people made a hero.'

'It made sense,' Abhi clarifies. 'We needed a face. We needed to raise the profile of the movement and leverage the issue. It was a perfect opportunity.'

I put in my two-bit. 'You were a perfect martyr, if something happened to you in jail, and even if nothing did.'

Abhi nods his head. Debashis' frown nearly distorts his face. I light a slim cigar I've been saving for an excuse; this seems as good a Che Guevara moment as any.

'Havana?' Abhi queries.

'No, Dominican. It's become a little dry.' I turn to Debashis. 'Abhi says you're a hi-tech Maoist. Are you?'

He's close to exploding. 'We've just met,' he snarls. 'Do you expect me to open up to you already? I wouldn't even have met you, or been here, if not for Abhi-*da*.'

'I appreciate that. But what are you? Are you a yuppie, or a Maoist?' I wave the cigar. 'I don't mind a bit of the good life now and then if I can afford it; I work for it. But I can't ignore what's going on around me, all the rubbish. What is it for you? I want to understand.'

Debashis fixes me with an unblinking stare. I haven't really noticed a left-winger blink, B onwards. I've ignored it like I would a stifled cough, an idle scratch on the neck or elbow.

'I'm doing both,' Debashis allows after a couple of minutes of silence. 'Activism and my work. It's like living two different lives. I do it, I'm doing well. I work morning to night.' He pauses. 'But sooner or later—sooner than later—I will have to take a decision. It will have to be one or the other.'

We are all quiet for a while. Then I tell him he seems to be in too deep, his anger and feelings too strong, to give up 'activism'.

'I think so too,' he admits.

'I'd like to see you a couple of years from now,' I

continue. 'See which way you have gone, what you have become.'

'I'll have to decide in the next six months to a year,' he says. 'See you.'

And he's gone as quietly as he came, the laptop revolutionary.

He's very angry, I tell Abhi as we settle down to a simple meal of leftovers. Abhi smiles, says nothing.

I'm spreading my own little revolution against colonial vestiges in Goa, I say. I've been teaching my daughter some twisted grammar. One person from Portugal is a Portugoose. Two and more are Portuguese. He laughs, but won't talk any more about Debashis.

Abhi retires to his room; I can hear strains of the *Internationale* behind closed doors. I lie down on the divan under the watchful eyes of Charu Mazumdar and am instantly asleep.

18

With Ramji as guide, I set off to meet Kanu Sanyal. Ramji is a sometime house painter, when his family—a wife and three young daughters—is close to starving. At other times, he is a revolutionary, an acolyte of the original Naxalbari co-leader and key dissenter.

'Kanu-*babu*' forgot to give Ramji any money yesterday. The family would have gone hungry but for a comrade giving him Rs 20. That bought a little oil, some salt, a kilo of rice cooked in the fire of scavenged straw, woodchips, and peels of banana and maize. The money is over, so the visit to Hatighisa is a bit of a treat from me. Rs 2 for a small cup of tea. A packet of Good Day biscuits for Rs 10. And the Rs 10 bus fare. If Ramji weren't accompanying me, he would walk and hitch a ride for the 25 kilometres from Siliguri to Hatighisa, or beg a neighbour for a bicycle. 'This is the price of politics,' he tells me cheerfully, as we settle into the minibus for the 45-minute ride.

Kanu Sanyal's home is a 15-minute walk in from Hatighisa post office, through a neat village with houses mostly made of bamboo, thatch and mud bricks—some with stunning, twisting columns of mud at the entrance. Children play in the rivulet of Manja Nadi—the main stream is diverted to irrigate tea gardens. Women bathe and wash clothes a little distance away. There are clusters of bamboo groves, animals out for a foraging stroll: mothers leading chicks, ducklings and piglets. The inhabitants of the village are mostly tribals from Bihar, Jharkhand and southwest Bengal, brought as tea garden labour, Ramji informs me. His steady chatter doesn't intrude on this tranquillity.

'I'll fight,' he tells me. 'Kanu-babu fights, so we fight. We never take our troubles to him. He gives me money for the bus fare but I walk, because I can buy rice with the money.' Cadre talk. Follow the leader. It isn't difficult to understand why. While many Naxalites from the old days are either killed, dead of natural causes, or re-assimilated—a surprisingly large number—into the urban elite they came from, Sanyal is among the few on-ground leaders and participants who still live in and around the ground zero of 1967.

—

Home for Kanu Sanyal is a two-room mud hut, gleaming with a recent coat. The single door to the hut is open, and I can look straight in at his pantheon on the wall: Marx, Engels, Lenin, Stalin and Mao. On the floor covered with reed mats and plain handwoven local rugs, is an old manual typewriter. Some files are scattered on the floor, some newspapers; a mattress, pillow and hint of mosquito netting.

He is sitting on a wrought iron stool on the veranda, leaning back on a wooden roof-support, dressed in pyjamas and a once-white sleeveless sweater; I look for the frayed shirt-collar of the I-don't-give-a-damn-about-such-things communist. It's there. As are basic sandals, thick-lensed spectacles. I start to take my shoes off.

'Why are you taking your shoes off?' he snaps. 'This is not a temple.'

'I don't want to dirty your floor. I can see it's been freshly layered.'

'It's mud. It can always get another layer.'

He has other guests. A reporter from a major Bengali daily, and a two-man crew from a Bengali news channel. Elections to Bengal's assembly will begin in six days, so this is sound-bite time. I sit quietly; listen to the retelling of a slice of history.

'...And so...we were all part of CPI (M), Charu-da, me, others,' Kanu-babu resumes. 'But we all felt a little stifled. There was pressure from the government; we were in and out of jail quite a lot. And in between, many things happened, it was like a flow.

'In 1964, Charu-da wrote an article which was published in *Amrita Bazar Patrika*. In it, he wrote how there should be small armed groups and these groups should kill class enemies— finish them off.' He uses English for emphasis here and then continues in Bengali. 'Me and others disagreed with this suggestion. The party was also upset. They wanted to expel [him]. The party secretary came to Siliguri. We stood by Charu-da. We said, "How can you expel him without a show-cause [notice]. They agreed. Charu-da also withdrew from his stand and promised in future he would show his writing to the party before publication.

'So while we disagreed with him, we supported him in this regard. But he wanted revolution. Instant revolution. I didn't believe in that.'

Daily decides to get smart here. He drawls arrogantly in Bengali, leaning back on his plastic chair, one leg over the other, foot flapping near Kanu-babu's face. '*Ta theek, biplob to aar gachch thhekey porey na...besh, besh.*' That's right, revolution doesn't readily drop from trees, does it...?

Kanu-babu shuts him up with an impatient flap of arm. Rebuked, the man lowers his foot, straightens up. He looks at me, embarrassed. I look away to stifle laughter.

Meanwhile, the undergraduate class in revolution—Revolution 101 if this were America—continues.

'He wanted small guerilla groups to go and kill, take over land. We felt that was wrong. I...we...felt that farmers and workers should first take over land'—he uses the Bengali word *dakhal* to express it—'and then defend it.' A matter of nuance.

'So, there was a difference already?' Daily moves in.

'Yes...'

'*Besh*,' Daily swiftly intervenes, sensing a 'quote', and lays the trap for it. 'So you don't believe in armed revolution?' He uses the phrase '*soshostro biplob*'.

'No,' Kanu-babu barks. 'I believe in it, but objective conditions need to be there. It cannot be forced.'

'So the Naxalite Movement...' I wade in, trying to cool things down, only to have Kanu-babu slash my throat.

'The media called it that. We did not. People just added another 'ism'. For us, it was Communism, not Naxalism.'

TV steps in with 'Then what happened?'

'We were back in jail. Meanwhile, conditions had built up in north Bengal. Things moved very quickly—too quickly to even keep track. That's how it was in '67. I wasn't really keeping track of the argument in the party. What Charu-da was saying...I was either in jail or underground.

'Then, almost suddenly, the party was formed. CPI (ML). We had differences with CPI (M). Many of us didn't agree with the charter of armed revolution by just cold-blooded killing, but we joined up. We were for armed revolution but not in this manner.

'We went underground from 1969 to 1972. During this time, I also went to China.' He is deadpan in delivery. '*Mao-er shongey amaar dekha holo*.' I met Mao. 'After talking to him, discussing the situation in India, I became even more convinced that the way was not correct. Mao talked to me about how the movement began there. At one time they had only 150 muzzle-loaded rifles. But they worked among the people, built up popular support. He told me, "You won't need help from anyone outside if you have popular support."'

TV doesn't want history. He wants a sound bite. He asks Kanu-babu his views on the situation in Nepal. 'Do you think King Gyanendra will go?'

It's 11 April, the sixth day of Maoist-backed nationwide demonstrations by an alliance of seven political parties, calling for the king's abdication at the least and failing that, his head. It has brought citizens on to the streets of Nepal. It's reminiscent of the pro-democracy agitation in 1990. But this is much bigger, angrier, more we-have-nothing-to-lose. There are daily reports of police beatings, arrests and shooting. Nepal has been shut down, but not its people.

'You cannot compare the situation in Nepal with the situation in India,' Kanu-babu replies. He says he can't, and wouldn't like to, comment on what's happening in another country. 'And anyway, I cannot foretell events. I'm not an astrologer but a Communist. But I agree with their stand against monarchy.'

TV switches tack, asks about the political situation in Bengal. 'In West Bengal there is no option to the Left Front except Congress. Is Trinamool an option?' He mentions the Congress breakaway, at the time aligned with the BJP—its chief, the tough-talking lady with a strong sense of drama, Mamata Banerjee, would in some months star in the protests at Singur, and later Nandigram. 'No...We must fight at every level. I do not believe in electoral politics but we take part in it because it suits us,' the answer is roundabout, but is important for its admission of approach, that some revolutionary parties have decided to do what it takes to keep going. 'People tell me at election meetings, "If you win elections you will become just like the others." I tell them we are different, but they don't believe me. And they are right.' He spits it out: 'Shob chor-er dol.' All parties are thieves.

Daily and TV leave, satisfied they have usable quotes. Elections in north Bengal are due on May 8; elections to the assembly in this relatively small state are being staggered over four days spread across several weeks for security for voters and to avoid rigging of votes—the first mainly on account of the Maoists.

(The Marxists would win those elections by a large margin. Buddhadeb Bhattacharjee would return for a second term as chief minister. But the Revolutionary parties never expected to derail Bhattacharjee; they want a toehold into the system as strategy. Kanu-babu has openly trashed the approach taken by CPI (Maoist) and, in turn, they think him too soft—as they do parties like CPI (ML) Liberation. But there is a section of the Maoists, dismissed as 'revisionists', who believe, according to discussion reflected in internal documents, that there is a need to participate in electoral politics if only to upstage the system from the inside out. To quote Kanu-babu, 'It suits us.')

Kanu-babu turns to me, and continues without a break, eager to talk. 'It all broke up, do you know? CPI (ML) broke into many factions. Even I led a faction.' CPI (ML-Kanu Sanyal). 'Then in 2005 I again formed CPI (ML). This is the old name. The original name.'

Dipu Haldar drops by, a stout, stern-faced lady who is major domo to Ramji's street lieutenant—he is all but invisible in a corner, discreetly nibbling on biscuits. I've seen her go about here and there on a bicycle before. Now she sends off a young boy to fetch the day's papers from a kiosk on the highway.

I want R-101 to continue. How can you tell when the time for revolution, armed or otherwise, is right? I ask Kanu-babu.

'Hmmm,' he replies. 'The Paris Commune failed because objective conditions were not right.'

On March 18, 1871, workers in Paris took over the city from "bourgeois rulers". Ten days later, they established the Paris Commune, which 'reds' of all shades claim as the world's first proletarian state, a classic by-the-people-for-the-people 'liberated zone'. The Commune, born out of the chaos of Franco-Prussian war and abject conditions of workers and destitute, 'lived for 72 days and fell, after heroic resistance', says the hefty book on writings by Marx and Engels on the Paris Commune I bought in my last year of high school in 1981 for Rs 3.25, the price of a ticket at the movies.

'Storming heaven', Marx called the move to establish the Paris Commune—basically, laboratory Communism. During its brief existence, the Commune executed a range of orders, from banning conscription to writing up measures to reimburse rent for three quarters, and even freeing 'public prostitutes' from their 'degrading' slavery. It never got around to 'mental emancipation', as 'reactionary forces'—'the centralized state machinery' of absolute monarchy—struck back and broke up the Commune.

Short and sweet: it was ultimately too ambitious, too rushed, too disorganized, underpowered—under-armed and under-supported. It took till 1917 for the lesson of the laboratory experiment fine-tuned by Lenin and his colleagues to work itself into the Russian Revolution. QED.

'Yes,' Kanu-babu looks bemused. 'In Russia, momentum built up, and it happened in 1917. Not before. Not after.'

I repeat my question: how do you gauge the right time for revolution?

'There are four stages,' he replies, as if lecturing a student. 'In the first stage, you talk and they listen to you but they will forget what you say as soon as you leave.

'At the next stage, they will listen to you, but there won't be any understanding.

'In the third stage, they realize something needs to be done, and they might want to do it, but something holds them back.

'In the last stage, they are ready to move—do anything. They are completely convinced.' He stops to change position, limber up a bit. 'Charu-da moved too early,' he says in refrain. 'He said, "Bring everything, anything—farm implements, swords, bows, arrows, snatch guns from police..."'

But still, I insist, how do you really know when the objective conditions are right?

He smiles, and tries again, but he doesn't snap; for the first time in the past hour, he is patient, calm. 'When you light a fire under a pan of water, it gives out a bit of steam—but that doesn't mean the water is very hot. It needs more time to boil. Different people have different boiling points. In a people's movement, individual feeling, individual anger must first become crystallized for a people's movement to succeed.'

'Take the case of this farmer,' he continues, eyes pinning me to the chair. 'This is from half-a-year ago. He lives about eight miles from here. He came to me, complaining that his land was being grabbed by a local landlord through encroachment, and by using local village authorities. I told him what to do but he didn't listen. Then they came to break his house down, claiming that too did not belong to him. So he went along with his entire family and killed the landlord. That was *his* boiling point.' Kanu-babu is now trying to get the man out of jail.

He pauses to sip tea. 'There is a situation in the gardens.' Abhi uses the same phrasing. Naxalbari DNA. 'Thousands of workers are being discriminated against and ill treated. We have to assist the motivation of the people.'

Is that why you stay here, I ask, preparing to leave. Why don't you stay in Kolkata, motivate students and intellectuals like they do in Hyderabad, Delhi?

'You need to be with the people to know what they feel, what they think, how they live. They need to see you. You need to see them.'

—

Ramji catches up with me ten minutes later. He's grinning from ear to ear. Kanu-babu has given him Rs 150, and that will keep him going for a few days. I give him Rs 10 more for his bus fare back to Siliguri. He clutches what remains of the packet of Good Day biscuits—not much; he's shared some with Kanu-babu and Dipu Haldar.

19

The crowded bus crawls as it nears Panitanki. Parked trucks with Indian and Nepali number plates take up half the width of road, a two-kilometre-long line that snakes to the main junction of the dusty, baking border town. For six days, not a single truck or bus has crossed the Mechhi river into Kakarbhitta, across the border, the result of what has come to be called Jan Andolan II, the second people's movement after the first that had won patchy, illusory democracy 16 years earlier. Nepal's easternmost district of Jhapa is firmly in the control of the Maoists. Just three days back there was a big 'action' in the region; truckloads of Maoists swept through several towns.

So the stalled trucks wait. They will wait as long as they have to: they carry precious cargo for land-locked Nepal, consumer durables and chemicals—this is by treaty with India. Petrol, timber, pre-cast concrete pillars to support electric cables, liquefied petroleum gas, even salt. When calculated across several such transit points along India's border with Nepal, the obvious hardship and economic loss of total closure is staggering for any nation, let alone one as wrecked as Nepal through nearly 250 years of government negligence and, now, a decade of civil war.

But the mood is almost festive in Panitanki. Truckers have created a new town of loud songs from Hindi movies and raucous Nepali radio, instant kitchens on the side of the road, robust jokes and curses. Markets are open and full. Indian and Nepali currencies—here and in Nepal, IC and NC in exchange ratio of 1:1.6—fly freely, as happens in any border town. But even more now, as entire families, old to young, come by from Kakarbhitta on foot, bicycle and rickshaw to shop for groceries, sweetmeats, bangles and *bindi*, shoes, utensils, recharge cards for mobile phones. Near the border, communication and entertainment airwaves fly freely too, and almost unchecked, say intelligence officials—like revolutionaries, terrorists, arms, equipment and drugs.

Subodh the rickshaw-wala agrees to take me to Kakarbhitta and back for 20 Indian rupees, and we set off through the crush, and through the border. The long, high span of the bridge provides a bird's-eye view of the river. It's an extension of Hatighisa-idyllic. Men and women bathe in the clear shallow rivulets of the Mechhi, a cluster of children lie on their bellies or on their backs, letting the river flow past them, soaking up the sun like happy geckos.

Roughly halfway across the bridge, the river socials dry up. Just some cattle, no people. Then the formal border post, with a grand whitewashed archway. Subodh says I must get off and walk past the gate, past the Royal Nepal Army (RNA) sentry posts with machine-gun emplacements and walkabout soldiers with automatic weapons. That's the rule for all vehicles. Two teenage Nepali boys have broken convention, riding in, so a soldier makes them get off and as punishment carry the cycles above their heads. Nobody checks papers and bags, including mine; nobody walks up to the immigration and customs counters, neither do I. Perhaps my simple cotton tunic, faded jeans, everyday Velcro strap-ons and small backpack and Indian face makes for a commonplace package. I pass a couple of sub-machine gun toting soldiers, a young boy brewing tea in the shadow of the massive gateway, and I'm in Kakarbhitta.

The main street is empty save a few people standing about in knots near rickshaws and a couple of tea stalls and cigarette shops, seeking whatever shade they can in the blazing sun of early afternoon. Some restaurants are open too, but nothing else. The huge bus stand to my right is empty except for a dozen or so carelessly parked buses, the area enclosed by a rabbit warren of narrow lanes and cheek-by-jowl houses of exposed brick so common even in Nepal's larger towns. A signboard for Mechhi Chamber of Commerce and Industry is lost among other pitches, for mobile phones, instant noodles, Orangeboom and Tuborg beer.

It's a picnic in the town. Families and friends play carom, chess and ludo seated on tiny stools just outside houses, or just chat and look around. Some households have put out strips of meat to dry, others red chillies. I'm ravenous—having had nothing but tea all day—and settle in at the tiny Fewa Hotel. They have exactly what I want, a deep brass *thali* with heaped coarse rice, dal, a dry dish of diced potato and bitter gourd, a potato curry, pickle and 7Up. A gaggle of young girls go past talking of friends who work in 'Bangalore-Mysore'. An elderly retired soldier sits across me and orders fried pork and beer. We smile companionably, and watch TV.

There's news on Nepal 1. There's a raging fire at a school in Lucknow; many children are feared dead. It cuts to Mumbai and movie star Salman Khan in jail, in a case of poaching black buck in Rajasthan. Then it cuts to RNA chief General Pyar Jung Thapa trashing the Maoists; the voiceover soon backs a shot of rows of captured weaponry: machine guns on tripods, AK-47 and AK-56 automatic rifles, clusters of hand grenades. Fried Pork and Beer grins and winks at me, flaps his right hand in negation and goes back to watching. I don't know what to make of it. Does he support the army? Or is it pro-Maoist dismissal aimed at the general: Enjoy being on TV while you still can; the general will lose his job in a matter of months. There is now a promo for a new programme. A young man grins into the camera. 'Only ak-sun!' he shouts. 'No ten-sun!'

As I step out, the lane is transformed from picnic to protest. A sea of red flags is coming towards me; the lane is choked with people, shouting men, women, youngsters, children, yapping strays in procession. The flags are mostly of the Communist Party of Nepal (Unified Marxist-Leninist) [CPN (UML)]—essentially, Nepal's version of India's CPI (M)—and one of its factions. Then a handful of Nepali Congress flags, and the white banners of the Nepal Mahila Sangh. Overall, the Maoist flags are low-key, of moderate size—simple white hammer and sickle on blood red. I guess you don't need overkill if you control the territory. And this, after all, is in partnership with mainstream political parties—the Seven Party Alliance—to rock the king off his perch.

I step back into Fewa Hotel to let them pass. There must be 300 or so people. And more join them. Jean-clad youngsters in stylish anti-glare, teenage girls in pigtails, elderly women beating on brass and stainless steel plates. It's a joyous funeral procession, complete with burning incense sticks on three biers the crowd carries, decked in marigold. I follow them.

We make a circuit of the town and end up at the bus stand. There the biers are placed on the ground, and women fall upon the shoe-garlanded effigies with brooms. One bier has written on it 'Rajtantra'; the monarchy, symbolizing King Gyanendra. The second's label reads 'Grihamantri'; that would be Home Minister Kamal Thapa. The third one is labelled 'Pracharmantri'; that would be Information and Communications Minister Shirish Shumsher Rana. Both ministers are key disseminators of the king's will and testimonial. In Kathmandu, over a dozen are dead and several thousand injured on account of shoot-at-sight and beat-at-will orders.

All the while, the crowd swells. The slogan shouting continues and a meeting is announced for 13 April. I expect RNA troops to arrive any second; the border post is less than 200 metres away and they must have heard the commotion. But here…it suddenly strikes me; there isn't even a trace of police. I'm told that these days, in several places, especially the hill areas of western and eastern Nepal, the police are in compact with the Maoists; they stay in their barracks and the Maoists pretty much do as they please. But this is still unusual. And RNA soldiers at the border are pointedly keeping away, too. I think to myself as I locate Subodh for the trip back: I don't know how many more days King Gyanendra will last in Kathmandu—but here, at the far edge of his notional kingdom, he's already history.

———

There's too much Naxalism/Maoism in my head; I need a time-out. I decide to go to Kalimpong and stroll around, see the hills, pick up some Kalimpong cheese, which enjoys cult status in the east. My train to Kolkata leaves only after 7 p.m. I have the whole day.

At Sevoke Road in Siliguri, a steady stream of battered Mahindra jeeps ferry people to Kalimpong and back. Co-passengers are shovelling in quick breakfasts of lemon tea and platefuls of steamed momo. Others read newspapers. Rs 50 buys me the last remaining seat on a jeep that leaves in ten minutes.

Canned sardines have a better life. My seat is in the back row, near the window, above the wheel. I have to sit twisted at the waist and stick my face out of the window to avoid luxuriant hair on the head of the lady in front from suffocating me.

'They are breaking the law,' the elderly Bhutia gentleman to my right grumbles in empathy. 'They are supposed to take 1+10. But they squeeze in 1+11.'

The Mahananda Sanctuary to the north is lush forest that merges into towering hills of the lower Himalaya after Sevoke railway crossing. The railway track here heads east to Alipurduar, the stated centre of Kamtapur Liberation Organisation, a relatively new formation fighting for the rights of ethnic Rajbonghshi tribal groups; all of the state in the north barring Darjeeling hills comes under their stated footprint. The track goes further east into Assam, first into the territory of the once-feared Bodo militants fighting for Bodoland, and then, further east, into territory ravaged by the ULFA, currently under on-again off-again truce with the Government of India. (The truce would last scant weeks, and the region would resume its play of bloodshed.) Indian intelligence agencies now suspect ULFA of passing hard cash and occasional shipment of arms and ammunition to Indian Maoists, adding to the logistics network that the Maoists in southern and central India have with LTTE.

There are also intelligence reports of Nepal's Maoists training in the forests of Jharkhand and Orissa, being treated for wounds at 'field' hospitals as well as those in cities like Kolkata, Jamshedpur and Siliguri.

There's a large army base in the Mahananda forests, which we pass in our deafeningly noisy jeep. But I can't help wondering what even well-trained troops would do in an area of thick jungle that leads from Nepal to this stretch of India. The terrain seems even more forbidding after crossing the Teesta River, as we leave behind the highway to Bhutan and the left-fork to Darjeeling. It feels a bit like the insurgency-friendly pipeline of the Pir Panjal range of Jammu & Kashmir, a maze of heights, forest and ravine leading into Pakistan. India's massed military and paramilitary forces have battled there since 1989. So far, the objective conditions for peace have proved entirely elusive.

Kalimpong town is a mess of choked traffic, choked sidewalks and choked markets, inundated by colourfully dressed locals, and loud visitors from the plains of Bengal; large parts of it resemble Siliguri at 4,100 feet. It's profane. I duck into Mr Sood's tiny grocery that displays homemade meat and bamboo pickle.

'Sorry, but do you by any chance keep Kalimpong cheese...?' I begin.

'Yes, yes,' he is brusque.

In frenzy, I buy three kilos.

There is still a little time before I head back to catch my train, so I find a tiny cyber café near the taxi stand. A bunch of emails are waiting for me with news, views, updates.

NDTV anchor Barkha Dutt and Kashmir specialist with *The Hindu* Praveen Swamy, and a bunch of other journalists have been awarded the year's prestigious Ramnath Goenka Award for Excellence in Journalism. There's another winner, C. Vanaja, for her documentary on the Maoists of Dandakaranya. It rings a bell: a name from A's briefing in Delhi.

There's more news.

The government has agreed to review the height of the Sardar Sarovar Dam and the resettlement of displaced persons, but is unwilling to link the two—the state wins. Kannada film star Rajkumar has died of natural causes and his fans in Bangalore have beaten up people, smashed stores, burned buses; inexplicable emotion that so often in India accompanies the death of a well-known person. The Sensex has tanked 307 points—'you would have been a braveheart to survive the markets on Wednesday', I read a news update. Crude oil prices have eased to a little over $69 a barrel. England have trashed India in a cricket one-day international at Jamshedpur, the only place in Jharkhand conspicuously free of Maoist graffiti and overt influence—yet. Affairs of the relatively well-run city are managed by the Jamshedpur Notified Area Committee, comprising civic officials and senior executives of Tata Steel, the company that birthed the 'steel town' more than a century ago. Santhal tribals of the area were evicted to make way for the eventual industrial complex and township, but that is another story, another history.

A record 3,00,000 students have qualified to appear for entrance examinations to the seven campuses of Indian Institutes of Technology, the country's pride and joy; one in seventy-three will make it. Bank credit has grown year on year by four per cent. Hollywood strato-stars Brad Pitt and Angelina Jolie are in Namibia, 'at a secluded beach resort, prompting speculation that their baby will be born in Africa...' The police in Mumbai have filed a case against John, the motorcycle-idol from the poster on Punjab-da's crumbling hut, for negligent driving.

And 'Naxal extremists' have blown up the Bansinala railway post in Bihar's Gaya district.

The world is real. I was mistaken, that's all.

On the way back, my neighbour in the sardine-can jeep, a middle-aged Nepali gentleman, falls asleep as soon as we leave the precincts of Kalimpong and leans heavily on me. By the time I spot the calm, emerald-green upper reaches of the Teesta through foliage at an excruciating hairpin bend, he has begun to drool. It's time for war.

'Maobadi!' I fiercely whisper into his ear.

He wakes up with a start.

BOOK III

A revolution is not a dinner party, or writing an essay, or painting a picture, or doing embroidery; it cannot be so refined, so leisurely and gentle, so temperate, kind, courteous, restrained and magnanimous. A revolution is an insurrection, an act of violence by which one class overthrows another. A rural revolution is a revolution by which the peasantry overthrows the power of the feudal landlord class. Without using the greatest force, the peasants cannot possibly overthrow the deep-rooted authority of the landlords which has lasted for thousands of years. The rural areas need a mighty revolutionary upsurge, for it alone can rouse the people in their millions to become a powerful force...To put it bluntly, it is necessary to create terror for a while in every rural area, or otherwise it would be impossible to suppress the activities of the counter-revolutionaries in the countryside or overthrow the authority of the gentry.

—Mao Tse-tung, 'The Question of "Going Too Far"', A Report on an Investigation of the Peasant Movement in Hunan' (*Selected Works of Mao Tse-tung*, The Maoist Documentation Project)

20

April 2006, as it turned out, would be the 'it' month for Maoism and responses to the movement.

In India, as elsewhere, a problem or solution isn't sanctified until the head of state or government imprints it with a word or two. It doesn't matter if the nation has seen, heard or suffered for years. This imprimatur is 'it'.

Prime Minister Singh presided over a meeting on Naxalism on 13 April in New Delhi—six days before the international investment rating agency Standard & Poor's upgraded its outlook on India from 'stable' to 'positive', and Maoists blew up an armoured landmine-proof vehicle in Gadhchiroli district of Maharashtra. Perhaps eager to impress upon Singh its organizational acumen, the Ministry of Home Affairs put a massive banner on the dais for the meeting. The following day, the image that made front-page across the nation was of a Prime Minister with hand covering his face, and 'NAXALISM' big and bold on the banner behind him. This wasn't an overstatement. Speaking at the meeting, the Prime Minister had said: 'It would not be an exaggeration to state that the problem of Naxalism is the single biggest internal security challenge ever faced by our country.'

He had also raised an alarm a year and a half earlier, when, on 4 November 2004, he told a conference of directors general of police and heads of police organizations what they already knew, that 'large swathes of tribal territory from Andhra Pradesh in the south to the border of Uttar Pradesh and Bengal in the north and east respectively have become the hunting ground of left-wing extremists.' This was just weeks after the announcement of the merger of the MCC and the People's War to form CPI (Maoist), and the failure of peace negotiations with the Y.S.R. Reddy government in Andhra Pradesh. Clearly, there was a threat perception, but senior government officials, even outside the precincts of the Home Ministry, continued to downplay the situation. Then Defence Minister—later Minister for External Affairs—Pranab Mukherjee would claim in January 2005 that 'Naxalite activity...has caused some concerns but it is manageable and there is no need for anyone to panic. The problem is being dealt with.'

Evidently, not with dispatch. The year 2005 would prove to be the bloodiest in modern revolutionary history, with casualty figures exceeding those of the North-East. And 2006 began badly, too. In February, alone, ten Naga Armed Police personnel were killed and eight injured in a landmine blast in Dantewada; eight CISF troopers were killed when CPI (Maoist) cadre attacked a major store of the National Mineral Development Corporation, also in Dantewada, and escaped with 20 tonnes of explosives; and at the end of the month, on 28 February, 26 Salwa Judum members were blown up at Eklagoda.

In March, the headlines, only marginally less violent, had shifted to Jharkhand and Bihar. Maoist women dressed as members of a marriage party ambushed a CISF and police camp in Bokaro, killing seven. Over a hundred Maoists attacked Umaria police station in Bihar.

The word was out, through an official Home Ministry leak, even before the big meeting on 13 April: anti-Naxal forces would have renewed government sanction. All increases in expenditure towards raising more forces and training and arming them would be fully underwritten by the Home Ministry under the head of Security Related Expenditure. The anti-Naxal Greyhound force in Andhra—police volunteers to this well-trained force are better trained, better equipped and paid 50 per cent more than regular Andhra police—would be beefed up and let loose, and clones would take wing in Chhattisgarh, Jharkhand, Orissa and Bihar. Alongside, all

Naxal-hit states would be urged to form special intelligence units to deal with Naxalism.

When the Prime Minister met chief ministers and officials of the 13 'officially' Naxal-affected states, it was basically to read out the riot act to the Maoists, and, at the same time, give it a populist spin so as not to appear anti-people. This, for all practical purposes, would be the Government of India doctrine.

Prime Minister Singh articulated the point about the central government contributing funds to combat Naxalism and dealt the socio-economic card with some elegance. 'Our strategy, therefore, has to be to walk on two legs—to have an effective police response while focusing on reducing the sense of deprivation…' He spoke of the undeniable need for good governance, 'effective implementation of development programmes, periodic monitoring and ensuring there [are] no leakages.' He added: 'We are dealing, after all, with our own people, even though they may have strayed into the path of violence.'

On Independence Day, some months after this comment, the Prime Minister would take a harder line against Left rebels in his address to the nation. 'I want those who have mistakenly taken to Naxalism to understand that in democratic India power will never flow from the barrel of the gun. Real power flows from the ballot box. At the same time, our state governments must pay special attention to the welfare of our tribals and small and marginal farmers,' he said, perhaps driven by his recent visit to Vidarbha. He then took off his velvet gloves. 'It is their distress that Naxalites exploit. The path of violence can never solve the problems of the poor. Our security forces will respond appropriately to the violence unleashed by Naxalites.'

Disturbingly, through these months, nobody took a call on the Salwa Judum. To either stop the tactic that combines protection, fear, intimidation and scorched earth. Or even to spread it. So, Chhattisgarh would remain the state-mandated laboratory of combat with the Maoists. To withdraw would mean accepting defeat. To persist, a calculated risk.

Salwa Judum. Tricky business. The Home Ministry and higher-ups have hinted more than once about extending the play beyond Chhattisgarh, but so far no other state will have it. These states would rather induct more tribals and rural-folk into various security apparatus for jobs and consequent loyalty; they haven't yet bitten the poison pill. Not even West Bengal, with its long history of utter ruthlessness by the Left for any dissenting Left—certainly extreme Left.

'Salwa Judum is a double-edged sword,' Bengal Armed Police chief Majumder told me when I pressed him on the point.

'Instead of gunning for the Naxalites we are creating another group and making them professional, licensed goondas.'

'That's exactly what's happening in Chhattisgarh...' I offer.

'Licensed goondas. You had good intentions, but then...' he trailed off with a disgusted look. 'If the government announces that you're my agent against the Maoists, does the government protect you? You're not a VVIP. All these [Salwa Judum] people are sitting ducks.'

'What do you think they should do with the Salwa Judum?'

'Disband it. The government should say, "It has failed". Disband it. And then do whatever has to be done.'

'They aren't going to do that,' I said. 'It's become a prestige issue for the administration.'

'That's a problem. Once you have taken on more than you can digest...' He quoted a line from a poem by Rabindranath Tagore, about how it hurts to remove a beautiful jewelled necklace, and yet, how wearing it can choke a person.

'What happens now?'

'The barrel of the gun is not going to solve these things. Police, security forces, these are used just as firefighters. There's fire, throw some water on it. The flames will die down a bit. But tomorrow the fire will burn again.'

Ajay Mehra, director of the Centre for Public Affairs, and commentator on Naxal issues, described this 'popular façade of resistance to Naxalism' to me as 'basically using people as cannon fodder'. And this was inevitable, he said, given what kind of police force the country gives itself. 'Police roles are not clearly defined...what is the police to do? They were not even formally invited for the 13 April meeting called by the PM. If the police do not know their role with regard to internal security, and forces are not modernized, if they are not sensitized, then, among other things, incidents of human rights violations, which the police practice on a daily basis, will continue.' And the preferred approach of the police in 'disturbed areas' would be to let the army handle things, or encourage and arm people to butcher each other.

According to Mehra, whose father retired as a police officer in Bihar, the Salwa Judum is another, dangerous proof that government actions are not organized but ad hoc. It is to him symptomatic of another basic problem with the nation: the Indian state is not constitutionally equipped to deal with internal security in a cohesive manner, as federal provisions largely delegate responsibility to state-level action—and that's where planning breaks down.

Observers and analysts such as Mehra and Ajai Sahni and several police officials and bureaucrats I spoke to feel the attitude derives from the ambiguity of provisions in the Indian Constitution when these are married with reality. A case in point is Article 355 of the Constitution, which states: 'It shall be the duty of the Union to protect every State against external aggression and internal disturbance and to ensure that the government of every State is carried on in accordance with the provisions of this Constitution.' While Maoism would come under the ambit of this protective umbrella, law and order— or lack of it, due to Maoism—is listed as a 'State Subject'. Therefore, the Union government cannot step in with regard to a local issue until the state requests it. And, to complicate matters, each state is absolutely free to deal with a law and order issue in the way it feels is appropriate.

Andhra Pradesh and Chhattisgarh are prime examples. Both can—and have—taken a cue from the Home Ministry's prompt clearly spelt out as policy in its Annual Report for 2003–4—an agreement reached by a conference of chief ministers of Naxal-affected states—and pretty much reiterated every year since:

'On the one hand, there is a need to remove all the shortcomings in intelligence sharing and [to mount] well coordinated anti-Naxalite operations by joint task forces of the concerned States. On the other hand, greater emphasis needs to be given by the States to accelerate the physical and social infrastructure in the affected districts. The Central Government has adopted a multi-pronged strategy to tackle the problem of naxalism which includes modernization and strengthening of the State Police Forces, better training to police personnel, Special Task Forces for intelligence...focused attention on developmental aspect and gearing up of the public grievances redressal system and encouraging local resistance groups at the grass roots level.'

But the states have reacted to it in very different ways. For example, Andhra has Greyhound, the specialized anti-Naxal force with skills honed in a decade of striking back. Chhattisgarh—newer in the game as it administratively became its own master only in 2000—does not. Batches of its police, like police from several other states, are only now graduating from the practically brand new Counter Terrorism and Jungle Warfare College in Kanker district. It will be several years before the full effect of this training is felt across the state.

For Andhra, 'encouraging local resistance groups at the grass roots level' has meant developing 'Cobra' teams of anti-Naxalite forces made up of local tribals and others, under the firm operational control of the Greyhounds. Infiltration has meant turning around disaffected elements, as Andhra's former director general of police H.J. Dora revealed. He gave the example of picking out a Lambadi tribal with a grouse against the Naxals—they took away his land and supported a rival—and set a police constable from the same tribe to develop rapport and feed on his resentment. Two dalams of Naxals in northern Andhra were thus decimated with the help of just one 'turnaround' (who, Dora insisted, would not be armed 'at any cost').

'You need intelligence that is actionable,' said Dora. 'I have to win over one fellow. Then another. And another.' He reeled off names of some of these early tribal 'turnarounds': Bapulal Lambada, Chadmal Tunda...

Chhattisgarh, for its part, took resentment and turned it into the fearsomely disruptive bulldozer of Salwa Judum, providing even minors with guns.

Andhra has completed the restructuring of several of its police stations in the interiors, learning the hard way. Perimeter walls were used by the Maoists as shelter; these are now of barbed wire or razor wire. Country dogs provide another layer of alarm—and defence. There were no positions for lookouts on the roof; now there are, and with alarm sirens. Where there were lookouts, they were not linked by communication apparatus with the control room below or in the nearest police headquarters; now they are, with high-frequency transceivers. The Maoists would shoot out exposed communication and electric cables to incapacitate police posts; these cables are now placed underground and within the building, and there are generators to back up electricity failure. There weren't properly placed firing emplacements, just basic sandbagged and brick positions; now there are strengthened turrets covering all vulnerable directions. Living quarters of policemen would often abut compound walls, leading to several cases of Naxals attacking these in the course of destroying the police stations; quarters are now more secure inside the main structure. Few policemen wore bulletproof vests; in several outposts these are now standard issue.

When former chief minister Chandrababu Naidu barely escaped death in a landmine blast triggered by the Maoists in 2003, Andhra's police officials attributed it as much to divine intervention—the site was close to the Tirupati temple—as to reinforced, bulletproof cars they had commissioned for VIP travel.

Chhattisgarh's police is primitive in comparison. Most

police stations do not have the new features and reinforcements that stations in Andhra do. The central government funds have made little difference.

But at least Chhattisgarh is better off than Jharkhand. The office of the Comptroller and Auditor General of India published a report in 2005, pointing out that a state-level 'empowered committee' chaired by the chief secretary of Jharkhand purchased SUVs for ministers and VIPs worth Rs 157 million (Rs 15.7 crore) for the 2004–5 financial year, using money meant for the police to construct 'police lines' in a few disricts and to purchase vehicles for patrolling.

At the meeting on 13 April 2006, many chief ministers cut through the Prime Minister's two-tone talk as so much soft butter and pitched for an entire laundry list, including helicopters and even unmanned aerial reconnaissance vehicles for monitoring Naxal movements. Chhattisgarh's Raman Singh made a random pitch for a ratio of 1:10 to combat Naxals. Or, a mammoth force of 40,000 security personnel exclusively to deal with an estimated 4,000 Naxals in the area. This when senior officials and advisors involved in counter-insurgency clearly advocate not having huge forces. Former Andhra Pradesh police chief Dora, for instance, suggests the use of 'small, well-trained, cohesive groups—with purposeful attack.'

'And I heard one chief minister say'—I was later told by an intelligence official in Delhi about Orissa's Naveen Patnaik— 'that for every Maoist we must have nine paramilitary.' That's one less than what Chattisgarh's Raman Singh suggested. Random equations. 'A professional, well-trained policeman can take care of nine people. Unfortunately...' the intelligence man grumbled into silence.

Bihar's Nitish Kumar raised his legitimate concern at the meeting about Nepal's Maoists triggering a spillover of manpower, arms and ideology across that nation's entirely porous border with India—a border his state shares with Uttar Pradesh and Uttarakhand. Others had little to contribute. Maharashtra's Vilasrao Deshmukh even found time for a nap.

His wake-up call was yet to come, despite large parts of Vidarbha—where farmer suicides were rising—slipping out of his grasp.

But at least Deshmukh was present. Six invited chief ministers did not even show up for the meeting with the Prime Minister of the country and instead sent their representatives.

'The Naxals won't win,' Ajay Mehra had prophesied during my conversation with him. 'But they don't need to. They just need to be there.'

21

The conversation next to my table at Café Bhonsle in Panaji is animated. In Goa, anytime is good for a bit of wordplay. Even at 7.30 a.m., as I drop in for chai, a quick breakfast of mix-*bhaji* and *pao* and a scan at newspapers and magazines I collect from the kiosk outside. But the editorializing near me is more interesting.

The manager and a patron are talking. The topic, unsurprisingly, is about *bhaille*, 'outsiders' who are increasingly moving into relatively prosperous, tourism-driven Goa in search of better prospects. Over the past two years, bhaille (*bhailo*, in singular) references have included those from outside who buy land in Goa; those who operate businesses in Goa; sometimes, even people like me, who have relocated to pursue writing or other non-intrusive vocations. But among the majority, the targets typically are daily wage labourers and workers in the hospitality trade from dirt-poor areas of northern Karnataka, southern Maharashtra, Uttar Pradesh, Orissa, West Bengal and Nepal.

Today's hit is against people from Orissa.

'These Orissa people, no? Most are below poverty line. But after they come here they change their colours, no?'

The manager nods.

'What happened, no?' the patron continues with his tirade.

'We Goans are relaxed, no? We don't do their work, so they will come.'

'But Goans go abroad and all, no?' Café Bhonsle offers. 'Clean toilets and all. *Why* go do that? Why not stay in India, no?'

'Because we have people from Orissa and all, no? Below poverty line. They are below *our* poverty line, no?'

And so they will go wherever food and shelter beckons. India isn't free from poverty, caste, religious bigotry, corruption, deep regional prejudice. And, as sometimes evidenced during elections, a lot of India isn't free to vote for who it wants, either. But yes, people can move wherever they want. In that, Indians are free. Indians are free, too, to ignore misery in their own backyard without realizing its volatility and destructive capability.

The local paper I scan, *Gomantak Times*, has a front-page story on the utterly miserable of Goa, far removed from the sun and sand of the western strip. The last of the three-part article argues, 'Politicians thrive, Dhangars strive.' It is about how the nearly 8,000-strong Dhangar community of Goa, nature-worshipping cattle and goat herders who live in the hilly areas of the tiny state's densely forested east, are being denied the classification of Scheduled Tribe as both Congress and BJP clamour to take credit. This classification would enable the Dhangars, over some generations, to claw out of extreme poverty and neglect through reservations in state-funded education and government jobs.

But it wouldn't necessarily guarantee them respect. Their tribal brethren, the adivasi Kunbi, Velip and Gawda are today, despite official classification as tribals, little more than token presence in handicraft fairs and gawdy *carnaval* parades that float through Goa's major towns in pre-Lent exuberance. As adivasis, they have the right to be called Goans, but remain socio-economic bhaille in class-conscious, colour-conscious Goa. And the Scheduled Tribe classification would certainly not grant the Dhangars rights to the forest they inhabit, the owner of which is the government. And this, in turn, would ensure that then, as now, government would again not 'recognize' them and therefore they would simply disappear into the cracks of development—no state-sponsored primary healthcare in or near their hamlets, no state-sponsored schools, no cables carrying electricity, nothing at all. As with their kind across the state border in the jungles of Karnataka, Dhangars would be non-persons, prime fodder for extortionist forest officials—and, if they choose, catchment area for the Maoists.

But even Goa's poor, rarely spoken of in this 'party' state, can fight back. Reach the boiling point, to use Kanu-babu's phrase.

On 28 December 2005, a group of villagers from Saleli in the northeastern Sattari *taluka*—revenue district—attacked and killed a politically connected owner of quarries and stone-crushing units, a man of the same clan as Goa's chief minister Pratapsingh Rane. It stunned Goa, where rampant corruption in land sharking, mining and the drug trade are well-known and well-documented but rarely prevented; villagers are known to be absorbed in far more local issues, like quarrelling over the intruding branch of a guava or mango tree over a neighbour's wall. Saleli was rebellion.

The murdered man, Prithviraj Rane, was *khase*, hereditary chieftains by another name who continue after Goa's incorporation into India in 1961 as all-encompassing landlords and political fulcrum. The villagers wanted a control on stone-crushing plants—the village had 13 such units servicing 48 mines of meta-basalt and meta-granite, and two hot-mix plants. The area's coconut, cashew and jackfruit plantations lay covered in dust and muck, most streams were unusable, and noise blasted the area from dawn to dusk. Prithviraj claimed that his family owned Saleli by virtue of a land-lease system known as *mocasso*, so he could do pretty much what he wanted. And so, there would be yet another stone crushing unit, duly cleared by compliant government agencies. Any protest met with intimidation, and registered complaints against illegal mining and misuse of reserved forest area were ignored for several years—documented since 1994, according to New

Delhi-based Centre for Science and Environment. Perhaps Prithviraj was emboldened by the fact that his family had political sway over the area. But the villagers had enough, and a group of six just killed him.

Then, as the men surrendered or were caught, and over a hundred were jailed, Saleli's women sat in protest at the village temple on hunger strike, demanding their menfolk be released and action be taken against mining and crushing units. On 3 January 2006, farmers from 60 villages took out a protest march in support of Saleli's people. Within a week, show cause notices were sent to the stone-crushing units and they were temporarily shut down. It was too politically volatile for Chief Minister Rane—married into Nepal nobility, incidentally—to bury.

There could easily be more Salelis. Agricultural and forest land across Goa is being converted and sold to real estate developers and mining operations. Public pressure has put a government-mandated blueprint for land conversion and use, Regional Plan 2011, on hold, but critics maintain loopholes will be created for business as usual.

Later in the morning, after finishing up at Café Bhosle, as I cross the tiny bridge across Ourem Creek, which links the Latin Quarter of Panaji with the business district of Patto, to buy a bus ticket to Hyderabad, I notice a loud red splash on the brightly painted blue. It wasn't there the previous week. '*Nepal Rajtantra Murdabad! Gantantra Zindabad!*' Down with Nepali monarchy. Long live the people's republic.

The exuberance of Nepali bhaille.

22

Hyderabad, Cyberabad, Hyperabad. It takes forever to get there. Close to fourteen hours from Goa, skirting the northern borders of Karnataka with Maharashtra. The route allows for minimum possible time in Andhra Pradesh and skirts emerging

Maoist areas of influence in Karnataka. I've been up since 5 a.m., when the bus stops for the first of many checks almost immediately after we cross into Andhra Pradesh from Karnataka, not too far from Bidar.

The usual. Two tired policemen clamber up and inspect luggage on racks and near footrests, while another inspects the luggage hold. The search is perfunctory. Either they can smell an extremist when they come near one, or because this is an air-conditioned bus, we're all spared rude tone and brusque queries—how can Maoists travel in relative comfort? Their hair-trigger bosses haven't told them that all Maoists don't walk around in olive green, carry guns and scream destruction. Or maybe I'm just tired after a long ride and the policemen just want to go home after a long, tense, spirit-crushing round of duty.

The sun brings with it familiar pointers in Medak district, the old stomping ground of Indira Gandhi. She was famously elected to parliament from this constituency, signalling a political comeback after over two years in the wilderness following the Emergency. She still holds a cachet, I see, as we pass the industrial town of Patancheru 30 kilometres from Hyderabad. There she is, smiling from a billboard with trademark white slash in her hair. Y.S. Rajasekhar Reddy, of Indira's and now her daughter-in-law Sonia Gandhi's Congress, is the new chief minister of Andhra, after the tech-savvy poster boy of IT and globalization, Chandrababu Naidu, was voted out in the last assembly elections. And so, 22 years after she was gunned down by her bodyguards, Indira is summoned to lend credence to a new rural development programme that the state government has just launched: Indiramma.

Literally, it means Mother Indira. That takes care of sycophancy to dynastic Congress leadership. But it's actually an acronym that will surely rain rose petals on the person who thought up the double entendre of political economy: Integrated Novel Development in Rural Areas and Model Municipal Areas.

Indiramma, the programme, seeks to cover in stages every

gram—village—panchayat in the next three years and provide what the state has not in decades. Primary education to all; health facilities where there are none and better facilities where there are some; drinking water; pucca houses with latrines; drainage; electricity connections to all households; roads; pensions for the elderly, widowed, disabled; even better pre- and post-natal supplementary nutrition, and nutritional care for adolescent girls.

The plan was officially unveiled in Medak district in February 2006 by YSR with an announcement that Rs 230 billion (23,000 crore) would be spent over three years to upgrade 21,000 villages. And it was launched in April that year, though without any concrete indication as to where the funds would come from. If at all this saturation coverage succeeds, the Maoists won't stand a chance. If it doesn't succeed—as, besides sourcing of funds, Indiramma will also need to deal with corruption, to which there is no known point of saturation in India—the Maoists will gain propaganda leverage. According to several estimates, only between 10 per cent and—if some degree of honesty is factored in—20 per cent of funds reach where they are intended. By this logic alone, committed application of the Indiramma salve on Andhra's wounds would take about 15 years to heal—best case. If the three-year programme is not extended by Reddy in 2009, were he to run for and win elections, or by his successor, then the urban–rural, rich–poor divide would continue to fester.

So it goes.

We're on Hyderabad's Ring Road before I know it. The bus turns right, avoiding the city; it will curve in a huge arc all the way around the city to deposit us in front of the army camp at Golconda. But before that, we travel through the Indian Dream of the suburbs. To our left, large outcroppings of rock and modern office buildings, temples to BPO, technology, modern enterprise. It even has a name: Hitec City: Hyderabad Information Technology & Engineering Consultancy City. To our right, sprawls of elegant suburban housing. In between, multicoloured splashes of bougainvillea, fiery orange gulmohar, and broad tree-lined avenues. Neat, organized. Quite lovely, really.

Then I make the mistake of looking at the Andhra Pradesh road map in my hand, and of course I search for the Andhra of Mao's army. Distance from Hyderabad to Mahbubnagar in the south: 103 kilometres. To Kurnool: 208 kilometres. North to Adilabad, near the Maharashtra border: 302 kilometres. Karimnagar to the east of that, in deepest Telengana: 158 kilometres. Khammam: 198 kilometres. And beyond, into barren land, forest, hills. The ring of fire. If there was an insurgency this close to New York—or New Delhi—it would be an army camp.

—

Futuring is a dynamic business. But broad projections can be made based on logical progression.

For me, an extreme scenario would be that in the next 20 to 30 years there would be implicitly gated City States and massive urban belts. India's staggeringly populous large cities will grow into City States—they already are in many ways. So we could have the states of Delhi, Mumbai, Kolkata, Bangalore, Chennai, Hyderabad, Pune, Ahmedabad, Baroda, Chandigarh, Thiruvananthapuram, Kochi... Perhaps those that are relatively close, like Mumbai and Pune, Ahmedabad and Baroda, Bangalore and Mysore, and Delhi, Jaipur and Chandigarh will coalesce into gated states, peopled by several tens of millions each. Each such urban agglomeration would have its captive hinterland for food and water. Each would trade with the other; become new federal units in the future Republic of India. State boundaries as we now know them would become meaningless. The Urban State will constitute the key administrative unit of the future.

Already there is what is loosely called the National Capital Region, roughly a 50-kilometre radius around Delhi. This urban sprawl is snaking southwest towards Jaipur, and north towards Chandigarh. Mumbai has grown to Navi Mumbai, and will soon stretch across the bay into mainland Maharashtra to form a gigantic basin of industry, trade and habitat—if agitating farmers permit Reliance Industries Limited to acquire land for this private initiative.

The government of Karnataka has approved a proposal of the Bangalore Metropolitan Regional Development Authority to decongest Bangalore by developing five major satellite towns and seven 'intermediate' towns. These will be linked to two massive concentric circles of ring roads, the inner one of 178 kilometres and the outer, 283 kilometres, further interlinked with radial roads of over 260 kilometres to include in its embrace commuter habitats and circles of business, food and livelihood. This huge exercise, for which Rs 34.3 billion (3,430 crore) is the estimated cost just for developing roads—boosting infrastructure of the towns would require several times that amount—would involve acquiring 75,000 acres of land. Cars would zip around at 180 kilometres per hour on six-lane roads, which would also provide space to 'carry' power and optical fibre cables and sewage pipes.

Hyderabad, too, is growing. The Hyderabad Growth Corridor Limited has already issued large advertisements in praise of its Outer Ring Road, 162 kilometres of access-controlled, high-speed expressway. 'ORR—The Road to a Flourishing Future', it trumpets, 'Making Hyderabad a Global Metropolis'. This is set amidst images of swirling, looped ribbons of road, and a photograph of a smiling YSR and promises of 'innumerable satellite townships which will propel the city to the forefront of global business activity'.

All such City State regions could, in the not too distant future, be 'in'. What lies away—in effect, rural—would be 'out'. Out of sight, possibly out of mind; the sole purpose of its existence to service the urban agglomeration. And those that are uprooted, such as farmers evicted by massive acquisition of land, would either fester in 'in' slums, or fester in the shrunken and forsaken 'out'.

Let's call these In-Land and Out-Land.

The have-nots in In-Land could provide tinder for trouble. And more will arrive everyday from Out-Land, in the absence of rural or agricultural growth. Many of those who do not— or cannot—will provide tinder in Out-Land.

The chairman of the National Commission on Farmers, M.S. Swaminathan, in 2006 sounded a caution at the convocation of a local university in Nagpur, gateway to the suicide land of Vidarbha. 'Our farm population is increasing by 1.84 per cent each year,' he said. 'But the average farm size is decreasing each year. The cost-risk-return structure of farming is becoming adverse, with the result that farmers are getting increasingly indebted. Marketing infrastructure is poor, particularly in perishable commodities.'

'No wonder,' added the man who is arguably credited with India's once hopeful and now faltering Green Revolution, 'a recent NSSO [National Sample Survey Organization] survey revealed that 40 per cent of our farmers would like to quit farming if they have an option. Unfortunately, there is little option for them except to move into urban slums.'

Therefore, using a back-of-the-envelope calculation, over 250 million, or 25 crore, people at the very least are potentially at risk of giving up in Out-land, upping their lives and moving to In-Land. Each year the pressure will build. Who will take them? Where will they go? How will India cope with this swell—even with increasing concentric circles of urban habitat?

This remainder of India, beyond the urban pale, would likely be abdicated by the central government, if there is one, to bands of various 'people's governments', Maoist or otherwise. (This isn't at all improbable—it has already happened in the Dandakaranya region and vast chunks of Jharkhand and Orissa.) These forgotten Out-Land areas would likely keep in touch with each other, even form loose agreements with the City States, to permit passage of goods and people. As long as the Out-Land areas don't directly threaten the City States, these could, theoretically, continue at will. The Republic of India could become the Republic of South Asia, a gathering of always-on-the-edge confederacies.

A worse case scenario, besides the disintegration of India—something that many feared even in the *India Today* opinion poll of 1997—would be rampant warlordism in the areas of Out-Land, of present-day Other India.

If ever today's still largely rural, increasingly ignored people's movements gather steam and are carried to the cities where the urban intelligentsia and the urban poor combine to even partially reflect the Urban Perspective Plan of the Maoists, there could be chaos. India's cities are largely slum. The deprivation and anger there is already tinder for slumlords and politicians, who cynically feed off the lowest common denominator. As it happens, only the Maoists, apart from pan-India political entities such as the Congress, to an extent the BJP, and lately the Bahujan Samaj Party, are engaging the lowest common denominator in the widest possible area. The Maoists seem to be doing it as well as the others.

A 'Unity Congress' of CPI (Maoist) in the last week of January 2007 in the forests of Jharkhand, after electing a new central committee and re-electing Ganapathy as the general secretary of the party, passed several resolutions. Among other things, these focussed on combining rural, worker and urban issues and mentioned '...massive attacks on the working class and vicious attempts to bind labour hand and foot, which has facilitated a massive loot by big business...Wage freeze, VRS, dismissals, curbs on recruitment, anti-labour Court Judgments, de-facto ban on strikes, etc, are leading to greater and greater impovirisation (sic) of the entire working class.'

The party's suggestion: militant workers' movements. This plays on the vulnerability that results from the state acquiring land—often through pressure and by offering rates below market—on behalf of big projects. When the process should, ideally, be a direct transaction between business and those who wish to sell land, with the state intervening only to protect the interests of those who sell and also those who choose not to.

'The 300 planned SEZs are all set to create de-facto

foreign enclaves within our country by grabbing lakhs of acres of prime agricultural land by the foreign and local sharks. Together with this, to turn urban centers into elite enclaves and pave the way for big business retail chains, ruthless demolitions and eviction of lakhs of people are taking place, demolishing slums and even permanent housing. The Unity Congress of the CPI (Maoist) calls on the people to resist the seizure of their lands and houses and beat back the demolition hordes by whatever means possible.'

Like major political parties, CPI (Maoist) doesn't just want a slice, it wants it all. And it plans to do it without fuss, without co-opting Ganapathy—who, Naxal watchers say sometimes uses the aliases Ramanna, Srinivas and Chadrasekhar—into the revolutionary pantheon of India. (Unlike in Nepal, where 'Prachanda Path', the way of Prachanda, is part of iconic sloganeering and his face adorns the party's website, protest banners, and even T-shirts that rebel soldiers wear.)

Driving into Cyberabad, I wonder how far the chaos is.

—

Venu will see me, but first he needs to take his uncle P. Varavara Rao to a doctor. He's just been released from jail after more than seven months under IPC Sections 121 to 124A and a few other statutes enacted by Andhra Pradesh. He's out on bail, and not keeping well. It's the price VV, as he is commonly known, pays for being poet-ideologue of Andhra's revolutionary movement, a leading light of the banned Virasam—Revolutionary Writers' Association—and above ground spokesman for CPI (Maoist). Venu—N. Venugopal—formerly with the *Economic Times*, the country's biggest business paper, is both dutiful nephew and acolyte.

I do things to kill time, and there isn't much to do at Shree Venkateshwara Hotel at Lakdi ka Pul, a busy, noisy area of old Hyderabad, so far from Hitec City and the elegant bungalows of Secunderabad. There are no posters in this part of town welcoming delegates to the ongoing 39th Annual Meeting of the Board of Governors of the Asian Development Bank (ADB).

For starters, I tuck into some breakfast. The menu at Shree Venkateshwara's coffee shop advertises 'MLA Dosa', the most expensive dosa at Rs 35. All around me are wealthy businessmen—mostly contractors—dressed in crisp white shirt and dhoti, shirt and trousers, and the perennial Indian favourite: the safari suit. The lesser among them wear gold-plated watches and pens. The greater retain gold watches, but for pens they have black or mauve ones with tiny white blossoms on the cap: Mont Blanc. To make up for my lowly status I sternly order buttermilk and an MLA Dosa. It's as plump—and as rich, as VV and I will joke later—as an MLA.

Bloated, I stroll across the road to Krishna Complex, a cluster of dingy travel shops, eateries, a barbershop, and the area's only cyber hole in the wall. Two British boys I earlier saw at the coffee shop, accompanying their parents who are visiting on a cheap medical holiday, India's newest tourism offer, occupy two of the terminals. At Rs 15, an hour of surfing here costs only as much as my breakfast glass of buttermilk.

My in-box has the usual mix of news and updates. Abhi has sent me a message about evictions in Sikkim. There's another from a dummy address about a revolutionary contact in Punjab. A message from Maoist Revolution, an Internet user group, saying that I have been approved for membership. And another, from the People's War user group—where again I was recently approved as member—promoting a book, *Dispatches from the People's War in Nepal*, by Li Onesto, well-known writer in global Left circles. There's also a link for a related video on CNN.

The desktop revolutionary. It can begin as easily as this.

'Andhra Pradesh has a history of defiance,' Venu says. 'People anger easily. There's a reason. Take Mahbubnagar. It has a population of about 17 lakh. Ten lakh are out of their homes on account of extreme poverty. It has been this way for the last 23 years, since NTR'—former chief minister N.T. Rama Rao, Chandrababu Naidu's father-in-law—'who said, "I am adopting Mahbubnagar, the problem will be solved." All whitewash.'

'There's desertification in Anantpur. Adilabad to Srikakulam is covered with thick forest. Exploited tribals live there; they constitute 20 per cent of the state's population.'

'Tell me,' he switches tack, perhaps to throw me off balance. 'Do you know _____?' He mentions a well-known journalist in Goa.

Of course, I say. We meet now and then.

'And you were at *India Today* from...?'

'1991 to 2002.'

'And then...?' I detail it.

'And you went to...?'

Delhi University. St Stephen's College.

'Ah, Stephen's!' Venu smiles.

'Very bourgeois. Elitist and all that. So sorry.'

'No,' he insists. 'Stephen's is the hotbed of Naxalism.'

Was. I had a teacher at school who went to St Stephen's, and he was full of stories of how in the late 1960s and early 1970s, rooms at the college hostel—which Stephen's tradition pompously calls 'residence'—would out of the blue be locked for weeks and months, a signal of its occupant having taken off to join the Naxals. Of how on a few occasions parents of errant urban revolutionaries—those who had a change of heart after seeing the violence Naxalism involved—would receive the bodies of their sons in trunks, hacked to pieces.

A critically acclaimed movie from 2005, *Hazaaron Khwaishein Aisi*, talked about that time and place, Stephen's and Delhi included, about students drawn into the brutality of instant revolution in Bihar, fighting the upper castes, tangling with vigilante bands and police. A friend, Vivek Bharati, several years my elder, and a former journalist, World Bank analyst and currently advisor to the Federation of Indian Chambers of Commerce and Industry, once wonderingly spoke to me about his first day at Stephen's in the late 1960s: 'There was a red flag on the cross. It was the first thing I saw.'

In my time, the early 1980s, the institutional cross on the main building at St Stephen's was once adorned by pranksters in a different way: with underwear filched from the changing room that the ladies' basketball team used. At the cusp of the initial loosening of India's controls by a youthful Rajiv Gandhi, it was less about life-claiming politics and revolution, and more about preparing for entrance examinations to business schools, scoring high grades to slip away to American universities. Perhaps some did dream of changing the country through media and high-octane service in the bureaucracy. Batik had gven way to banking.

'Did you know anyone from PUDR at Stephen's?' Venu persists.

None, I say. The closest I got to the Left was when in my first year a very pretty girl of the Students' Federation of India asked me to buy a subscription coupon for the youth wing of CPI (M). I bought the entire booklet. I never saw her again.

I give Venu and his companion a copy of my first book, as combined CV and ice-breaker. Now, can we please get back to the business at hand?

Venu smiles. His companion Vanaja, silent all this while, says, 'You look like police, with your short hair.'

She smiles apologetically. I'm brought tea and a bowl of warm, sweet *payasam*.

I first met Vanaja on the cover of *Smarana*, the CD that A, the active revolutionary, gave me in Delhi several months ago. The sleeve of the CD, a documentary on the parents of revolutionaries from Andhra Pradesh speaking heart-rendingly about their children, dead or still underground young men and women, carried her email address. We exchanged emails, and then corresponded after she received one of India's most coveted awards in media, the Ramnath Goenka Award for Excellence in Journalism. It was in the category of 'Uncovering India Invisible'. The documentary that won Vanaja the award was on her travels through Dandakaranya in 2005, in the company of Maoists, recording their lives. A fortnight in the 'liberated zone'. The award jury took note. The Prime Minister of India personally gave her the award. Montek Singh Ahluwalia, now irrevocably 'Macro Man' to B, was at the ceremony too; there is a photograph of him conversing with Vanaja on her blog.

And there she was again, on a prime-time show and debate on Naxalism, aired by CNN-IBN on 16 April, with extensive footage from her DK visit. The programme ran for close to an hour, and made compelling, disturbing viewing, with some unintentional humour provided by India's Home Secretary. It went something like this:

Rajdeep Sardessai (the presenter): A massive one-third of India is under the control of the Maoists. 170 districts where the state has no say...it's by far India's greatest security challenge...

Maoist block chief Sannu and divisional commander Ganesh Uyike talk about how the Janatana Sarkar works a cooperative system; Adivasi elders detail how forest officials and the patwari took money for them to live, forage and graze animals in the only home they know, and made their life a misery on account of them not having the all-important patta, land ownership paper, that says they can rightfully live in the forest.

Vanaja (after a clip showing Maoists helping with irrigation in a no-irrigation zone, and helping farm fish): This has certainly added a new dimension to the violent image of the Naxal movement.

Chhattisgarh chief minister Raman Singh (in Hindi): ...60,000 people should get pattas. We have been ready with these pattas based on the Forest Conservation Act 1980. We can give it to them tomorrow...

Divisional Commander Uyike: ...we will have Janatana Sarkar groups ranging from 500 to 3000...

Brig. (Retd) B.K. Ponawar (director, Jungle Warfare School, Kanker): ...They have got the weapons, they have got the training, they have got the ideology in place—and they are gradually spreading this red carpet.

Mahendra Karma (leader of the Salwa Judum): ...by the end of this year we will be in all villages in Dantewada and in a position to finish Naxalis.

Commander Uyike (after a Maoist dance troupe ends a performance with shouts of 'Adivasi Kranti Zindabad' [Long Live the Adivasi Revolution]): ...we want to replace the concept of giver and taker...98 per cent of the people here are farmers...they plant a single crop...there is no irrigation, the rest is up to God...[the state] should give 80 per cent of funds for irrigation...

Cut to a panel discussion with, among others, Home Secretary V.K. Duggal, and revolutionary balladeer Gadar on satellite link from Hyderabad.

Sardessai (to Duggal): Would you say this is the biggest challenge?

Duggal: Well, I can't say it's the biggest challenge, but I'll say it's one of the challenges. India is a vast country with multidimensional challenges.

Sardessai: Are you playing it safe? 170 districts, 10,000-strong army...

Duggal: You know, you know, Rajdeep, you have known me for a long time, so...are these in all districts? Or part of districts? In only 500-odd police stations...of course, there is a problem.

Sardessai: Gadar, is it true that the Naxals are now killing innocents with their violence?

Gadar: Yeh violence nahin hota hai. Yeh aag hota hai. [This is not violence. This is fire.] (Starts singing) Aag hai, yeh aag hai/ Yeh bhookey pet ki aag hai/ Yeh aansuyon ki angaar hai/ Yeh jangal ki lalkaar hai [This is a fire/ Fire from empty bellies/ The spark from tears/ The war cry of the jungle.] (Stops singing). So the violence is of the sarkar. The people are only retaliating. The state has become a terrorist.

Sardessai: Mr Duggal, do you agree that Naxalism is not only a law and order problem but a socio-economic problem?

Duggal: I...I...I...the point is, India is a vast and varied cultural milieu...

'I don't get a sense of a plan, you know,' I tell Venu. 'In Nepal, it's crystal clear. The Maoists there state intentions in public. They rally the masses, and they go about their business. I can as a tourist walk into a Maoist area. Here, it's light and shade. I'd probably be killed either by the Maoists or security chaps. I don't even get much of a sense of what the Maoists are doing here. No sense of a plan. Not even in *People's March*.'

'You don't get this in *People's March*?' Venu is offended. 'I think you do.'

I promise to look harder in the CPI (Maoist) mouthpiece.

'It's not possible to spell out strategy in detail. But I think you will get enough of an indication.'

'As you say,' Venu continues, 'it's different in India. Unlike Nepal, here the middle class is greatly swayed by consumerism. Here, it is much more complex. But really, in a revolutionary situation you cannot say what is going to happen tomorrow. You can't have a two-, five-, ten-year corporate plan. Even if you do, things change from day to day—it's very fast-paced. You have to react quickly. Sometimes what could take years can be accomplished in a matter of days. But if you read *People's March*, you will get some sense of it.'

'Do you see?' Venu nudges me along, and I get a sense, again, of the Maoist Urban Perspective Plan playing out. 'Many anti-imperialist and anti-establishment forces are coming together. The anti-ADB protest here. The protests against the

217

Sardar Sarovar project in Delhi and elsewhere. People are getting more vocal, more angry, more frustrated. And a time is coming when their weight will be more than the weight of the state, of the bourgeoise, the capitalists.'

It fills me with a sense of the bizarre to be discussing revolution in a living room, with tea, surrounded by family, when the state—the Centre as well as Andhra—has banned CPI (Maoist) and all its front organizations. Where else would you have all this—freedom of speech and expression, and near-total state domination at the same time? No blacks and whites as in Nepal. As always, India is full of grays.

'It seems the fount of wisdom has turned from India to Nepal, reversal of order, don't you think?' I venture with Venu. 'Not too long ago, Nepal took lessons in revolution from India. Now, in about ten years, they're leveraging the country, and the king is out.'

On 25 April 2006, King Gyanendra finally gave in after having failed to crush public protests across his stricken nation, and said he would reinstate parliament, which he had dissolved in May 2002. Nepal's Maoists, who had steadily pressured the monarchy to near-impotency till growing public anger against the king delivered the final blow, would now work—on the face of it—with the Seven-Party Alliance towards peace, administration, elections, a new constitution, and writing the monarchy out of the picture. On 3 May, Nepal's new government—minus the king—formally declared a ceasefire with Nepal's Maoists. (Incredibly, the Maoists would join the new government in November 2006. By September 2007, however, the dream would be over. The Maoists would pull out of the government. They would renege on an earlier agreement to push ahead with elections to a constituent assembly, and allow that elected body to decide the fate of the king and the future of Nepal's polity. Nepal would be back on edge.)

'Here,' I go on, encouraged by Venu's silence, and state the obvious, 'revolution is nowhere near consummation.'

Venu's smile freezes.

I can't seem to stop. I remind him of the elections in West Bengal. On the same day as the Nepal announcement, West Bengal went to polls in the fourth of its five phases, blanketed with 400 companies of paramilitary forces in the three districts of Birbhum, Bardhaman and Murshidabad—the first two being 'Maoist districts'. Government officials, of course, boastfully called it 'peaceful', unmindful of staggering irony, but the fact was the area's Maoists couldn't do a thing to disrupt the elections that they had given a call to boycott. So, what can India's Maoists do if such application of massive force is replicated across the country—through the mechanism of intimidation, surrender-and-be-rehabilitated, or outright killing?

Venu is too sharp to not see it. But he remains quiet, letting me go on.

I offer a peace pipe. 'The people I talk to in India point to Andhra as the fount of revolution in this country, a place where revolutionary spirit is active. Even Kanu Sanyal told me that...'

'But he came to Vijaywada and strongly criticized Andhra Maoists.'

'Yes, he criticized you guys to me, too. Maybe he believes his way of revolution is better than anyone else's.'

We all laugh.

'There is a lot of repression,' Venu says then.

'The DGP is an insane man,' Vanaja cuts in. 'We have decided to not do stories now.'

DGP Swaranjit Sen. A dapper man fond of cravats, who carried forward the legacy of predecessors like H.J. Dora—the architect of anti-Naxal operations in Andhra—and S.R. Sukumara. He ran a steamroller across rebel strongholds in the Telengana region and the Nallamala forests to the north of the state. Not too long ago, dalams—armed squads—would roam with impunity in Medak district, between 30 and 40 kilometres from Hyderabad. When I met Venu and Vanaja, that was over. The 'guerilla zone' of North Telengana, the area north of Hyderabad, was in remission. And several of its key arm, the People's Guerilla Army, were believed to have gone into 'organization' mode, trading in olive green for mufti, back to the basics, blending in, regrouping, waiting for an opportune moment.

After Sen, who would retire in December 2006, a new man would assume charge. Eventually, he too would go, adding to the changing landscape of politics and administration, the cat and mouse game of rebels versus the state. In the business of revolution, it's all about tides: high, low, ebb, flow. Historically and cyclically, Tebhaga, Telengana, Naxalbari and Srikakulam redux.

But Sen's departure is still some months away as I ask Venu, 'What about here, in the city? Isn't the sense of deprivation and exploitation in big cities as extreme as in the countryside?

'You have to be more careful in an urban area,' Venu allows. 'Things can't be that obvious. You have to work with fronts...The cities are like tinder. One day, they will catch fire and burn everything down.'

Venu says this calmly. And when I think about it later, it does make sense. Cities are indeed like tinder—things only have to get unbearable for a large enough group of the dispossessed and an explosion is a given. Because there's nowhere to run to. In the countryside, you run to the next village, town, city, if something goes wrong—a riot, drought, floods, caste killing, rape, vendetta, displacement on account of a project, loss of land. Wash dishes, break stones, work as a coolie, make tea, help build condominiums, rent a rickshaw, somehow you survive. But where do you run to from the city? To another city?

Already, in places like Kolkata and Hyderabad, revolutionary activity takes place just a few hours' drive away. From Mumbai the zone is a little further—an hour's plane ride to the east, but it could be a lot closer if Nashik, a key area for development in the Maoist Urban Perspective Plan, is considered.

Chaos, according to activist and senior Supreme Court

lawyer Prashant Bhushan, would derive from the 'power-crazed libido of the elite' who are these days 'low on moral bearings', in compact with a State and its perpetrators similarly driven by such libido, and similarly adrift from the reality of poverty and anger. He provides small, as yet ignored examples of where our cities are heading. He speaks of 2,00,000 slum dwellers of the Yamuna Pushta area of Delhi moved lock, stock and anger to the outskirts, at Bawana, without provision for sanitation and water. 'I won't be surprised if many are driven to be criminals or join the Naxals—who are becoming more prevalent.'

'The state is clueless,' Venu continues. 'They don't know what to do. You know, I was in Vijaywada in 1988. There was some trouble related to poor people being beaten up by the state. The town erupted. In the main road I saw people picking up Sony colour TVs—then TVs were quite new—and smashing them on the street. The anger of the have-nots against the haves is very strong, very obvious.'

But we've had economic reforms since then, I counter. More people can have Sonys, and a lot cheaper.

'And more people will never be able to afford it. It's not just about a Sony TV, that's just a symbol, like any consumer brand. I believe that anger persists and has spread to more towns and cities. They can explode anytime.' I wait for his smug smile. It doesn't come.

What's it like living here in the overground-underground? Do you get threatening calls? Are your phones tapped?

'Of course. My calls are recorded. I used to get threatening calls quite often.'

'They would call anytime, the mafia-police,' Vanaja intervenes. 'They would threaten to kill Venu, and tell me in detail how they would send me his body in pieces.'

'Did you complain?'

'Yes,' says Venu, sipping tea. 'At the local police station. Nothing happened. Then I wrote to the chief of police. Then to the chief minister. Still they didn't stop. Then I wrote an open letter to the chief minister, saying police don't have to come to my house to shoot me. I will come to the Secretariat and they can shoot me there, in front of everyone. A newspaper published it. The calls stopped after that.'

Venu excuses himself, saying he needs to collect VV's medical reports. Vanaja sees me to the door, and offers some advice about just walking into a zone, solo.

'If you go into a village, then the sangham will put you in a room, a hut, a kind of holding area, till the squad come to question you, find out who you are. It's dangerous to just walk in. Anything can happen. It's very tense out there.'

'In Chhattisgarh?'

'Anywhere.'

'What was it like for you?' In the publicity shots for her award, she looked quite at ease, in denim and sneakers, with her camera among a group of smiling, curious Maoists dressed in olive. You could walk to a playground, a street corner, a slum or an office block and have a similar effect. Everybody likes being on camera, the same as everybody wants a better life.

'You see the dedication, the desire to bring about change. The tribal boys don't want to be in the sangham or the other teams, like development teams. They want to join the squad. The prestige is in wearing the uniform.'

Maoists, she insists as I leave, are human, too.

23

The door to the second-floor apartment near Nalgonda Crossroads is open. I ring the bell, and VV arrives.

'Weren't you supposed to phone before coming?' he admonishes.

'Yes, I'm sorry. Thought I'll take a chance. See if you're feeling all right.'

'I'm always all right. Come in.'

There's a framed poster on the wall near me. It's a quote by Marx quoting an anonymous worker:

But, because I tried to extend your liberties, mine
were curtailed.
Because I tried to rear the temple of freedom for you
all I was thrown into the cell of a felon's jail...
Because I tried to give voice to the truth, I was
condemned to silence...
You may say this is not a public question!
But it is!

'Remembering Dr Ramachandran,' a line at the bottom says. 'Vice-president of APCLC—AP Civil Liberties Committee—killed by police in Mufti, '85.'

'Shall we go inside, to another room?' VV suggests, after giving me some time to absorb the message. 'It will be more quiet.'

It's his bedroom, cluttered with papers and books. I'm not surprised to see Mao there. There's his profile with exhortation in Hindi: '*Vargsangharsh ko hargiz na bhulo.*' Never forget class struggle. Nearby, there's a quote from Che: 'It is better to die standing than to live on your knees.'

We settle down, and I switch on my tape recorder. 'Three hundred million below the poverty line,' I begin, hoping to get down to business immediately—

He cuts me off, and goes off at a tangent. 'Whenever the government or the establishment talk about people's movements or alternate politics or, in today's context, the Naxal movement, they say there's a corridor from Nepal to South India.'

'Pashupati to Tirupati,' I say, using a phrase made popular by former home minister and former BJP president L.K. Advani, linking Kathmandu's famous temple to the one in Andhra Pradesh.

'Pashupati to Tirupati,' VV echoes. 'Not once has the *revolutionary* leadership in Nepal or India said anything about a corridor. The revolutionary movements are homegrown, and essentially internal. The external aspect is only the political, cultural and ethical—moral—support that the revolutionary party of one country lends to a movement elsewhere.'

It didn't stop Mao's China from extending help to Vietnam, or Russia doing much the same, in Vietnam and elsewhere. But I keep my own counsel. I don't want to stop VV's flow.

When Naxalbari happened, VV was a lecturer. A writer friend, Rama Rao, and he read a small news item in the papers that there had been police firing in a place called Naxalbari and people had been killed. VV recalls Rao telling him, 'From now on the map of India will not be as it was yesterday.'

'That alternate reality has come,' this diminutive, shrunken man tells me. 'There may be ups and downs, but even in spirit, you see alternate thinking in everything—culture, politics. Take this ADB meeting going on now. Except for one or two intellectuals, no intellectual—even if they may be critical of ML parties or Maoists—is appreciative of ADB, the World Bank, etcetera. That is the real picture.'

VV stops for breakfast. A small plate containing two slim dosas with chutney, which his wife brings. I've already breakfasted, but I accept a snack of sweetened ragi.

'When Charu Mazumdar said the comprador-bourgeois, the stooges of imperialists, are exploiting this country, people may have laughed at that jargon,' he resumes through his meal. 'But any true intellectual today will argue that we have become a neo-colony to American imperialism. This thinking is driven by Naxalbari and alternate politics.'

'This country is as much mine as it's yours,' I can't stop myself. 'And I'm concerned about where all this is going.'

Typically, he comes at me at a tangent. 'Recently I read an article by Chomsky where he says people near New York are upset; they say, Why should we sacrifice everything to facilitate people to be in New York, to go to New York? Today this applies to so-called Greater Hyderabad. As you know, an eight-lane ring road is coming up. For that, people of Rangareddi, Mahbubnagar, Nalagonda, Medak are losing their land. They are being displaced, uprooted. So this rural conflict with the urban areas is a real danger.'

I tell him my pet theory about In-Land and Out-Land.

'You have coined a word—Urban State,' VV tells me after

patiently hearing me out. 'It's true. It's like what people said earlier, a contradiction between Bharat and India. But how much really is India and how much is Bharat? And how much Bharat is there even in urban areas? When you say "Urban State", how much "state" is there in the "Urban State"?' It feels a bit strange to be on the same side as a revolutionary, though my personal conviction about violence as means to a goal is divergent.

'To put it simply, the direction to people is to get people's power,' he finally spouts doctrine. 'Like all power to the Soviets. Like all power to the communes in China. Here, when you say all power to the people, it's *Gram Rajya*. What I'm saying is...like the Paris Commune—Marx talked about primitive communism. It was not Utopia. He had seen that primitive communism is direct communism.'

'So it was good in thought and spirit but shabby in execution?'

'Maybe, yes. Later he may have realized that if you don't have a strong party you cannot implement it. Take Bastar and Telengana. They have implemented it in very rudimentary form. You will see that the political power will be in the hands of the people, the weak classes, and their economy will be a self-reliant economy. They have formed Village Development Committees. The first thing is, land to the tiller—only the tiller will own the land. Whoever wants it will have to benefit from the fruits of labour. Then, there [can be] land use, primary education, primary healthcare.'

All these, VV continues, will be in the hands of the Village Development Committees which will be guided by the Gram Rajya Committee.

'Naxals have implemented these in various places,' VV says. 'In North Telengana they have built a dam involving people—in just six months. They've been doing work not done for several decades. That is the political programme of the party, to show that it can work: don't take anything from the government; don't participate in elections; implement your alternate politics, your own development programme.'

'The government is waking up now,' I counter. 'In Chhattisgarh they are getting the Border Roads Organization to build roads to connect villages, if only to get troops in. I hear the government of Jharkhand is planning to do the same thing...'

'But it's nothing new. In 1992 Indo-Tibetan Border Police and the Border Security Force were brought to Andhra Pradesh to deal with Naxals...That's how it is. One day, the Prime Minister talked about Salwa Judum in 13 different states. Another day he said, "We must give voice to the voiceless." That explains the character of the state.

'And they are creating roads not really for Ganapathy'— the Maoist chief widely believed to be in Bastar's inaccessible Abujmarh forest area—'but for multinationals to enter.'

It is understandable why many—and not just Maoists— would think that. Chhattisgarh has massive amounts of coal, iron and manganese ore, tin ore, bauxite, limestone, dolomite and quartz. Diamonds are the future—healthy Kimberlite pipes have been discovered in Raipur and Bastar districts, and this is revealed in the government's own public relations document titled *Chhattisgarh: Rich Resources, Shining Success, High Hopes*. There's also gold in Kanker, Bastar, Jashpur, Raigarh and Raipur. And uranium in Surguja and Rajnandgaon.

It's a widely held belief in Maoist and NGO circles that the government has woken up to the Maoist threat only after it realized how much money there was to be made from these resources, all of which are either in or near Maoist strongholds. They also believe the move will further weaken the rights of tribals and marginal farmers to their land. Basically, that the political economy of displacement on account of big industry and mining will visit Chhattisgarh, mirroring a battle currently being fought in neighbouring Orissa between the state and the mass activism of tribals, farmers and NGOs—several of these last suspected to be Maoist front organizations.

When VV last went to Kerala, he says, a big hunt was going on for Veerappan, the notorious sandalwood smuggler, elephant poacher and killer of over a hundred security personnel.

He operated with impunity in contiguous jungle areas of Karnataka, Tamil Nadu and Kerala. He was finally killed in October 2004 by a special task force from Tamil Nadu, raised specifically to hunt him, amid general speculation as to why it took close to twenty years to track and eliminate him. Theories have ranged from politicians and policemen receiving a cut, to the man being used by different parties to influence local elections, before he became too much of a political hot potato.

VV parades another, somewhat paranoid theory. 'The central government wanted to give that forest area to multinationals.'

He then reinforces that notion with a saying in Telugu: 'When it comes to the interest of the zamindar, the interest of the bandicoot will be sacrificed.' He unleashes a deep-throated chuckle. 'The small thief will be sacrificed for the big thief.'

'Anyway,' he continues, 'these are the issues. The problem is, in a relative period of peace, the people's movement could provide and show an alternate development programme.'

'Are you saying it has moved from relative peace to conflict—full conflict?'

'Yes. Full. So, in Bastar, for example, the government has told organizations and those like Salwa Judum to enter these areas and cut these [the Maoists'] development programmes.' This, of course, is the opposite of the government position, which accuses the Maoists of preventing development. Strong-arm takes on strong-arm. Both schools of development suffer.

'How do you see the movement progressing?'

'For a Maoist,' VV adds, 'the capital is the last citadel to be conquered. If you can isolate the Urban State...when you can make an enormous base, and continue a guerilla struggle, and use all your guerilla tactics and mass-line politics under party leadership. To capture Peking was not a difficult thing for him.'

Him. Mao.

He had it all mapped out by 1947, the doctrine of stooping to conquer that his acolytes here in India practice—and have practiced to tremendous effect in Nepal—aided by crumbling, obtuse governance.

It's easy enough if you follow the ground rules and wait for the tide. Mao had put it down as a ten-point strategic and tactical programme—'Principles of Operation':

1. Attack dispersed isolated enemy forces first; attack concentrated strong enemy forces later.
2. Take small and medium cities and extensive rural areas first; take big cities later.
3. Make wiping out the enemy's effective strength our main objective; do not make holding or seizing a city or place our main objective...often a city or place can be held or seized for good only after it has changed hands a number of times.
4. In every battle, concentrate on absolutely superior force (two, three, four and sometimes even five or six times the enemy's strength), encircle the enemy forces completely, strive to wipe them out thoroughly and do not let any escape from the net...Strive to avoid battles of attrition in which we lose more than we gain or only break even. In this way, although inferior as a whole (in terms of numbers), we shall be superior in every part and every specific campaign, and this ensures victory in the campaign...
5. Fight no battle unprepared, fight no battle you are not sure of winning; make every effort to be well prepared for each battle, make every effort to ensure victory in the given set of conditions as between the enemy and ourselves.
6. Give full play to our style of fighting—courage in battle, no fear of sacrifice, no fear of fatigue, and continuous fighting (that is, fighting successive battles in a short time without rest).
7. Strive to wipe out the enemy when he is on the move. At the same time, pay attention to the tactics of positional attack and capture enemy fortified points and cities.
8. Concerning attacking cities, resolutely seize all enemy fortified points and cities that are weakly defended. At

opportune moments, seize all enemy fortified points and cities defended with moderate strength, provided circumstances permit. As for all strongly defended enemy fortified points and cities, wait until conditions are ripe and then take them.

9. Replenish our strength with all the arms and most of the personnel captured from the enemy. Our army's main sources of manpower and materiel are at the front.

10. Make good use of the intervals between campaigns to rest, train and consolidate our troops. Periods of rest, training and consolidation should not in general be very long, and the enemy should as far as possible be permitted no breathing space. These are the main methods the People's Liberation Army has employed in defeating Chiang Kai-shek. They are the result of the tempering of the People's Liberation Army in long years of fighting against domestic and foreign enemies and are completely suited to our present situation...our strategy and tactics are based on a people's war; no army opposed to the people can use our strategy and tactics.

In India, it will need 'very hard work' to break the legitimacy of Parliament, the established systems, VV says. But that will make revolutionary instincts sharper, come to party and cadre alike as a 'blessing in disguise'.

'It is moving to a definition—organize the broadest movement against the state,' he articulates the way ahead, reiterating the gameplan unveiled in 2004, of taking along every kind of dispossessed, oppressed and angry group. 'The future is in organizing all those who are affected by the state.'

'Is violence the only way?' I ask. 'Or is it one of the ways?'

The reply comes in another curve. 'You need different types of struggles to capture state power. Marx says,' VV paraphrases here, 'those who are sitting at the peak are not sitting only with goats; they are protecting the peak with arms. The exploiters who have come to power are maintaining their power with arms. So if you want to overthrow them, you have to use arms. That is not the only way. That is one of the ways. That is the inevitable way.'

'But what is the situation among revolutionaries in India to reach that goal? When you look at Nepal, it seems much simpler...'

'In Nepal, it may be a simple belief today, but it wasn't ten years ago. In India our belief is being strengthened each day. We see the class serving imperialism getting isolated day by day...'

'Isolated? Or exposed?'

'Exposed more than weakened. Today, nobody will accept government as a welfare state. Nobody.' VV claims that went out of the window years ago. 'In Nehru's time, from independence until 1964, there was an illusion of welfare state. During his daughter Indira's time there was the illusion of "*Garibi hatao*".' Even the state, he contends, is not claiming to be a welfare state any more. 'In the name of transparency, the state claims it cannot look after the welfare needs of the people.'

But how would the revolution leverage this immense toehold, I venture. There doesn't seem to be a sense of unity. There are numerous factions, all eating away at the periphery of the movement and weakening its core. Aren't we looking at the splintering of the armed movement?

'It's not true,' VV blazes for the first time in our conversation. He then cools down. 'Some southern intellectuals are also saying [that] besides a change of name there is little difference between People's War of earlier times and People's War post merger. That is also not true.'

'This unity is just two years old,' he clarifies. 'There are also various parties active in Bihar, Bengal, Delhi, Punjab and other places. That's why this talk [of disunity] is there.'

Indeed, he insists polarization will take place along other lines, with 'CPI (ML) parties' taking to parliamentary democracy, like CPI (ML) New Democracy, CPI (ML) Liberation; 'they are slowly taking the line CPI (M) did after its split with CPI in 1964'.

'Yes,' I try to lighten the mood a bit. 'Radicals in Bengal joke that the biggest obstacle they face there today is the CPI (M).'

VV laughs out loud. 'CPI (M) and Chief Minister Budhhadeb Bhattacharjee going all the way to implement the World Bank programme, like Chandrababu Naidu did earlier in Andhra, or YSR today.'

And this is the reason, VV says, why revolutionary strategy is being continually revised, refined, honed and applied after each phase of a people's movement, in each area, after each setback—like a counter-offensive by the government of Andhra Pradesh even as we speak. It's the Andhra tradition, as it were. From 1977 to 1985, radicals who went underground during the Emergency and even earlier meticulously surveyed the 'revolutionary situation', particularly in the Telengana region, following the example of the Hunan Survey that Mao had undertaken.

Such surveys have become the hallmark of India's post-Naxalbari radical Left. 'Reports from the Flaming Fields of Bihar', edited by CPI (ML) Liberation guru Vinod Mishra and brought out in the late 1980s, for instance, is a classic text of detailed historical and socio-cultural review, and strategy for unifying the farmers and workers of Bihar. A series of People's War Group documents, including the 'Karnataka Social Conditions and Tactics' of 2001, have in detail mapped internal contradictions within the movement, and the way ahead. Every armed action is analysed for what went right and wrong in a layer that begins at the operational level and goes up to the Maoist Central Military Commission. Every stage in the penetration of ideology is analysed by state committees and, ultimately, the CPI (Maoist) Presidium.

Post-Emergency radicals in Andhra went ahead to oppose and expose Indira Gandhi's '20 Point Programme'. The intentions of this programme were noble more than 30 years ago, and remain noble today: poverty alleviation, support to farmers, welfare for labour, health and education for all, empowerment of scheduled castes, tribes and women, improvement of slums, better use of irrigation water, aforestation, food security, and so on. India's abysmal track record in all areas marked by the 20 Point Programme—even claiming bumper harvests and overflowing stocks of foodgrains means little in the face of starvation deaths—suggests that for the Maoists to convince the trodden and beaten of their cause would not have been too difficult.

Surveyors of the radical Left mapped the areas to gauge whether the programme was indeed being implemented. When they discovered it to be largely hollow, a 'go to the village' campaign began.

The Radical Students Union, Radical Youth League, the Rythu Coolie Sangham or agricultural labourers association, and the cultural wing, Jana Natya Manch—of which Gadar is ageing poster boy and icon—began to fan out into villages, form sanghams, occupy land. First with Telengana as focus, then radiating outwards. This continued practically unabated until 1985, when chief minister N.T. Rama Rao, popular actor turned populist politician on an anti-Congress, pro-Andhra identity platform, used TADA, the Terrorist and Disruptive Activities (Prevention) Act, 1987 to clamp down on all left-wing cultural programmes, songs and meetings. The radical Left, expectedly, pilloried this, calling NTR 'Drama Rao'—a key platform of his election campaign had been to win over the radical Left; he even called the Naxalites 'desh bhaktulu'. Patriots.

Today's movement, especially in Andhra, VV maintains, is riding on the hard work, application and adaptability learnt over 30 active years.

—

'If the state is so bent on destroying revolutionaries, why aren't people like Gadar and you in jail at this moment?' I've waited a while to ask this.

'I was released yesterday. I am on bail. I'm implicated in six cases.'

'Treason against the state?'

'*Haan*.'

'But from a human rights perspective, you do have the freedom…?'

'I have the freedom, and that's why I'm saying the state does not tolerate. When you say, "not in jail", you need to see the stages. I was an emissary for the peace talks. In October 2004, four [Andhra] ministers and four of us, including Ramakrishna'—the state secretary of People's War—'were sitting across and talking peace at the Manjira Guest House. We were treated on par with the ministers to the government, as emissaries. Maybe today I'm out [of jail], but what happens tomorrow will depend on conflict between the revolutionary movement and the state. It's not always the same relation.'

He is angry. 'Yesterday they talked with Ramakrishna. Today, as most wanted man they will kill him. It has happened before with our emissaries. Priyas was representing a CPI (ML) general secretary in the talks. He was killed in a fake encounter.'

There was also a hit on Gadar as far back as 1997. A senior police officer from Andhra told me about how a person was 'hired to neutralize Gadar'—he refused to say who had hired him. Gadar himself and several others of the movement have always suspected the police of stage-managing the attempt. 'This poor chap stood behind Gadar with a 9 mm pistol.'

'Why "poor chap"?'

'He was nervous, *na*. After all, Gadar is a major Naxal leader. This chap was shaking. His hand was shaking. He pumped some bullets into Gadar and ran off.'

Gadar survived. Doctors plucked two bullets from him. He still walks around with a third embedded in his back; it was medically too tricky to extract it.

'But you *can* talk, right?' I persist with VV, eager after a fashion to stress the Catch-22 dichotomy in India that guarantees a person to speak freely and at the same time enacts laws to put him in jail for doing precisely that.

'Okay, you can talk,' he admits. 'I even went to Orissa. I talked to the chief minister of Orissa, Naveen Patnaik. In fact, when peace talks were going on here, he too was interested to have talks, so he invited me.' That was in September 2004, more like exploratory dialogue, ahead of the structured peace talks in Andhra.

'I talked to him for two hours. I put forward a proposal, that you bring a law like 1970 in Andhra, giving guarantee to adivasis for right to land'—VV recounts the 1970 Act without a trace of irony—'don't implicate adivasis in any cases, and implement land reforms in adivasi areas. But of course he didn't do that.' Among other things, Patnaik insisted that rebels should not set any conditions for talks. To nobody's surprise, nothing happened.

In Andhra Pradesh, though, the talks went through a proper cycle, even if the ultimate outcome—failure—was to many of little surprise, seeing in 2004 a reprise of a similar attempt in 2002, when Naidu was chief minister.

In June 2004, the state government announced a three-month ceasefire, just over a month after YSR assumed office. The word had already gone out to security forces to go easy, halt operations against the Naxals. The ceasefire was extended as peace talks began in Hyderabad on 15 October. By then, the merger of the People's War with MCCI to form CPI (Maoist) had already been announced to the media—fait accompli since 21 September, and a result of on-again off-again discussions between the two major groups since 1992, an indication of how far back rebel leaders had foreseen a need for revolutionary merger and consolidation. The announcement was widely interpreted both as pressure on the government during talks and an indication that this unified rebel group had no intention whatever of seeing the talks through, that playing along with the government's peace overture was merely a ploy to regroup, consolidate gains, use some months of peace to dig deeper and spread further.

As it happened, talks broke down on 18 October over a wide range of disagreements, primary among these the withdrawal of criminal cases against those overground and underground, armed as well as sympathizers, and no state harassment in any form. The Maoists, of course, wouldn't lay down arms.

An uneasy peace continued in Andhra even as Maoist operations were being undertaken in Bihar, Jharkhand and Chhattisgarh. Other states, meanwhile, were hitting back at the Maoists in any way they could.

Gradually, 'peace' began to unravel, quite publicly. YSR announced in mid-December, quoting intelligence reports, that 'several roads had been extensively mined'. On 17 January 2005, CPI Maoists' Ramakrishna and CPI (ML) Janashakti's state secretary Amar announced they saw no point in going ahead with talks. On 20 January, Director General of Police Swaranjit Sen revealed, in continuation of YSR's statement, that nearly two tonnes of explosives had been planted across the state. On 1 March, the Maoists in Andhra killed six people, in apparent retribution for collaborating with the authorities against them. By August, it was all over. Andhra banned all Maoist organizations. And VV, along with others, was in jail.

—

It's a while after failed talks now. In places, the Maoists are on the ascendant and elsewhere, as in Andhra, on the defensive. As VV and I chat, Nepal's Maoists and the establishment are heading for talks to discuss assimilation of the Maoists into society, and into government. So I persist with the ideologue-negotiator. 'What would now bring the revolutionary front and the government, whether in states or centre, to the negotiating table?'

'The first thing is to declare ceasefire,' VV says. 'You need to create congenial atmosphere for talks. Then other things will develop.'

For that to happen, and for real progress to come about, he insists, three conditions would need to be met.

'One is the restoration of democratic rights.' That is, right to speech, right of association. No illegal arrests, no 'encounter killings', no 'missing' cases or disappearances.

The second, he says, is land reforms, and it would be a prerequisite for negotiations anywhere. This demand is also the most explosive and contentious in a grossly inequitable but growing economy like India. It has formed the basis of all major left-wing armed movements, Tebhaga and Telengana onwards. It involves taking 'surplus' land, holdings of big landlords, and wasteland, and distributing it among the landless—land to the tiller. This has always been fair game for demand and distortion. And for a change, the Maoists and the Marxists have been on the same side, protesting both inequity and the wildly fluctuating figures of exactly how much land is, as it were, up for grabs.

In 1967, Naxalbari Year, a government committee—the Mahalanobis Committee—was tasked with finding out the extent of surplus land available in India for distribution on the basis of a maximum of 20 acres per family. The answer: 63 million acres. But when Parliament was informed by the government in 1970, reveals the 28 August 2005 issue of *People's Democracy*, a weekly published by CPI (Marxist), it claimed that 43 million acres could be 'made available'. This dropped further in 1971–2, when a National Sample Survey put the figure at 12.2 million acres. 'The official estimates of land distributed, as informed by the government in Parliament last year [2004],' says *People's Democracry*, 'shows that out of the original estimate of surplus land of 63 million acres only around 7 million acres was declared surplus, of which just 5.4 million was [ever] distributed.' The reason: 'Many States adopted land reform legislations. However, the powerful lobby of landlords and their representatives in different governments has ensured that the laws enacted by the States remain on paper.' It claimed that while only 1.6 per cent of total landholders occupy approximately 17.3 per cent of the total 'operated area', nearly 60 per cent of landholders together operate only 15.1 per cent of it.

That land redistribution can be done, and makes a difference, is best—perhaps only—seen in West Bengal. It has over the years declared over 1.3 million acres as surplus, and distributed over a million acres. This is seen as a key reason—besides allegations of political intimidation during various elections—that has kept the CPI (M)-led Left Front government overwhelmingly in power since 1977.

'We believe there is an estimated one crore [10 million] acres of surplus land in the hands of landlords, the state and Indian and multinational companies in Andhra,' insists VV. The state government, during peace talks, threw at the Maoist team figures of between two and three million acres of surplus land, though official records show much less than a million. 'We said, You don't have to take our word for it, set up a commission with your experts. They formed a six-member committee, but nothing happened—it is only on paper. I think they have shown distribution of three lakh acres and that also wasn't the real picture.'

The third condition for negotiations, says VV, is self-reliance. 'The whole World Bank development programme.' Just junk it, he says.

'And WTO?' I suggest. 'Calibrate the approach...?'

'*Not* calibrate. Come out of WTO. That would be the ultimate demand.'

The Maoists want a lot of things—like prohibition, for instance—many forced by inequity, and many by plain dogma. It doesn't always work in a declared free nation. I can't help thinking why the Maoists in India assume that people will protest against the state but they won't against rigid Maoism if ever that becomes the state. The Salwa Judum, for all its ills, took root in intimidation and control by the Maoists. In dirt-poor Adilabad district in northern Andhra, several tribals have opted for intimidation by the state over intimidation by the Maoists. A Gond tribal dalam commander even walked off to the police with three colleagues, claiming the local Maoist hierarchy had begun to discriminate against tribals, keeping them away from planning and other 'important' roles, and that things were better under a former tribal commander.

If cracks and corruption can appear in the establishment, they can appear in the anti-establishment.

What would it be like if ever revolution were to succeed in India, enough to impose its imprint beyond tribal and caste-roiled areas? Most probably, instant justice, dogmatic and Puritanical life, Soviet-style post-revolutionary rot, vast May Day parades.

Perhaps even brutal China-style state control and a repeat of the Cultural Revolution of Mao himself, that ended up killing and damning millions of unbelievers. It is 40 years since the Cultural Revolution, which came close on the heels of that other great disaster, the Great Leap Forward—through which Mao collectivized China's farmers, and drove them to inefficient industry, inefficient distribution system and, helped along by three years of bad weather, massive famine. This was sought to be corrected—indeed, the path of revolution was sought to be corrected—in 1957, when Mao invited party colleagues to 'Let a Hundred Flowers Bloom', through criticism and ideas. When they did, by the thousands, Mao let loose a paranoid party cleansing on a scale rivaled only by Stalin, and eventually clamped on China the Cultural Revolution. It lasted a full decade until the death of the Great Helmsman in 1976.

In Shanghai, the symbol of China's berserk growth, new schoolbooks dismiss Chinese communism before 1979 in a sentence, and mention Mao once, in a chapter on etiquette. But repression in China continues to this day. The country's economy, which India seeks to emulate, is wracked by protest and rioting opposed to land grab by officials—seizures of land by corrupt officials to make money, and by the state to hand over to eager businesses. In November 2006, over 10,000 villagers fought with police in Sanzhou village of Guangdong province, accusing provincial and local officials of illegally seizing land and selling it off to developers from Guangdong and Hong Kong. Singur, Kalinganagar and Nandigram in full flow in Mao's homeland.

And why should anyone presume that the post-revolution Indian state won't resemble the endgame in Nepal, fragile power-sharing that craves emphatic control and emphatic peace at the same time—and fails.

From available historical evidence, a Maoist state might do little else but backslide all of India's hard-won victories despite the mire of grand corruption and the utter small-mindedness of administration.

As it is, what VV suggests is difficult. It will take nothing less than full-scale, riotous peasant and worker movements for India to even consider pulling out of WTO—an act of last resort. Land redistribution will remain a fiddle and miasma—there is simply too much at stake for the fat cats of government and business. The guarantee of rights is approached more easily, with active NGOs, courts and the Right to Information Act—unless the whole bag is declared void under some manner of draconian emergency. There are never any guarantees against that.

In hindsight, it's easy to see why talks in Andhra failed, beyond the easy reasoning that the Maoists didn't want peace in the first place. And why talks in Orissa did not move ahead. And why talks in any other state or at the national level will have little impact in the face of extreme-Left demands. The irony is that groups demanding regional identities, ethnic identities, even socio-economic identity and redress can actually be approached—as in India's northeast, as with reservations based on caste and tribe. Unlike these, pure poverty and deprivation have no strict geography. There are no demarcated boundaries for the negotiating table, just an increasing red splash, which now seeks to co-opt available leverage from any public grouse whatever.

The Maoists also gloat, pyrrhically, at a hated system without really having a viable alternative. In a way, it's like saying, 'It's a good thing all people are suffering, one day they will wake up and understand we are right.' Meanwhile, people suffer.

And so, the state will continue to attack and counterattack. So will the revolutionaries. With lesser numbers, the revolutionaries will time and again be forced to surrender, withdraw, lick wounds—possibly, be driven close to annihilation, as they have been time and again. But ever-larger numbers in Out-Land and pressure-cooker In-Land will, every now and again, tear the fabric of facile normality to force change.

There will always be extremist outfits led by leftist thought or pure anger to combat the state, looking for more crumbs and the elusive god of parity.

There is an old Chinese curse, centuries older than Mao, now made popular by speakers at power seminars around the world and, these days, in India too: May you live in interesting times.

24

As India's economic growth gathers great pace, it looks like the times will only get more interesting. For their part, the Maoists are willing to wait for as long as it takes. Meanwhile, they will diligently blueprint master plans, and every now and then, update them for tactical application, try and move ever inward from rural areas of operation. As they mention in the Urban Perspective Plan: 'As Com. Mao says, "the final objective of the revolution is the capture of the cities, the enemy's main bases", and this objective cannot be achieved without adequate work in the cities.'

There is no ambiguity here. And the Maoists are not remotely in a state of denial about the movement's current level of play in urban areas. 'The cities and big industrial centres are the strongholds of reaction where the enemy is the most powerful,' the document flatly admits. 'In these places the police, army, other state organs, and other forces of counter-revolution are concentrated and are in a dominant position from which they can suppress the people's forces. At the same time our Party's work and organization is extremely weak [in the cities] and generally cannot achieve a dominant position till the final stages of the people's war. It is this objective reality which determines our policy towards work in the urban areas.

'In such a situation, where the enemy is much stronger, we cannot have a short-term approach of direct confrontation in order to achieve "quick results". Rather, we should have a long-term approach. The task of the Party is to win over the masses, including the vast majority of the workers, and to build up the enormous strength of the working class in preparation for the decisive struggle in the future. Now is not the time for this final struggle between the revolution and counter-revolution...our policy should be one of protecting, preserving, consolidating and expanding the Party forces, while mobilizing and preparing the broad urban masses...'

It lists three 'main objectives' of work in cities and towns: 'Mobilize and organize the basic masses and build the Party on that basis'; build an 'united front' of workers and the disaffected against 'repression', 'Hindu fascism' and 'globalization'; and undertake 'military tasks' that are 'complementary to the rural struggle' performed by 'PGA and PLA in the countryside'. These, the document chillingly notes, 'involve...infiltration of enemy ranks, organizing, in key industries, sabotage actions in coordination with the rural armed struggle, [and] logistical support, etc.'

But the primary objective is the first, without which points two and three would not work.

For this, the plan lists three kinds of mass organizations. 'Secret revolutionary mass organizations, open and semi-open revolutionary mass organizations, and open legal mass organizations, which are not directly linked to the Party.' It adds: 'Urban work within the third type of organizations can further be subdivided into three broad categories: a) fractional work, b) party-formed cover organizations, and c) legal democratic organizations.' All activities, current and future, are minutely detailed (*See Appendix*) and constructed around the superstructure of all of India's major metropolitan areas.

The application of thought, the sheer thoroughness of it, is impressive. These aren't thugs planning, whatever police officials might claim in their spin. The planning is done by the lucid and the educated, and without a hint of emotion or naïveté—if at all, that belongs to the old days, between 40 and 20 years ago.

—

In the 'old' days, some Naxal leaders, when captured, were known to play a civilized game of bridge with their captor police officers—'class enemies' separated by little except which side of the fence they were currently on. Nishit Bhattacharya, Azijul Haque, Romen Saha, all intellectuals, had formed the underground CPI (ML) Second Central Committee in the late 1970s, breaking away from yet another post-Charu Mazumdar breakaway, CPI (ML) Mahadev Mukherjee. One of them was arrested twice and locked up in Calcutta's Presidency Jail, in the 1960s and then in the 1970s, but he escaped both times. Each time that he was arrested, he gave as his father's name that of his physics teacher at university, Professor Prasanta Chandra Mahalanobis—who later helped craft India's five-year development plan format—and his address as C.N. Roy Road. In the mid-1980s, he was tracked to Siwan in Bihar, and arrested again by his old captors—because he had used Mahalonobis's name yet again, this time as an alias because he had gone underground. It wasn't the cleverest thing to do, and of course he knew it. Asked why he had done it, then, the answer was childish in simplicity: 'I like to honour my professor.'

Another leader, arrested after an operation that he had masterminded, 'broke' in jail after 48 hours of interrogation. At first, he would refuse to mention his place of shelter in Calcutta, but all of a sudden he gave in, and mentioned that he used to stay in the government quarters at Satragachhi, across the Hooghly river from Calcutta, at the home of an engineer from All India Radio. When the police officer asked him why he was giving them this information, the leader replied that he had read newspapers for the preceding fortnight, and these had mentioned his capture. As a rule, his party followed the practice that if a central committee member was arrested they would abandon the use of any shelter he had ever used. A fortnight would have been enough time for word of his arrest to have reached the party.

Evidently not. Lack of information and lack of discipline led to eight senior members of the party being arrested from the apartment over several weeks. Police had moved in, laid a trap. As one member of the group walked in, he would be incapacitated, spirited away at night, and the trap set again. When one of them later accosted the bridge player in jail who had directed the police to the hideout, he would say, 'You broke the rule, you suffer.'

Gentlemen-Naxals, out to set the world right for others.

That was then. The Naxals of today aren't known to play bridge. Sabita Kumari, for instance, does not. She doesn't endlessly argue over what intellectual approach in the movement is the right one. She doesn't need others to set her world right; she is quite capable of giving it a shot on her own.

Marked for ascendancy in the Bihar-West Bengal area, the 22-year-old is now a Maoist poster girl—masked, carrying an AK-47—after her statement to *The Week* magazine in the summer of 2006. She had killed five people, she said. And: 'I will murder at least a hundred if I remain alive for another ten years.'

This graduate from a small college in remote Daltonganj, Jharkhand, was expected to become a teacher—at least this is what her parents expected. That was, as Sabita tells it, before moneylenders killed her two younger sisters as the family resisted attempts to take over their land in Pabira village. When Sabita went to complain to the police, she was asked to provide sex.

In November 2005, her squad broke into Jehanabad Jail to free hundreds of colleagues. By November the following year, Sabita, who speaks a smattering of English in addition to Hindi and Bengali, would be seasoned enough to lead her own pre-dawn raid in Belpahari, the Maoist touchstone in the West Medinipur district of Bengal. It was to stall a road project begun under the Prime Minister's Gram Sadak Yojana. The team burnt eight vehicles that belonged to the project—a completed project would mean better access for security forces. But this wasn't before the raiding team that largely comprised women had encircled a nearby post of the Indian Reserve Battalion, raised to lend muscle to the police and take some pressure off the CRPF. The Maoists fired at the camp for a couple of hours, yelling at troops to come out. None did.

Meanwhile, Sabita also gave orders to her colleagues to disable vehicles, asked labourers to keep away, pasted Maoist posters in nearby buildings except the three they blew up, and melted away.

Sabita's stated mission is to 'establish the rule of the people in India'.

—

On my way out of Hyderabad, the departure area of the airport is a mess of noise, serpentine check-in queues, overflowing garbage bins and harassed airline staff. It's early afternoon, and every flight out, full fare and budget, is packed. Both ADB delegates and anti-ADB protestors are headed out after 'seminaring' in Cyberabad.

They pass each other, look for their own kind. Power dressing and expensive luggage festooned with stickers of the ADB conference and frequent flyer tags mark the bankers and economists and the aid-brigade. Their enemies too are power-dressed and power-geared, in T-shirts—the ADB logo contained in a circle and a thick red line slashed through it—or handspun shirts and kurtas, jeans, tote bags. Some display frequent flyer tags, though most have only cabin baggage tags of budget airlines. But they do carry other weapons common to both species: smart laptops and mobile phones.

It's a fly-by circus.

I squeeze into a small cyber-booth after rudely tapping an anti-ADB protestor engrossed in a chat room. He tugs his goatee, glares at me and gets up. I'm anxious to see if the *People's March* website has a posting about the ADB conference, if there's any angst-ridden spew from Maoist user groups.

There's nothing from *People's March*, but I get a revolutionary quote primer from my Maoist news group.

'A people who want to win independence cannot confine themselves to ordinary methods of warfare. Mass insurrections, revolutionary warfare, guerilla detachments everywhere—such is the only way.' Frederick Engels.

Then another: 'There is no revolution without violence. Those who don't accept violence can cross out the word revolution from their dictionary.' Malcolm X.

And another, this one by General Vo Nguyen Giap, scourge of America in Vietnam, revered for his grit and strategic brilliance, and given an official red-carpet welcome by 'socialist brother' India on an official visit just a few years ago: 'Violence is the universal objective law of all thorough national liberation revolutions.'

This talk comes at a price.

I browse the *People's March* site, www.peoplesmarch.com. It's dead. I get a 'This page is unavailable...' prompt. I dial the mobile number of K. Govindan Kutty, Kochi-based editor of *People's March*. There's another prompt: 'The service to this line is temporarily unavailable.'

The security establishment had cut in.

But Kutty would switch numbers soon enough. He was back on call some months later. The *People's March* website, its server access blocked by the government—as acknowledged by the minister of state for home S.P. Jaiswal in Parliament—was back, too, on a service run by Google.

25

I can't catch the screening of *India's Moment of Truth in Jharkhand*. It's on at India International Centre, Delhi's premier snob-intellectual watering hole, at 6.30 p.m. The poster seems emphatic and attractive enough. 'The crisis of Adivasi agricultural livelihood. *Ab aur waqt nahin* [Time is running out]. Can the loss of an entire people be our gain?'

It's not that I don't want to go. It's just that I'm at the competition, India Habitat Centre, and there's a seminar on at the same time on Nepal. Two people are addressing it. Siddharth Vardarajan, deputy editor of *The Hindu* and Nepal tracker, is one. He scored recently with an interview of 'Prachanda', the Fierce One—now nearly as famous as Che and 'Chairman' Gonzalo of Peru, longtime leader of Shining Path guerillas—after he led the first extreme Left movement in this century to have subdued a country.

The second person speaking at the seminar is Hari Roka, there to present the views of Nepal's Maoists. He is an occasional writer on Nepal issues in the *Times of India*, and a PhD student of economics at Jawaharlal Nehru University. Nobody is sure how long he's been around in JNU.

This is just over a month after the king was forced to concede defeat in the face of continued people's protests and restore democracy in Nepal in late April 2006. The wires, papers and TV channels have been burning the past several weeks. It's as if May Days have broken out across the world of revolution. The Peoples War user group has emailed me crowing details of how, on 1 May, Bolivia's President Evo Morales, fresh from a visit to Fidel's Cuba, has nationalized the country's natural gas business. The Maoist Communist Party of Italy (PCM-Italy) exhorts, 'Let's go to Nepal! Let's contribute to the Nepali revolution!', and has called a meeting where Maoist colleagues from Italy, France, Turkish Kurdistan, Nepal and India will work a plan. 'Zia ur Rehman' invites me to New York to join a weeklong meeting at Columbia University to 'Build the Left, Fight the Right'.

The United We Blog web log has an update on Prachanda's ten-point 'roadmap to peace' calling for, among other things, a declaration of ceasefire, release of all political prisoners, dissolution of the old parliament and constitution, the setting up of electoral constituencies by ensuring representation of people from all classes, castes, sectors and gender, restructuring of all state structures, including the Royal Nepal Army, and holding elections to a constituent assembly under 'reliable international supervision'.

Meanwhile, a Nepali Congress legislator of the reconstituted House of Representatives, Devendra Raj Kandel, has gone to town saying the Maoists had asked him to 'donate' 1,00,000 rupees, and as he had not, he was being threatened. Madhav Nepal, general secretary of the Communist Party of Nepal (United Marxist Leninist) CPN (UML), a member of the Seven Party Alliance (SPA), has bluntly stated, 'The Maoists have been extorting money on the excuse of feeding their 20,000-man army.' And Baburam Bhattarai has asked people, especially businessmen, to be patient, to put up with such demands and extortion, till such time as the Maoist cadres were integrated into the mainstream.

And in the middle of all this action, a key development has taken place: on 18 May, King Gyanendra lost all his powers.

Through the tumultuous months that led up to the triumph of the people's movement in Nepal, the hand of India and the United States lay heavy. As the Maoist insurgency began to peak, and Gyanendra proved increasingly obtuse, the US and India began to panic about the spillover of Maoism and a possible game of Chinese chequers. When Gyanendra finally conceded defeat, the Indian media wrote copiously about how his hand had been tipped in favour of restoring the House of Representatives—in effect, signing his own warrant of ouster—after India's high commissioner to Nepal, Shiv Shankar Mukherjee, convinced the king, after having first convinced the chief of the Royal Nepal Army (RNA), that there was no other way out.

In this the Indian government had over-ridden objections from its own army and intelligence establishment, which preferred a heavy-handed king and royal army to the unknown of mainstream–Maoist partnership. It had also over-ridden objections from the United States. Through 2005 and up to the time Gyanendra caved in, the US ambassador in Kathmandu, James Moriarty had publicly urged the Seven Party Alliance to delink from the Maoists, essentially arguing that Nepal's Maoists wanted to establish a violent swathe like Khmer

Rouge did in Cambodia in the 1970s, and couldn't be taken at face value.

On 13 Febraury 2006 Ambassador Moriarty had delivered the diplomatic equivalent of calling the Maoists duplicitous liars. Referring to the stand-off between the monarchy and the Seven Party Alliance—'the two legitimate political forces'—he said, '...the Maoists will only continue to gain advantage—in the countryside, among people tired of the King–parties standoff, and among others who desperately believe, or want to believe, that the insurgents will shed their ideological stripes and join the political mainstream. Alas, wishing that something were so does not make it that way, as we learn in life.'

Then, on 3 May 2006, the US assistant secretary of state for South Asia Richard Boucher, after a meeting with Nepal's interim Prime Minister Girija Prasad Koirala, said the US would not remove the Communist Party of Nepal (Maoist) [CPN (Maoist)] from its list of terrorist organizations. 'They have to change their behaviour,' he said, and added, 'We need to work in close coordination with countries like India to move ahead with Nepal's political process and economic development.'

It appeared the US was keener on outright crushing of Maoism, while Indian officials were keener to run the risk of containment, assimilation and, therefore, the diminishing of Maoist influence. Settle Nepal, and in turn, over time, India could work to settle its own house.

The way ahead was clear much earlier. The International Crisis Group (ICG), a highly networked think tank comprising former heads of states, diplomats, lawyers and economists, had this to say in its Asia Report No. 106 of 28 November 2005, titled 'Nepal's New Alliance: The Mainstream Parties and the Maoists': 'The Maoists' statements of 2004 and 2005 have consistently stressed the desire to move forward politically. Since Indian support for a hard-line military approach had thwarted their political progress, they will welcome any change in New Delhi's thinking. As the present dialogue is the best political entry vehicle they are likely to get, they have good reason to agree and adhere to a reasonable agenda. Likewise, the present situation probably offers India its best opportunity to broker a political solution.'

The meetings that finally set up the Maoist–Seven Party Alliance matrix took place in New Delhi between 16 and 18 November 2005. The 'crucial meeting' was held on 17 November, and had only Girija Prasad Koirala and Krishna Sitaula of the Nepal Congress; CPM (UML)'s Madhav Nepal and his colleague K.P. Oli; Janamorcha's Amik Sherchan and his colleague Comrade Prakash from the party's underground wing, Unity Centre-Masal; Krishna Bahadur Mahara—one of the three future Maoist peace negotiators; and Prachanda and Baburam Bhattarai.

According to the Asia Report of ICG, 'At the table, the Maoists agreed in principle to multiparty democracy, respect for human rights (including political freedoms) and eventual disarmament, while all parties agreed to work towards a constituent assembly.' The matters of restoring parliament and what to do with the monarchy were stickier, and were deferred on account of the absence of common ground. The 12-point agreement was announced by the two sets of allies on 22 November 2005.

In public, however, both the Maoists and the Seven Party Alliance vehemently denied that meetings took place at all.

B, who had sneaked into the meetings, had a more entertaining and colourful version than the ICG's academic tone. The meetings took place in protected rooms at Vigyan Bhavan—Delhi's pre-eminent government-run convention venue—and the residential areas of Malviya Nagar and Khirkee Extension in south Delhi.

'Reps of the Seven Party Alliance, envoys of the US, UK, EU, India were there, along with chaps from Indian intell, and some others I couldn't make out,' B recounted to me. 'Of course, Prachanda and Baburam Bhattarai were there.'

B related it in his typical throwaway manner. 'The West urged Nepali parties to delink from the Maoists and go for constitutional monarchy. Madhav Nepal said, Nothing doing, we're doing a deal against the king. Indian chaps wanted the declaration to be made in Delhi, but the Maoists and the parties insisted they would announce it only in Nepal—which made sense, you know, or Nepali *janata* would think outside folk had brokered the whole thing! The West was screaming the loudest. As a last-ditch attempt to stall the deal, the Yank said, "What will you do if the RNA [Royal Nepal Army] walks in?" The Maoists played it cool. They said, "Walk in where? We have 75 per cent of the country."'

—

For all the hoopla around Nepal, the Habitat Centre seminar is thinly attended, about 50-odd people in Gulmohar Hall, a room that can take a couple of hundred. Hari Roka scowls, Siddharth Vardarajan looks quite at home at yet another seminar, and Major General (Retd) Afsar Karim, the moderator, looks around politely at the thin attendance.

As I expected, Hari makes up in bluster what the room lacks in attendance.

He thunders, after exceedingly polite and vague introductory remarks on the need for a 'new democratic model' by the general: 'I don't know why people in India keep going on about Nepal being a high-caste Hindu country and Gyanendra being the king of all Hindus.' This hit is aimed at, among others, the Hindu nationalist BJP, whose members made noises when Nepal was declared a secular nation after the 'people's coup'. 'Not Hindu, not high-caste, Nepal is full of *janjati*. Only 30 per cent are Brahmin [known in Nepal as Bahun] and Chhetri [the warrior caste]; 20 per cent are Dalits; and 30 per cent are janjati and tribals. The rest practice other religions. Seventy per cent people are BPL [below the poverty line].'

He angrily reels off more numbers.

'Over the years, one trillion [Nepali rupees] has been taken out by government officials and politicians. Fifty billion has been marked as bad debt. The finance minister has claimed a deficit of eight billion. Just recovering the sums will make Nepal liquid...

'The monarchy gave us poverty and anxiety,' Hari concludes, glowering. 'And now India wants a Marshall Plan for Nepal. We don't need intervention from outside.' He stops, breathing heavily.

Siddharth doesn't yet live in a country at such terminal crossroads. Neither is he flush with victory of a personal political battle. It allows him to be more even-toned.

'There will be necessary involvement of the Maoists at every stage,' he gently suggests. 'People tend to underestimate the role the Maoists have played in the people's movement, the pressure they have brought to bear on the monarchy these past years and especially in the past six months or so. People will make a great mistake if they underplay the role the Maoists had [as] the backbone of protests, in pressuring Gyanendra to step down, and pushing...the political parties to force the pace.

'It's a delicate phase. Things could easily slide into anarchy if the government and the Maoists are unable to come to an understanding.'

Siddharth rounds off his chat with a few quick observations. It's great that the Maoists have themselves agreed to third-party mediation, especially by the UN, which is seen by many in that country as being largely influenced by the US. If political parties don't move quickly and transparently, people are again likely to take to the streets. And, he reminds the audience—the Maoists have said they won't give up arms before attending any talks. It's a scary thought: a process on pure trust and complicity with absolutely no safeguards in place other than people not wanting another descent into chaos and civil war.

'The Maoists have all along astutely played their cards, calibrated each move,' Siddharth is frankly admiring. 'It will be interesting to see where it all heads. What will be the contours of the constituent assembly? Will the Maoists be absorbed into the RNA—now the NA [Nepal Army]? How will rebels integrate into the mainstream?'

Hari butts in angrily, springing forward in his chair, as the gathering breaks into gentle chuckle.

'Don't worry. We will do it. If we don't get any *help* from friends, we will do it. We do not need interference from anyone—India, United States, European Union…The People of Nepal are capable of taking care of themselves.' Then he cuts viciously into Indian stereotypes of the Nepali. 'They are not only Bahadurs, cooks, servants, maids and'—he swallows—'in India.'

'Bahadur' is a reference to the ubiquitous Nepali security guard at homes and offices, insultingly, or at best callously, called Bahadur without exception. The blank word in Hari's diatribe, I suspect, is 'prostitutes'. (A million Nepali citizens, of a population of nearly 27 million, are estimated to live and work in India, their earnings greater than Nepal's exports. An ADB report from 2006 estimates 2,00,000 commercial sex workers of Nepali origin in India, a quarter of them minors.)

Hari sounds a final pulpit warning, in his own way underscoring the point made earlier by Siddharth. 'Everything that is being talked about now by the political parties, everything that has become part of the people's demand, SPA's demand, was put forward first by the Maoists. The Maoists talked about this "new democracy", abolition of monarchy, formulation of a new constitution—these are all democratic demands put forward first by the Maoists.'

No contest. The Maoists did all this, as the political parties frittered away the gains of the first flush of Nepal's democracy in the early 1990s and sank into the same corrupt torpor that they had accused the monarchy of. It's a key reason why the Maoists walked out of Nepal's parliament, and took to the gun in 1996.

—

Later, we relax over drinks at the cozy bar of India Habitat Centre. It has colonial-club plush furniture, dark wood and green leather, and framed old advertisements for alcohol and good health.

'You're hoarse,' I tease Hari.

'All this talking,' he replies. 'But I can now speak freely. I have been in and out of jail for seven and a half years for my beliefs.'

'He's been giving speeches at meetings in Kathmandu all last week,' Siddharth joins in. 'Wherever I went, Hari was there. He's a big shot.'

The friendly jibe cools Hari down a bit. He smiles.

As Siddharth and Hari get into a huddle to exchange political gossip, Hari's friend Bela Malik offers an insight into another application of Nepal's workforce in India. The Maoists have begun indoctrinating Nepali workers in India, she says. Their political awareness is increasing daily, and with it a sense of empowerment. It's been going on for some time in 'the Delhi region', she says, home to several hundred thousand Nepali workers. 'My helper discusses political theory and rights with me.'

All this is, apparently, being done to prepare a ready force that can be sent into Nepal for protests and other activities if there is ever a need. Seeing my incredulity, Bela writes on a napkin the name and email address of a person tasked with keeping this programme in shape.

Siddharth and Hari return to the conversation, and I bring up the question about the future of Maoism in Nepal, about all the chatter in Maoist websites on the primacy of the movement in Nepal.

'You guys seem to be the kings of RIM these days.' I use the acronym for the Revolutionary International Movement, a loose coalition of the extreme Left all over the world that was grandiosely announced in 1984. Besides Nepal and India, the coalition includes Maoist revolutionary organizations from Bangladesh, Sri Lanka, Afghanistan and Iran.

'We will very soon move away from RIM,' Hari says softly, so quietly we almost miss it in the hubbub at the bar.

On the face of it RIM means little beyond expressing solidarity—in the same manner I had seen, during my childhood, Naxals splashing graffiti to express fellow feeling for, say,

Peru's Shining Path guerillas. But in 2006 networking has moved from messages on walls to messages on the Internet. Leftists crisscross the globe to attend meetings. Indian intelligence agencies haven't yet begun to investigate global leftists in the same manner as they probe jihadist links. These days, networking means everything from safe houses and arms supplies to safe bankers. In a limited sense, in South Asia, it can also mean participating in Maoist plenaries, as Nepal's Maoists are known to have done in the jungles of Jharkhand and Orissa. Or help with hospital facilities, share notes on explosives technology, military tactics and scores of other things.

'What about CCOMPOSA?' I ask, referring to the South Asian Maoist coalition. 'Will Prachanda and his acolytes walk away from that too?'

Hari nods.

'You guys are changing.'

Hari brushes away my surprise, and also answers my implicit query. 'The difference between us and the Indian Maoists is that we are now fighting for a new capitalism. Indian Maoists are fighting for socialism.'

In the complicated, semantically tuned world of the revolution, qualifications have already begun. It will be interesting to see where things head from here in the 'revolutionary zone' of South Asia.

—

Roughly two months later, I am sitting in Pilgrims Feed 'N' Read Restaurant & Bar in Thamel, the cult tourist district of Kathmandu made of exposed brick, narrow lanes and a mesh of telephone and cable TV wiring. 'Live for others', the menu suggests, quoting Sufi wisdom. 'The candle does not burn to illuminate itself.' Attar, a Sufi poet who the menu claims inspired Jalal-ud-din Rumi, adds his bit: 'The chain of steps determine the path, but the first step makes the path appear.' I could be reading Mao.

By the time I decide on a plate of potato fries, I see the final quote. It's from the management: 'Let us all do what we can to bring hope, peace of mind and peace on earth.'

Now that peace has broken out—somewhat—'all' could perhaps begin by clearing up the garbage outside. It is piled up high here, uncollected for several days. I have visited this area for the past 20 years, and never have I seen the spill of refuse this acute. Thamel, awash after a sudden mid-July downpour, stinks.

The state of disrepair is evident across Kathmandu, wrecked by the concert of limp administration and revolution. The city's showpiece street, Durbar Marg, that leads right to the gates of Narayanhity Palace, where Gyanendra, the king in suspended animation, lives, is a mess of cracked sidewalks. On the streets, the destitute and beggars seem greater in number. Some lie by the wall of the palace. According to estimates by human rights organizations, up to 2,00,000 people displaced by internal conflict have swarmed Kathmandu, broken inhabitants of a broken country, one that several among global media have concluded is a failed state.

In the midst of this destitution, new designs of state are visible.

The disembarkation card at Tribhuvan International, the country's only jetport, has lost the royal crest and the word 'royal'. His Majesty's Government is now Nepal Government. The ageing Boeing 757 jet parked on the apron looks curiously whitewashed. It takes a while to sink in: the livery is hastily changed from Royal Nepal Airlines to Nepal Airlines. The armoured cars and the sandbagged machine gun emplacement outside the creaky airport are gone. Security is nearly peacetime's worth, with two watchful army men with automatic rifles who form a casual roadblock. After a massive show of strength on 2 June in central Kathmandu, when several hundred thousand Maoist cadre and sympathizers filled the city's largest open-air space down the road from Narayanhity Palace, the Maoists have settled down. For all practical purposes, they have won. For better or worse, red fire has stormed the citadel, in copybook Mao—a mere ten years from start to current state of play.

As I walk to the Himalaya Hotel in Kupondole, across the Bagmati river choked with refuse, into the southern part of the city, Maoist cadre are painting up a sprawling wall adjoining the hotel with fresh red on white. '*Ne-Ka-Pa (Maobadi) Jindabad*', using the Nepali equivalent of CPN (Maoist). On an impulse, I raise a closed fist to the two, and ask in Hindi if I can borrow the brush, saying they can always paint over if I mess up. Reluctantly, one hands me the brush. I add an exclamation mark after 'Jindabad'. Long live!

We have a good laugh, shake hands, and carry on. It's the first time ever I've painted political graffiti; there's a guilty-schoolboy aspect to it.

Three months earlier, like them, I would have been beaten for sure, perhaps jailed—possibly shot at—for daring to do that. Broad daylight would have been out of the question.

Times have changed. The signs are everywhere.

It's good to see Yubaraj Ghimire hasn't changed much, except for a little less hair, and tired eyes. Former colleagues in Delhi at *India Today*, we're meeting after several years. For one of Nepal's best-known and plugged in journalists, he's unaffected. Simple cotton shirt with rolled up sleeves, slightly crumpled trousers, scuffed sandals, a notebook and cheap ballpoint pen sticking out of his shirt-pocket, modest mobile phone.

In mid-June 2001, the government jailed him for several days for publishing an opinion piece by the Maoist deputy Baburam Bhattarai which suggested that the 1 June killing of King Birendra and much of his family by the crown prince, Dipendra—who later killed himself, according to the palace version, over his parents' refusal to let him marry his beloved—was really an international conspiracy, and that Gyanendra and his cronies, thought to be harder on the Maoists than Birendra, were the direct beneficiaries. Bhattarai also wrote that the people should reject Gyanendra, and suggested the army should, too. That was in *Kantipur*, the country's largest

Nepali-language newspaper which Yubaraj edited then. He now edits *Samay*, a weekly in Nepali. It's doors are still open to all shades of opinion.

How's the king, I ask him, settling down to some weak coffee in the hotel's lobby, as UN officials, along with several NGOs, the providers of Nepal's bread-and-butter aid and expat revenues, ensure steady traffic in the lobby.

'He's very tense. But he's still trying to play. He won't give up.'

'Even for the others,' he continues, 'it's a sensitive time. Talks are on; interviews are being given for maximum impact.'

All through the previous month, Nepal's Maoists have ratcheted up the rhetoric for maximum leverage. In early June, Prime Minster G.P. Koirala's goodwill visit to India had the shadow of the Maoists over it—even moderate leftists in both Nepal and India made threatening noises in the Nepali media against Koirala's signing anything that went against the wishes of the 'people of Nepal'. From the point of view of Nepal's new work-in-progress establishment, the concern appeared justified; India had only late into the people's protests capitulated to the idea of Gyanendra's ouster. On 15 June, just a day before signing an eight-point pact with Koirala on a wide range of issues—from agreeing to draft an interim constitution to holding elections to a constituent assembly—Maoist chief Prachanda had turned on the heat. Speaking to Reuters in Pokhara, he bashed 'so-called King Gyanendra and his son Paras who [are] goons and smugglers'. 'If [the king] abdicates, then the people may accept he has room for survival,' Prachanda had continued. 'But if he does not, people will take action, and he may be executed.'

Yet, talks, too, continued and the Maoists had yet another interim deal on 16 June, after a ten-hour marathon meeting between Prachanda, Koirala and their representatives. This was the third agreement with their allies since the Maoists agreed on the anti-monarchy people's movement compact in Delhi in November 2005. This was widely seen as another crucial step towards peace and a stable Nepal.

On 17 June, India's moderate Left of the CPI (M) and CPI—sworn enemies of India's Maoists—were crowing about developments in Nepal, telling media that the concept of people's power 'through the bullet had been repudiated'. CPI general secretary A.B. Bardhan spoke of how the accord in Nepal would have 'far-reaching repercussions not only in our subcontinent, but over Marxist extremist thinking all over the world'. It was entirely consistent with the bizarre world of realpolitik. After all, the person who had soothed the ruffled feathers of Nepal's Maoists in April, as India's government scrambled to save itself the embarrassment of rooting for Gyanendra when the ground situation was blindingly clear about his imminent ouster, would be none other than a top leader of India's mainstream communists: CPI (M) Politburo member Sitaram Yechury, a friend of Prachanda's and Bhattarai's.

But Bardhan and his colleagues in the moderate Left missed—or, more likely, papered over—a crucial point while celebrating. Nepal's accord came about primarily because of the pressure the Maoists were able to bring through extensive, prolific use of armed action. If there is ever a signal to go out to the subcontinent's Maoists, it is this: nobody is going to talk to you unless you leverage enough influence. In other words: if you can, fight some more. There is another, more disturbing message, aptly demonstrated to the marginalized and poor in Nepal, India and elsewhere: if you don't commit violent acts, the state and the privileged won't give a damn about you.

The game in Nepal is hardly over. Prachanda himself hinted as much in the third week of June, when he spoke of an 'October Revolution' by Maoists if talks failed. In July, Bhattarai was even more belligerent, in comments aimed at government negotiators and global observers: 'Let us be clear. We'll never surrender our arms. We want the restructuring of the state and the army. In that restructured army our army will also be integrated.'

As Yubaraj and I talk in mid-July 2006, Maoist negotiators—Krishna Bahadur Mahara, Dev Gurung and

Dinanath Sharma—are deep in conference with counterparts in the interim government over the exact schedule for the formation of the future government and Maoist participation in it, the role of the monarchy and the rehabilitation of the Maoists' cadre. Meanwhile, the cadre, now in peacetime mode, continue to openly exercise and practice drills a mere two-hour drive east of Kathmandu, in Kamidanda, happy to pose for photographers in camouflage gear, with epaulettes with PLA (People's Liberation Army) stitched on in Devnagari script. They wear the same gear while playing soccer to unwind between drills and media photo-ops. But nobody is fooled with that soft play.

City-based cadre are fanning out, demanding money for the party and jobs for cadre from businesses across Nepal, including Kathmandu's lucrative casino industry. My friends and contacts speak of the Maoists continuing with their formulaic donations, even from farmers, teachers, government servants—usually five per cent of their salary; those with family members overseas contribute more.

Even conmen are getting into the act. The previous evening, during my stroll through Thamel, I glanced at the bit of recycled newsprint that held roasted gram I'd bought from a street vendor. It had a clever headline in Nepali outlining a sober truth: *'Maobadi ka nam-ma Khaobadi.'* It punned Mao with 'khao'—eat—to tell a story of five men who had recently posed as Maoists to pressure people for donations.

'There are a lot of concerns about the Maoists,' Yubaraj says. 'What they want—the forward path is not clear.'

'You mean, about disarming and integration? It's quite scary. How do you put 10,000 combatants and tens of thousands of militia back into society? Is everyone going to listen or will some break away and continue fighting, or turn into local warlords or thugs?'

'Exactly,' Yubaraj says. 'There are some cadre who are calling Prachanda a capitalist.'

A senior Maoist leader, Ram Bahadur Thapa, who goes by the *nom de guerre* Badal, had a row with Prachanda about negotiations with the government. When later pressed to clarify the point, he was blunt with anger: 'There is an issue of whether the Maoist leadership [should] join the government, be like UML. I will not join the government or become the President. If I do so, then I will become...a Pajero-man.' Badal admitted he had plans to rebel against the party. 'It is everyone's birthright to rebel. There will be rebellion if any party leader does injustice to the people and cadre...Every citizen should rebel against anyone betraying the nation and the people.'

Clearly, it's going to be a long, slow road to peace. And in how Nepal proceeds or falters, even fails, will evolve the script of any Maoist movement in South Asia.

I tell Yubaraj how Indian Maoists have already begun an expected ideological distancing from the Nepal movement, gone ahead and questioned the peace process.

'Yes,' says Yubaraj, he knows about that.

CPI (Maoist) spokesman 'Azad' made the Indian party's stand clear in Maoist mouthpieces, replete with revolutionary angst against his Nepali comrades. 'We think that Maoists forming a government jointly with the comprador-bourgeois feudal parties such as the reactionary Nepali Congress, revisionist CPN-UML and the other parties of the ruling classes will not really work out as they represent two diametrically opposed class interests. It is a wrong interpretation on the question of the state in Nepal to expect a possibility of peaceful transition from the CA (constituent assembly) to the NDR (New Democratic Republic).' Even some reforms, he insists, will not solve the basic problems of the people as 'you cannot smash feudalism and throw out imperialism from the soil of Nepal by utilizing the old state, whatever embellishments one might do to give it a refurbished image. Nothing short of a revolutionary upheaval of the masses can achieve the above objective.'

'You think the Indian chaps are upset they may lose a revolutionary bulwark in South Asia?' I ask Yubaraj. 'Or is it the truth, a real concern about Nepal's anti-monarchy alliance being unsustainable? After all, Indian Maoists aren't these days ideologically averse to working with various non-Maoist groups to achieve revolutionary goals.'

Yubaraj looks out at the tiny rock garden beside us, and absently taps his mobile phone.

'You know, with so much poverty and corruption in South Asia, it's very easy to spread the message of revolution and armed struggle. It's more difficult...In some ways it's easier to deal with a state of conflict, because there's a goal. Now, because that goal is achieved, you don't now what you will do...with peace.'

'Did you tell that to your Maoists?'

'I have been open about everything. When I felt the government was doing wrong I wrote about it. When I thought the Maoists were doing something wrong I wrote about that too. They didn't like it, but to be fair, they acknowledged it. Right now, quite a few things are unclear. How will the disarmament take place? How will the monitors work? Will cadre be willing to give up arms?'

There are many more issues. Land reform, a Maoist demand, will likely be tricky. Especially radical redistribution, let alone reverse distribution—return of land that the Maoist cadre have grabbed across Nepal, for reasons ranging from 'noble' communist pursuit to some villager daring to attack a Maoist or refusing to make a 'donation'. Institutions and elections too are a major point of evolution. Economic policy and gender, caste and ethnic issues are others.

This last is of great concern to Yubaraj. As part of their people's war strategy, he says, the Maoists diligently cultivated Nepal's numerous tribes, and ethnic and political interest groups, from the Newaris in the Kathmandu region to the disenfranchized Madhesis (people of Indian origin) of the terai, the southern plains that form Nepal's most densely populated but in political terms most under-represented region. Now, having achieved controlling interest in Nepal, as it were, the Maoists would need to deliver to each of these impoverished or neglected groups. Or else the danger of breakaway groups— now armed and indoctrinated in gritty protest and survival— could spark trouble.

Yubaraj could hardly have known how true his concerns would ring. Days after an interim parliament was constituted in January 2007, with CPN (Maoist) snug with 83 seats in the 330-member parliament, the same as CPN (UML) and only two less than the Nepali Congress, clashes between Maoist cadre and Madhesi protestors, mainly from the Madhesi Janadhikar Forum (MJF)—uneasy allies until then—would break out. A key issue would remain under-representation in the remaining seats of parliament, divided between other Seven Party Alliance allies and several representatives of ethnic minorities and economically weaker sections. By the end of February, nearly thirty, mostly Maoist cadre and sympathizers, would be dead, adding to the estimated 13,000 that died in the decade-long insurgency. Interim Prime Minister Koirala and Prachanda would promise redress of the issues of political under-representation. The interim government would invite MJF, the Madhesi People's Rights Forum and the Janatantrik Terai Mukti Morcha for talks.

Even that wouldn't help, as talks wouldn't get too far. On 21 March several dozen Maoists would lose their lives in clashes with supporters of MJF, and the Forum's leader Upendra Yadav would blame the Maoists for provoking attacks. A day later, an event of supreme irony would take place. A livid Prachanda would allege that royalists, Hindu extremists from India and 'other foreign powers' were behind the attacks against the Maoists. In much the same way as the establishment had earlier demanded a ban on CPN (Maoist), Prachanda would demand that MJF be banned.

There would be other embarrassments, too. There would be talk of how Belgium's secretary of state for administrative simplification, Vincent Van Quickenborne, was made to pay 'tax' to the Maoists during a visit to the Myagdi region. In March 2007, hoteliers in Kathmandu would strike and take out a procession to protest Maoist collectors beating up a hotelier upon his refusal to pay up.

After my meeting with Yubaraj, I stroll down towards Lalitpur and the bridge. The Maoists have set up a base there for trade union activities.

The place is easy to find. Take a right from the massive Maoist banner that runs across the road, and look to a Maoist flag, simple hammer and sickle on blood red, flying atop a four-storey building. People wearing Maoist badges crowd a nearby tea stall. A receptionist waves me up when I mention I'm looking for Saligram Jamarkatel, chief of the trade union wing. Small rooms stacked with posters on the way up are given over to ethnic interest groups and front organizations, such as for women, Newaris and Madhesis, each with a contact number pasted outside the room. Not a single door is closed—this is open season for interaction—but people behind the desks are either reading newspapers, listening to the radio or engaged in desultory conversation. It seems like a curious mix of people with little to do; and people who have suddenly been thrust into public positions and are getting the feel of it. It's too early in the Maoists' overground existence.

I'm invited in. 'I have read some of your articles,' Saligram Jamarkatel says in broken Hindi, apologizing that he can't speak it, or English, too well. My response in thanks is automatic: my Nepali is worse. He smiles.

I sit quietly for several minutes as he attends to two visitors seated in front of the compact trade union boss; I'm on a chair to the side. It's a cramped room, made smaller with protest posters and leaflets stacked waist-high on the floor. He juggles two mobile phones, and is both watchful and evasive when I pour out a number of queries, from concerns of extortion and hostage taking to pressuring businesses, and the future of front organizations.

I'm brought tea, but no answer or clarification. He continues to smile at me, every now and then glances at my calling card, uses his fingers like a Rolodex to flip it around.

'There is peace,' I say. 'But you still seem to be very careful.'

'You have to always be careful,' he says. 'You should go to our main office. Our people are there. You can ask them. Comrade Mahara, Comrade Sharma, Comrade Gurung.'

'They are busy in negotiations, aren't they?'

'Comrade Prachanda and Comrade Baburam Bhattarai are even more busy. We are all very busy. War is busy. Peace is busy.'

And then I'm off to the main office of the Maoists in Old Baneswor, towards the airport (the Maoists would in a few months shift to a larger address across town). The address is only a few weeks old, but my auto rickshaw driver says he knows where it is.

From the airport road at New Baneswor, we turn left to the older quarter. There's the Michael Jackson Dance Bar, yet another in Kathmandu's contribution to seedy nightlife. There's one near the Marco Polo hotel in Thamel, where I'm staying, called New Red Fire—quite far, as I could see from transvestite hangers-on outside and slim, pretty girls entering and exiting at regular intervals—from the other new red fire, Nepal's crucible of communism-capitalism. We go past Momo Mantra, another ubiquitous Kathmandu institution, turn the corner past King Stone Bar, which reeks of country liquor, and in a cul-de-sac is our destination. An incongruous chalet-style bungalow.

Dozens of people are shouting inside and outside, in preparation for a march. A mix of men and women with wood and cardboard placards, some with red banners rolled up around bamboo and wood staves. Neighbours peer curiously from windows and balconies in this middle-class neighbourhood, watching the circus. The driver of the auto rickshaw that brought me here meets a friend; after a backslapping hug and extended handshake, he disappears into the throng with the friend. The auto rickshaw is meanwhile draped in red flags.

I wade into the tumult of angry faces, made angrier by a stout lady screaming what to me is unintelligible, but it has the effect of whipping the crowd into a frenzy.

At the reception, a smiling Kogendra-ji is fielding shouted queries and physically preventing bits of the throng who want to storm into the building; a burly man is positioned at the entrance.

I locate my driver and ask him what the fuss is about, all the screaming and shouting.

'*Janjati*,' he says simply, to my query in Hindi. And then, 'Budget.'

A procession for tribal and low-caste rights, demanding more from the budget, announced the previous day, 12 July.

'*Yeh kya chahtey hain?*' What do they want?

'*Sab*,' he says. All of it.

They leave, and the shouts and sloganeering recedes as the procession winds its way through Baneswor.

The neighbourhood perches are empty. The circus is over for now.

It's easy to see why Kathmandu-based Maoist cadre are taking to the streets in minor protest. A day earlier, one of the three Maoist negotiators, Dev Gurung, had criticized the budget for 2006–7, Nepal's first under the shadow of Jan Andolan II, as 'regressive'. 'The government has continued to increase the burden of tax on the proletariat and middle-class bourgeoisie. Instead, it should have nationalized the property of the king...[and made] public the assets of the elite class and imposed progressive taxes on them.'

But Gurung is being uncharitable and dogmatic, as if making noise because he is expected to make noise as a leader of the revolution, to be seen as not giving in too easily to the machinations of former enemies. Figures tell the story. In the year of hyped renewal, expectations will always be high, and, as ever, there will be interest groups to take care of. This year, the Maoists are the most volatile interest group, with a need to be seen as doing right not just by the cadre but the nearly 80 per cent of Nepal's 27 million they claim to fight for. The army will want its own pound of flesh, so will business. And the Nepali Congress and CPN (UML), prime movers in the Seven Party Alliance, will use the budget to keep at bay the force that will certainly be their greatest counterweight: the Maoists. In the middle are caught the middle and consumer classes, and those in industry—the traditional drivers of a market economy.

The king is not paying taxes—yet. These will surely come if the Maoists are able to maintain pressure. Nor are his properties nationalized—yet. That too might come. As an indication, budgetary allocation for the Palace is reduced by 70 per cent from the previous year's figure of about 220 million Nepali rupees. The Hari Rokas of the world, as other Maoists, would be outraged; for them it means little, as no investigation has yet been ordered into the shifting of funds overseas by Nepal's royal family, and voices. But they ought to be pleased that nearly six times the Palace budget is earmarked to organize elections to the constituent assembly.

Finance Minister Ram Sharan Mahat has played a dangerous game to provide nothing at all in the budget to mainstream the Maoist army, in what is nothing but blatant chess play. 'Allocating a budget for its rehabilitation is out of the question until a formal understanding is reached with the Maoists.' It will bear pressure on the Maoists to move quicker in this bait-and-hook peace process, but it also means the Maoists' parallel economy will continue to thrive—as an army of 10,000 plus militia, need to be clothed, fed, housed and paid.

But, whether due to the influence of the Maoists or not, an impressive 43 per cent of the proposed 143.91 billion Nepali rupee budget has been allocated for education, health and drinking water, roads and electricity, agriculture and irrigation. Business and economists' lobbies may dismiss it as a 'populist' budget, but it isn't such a bad way to spread salve on the festering wounds of Nepal.

—

Evidently, my poring over papers and documents isn't the done thing at Thamel's Full Moon Bar. Patrons and waiters are beginning to stare. A band, a mix of young Nepalis and grizzled Europeans, arrives and calmly sets up for an evening of live jazz.

A waiter has had enough of my tame, low-cost tea

drinking. He comes over and suggests: 'Fat momma knock ya naked.'

Seeing my stunned expression, he explains kindly, among grins all around: 'Margarita. You like?' He points to the menu, by a guttering candle on a low table.

It costs 300 Nepali rupees. Nearly a week's income for many Nepalis. I say yes to Fat Momma. She and I will together contribute to the local economy. For that, I don't mind the joke at Full Moon Bar being on me.

A sudden breeze takes away the smell of Kathmandu. When the rot returns, I'm too busy with Fat Momma to notice. The music is nice too. In this cozy den, it's a happy, hip world, no revolution required for reconciliation. At the next table a young man in trendy haircut and clothes exchanges a cigarette and high-fives with a similarly dressed friend.

'*Jiyo*, bro,' they yell in toast.

Live, bro.

BOOK IV

'Dear Comrades,

    I am working in Jammu & Kashmir to prepare the ground for Marxism, Leninism and Mao thought. I am alone here. Therefore I need your moral support...

    Though it is very hard, but I think if I get all out support from your side I must get results here in Kashmir.

    With revolutionary greetings.

    R____ Chatterjee'

—From 'Maoist Revolution' Internet
Newsgroup,
20 August 2006

26

Gears churn out there. Attack, retreat, regroup, deal, negotiate, observe, plan—in no particular order and all at once, depending on the theatre of action, the stage of the 'revolution', the state response, the exigency.

B is quiet. I can't reach A. Hardly a whisper out of D. Maybe it's a result of reworking strategies in the shadow of Nepal. Maybe the Republic of India is beginning to reclaim land and governance it wilfully abdicated to the Maoists. Maybe factionalism is taking its toll among the Maoists.

In the shadowy world of the revolution and counter-revolution, the operative colour is more confounding gray than red.

Pressure, counter-pressure. On 11 May 2006, nervous Maharashtra police forced some tribal villagers to dismount from their bicycles and remove a roadblock on the Etapalli–Jarabandi road in Gadhchiroli. A tree had been placed across the road by the Maoists to hamper traffic and lure the police to ambush. A 25-strong team of police, including bomb disposal specialists, watched as the seven tribals, Dugga, Khabi Kullu, Chitka Potavi, Lebdu Gota, Ajit Kullur, Devaji Tarote and Maksi Kunjam, moved the roadblock and a low-intensity explosive blew up in their face. None died, but Dugga lost an eye, and the others were partially blinded or injured. The *Indian Express* later quoted Shirish Jain, Gadhchiroli's superintendent of police: 'Such operations are to be carried out by policemen entirely on their own to protect civilians. I have warned my men not to allow civilians to do it.'

On 13 May, the opposite played out in the hell zones of

Chhattisgarh. Angered by an attack by Naga Armed Police on the hamlet of Fandigua in southern Dantewada, the area's Maoists attacked a nearby Salwa Judum camp in the middle of the night. None of the Naga police near the camp, better trained and better armed, died. Four SPOs did. Foyam Kanna, Panduram Dulla, Mulki Sola, Funja Lachha. All local tribals, 18 to 28 years old.

On the same day, I was in the university town of Manipal in Karnataka, discussing the syllabus with the board of an institute of communication, when Maoists attacked an upper-caste schoolteacher across a few hill ranges. This is the heavily forested Udupi district, home to good education and Udupi town, which has birthed a sizeable population of entrepreneurs in banking and the restaurant business. The schoolteacher, Bhoja Shetty, didn't die. But I recorded the latest in a series of probing attacks—to intimidate local landlords, grab weapons from rural police outposts, destroy state-owned infrastructure. I'd heard already about Maoist graffiti and meetings among the region's landless labourers, people of lower castes and tribals.

These are the first steps in a Maoist show of strength to establish domination over an area.

—

Over a dinner of superb seer fish curry and rice at Manipal's Hotel Valley View International, I discuss Maoism in the area with some of Manipal's informed and influential. With the exception of one person, a well-known television anchor from Bihar, all dismiss it as idle fantasy. Ajay Kumar, of Star News (he would later move to *Aaj Tak*), knows only too well the reality of caste-ruination and Naxalism in his home state, and watches quietly. The Karnataka police have moved small contingents of anti-Naxal forces into the area, I tell them, and the director general of police is pleading for more funds and armoured vehicles for forest beats. The Maoists are here.

Before I can ruin dinner, Ajay Kumar diplomatically steps in and veers conversation to politics in Delhi. Everyone perks up. Talk, inevitably, turns to corruption and the compact of business and politics. 'They should be shot,' says a companion at the table, a senior functionary at Manipal, neatly slicing into the fish, suggesting a final solution for 'these crimimals and thieves'.

Middle-class India has for long been brought up on suggestion of extreme solutions in casual conversation. As a child, I frequently heard the Bengali version of the panacea for all ills ranging from corruption and rape to hoarding of subsidized food grain by traders and scalping of railway tickets: *'Shob kota-kay ekta dewaler shamney dar koriye guli diye udiye deoa uchit'*—All of them should be lined up in front of a wall and sprayed with bullets. At university in Delhi, the cry was more to the point: 'Shoot the bastards.' At clubs, a more politely structured 'The bastards should be shot.' On the streets, in evocative Hindi: *'Sab saalon ko uda do'*—Blow up all the shits. In one of the biggest movie hits of 2006, *Rang de Basanti*, a bunch of trendy youngsters disgusted with official apathy over the death of their fighter pilot friend kill the defence minister of India. In the comparatively downmarket *Betaab Badshah*, which I would watch later, in a bus from Hazaribagh to Ranchi in February 2007, the hero kills the corrupt chief minister of his state.

The Maoists—I say to the senior functionary in Manipal, perhaps intemperately, in the nature of such conversations— are actually practicing what we preach daily without a second thought. An elderly journalist who is also chairperson of a major media agency turns to me and gently asks, 'Are you a communist?'

I ignore Ajay Kumar's warning glance. 'No, sir, a journalist,' I reply, as politely.

I soon excuse myself, pleading tiredness. I don't carry a brief for the Maoists, I tell myself. If the Maoists wish to convince these well-meaning, cultured gentlemen, it's up to them.

The Maoists have waited a long time in this part of Karnataka, prepared meticulously, worked the lay of the land, the economy, and society.

In mid-2002, the Karnataka State Committee of CPI (ML) People's War, two years before its merger with the MCCI, prepared a survey titled *Social Conditions and Tactics—A report based on preliminary social investigation conducted by survey teams during August–October 2001 in the Perspective Area*. The 'Perspective Area' being Central Malnad, including parts of Udupi district, and the adjacent districts of Shimoga, Chikmagalur and Dakshin Kannad. In both Maoist and security circles this report has come to be called 'Karnataka SOCOTAC'. Liberally quoting Mao, Stalin and the movement's own *Strategy and Tactics* document—with a Government of India satellite map showing forest areas and a district map thrown in for easy reference—it offers remarkable insight into the mind of the Maoist, the detailed planning and argumentative conviction and old-fashioned spin-doctoring that goes into developing a revolutionary base.

Malnad is the forested ghat region of Karnataka comprising ten districts, from Belgaum in the northwest, across Goa, to Chamarajnagar in the south. It includes nearly half of Karnataka's forest area, nearly all of its iron ore and manganese riches, major concentrations of areca—betel nut—cardamom and other spices, and all of its famous coffee. It also has a high tribal population and, alongside, extreme caste prejudice— untouchability led to many being unable to take advantage of local development programmes, as it entailed working with those of relatively higher castes. The Maoist survey records a fairly large percentage of landless and poor peasantry and complete domination by the upper castes—Brahmins and Vokkaligas, among others. The landless received daily wages as much as 15 per cent less than the norm. In places, the survey recorded between 10 and 32 per cent of land without title deeds and consequent 'encroachment' by wealthier peasantry and landlords.

The survey, which refers to particular villages only with designated alphabets to maintain secrecy, recorded high indebtedness, racked by an average of 30 per cent a year rate of interest from private moneylenders. As many such moneylenders were also landlords—comprising four per cent of the population but owning a quarter of all land—inability to repay led in numerous cases to a member of the family, usually a youngster, being bonded as farm or plantation labour. It quotes one 'area commander' reporting the instance of a particular landlord in a coffee-growing region: 'Landlords keep labourers in debt bondage. Anyone who decides to leave the big landlord of T and go for work elsewhere must first repay his loan. The landlord does not provide loans to labourers who do not work for him.' Few break the cycle.

Moving to big-picture mode, the survey tracked the fall in prices of produce in some areas. Compared to prices in 2000, prices in 2001 are shown as between 27 and 60 per cent less for several categories of areca; pepper and cardamom at half the previous year's prices; and coffee, nearly 70 per cent less. Expectedly, daily wages too dropped, from 25 to over 40 per cent. All this is the overall impact of 'semi-feudalism', free-market pricing, lowering of import restrictions courtesy of WTO, and in some cases—like coffee—overproduction. Essentially, the squeeze is passed on to labourers.

In great detail, the survey notes which Brahmin landlord is 'known to break two whipping sticks on the backs of his tenants', where a landlord has a link with Mumbai's timber mafia, where Jain landlords have evicted tenants unable to pay rent, and which temples in the region have links with the high and mighty of India—a pointer to 'bourgeois' indemnity. And there is, too, a list of weapons in the surveyed villages: all the easier to know where to snatch weapons from to use against declared 'exploiters'.

And so, the survey recommends, the party must be built in the area by 'strictly secret methods'. These should include secret front organizations of women, coolies and Adivasis. The People's Guerilla Army militias should be built as village-level clusters, in turn guided by the Local Guerilla Squad assigned to that territory—one such squad would have under its care 800 square kilometres and four squads would form an interlinked team to control 3,200 square kilometres. The survey is realistic and accepts that 'reactionary forces' of the state will inevitably combat revolutionaries, so even if a fluid state of affairs prevails, in that neither the state nor the revolutionaries have clear control, the area would be seen to be successfully established as a Guerilla Zone.

At no time, however, would such development be in isolation from urban areas:

> In addition to our legal mass work, we must, in each town where our party organization exists, take up work under new covers. These covers should not be exposed. We have to allocate adequate number of cadres in Blr [Bangalore], Smg [Shimoga] and in towns around the PA [Perspective Area] to work among the working class.
>
> We must build organizations for the slum youth and organizations among various professionals and employees.

As in other such Maoist reports, there is no hint of any organizational self-doubt that the urban poor and dispossessed will unite and light a conflagration.

Between May and July, incidents of Maoists snatching weapons from guards of the Forest Department, especially in the Malnad area, too would increase. Shootouts between Maoists and police would take place. Maoist activities would spread a little closer to the bridge territory in the already Naxal-affected, drought-prone districts of Bellary and Raichur, not too far from the Telengana region of Andhra Pradesh.

Officials would also track Maoist intent further to the north in new areas in Vidarbha, the easternmost region of Maharashtra. If they looked at revolutionary material in their archives, surely this line would show up in sharp relief: 'The party of the proletariat...relies on the peasantry—the main force of the revolution—makes backward rural areas its main centre of work.'

—

Meanwhile, in large parts of Vidarbha, India's most recognized agricultural death row, circumstance, prejudice and state apathy is conspiring to prime newer areas for Maoist propaganda and covert activity.

Large numbers of farmer suicides have also occurred in Andhra Pradesh, Kerala, Karnataka and Punjab, but the crisis has been especially acute in Vidarbha. Between June 2005 and May 2006, alone, 520 farmers in the Vidarbha region, mainly cotton farmers, committed suicide. (This figure, according to the Vidarbha Janandolan Samiti, a local NGO, was a conservative estimate; they were still waiting for confirmation of several suicides from police records and other sources. By the end of 2006, the number of farmer suicides in the region would cross 1000.) On 22 May, as Maharashtra's chief minister Vilasrao Deshmukh made a long-delayed visit to the region, three more farmers killed themselves with pesticide on account of indebtedness to private moneylenders, crop failure and lower prices of produce.

Later in the week, P. Sainath, who published the path-breaking *Everyboy Loves a Good Drought* on India's scam-economy as told from the country's poorer districts, had yet another major article on Vidarbha's woes in *The Hindu*, where he is editor of rural affairs. He wrote of the fear '*anna*', or elder brother, evokes in the region among tribals and others. Anna is the moneylender. '...Bhima Kudamate, a Gond...took Rs 10,000 from him last season. "I had to return Rs 15,000 in six months." That is, interest of 100 per cent. "I sold my cotton but prices were so bad, I raised only Rs 10,000." However, anna has a home collection system, too. He grabbed all Kudamate's money and also seized his bullock cart and animals. "Now I hire a pair of bullock at Rs 1,000 a month." Yet, "we need him. What options do we have?"'

Sainath explains that anna is from Andhra Pradesh, among a tribe of moneylenders that have smoothly moved in from elsewhere in India to fill the gap left by the region's original moneylenders who run scared from the police—an act mandated by Maharashtra's deputy chief minister R.R. Patil. This bizarre instance of enforced economic Darwinism has had the same effect as the earlier crop of grassroots private moneylenders had: continued debt and brutal collection. Essentially, asserts Sainath, the state is reduced to callous, lunatic bystander.

'No less problematic is the Rs 1,075 crore [Rs 10.75 billion] "relief package" announced last year for crisis-hit cultivators,' writes Sainath. In a way, he claims, three-fourths of it was farmers' money being returned to them; the Cotton Federation, which buys all cotton in Maharashtra, would earlier deduct three per cent of the minimum support price for cotton that farmers received. It went to a corpus that leveraged loans from banks. The government had basically 'gutted the fund' to offer the relief package.

'Even though it's their own money, farmers are getting relief cheques for absurd amounts. In Koljhari, [deputy sarpanch] Tulsiram Chavan shows us one cheque that gives him "relief" to the extent of Rs 78. Others speak of cheques of Rs 5.' The reason for this, explains Sainath, is that in bad years many small farmers could not sell their cotton to the federation. They had to sell to the traders to whom they owed money. The traders then pocketed the federation's price. 'And so this year, the traders picked up the refunds meant for farmers. After all, their names were on the sale records.'

The international voluntary agency Oxfam has mapped out India's cotton suicide spiral. It began, says the report, in 1991, with the lowering of duties on cotton imports. With further liberalization and the lowering of duties to zero, import of cotton lint grew at a compounded annual rate of 75 per cent, which had the effect of slashing India's cotton prices—these went down by 55 per cent between 1996 and 2003.

Jolted by a series of suicides in 1999–2000 in Andhra Pradesh and Maharashtra, the government raised cotton import duties first to 5 per cent in 2000 and then to over 30 per cent, but it was too late. Higher input prices, shabby briefing on Bt Cotton seeds, drought—only ten per cent of the region is irrigated—and crop failure had already set in motion the deadly cycle of indebtedness.

Then, in early 2006, evidently immune to the farmer suicides, the government of Maharashtra reduced procurement prices for cotton from Rs 2,250 a quintal to Rs 1,700. A drop of over 20 per cent, not accounting for inflation. It further tipped the scale desperation's way.

Not all people driven to despair in Vidarbha kill themselves. On 19 June 2006 a farmer, Vijay Thakre, and his family beat a moneylender and his associate to death with sticks and stones in Pimpalgaon village of Akola district. For good measure, they also hacked the moneylender's body with axes. The moneylender, Danode, had loaned Rs 50,000 to Thakre after accepting in mortgage 13 acres of land that Thakre—a 'medium' farmer—owned. Thakre paid back Rs 3,00,000, six times the principal. But that wasn't enough for Danode, who took over Thakre's 13 acres under mortgage. A local politician of the Shiv Sena, Gulabrao Gawande, led a public campaign to get Thakre back his land. But Danode, confident in his own political connections, wouldn't have it.

Thakre and his family wouldn't have it either. So they did what they did. They had arrived at the 'boiling point', as Kanu Sanyal might say.

The Vidarbha region borders the Maoist-affected areas of Andhra Pradesh and Chhattisgarh. Given this, and the crisis among farmers and general backwardness, it isn't surprising that the four Maoist-affected districts of Maharashtra are in this area, including the Naxal stronghold of Gadhchiroli. In May 2006 the Maoists had given a call for a three-day shutdown to protest New Delhi's economic policies. There was talk that the Prime Minister was being pressured to visit Vidarbha, for long-overdue PR.

When the Prime Minister arrived in Vidarbha on 30 June, with the Union agriculture minister Sharad Pawar and Chief Minister Deshmukh, he listened at a neatly organized, sanitized gathering to three dozen pre-selected suicide-struck families. 'I am aware of your pain and sorrow,' he said to the farmers. Before he returned to Delhi, the Prime Minister announced a 'crisis mitigation package' of Rs 37.5 billion (3,750 crores) for six districts of the Vidarbha region, mainly for providing credit to farmers.

It would hardly prove a salve for seven farmers, who would kill themselves within five days of the Prime Minister's departure. The announced package had come too late for them; they were already more than a month behind any credit they could have used for summer sowing, or *kharif* season.

By July, the rate of suicides was quite dramatic: one farmer every five hours.

In January 2007, Chief Minister Deshmukh told a major Indian newspaper, 'Farmer suicides will be zero. This is my vision.' Perhaps he should have listened to the divisional commissioner of Amravati, Sudhir Kumar Goyal, who spoke of farmers struggling for survival in a flawed system amidst adversity, without adequate help and proper guidance. He wanted policymakers to focus on low-cost farming with micro-watershed development. 'We allocate Rs 450 billion for irrigation in 15 per cent of cultivable area and only Rs 40 billion for watershed development in 85 per cent of the [remaining] rain-fed area.'

But Chief Minister Deshmukh did not talk about these issues in his media interview. He finnessed. Maharashtra, he pointed out, accounted for only 15 per cent of the 1,00,000 farmer suicides in India in recent years.

'Did you know,' he asked, 'that in Mumbai 4,000 people commit suicide annually?'

As the Prime Minister and his advisors mulled over options to provide debt relief, by mid-July 2006 Andhra Pradesh, also a Congress-run state, had made a pitch in Delhi for a massive Rs 700 billion (70,000 crores) special package for farmers, most of the money to be spent on completing irrigation projects. It was audacious long-term thinking to pad short-term relief that the state had already asked for; 16 districts of Andhra, more than half of central and southern India's 'suicide districts', have been drought-struck for several years. Being a practical Bharat/India man, YSR also found time to discuss with

Germany's ambassador to India the possibility of Volkswagen setting up a factory in the state.

YSR eventually managed Rs 96.5 billion (9,650 crores) for agricultural relief—inclusive of interest waiver of loans to farmers and rescheduling of loans—through a special three-year relief package sanctioned by the central government. Maharashtra got Rs 38.7 billion (3,870 crores); Karnataka, Rs 26.9 billion (2,690 crores); and Kerala, Rs 7.65 billion (765 crores).

YSR did, however, lose out to Deshmukh on one count. On 29 November the board of Volkswagen signed a memorandum of understanding with the government of Maharashtra to set up a plant in Chakan, Pune, at an initial investment of Rs 24 billion. Until that happened, Volkswagen would commence rolling out its Passat model from the group company Skoda's plant in Aurangabad, just 400 kilometres northeast of Mumbai.

Simultaneously, an anti-Naxal security contingent was moved into Aurangabad, to pre-empt the rebels' expected march westward from Vidarbha.

Balanced development.

27

In mid-2006, activist Medha Patkar, fighting a losing battle against the authorities and the judiciary for a reduction in the height of the Narmada dam that would displace many more farmers and tribals, made a worrying statement in a lecture she delivered in Pune. Several organizations that had thus far believed in peaceful people's protest and due course of law, were thinking of asking for help from the Maoists, she said. 'The lobbies against which we are fighting are very strong. Hence, there is a growing feeling that we should rope in all those who are fighting for justice, including the Naxalites.'

(That happened soon enough. The People's Democratic

Front of India took formal shape by the end of June, co-opting NGOs and representatives of the Maoists, for a loosely structured people's protest network. It included Naxalite leaders from Punjab and Andhra Pradesh, and senior functionaries of 'ML' organizations. In effect, the broad front coveted in Maoist strategy documents. On 3 June 2007, Patkar would share the stage at a meeting in Kolkata with G.N. Saibaba, tagged by security agencies as a Maoist functionary, to work out a strategy for protest at Nandigram in particular and SEZs in general. Saibaba is a member of the Revolutionary Democratic Front, which helped band together the People's Democratic Front.)

The Naxals themselves, meanwhile, were lying relatively low during this period, eschewing big action—in what was clearly a period of reflection and regrouping—for exploratory stabs. They seemed content to keep things on simmer.

This included setting a huge stockpile of bidi leaves on fire in West Bengal's Birbhum district, and in the middle of June, shooting dead a local CPI (M) leader in Medinipur district. In Andhra, they blew up the house of a former Congress MLA in the Vishakhapatnam area, and killed a police constable in Mahbubnagar district. On 3 July, they bombed a police outpost in Gaya, Bihar, and on the same day shot dead an aide of Mahendra Karma in Nilwaya village of Dantewada, after holding the dreaded Jan Adalat.

The Naxals were lying low because the police and paramilitary forces were suddenly, fiercely, active. The squeeze was on. After a string of spectacular Maoist strikes and operations from late 2005 into the summer of 2006, the state was grinding into motion against the Maoists. And it was showing: after several months, the tide appeared to be turning the government's way, at least in terms of body count and holding operations. The prime-ministerial kicking of posteriors in April 2006 seemed to have prompted some sort of inter-state coordination.

On 9 June, Orissa announced its first coherent anti-Naxal carrot-and-stick policy, formally banning CPI (Maoist) and seven organizations it identified as fronts: Daman Pratirodh Manch, Revolutionary Democractic Front, Chasi Mulia Samiti, Kui Lawanga Sangh, Jana Natya Mandali—the local clone of Gadar's revolutionary troupe—Krantikari Kisan Samiti, and the Bal Sangham. A mix of Maoist worker, farmer, artiste and youth organizations. Alongside, as a carrot, it threw in a surrender and rehabilitation package beginning with Rs 10,000 upon surrender, double that if the Naxal surrendered with weapons; bank loans up to Rs 2,00,000, with a two-year interest moratorium; free medical treatment in government hospitals; even grants for building a house and for marriage. Following the example of Andhra Pradesh and Chhattisgarh, Orissa also announced that if there was a reward on a Naxal's head, it would be offered as rehabilitation payout upon his or her surrender.

Orissa also joined Chhattisgarh, Andhra Pradesh and Maharashtra in customizing its rehabilitation policy for people—mostly tribals, displaced by industry and development projects. Orissa's proposed payout was the most lavish among the states, clearly driven by its need to minimize popular protest against massive projects the government had signed, MOUs worth Rs 1,780 billion (Rs 1,78,000 crore)—with Korean steel major Posco, global steel behemoth Arcelor-Mittal and Tata Steel, among others. The steel plants and attendant iron ore mine leases promised as dealmakers—deal sweeteners—occupy vast chunks of Orissa's north and southwest portion, with tens of thousands of villagers and tribals in danger of being evicted. Then, there were power projects and townships to support these projects. Altogether, an estimated 1,31,000 acres of land for projects, and a minimum of 1,34,000 acres to expand residential areas around major towns.

NGOs and Maoist front organizations have systematically raised—and continue to raise, despite a ban—grassroots protest against these projects. In Orissa, though, they are on a relative low, despite having one of the Maoists' most feared commanders, Chalapthi, who heads the Andhra-Orissa Border zone's military commission, running operations in southern parts of the state.

Maoists would also suffer a big blow here in October 2006, when Budhni Munda, also known as Shobha, the wife of Prasad Bose aka Kishan—Maoist overseer of northern and western Orissa, Jharkhand, West Bengal and Bihar, former general secretary of MCCI, and second only to Ganapathi in the unified CPI (Maoist) hierarchy—was arrested by police near Ramjodi, near Lathikata police station. Her bodyguards were arrested along with her. The Revolutionary Democratic Front, by now widely recognized as a thinly veiled Maoist front, put out an appeal for a shutdown strike in the region and demanded her release. Neither worked.

Andhra Pradesh, for its part, had just turned up the heat and steamrolled Maoists. On 6 June, three CPI (Maoist) cadres were killed in what some newspapers termed an 'alleged encounter' with the police and teams of Greyhound personnel; among the dead was believed to be Chandu, division committee member of Srikakulam.

On 16 June, Andhra police killed a member of the State and Central Committee of CPI (Maoist), Mattam Ravikumar in the Nallamala forest area near Yerragondapalem. Ravikumar, who went by the *nom de guerre* of Sridhar and Anil, was an engineering graduate who actively took part in policymaking and propaganda. The following day, three more Maoists, including a woman leader of a platoon and a leader of a dalam were killed, also in Prakasam district. The next day, two, including a district committee member, were killed in Khammam district. The next few days were just as busy with Maoist body count. The twenty-first of June, to take a random example: two dead, including Jagadeesh, Khammam district secretary of CPI (Maoist). The group's state secretary, Madhav, called some newspapers to praise his 'martyred' comrades and accuse Chief Minister Reddy and Andhra's then chief of police, the dapper Swaranjit Sen—whom Venu calls a 'maniac'—of staging false encounters to kill Maoists instead of engaging them as soldiers of a movement.

As much as the Maoists are feared—and often reviled—for gruesome justice, the Andhra police are indeed notorious for their heavy-handed, extra-judicial style of functioning. According to the National Crime Records Bureau, in 2005 Andhra led the country with 55 custody deaths, followed by Gujarat and Maharashtra with 21 each, and Uttar Pradesh with 14. In three years, Andhra accounted for 144 out of 359 custody deaths. In most cases, while custody deaths were recorded, chargesheets were not filed, making it impossible to pursue trial. Fake 'encounter deaths' is another set of statistics, fuzzy at best; a prisoner 'killed while attempting to escape' is among the oldest, coldest, tricks in peacekeeping. Andhra Pradesh, along with several other states, has practiced it for decades. In May 1969, it earned anti-Naxal fake encounter spurs when it detained seven Naxals along with central committee member Panchatri Krishnamurthy at a small railway station, bound them to a tree and shot them dead.

After the Maoist losses in June 2006, Madhav vowed revenge. It didn't come. In a month, on 23 July, Madhav too was taken out of the equation, shot dead by police. Death in combat, according to the police; 'encounter killing' according to the Maoists. They would claim the same end for another key Maoist figure, Sudarshan, who they claimed was arrested in Bangalore in neighbouring Karnataka then brought to Andhra's Nallamala forests and 'encountered'.

Madhav and his colleagues had been beaten at their own game: networking and information sharing that had stood—and still does—the Maoists in good stead were now being applied against them. The state machinery was trying every trick in the book—and adding some—in its battle to reclaim territory. In Karimnagar, there was talk that in places the police were actively encouraging temple worship to keep the population away from the 'godless' communists. In another instance, Andhra police appealed to the secretary of the North Telengana Special Zonal Committee, Jampanna or Jingu Narasimha Reddy, who carries a reward of Rs 1.2 million, to surrender. The message was blatantly, cleverly targeted at

Maoist cadres and militia in the region: the reward money could help treat nearly 50 children with heart ailments; 250 villages could be provided with borewells.

Andhra Pradesh and Chhattisgarh exemplify greater coordination among various agencies of the state—and between one state and another. For instance, on 26 June teams of CRPF and Andhra and Chhattisgarh police destroyed seven Maoist camps in Bijapur, Chhattisgarh, killing five and driving away the rest. The fleeing Naxals left behind a dozen landlines, four pressure bombs, detonators, and about 750 kilos of rice and pulses, biscuits and other eatables—an army, any army, can't march on ideology alone.

—

As the relative success of the security forces continued into the last quarter of 2006, there was a seizure—on 8 September—that would indicate both how serious the Maoists are about their business, as well as increasing infiltration of police informers into Maoist ranks. Andhra police teams grabbed from separate raids in Mahbubnagar and Prakasam districts caches of 42 rocket-propelled grenade launchers, nearly a thousand empty rocket shells, spare parts for launchers, several dozen landmines, sticks of gelignite explosive, detonators, electronic weighing scales and live rifle ammunition. A Maoist courier in Mahbubnagar had showed up to take possession of a cache from the local office of a Chennai-based freight company, Kranthi Transport. He squealed to the police. That led to another raid in Prakasam.

Over the next two months, the Andhra and Tamil Nadu police cooperated to crack the modus and network, tracing it back from the initial find in Andhra to Ambattur, a busy industrial hub in Chennai. Investigators from Q Branch of the TN police, tasked with anti-Naxal work, recruited civilians, gave them parts of rocket launchers and shells and made them do the rounds of Ambattur, showing these to several small and medium metalworking units and asking if they could fashion similar parts. Finally, a manufacturer eyed a part and said a person called Raghu had wanted just such a design replicated. Following this break, the police traced seven units: Everest Engineering Company, Universal Cuts, Bharath Fine Engineering, Jai Tech Engineering Company, Shanthi Engineering Company, Arun Engineering Company and Dhanalakshmi Foundry. From the names, innocuous—like thousands of similar units scattered across India, some close to Maoist hubs.

In November, Raghu—or Thota Kumaraswany, also called 'Tech Madhu' in Maoist circles—who ran Bharath Fine Engineering and had been on the run since the seizures in Ambattur, came above ground in Warangal and surrendered to the Andhra police. On 4 November he appeared before media in a hurried police-managed meeting and talked about how he had trained cadre in the use of rocket launchers in the Nallamala forests, how the party had specifically given him the responsibility of developing a manufacturing network in 2004, how he was paid Rs 25 lakhs—2.5 million—for the rocket launcher project, and how Maoists in Andhra, despite the seizure of seven of their units, had upwards of 200 rocket shells with them. These rockets, Raghu said, were being tested.

Security analysts would express surprise at the level of workmanship, at how quickly a 'cottage industry'-style fabrication had taken place from the time Andhra police came across sketches and plans of rocket-propelled grenade launchers near the borders of Andhra and Orissa, which they claimed were modelled on the Russian RPG-7 and the American M-1. The intercepted launchers and shells displayed fine craftsmanship, on precision lathes, of the manual trigger, the trigger guard, the percussion cap—which fires the shell—and the shell itself.

Only a couple of months before the Ambattur raids, the subject of where the Maoists get their funds and arms had come up in a chat I had with Ajai Sahni of the Institute of Conflict Management.

'There's no problem of funding,' Ajai had said. 'Where's the problem? All the money is out there in the open—they just need to put a gun to a man's head and take it. They are taking cuts from contracts, including government contracts. They decide who gets contracts in certain areas. Contractors pay them off directly.'

'What about sourcing arms?' I asked. 'I was told they get some from Nepal, some from the LTTE.'

'Not to my knowledge,' Ajai was emphatic. 'The LTTE link has been there for a long time, but they don't really need the LTTE—and that is the danger of this movement; it's completely self-reliant. They took training from LTTE. Now they are manufacturing their own bombs. As far as weapons are concerned, a majority still comes from snatching and looting. If they loot an armoury and take 200 rifles it takes care of an entire region. And that's okay. This is guerilla war; they aren't going to confront your armies in numbers.'

The CPI (Maoist) was also manufacturing weapons, Ajai said. Besides IEDs—basic and sophisticated—sophisticated mortars, even missile launchers. 'Basic machine guns, too. In Chhattisgarh you'll see pictures of lathes in the jungles.' I had.

'They source a barrel from somewhere, stock from somewhere else, so you don't even know what they are manufacturing. I go to you and say, "*Yeh* tripod stand *banana hai, yeh* dimensions *hain...*" Machine gun stand, rocket launcher stand. They're manufacturing these things in Hyderabad and elsewhere—in any foundry area. They take the parts and put it all together in another place, a secret place.'

Several months after this conversation, there would be another impressive haul—and a surprising one—in low-key Bhopal, the capital of Madhya Pradesh, in January 2007. The assistant director general in charge of intelligence there, S.K. Raut, would reveal that the arms factory had been in operation for three years, and supplied weapons and explosives to Maoists in Chhattisgarh, Karnataka and Gujarat—the last a new frontier. An arms factory was in the pipeline, and the Bhopal factory planned to train recruits for it. Raut would say of the band of young men arrested: 'They are intelligent and well-educated, and speak English, Hindi and Telugu fluently.'

'But won't they be buying any stuff at all from Nepal, or the boys in Assam, through their Bangladesh routing?' I had persisted with Ajai. 'Surely they can't be manufacturing and looting all they need?'

'No, not from Nepal—not yet,' Ajai had said. 'But we do know that several Bangladeshi transports intended for the Maoists here in India have been seized from Assam.'

But all was not going right for the self-reliant Maoist army through much of 2006. After his surrender, Raghu, or Tech Madhu, the 34-year-old entrepreneur-Maoist, talked to the media about 'unilateral decisions' being taken by the Maoist leadership, who, he said, had lost touch with the cadre and with ground-level realities. The victories that the police and paramilitary forces were registering, almost every week, were partly due to differences within the revolutionary fold.

B had pointed to similar developments some months before this to explain a number of access roadblocks that I suddenly faced. 'In Andhra these guys [the Maoists] are completely infiltrated. They are reviewing their networks and strategy. You're an outsider. They are not even sure if you're a sympathizer, they have no guarantee about what you will write. I warned you about this.'

A contact in Hyderabad, in fact, had practically laughed at me when I requested ingress into Maoist zones in, and from, Andhra; and from anywhere possible into DK. 'Not possible here,' he had said on the phone. 'Try from Delhi. Try anywhere in the north. Not here.' Then he hung up.

I had already tried in Delhi. One senior-level contact, after a gruff phone conversation, asked me one afternoon to a designated place in R.K. Puram, a sprawling south Delhi zone of government housing. I showed up. He didn't. I dialled the number of his mobile phone. At first, a recorded message said it had been switched off. In a few hours, the message had changed: the number was no longer in service.

B would tell me later that calls from my contact's mobile had begun to be intercepted and he got wind of it before he was to meet me.

28

As the squeeze on the 'red army' was at its peak in August 2006, I returned to Chhattisgarh, the biggest—and messiest—theatre of action. My first appointment was with the bureaucrat-boss of anti-Maoism. On his turf.

It's a big name and designation, on a big nameplate: B.K.S. Ray, Additional Chief Secretary (Home), government of Chhattisgarh. When I visited in April 2006, he was busy organizing—*bandobast*, in bureaucratese—for the visit of L.K. Advani, the ageing warhorse of the BJP, on a 'yatra' to spruce up peeling image.

I remind Ray of it.

'Yes, very busy time. I'm busy now also,' Ray tells me with great courtesy over the phone. 'But you come. I will see you.'

'Thank you.'

'You work for Penguin, *na*?'

'No, no. I'm a journalist...writer...whatever...Penguin publishes me. I'm commissioned by them to work on this.'

'*Achha*, okay. I'm very busy but please come.'

Courtesy, often missing in the zone of Dantewada, is nearly overwhelming here. The security guards at the Mahanadi Gate of Mantralaya, the colonial-style building that houses government offices in the heart of Raipur, are shockingly courteous for a state under siege. The two heavily armed guards, who smoothly frisk me at the side entrance and check my small backpack, are extremely polite. I take the plebian way up to the second floor, by the staircase tucked into the far corner, although I am sorely tempted to commandeer the cavernous elevator, decorated with vines of plastic flowers, that is reserved for Chhattisgarh's chief minister and other VVIPs.

There is a wait; Ray is busy. His courteous staff offer me tea and turn a PC terminal a little my way: Sri Lanka are playing a cricket home series against South Africa.

'Sit, sit, please sit,' Ray receives me, barely looking up from a pile of files, jotting down something on a sheet of green paper, and signing letters. For several minutes I get a view of the top of his head, hair severely patted down with oil, flat around the crown and wavy on the sides. He mutters 'busy' every now and then. After five minutes or so of pen pushing, he realizes I'm still around. Either he's snowed under, or it's elaborate play-acting—possibly both.

'I'm also writing a book, you know.' Sign. Jot. Jot. Sign.

'Really? That's very nice. Non-fiction or a novel?'

'Novel, novel. You want to see?'

He hands me a printout of a chapter. It's filled with quotes and elaborations from philosopher Herbert Marcuse. At another place, one character asks of another: 'Naxalism is a failed ideology, isn't it?'

I read that aloud. 'It's still around, isn't it? So would you say that the state too has...'

'It's set in the sixties and seventies,' Ray cuts in. 'It's against Naxalism. I am proofing it now. Then I will show it to K.P.S. Gill.'

'Why don't you show it to a publisher instead?'

'After I am done, and K.P.S. Gill has seen it...So, tell me.'

I tell him.

He does a Pisda on me, launching into cause-and-effect: 'These people are taking advantage of systemic failures in development. The terrain is inhospitable. Development has not been uniform, so these Naxals exploit it. In my book I am criticizing the Naxals. I believe it is a failed system. Go ahead and protest, but like Gandhi—even like Nelson Mandela. Did he use violence? No, he stayed in jail and protested.'

He dismisses the Maoists with a flutter of his hands: 'These people are just thugs and extortionists. That's why in

Chhattisgarh you have a spontaneous popular movement against them—these tribals are fed up of the Naxals.'

'Surely they are also fed up of the state.'

'No. Naxals. Will you have some tea, coffee? Coffee? Okay.' He punches a button on his phone and orders, 'Coffee *lao*.'

He punches it again and asks for a number in Delhi. He turns to me and mutters: 'I'm very busy these days—too much. All these Naxals and other things.'

The call comes through. '*Ji*, hallo. Where are we meeting? In Home Ministry, *na*? From there only we will go for the meeting. The DG will come. Chief Secretary might also come. Okay, I will reach 30 minutes before and we will all go together.'

'You're busy,' I prod. 'Meeting about the Naxals?'

'Yes. That's the joint secretary, Internal Security. I'm flying to Delhi on the seventh.' He makes another call and asks for more files.

'I'm preparing for the meeting.' He goes off at a tangent. 'Do you know Lalit Mansingh?' he asks, referring to a former foreign secretary and then India's ambassador to the United States. 'Lalit Mansingh is my brother-in-law.'

I nod politely, accepting his extended credentials.

I notice a burly man with a crew cut and moustache seated to Ray's left across the desk—in the flurry of conversation I've hardly had time to focus on him. He ignores me completely even as he looks at me. I will later find out he's the inspector general of police for Raipur.

'What about the Naxals?' I urge Ray.

'*Achha*, why are you all coming to Chhattisgarh?'

'Who?'

'Journalists and all. What's the attraction?'

You're in the heart of India, a still relatively unknown heart, I tell him. There's the romance of the jungle and tribal culture. And then there's a raging Maoist concentration, and the out-of-control Salwa Judum. You've also enacted a gag law. We journos know that all we need to do is fly down to

Raipur, drive a bit and we're in the middle of a war zone. You've asked for it.

'Have you been to the jungle?' he asks suddenly.

'Yes. In Dantewada,' I admit. He scowls.

I shuffle the pages of his manuscript and attempt rescue. 'Your style is direct.'

'Yes, very direct. I write well.' He's smiling again.

'When do you write?'

'In the night. Late at night. Early in the morning. It takes away the tension. Oof, too much work these days.' He pats down his hair.

A call comes through. 'Big meeting in Delhi,' he talks into the phone. Then he assures the tinny voice: '*Tumhara* promotion *ho jayega*. Don't worry. Dilli *se aakey* we'll formalize, okay?' He hangs up and turns to me.

'The army is holding a special meeting. We will decide some strategy about what to do now.'

'What can you do?'

'My plan is to finish them. That is what we will do in Chhattisgarh. We will finish these criminals.'

'Do you write anything besides novels?'

'I have written poetry.' In 1999 he published a book of poems called *Dream Songs and Shadows*. One poem, a fractured outpouring of dilemma, is titled 'A Bureaucrat's Armour' and talks of a 'decision-making soul' suspended 'between positive and negative' and 'reconciling the opposites like a hot-cold beverage.'

'I am also writing some poetry against Naxalism,' he tells me. He expects the department of public relations of Chhattisgarh to publish it. (The book to be cleared by Gill would in several months be published as *The Revolutionary*. The poems would still be work-in-progress.)

Ray reminds me of Rajeev Kumar, a police officer in Bokaro, Jharkhand. He scripted a radio-play called *Ek Naya Savera*, A New Dawn, that went on the air on local stations of All India Radio. The plot revolves around a few youngsters going missing from a village, and ending up dead as Naxals.

Then a bunch of villagers educate other villagers about the virtue of staying away from 'anti-social' groups. The Maoists threatened to blow up radio stations if the show continued. The police persisted with 17 half-hour episodes aired on Saturday evenings.

The phone rings. Ray takes in news of a skirmish with some Maoists and gives his blessings for search and destroy. '*Achha*, situation *hai*? Encounter *chal raha hai*? *Achha, karo karo*. You don't worry. *Sabko khatam karo*, you understand. Finish them all. You have our mandate.'

He turns to me to explain: 'That was Surguja.' The northernmost district, bordering Jharkhand, Uttar Pradesh and Madhya Pradesh.

'The SP?'

'No, no.' The large man, watchfully silent through our exchange, comes alive like a crystal ball. 'The SP of Balrampur.' He sees my surprise and smiles broadly. Ray joins him in conspiratorial grin. Balrampur made quite a bit of news in 2005, when activists took out a peaceful 'yatra' through six states demanding employment guarantee and right to work for the poor. Economist Jean Dréze was part of this pressure group to build support for the UPA government in Delhi to enact a manifesto promise: a National Employment Guarantee Act. When the roadshow arrived at Balrampur and held a meeting, they were attacked by CRPF troopers in plainclothes. Dréze and some others were hurt. The CRPF men even held a gun to the chest of the driver of their bus, asking him to move along.

Things tend to be edgy in Naxal-Land.

Another call comes in, this time on the phone to Ray's left. He drops all pretence of putting on a show. '*Kaise ho*?' He looks at me as he speaks into the phone. 'Fifteenth August is coming, *na*? We should do something. Psychologically *kuchch karna chahiye*. Do an essay competition in schools. Something like '*Vikas ya Naxalbadi hinsa*' [Progress or Naxalite Violence]—something like that...We should advertise in the newspapers and invite schoolchildren to write essays against the Naxals. We have to tackle this with psychological warfare. Don't worry about the budget. DG *ke paas* budget propaganda *ke liye rahta hai.* Provision *ho jayega.* You give me the request and I will put a note out today only.'

He hangs up, looks up, smiles. 'I have to do this. We want to develop the place, but these Naxal people are not letting us develop it. They stop people from going to these areas.'

'Nice topic,' I admit. 'Development or Naxalism. But isn't it a bit heavy for schoolchildren? What will you do if a child says nice things about Naxalism?'

He ignores me. 'I have Z-plus type security,' he says, irrelevantly. This is just a level below the Prime Minister's security. 'What to do? This is how it is.' He pats down his hair.

'Isn't the Salwa Judum out of control?' I ask gently, copying his action, patting down my hair. 'A civil rights team from Delhi was almost lynched recently in Dantewada.' Among other things, SJ cohorts, building up to a lynch mob, had accused Ramachandra Guha—the columnist and historian—who was part of the 'independent citizens' initiative', of being a Naxalite active in the area. He'd never been there before. The group—Nandini Sundar was part of it, too, along with journalist and commentator B.G. Verghese, and Harivansh, an editor of the newspaper *Prabhat Khabar*—got away by the skin of their teeth, thanks to some timely intervention by Himanshu.

'Well, I gave them a letter [of introduction and safe passage]. This Nandini Sundar met me, I gave her a letter. But still, these things can happen. People have seen their friends and family killed.'

'But what about giving people—even children—guns all of a sudden? Isn't that a recipe for disaster?'

Ray goes cold. 'It's a spontaneous people's movement.' Pats hair.

'But both movements, as you call them, are far from spontaneous. Naxalism, Salwa Judum. These are deliberate set pieces, like chess.'

'Why are you media people always like this?' I take it he means: Why can't journalists shut up, why won't they listen only to the government's point of view?

Even the state's governor, E.S.L. Narasimhan, a former director of the Intelligence Bureau in Delhi, would allude to this. 'How do we counter the propaganda machinery? Glamourization of terrorists by the media must stop,' he would say while inaugurating a conference on Naxalism in Raipur in February 2007. 'Please cooperate with us in this fight.' It was as if the governor, required to be above politics and making partisan remarks, had gone back to his old job. The state's home minister, Ram Vichar Netam, would make the same point. Mahendra Karma would remember to mention it as part of his long discourse on the merits of the Salwa Judum, before leaving in a flourish in his SUV. Chief Minister Raman Singh would say it. Former chief secretary of Chhattisgarh R.P. Bagai would say it.

In the interest of national security, the media must change.

Displaced people too must change in the interest of the nation. 'Industrialization will inevitably lead to displacement,' Narasimhan would say at the conference. 'Vested interests exploit the agony of the displaced...We need to deny Maoists [these] catchment areas.' He would end with a flourish: 'I am confident that in five years we'll be able to get on top of this problem.'

The message would go out over and over again. Everyone must 'change' and 'cooperate' for this to happen. Only two sections would be exempt: politicians and the bureaucracy.

'Why don't you negotiate?' I ask Ray.

'We keep thinking we can negotiate. But negotiate with whom? There are no faces. Whom do we talk to?'

'The Andhra boys. They negotiated before, didn't they? They have overground faces. They are freely available to talk. But do you want to talk?'

Ray stays quiet. I'm not sure if he doesn't reply because he has no answer or because he doesn't want to give me one. Perhaps tactics have changed with their new advisor.

K.P.S. Gill, I know, does not believe in negotiations—in a few weeks, he will tell me that himself. Gill lays down the law— or else. The party that initiates negotiations is seen to display weakness. In Chhattisgarh, tripwired with ego, nobody is about to back down.

And ego is just one reason why the war will go on. Among others is money. It isn't just in Jammu & Kashmir and the North-East that the economy of war has spawned millionaires. Money meant for security and appeasement of the displaced and downtrodden mysteriously disappears in Chhattisgarh, Jharkhand, Maharashtra...

For vultures, peace is limpid nonsense.

—

Down the road from Ray, near the governor's house, is where Director General of Police O.P. Rathor maintains his office. Rathor is the antithesis of Ray. Smooth, unflustered, suave. A local raja had spoken to me of him in some awe as he climbed into his modest Japanese car: 'Do you know, the DGP drives a Mercedes!'

He also likes English tobacco, and is dressed smartly for the evening, in full-sleeve shirt and slacks. He is headed to the local club, Rathor tells me. There's a meeting of the committee, and he needs to attend, as he is on it. 'But don't worry, I still have time. They can start without me. How can I help you?'

'I need to talk to you about the Naxals.'

'Naxals, is it?' He curls his upper lip in disgust. 'Bloody nuisance. There's no Marxism, Leninism or Maoism about them. When I was young I at least sensed some ideology about the Naxalites. But these chaps [now] are nothing but thugs and extortionists.'

It's what B.K.S. Ray told me. But as with Ray, I don't want to tangle with Rathor, to tell him that while he may be right about some thuggery and certainly, brutality and extortion, he's dead wrong if he thinks there's no ideological core. These 'chaps' aren't woolly-headed youngsters, but led by several clever intellectuals herding anger and hatred, their own and that of others, and they won't give up without a fight. That's enough ideology for me.

'When I was at the United Nations...' Rathor tells me.

'Really?'

'Yes,' he fixes me with a pitying look. 'I was security advisor to the secretary general till 2004.' That would explain the car, brought home on expatriate entitlement, and the studied smoothness.

'When I was at the UN, this high-ranking Chinese diplomat came up to me and asked, "What is this Maoism that you have in India?"' It is clearly rhetorical, so I stay quiet. 'You can't move in these forests without their permission. You pay a cut and you can go in. Thugs. Extortionists. We'll get them.'

Then he throws a contradictory line, and that, to me, is symptomatic of the complete confusion with regard to how exactly to deal with the Maoists' present-day mix of urban and rural, slick and rough, educated and relatively illiterate, and their new-found ability of canny adaptability. 'These people, the leaders. They are well educated. You should read the pamphlets and press releases they put out. The language and grammar is perfect. I think it must come out of JNU or something. Did you study at JNU?'

'No. But I know what you mean.'

He switches gear. 'You see, the terrain is really difficult, quite inaccessible. And they have these bloody IEDs. If they didn't have IEDs we would have got them by now.'

I remind him about his meeting at the club. He smiles, puts through a call, and tells the person at the end of the line that he won't be attending, and to go ahead and take whatever decisions are required—'I'll endorse it.' He turns to me. 'I've cancelled it. We can talk.'

'Many thanks,' I acknowledge. 'Do you think the ongoing peace process in Nepal will bring an end to links with Indian Maoists?'

'It has brought an end to nothing. I don't think, firstly, that the so-called peace process in Nepal is going to hold.'

I agree with him, but this is not the time or place to discuss it. 'Let that be for a moment. Do you see Naxalism spreading in India?'

'I don't know about spreading, but it is difficult to contain if we [the security forces] do not get full support, not just with tackling it from a security perspective, but also from the administrative aspect. And these chaps have reduced the budget. We wanted over Rs 50 crore. We have got 18 crore in the budget—and this is supposed to be the most Naxal-infested state in the country.'

'So the system is not helping?'

'Not as much as it could. I even went to Delhi and made a presentation to the cabinet secretary. I told him, "Please give us Rs 500 crore to seal the borders of Chhattisgarh and the problem will disappear." The Cabinet Secretary said he understood our problem and that we would get what we need. He gave instructions to officials to follow up—but nothing has happened. We still have only Rs 18 crore for such a large state with such a problem.'

What about the proposed raising of India Reserve Battalions mandated by the Ministry of Home Affairs, I ask. Chhattisgarh will get a couple. Isn't that going to help?

'They will help a bit. But IRBs are to be shared by all [Naxal-affected] states. We need 50 battalions here—of what use are two? This is war, and it has to be fought in a planned, concentrated manner. We need to fight the guerilla like a guerilla.'

He quotes the adopted mantra of Brigadier B.K. Ponawar, who runs the Counter Terrorism and Jungle Warfare College in Kanker, a man at home spouting a mantra of Mao—'power flows from the barrel of the gun'—and of Charu Mazumdar—'one cannot be called a revolutionary unless he has dipped his hands in the blood of a class enemy'. The brigadier, a restless whippet of a man, talks of '360-degree battlefields', how policemen need to be able to walk 40 kilometres a day without breaking sweat, fully weighed down with weapons and equipment, ready to do battle. Train in rain or shine, be trained to take 'face-to-face' firing without flinching, get lean and mean—all in six weeks of the course. He terms it a necessity to engage in 'creeping reoccupation' of territory lost to the Maoists. Kanker is where anti-Naxal forces are currently being trained.

(And such training is as far as army association has gone thus far. Minister of Defence A.K. Anthony was quite clear during celebrations for Army Day in January 2007: 'It is not the job of the army to tackle Naxalites...The Naxalite problem has to be tackled by the state police forces and paramilitary forces.' It was a text clearly scripted by the army establishment. Half of India's 1.2 million army was already engaged in handling other counter-insurgency operations, the defence minister added; it was not keen to take on more.)

'Looking at it from your point of view,' I say to Rathor, 'why aren't you exploiting the factions in the various Maoist organizations?' I am playing something at him that D had shared with me, rumours that divisions among the Maoists, at least in the Chhattisgarh-Andhra region, were deepening.

'But they are like a hydra-headed monster,' Rathor bursts out. 'You cut off one head, a few more grow. It's like a cellular structure. We have an old Naxalite here, Sanyal.' I nod. That's Narayan Sanyal aka Navin Sanyal, senior Maoist leader and ideologue arrested in 2005 and incarcerated in Raipur. 'He talks politics and theory—he talks endlessly. But when I ask him about military tactics and movement, he says he knows nothing.'

'You believe him?'

'Not at all. They are all in touch.'

'Are Nepal's Maoists and our Maoists in touch?'

'One hundred per cent.'

'So some cadre are still in touch. All this talk by Nepali Maoist leaders of breaking links is hogwash?'

'Yes, hogwash.'

Just three days later, Azad, the spokesperson for CPI (Maoist), and Satya, spokesperson for CPN (Maoist) would issue a joint statement: 'The Communist Party of Nepal

(Maoist) and the Commuist Party of India (Maoist) jointly re-assert their firm commitment to proletarian internationalism, mutual fraternal relations on the basis of MLM. All tactical questions are being adopted in the respective countries on the sole concern of the parties operating in them...It is in the interests of the reaction that Maoists divide and split continuously. It is then no wonder that a section of the media has sought to exaggerate the difference in India and Nepal. The two parties once again re-assert their firm unity in the spirit of proletarian internationalism while continuing healthy debates and discussion on issues on which we differ...'

'Where do you see the conflict in India heading?' I ask Rathor.

'It's going to increase. Escalate. Become more violent. They are throwing everything they can at us.'

Why, to better a negotiating position?

'No, because they are getting squeezed. It will get worse before it can get any better.'

29

The guard rudely flags down the auto rickshaw I'm in at the gates of Rajkumar College, a private boarding school in the outskirts of Raipur set up in colonial times to educate the region's princes. S, a friend from my schooldays, now a contractor of security fencing who senses a great killing to be made in this state under siege, mentioned that the governing council of the college was in town. 'Come say hi, as you're around,' he had urged, promising an interesting evening. 'The council is peppered with erstwhile royals from Chhattisgarh and Orissa.'

At the gate, prompted by S's brief earlier in the day, I utter the magic words. 'HH Kalahandi. HH Mayurbhanj.'

The gates swing open. 'His Highness' is still a cachet in India. The guard gives me a huge salute. Evidently impressed, the auto rickshaw driver neglects to ask for more money when I'm let off near the sprawling main building.

Their Highnesses are casually draped across chairs in the vice principal's office. S is skulking around. He introduces me.

'Ah, so you're doing a book on the Naxals?' Udit, HH Kalahandi, pipes up. 'You should come to my place. Amazingly, there is no Naxal situation in my place, but in every place surrounding Kalahandi.'

'It's amazing,' I agree. Kalahandi, tucked into Orissa's southwest, bordering Andhra Pradesh and close to Chhattisgarh, has immense tribal deprivation and frequent starvation deaths— a mid-July article in *The Week* had mentioned tribals in the region surviving for months together on mango kernel and wild roots. Parents routinely sell off children to buy some food for themselves and possibly a less wretched future for the children. In places, the National Rural Employment Guarantee Scheme provides employment for just 15 days to a person in a year, against the policy's stipulated 100 workdays. In Chimrang village, literacy is zero. In Kachilekha village, officials hushed up 25 starvation deaths in 2005. In the absence of healthcare, midwives cut umbilical cords with sharpened stone. Two lakh people a year from the region migrate seasonally in search of jobs. According to the article in *The Week*, approximately Rs 7,000 crore—70 billion—has been pumped into the region over the last 20 years and successive governments have initiated several development schemes to insignificant result.

In 1943, Kalahandi sent rice to aid Bengal's famine-struck. A 1954 survey by the Planning Commission found that people received, on a very healthy average, 282 days of employment in a year. Yet in 50 years the region plummeted to among the poorest in India. There are an estimated 1,00,000 families living on less than Rs 250 per month—a little over eight rupees a day. If families that have earnings of less than Rs 500 and less than Rs 1000 a month are included, the numbers add up to half the population of Kalahandi.

The state government claims a staggering Rs 2,000 billion

(2,00,000 crore) will be injected into the area comprising Kalahandi and similarly backward districts of Bolangir and Koraput over the next several years, primarily on account of 46 projects related to metals and mining—South Korea's Posco, Arcelor-Mittal and Tata among them. Today, in the face of fear of safety, public protests against destruction of the environment, it's just pie-in-the-sky talk.

Meanwhile, Maoist front organizations are already active, and the simmering place is being primed to explode.

But it seems rude to remind the former ruler of Kalahandi of it. He's had a busy day of meetings, there's a dinner to attend—to which I'm invited. It wouldn't do to be rude to my hosts.

'Is it true what I've heard?' Udit, HH Kalahandi, asks. 'Is the Salwa Judum really a grouping of traders of the region who have teamed up against the Naxals?'

I've heard this too, I tell him, and it appears logical. The Maoists even accuse some of the country's biggest business houses of actively encouraging and funding the Salwa Judum to further their interests in establishing captive mines to feed their aluminium and steel plants in Chhattisgarh. But there's no proof.

'Ah,' HH Kalahandi leans back in the deep chair, fingering his moustache and flicking the top button of his embroidered kurta. 'So my information isn't wrong.'

'In this war everything is right and wrong.'

Before I get morbid S smoothly intervenes with 'And this is HH Mayurbhanj.'

'Just call me Praveen,' HH says genially.

'He's related to the king of Nepal.' S adds. 'Gyanendra.'

'Yeah, I heard. How's the king?' I inquire of Praveen. 'Low?'

'Yes, of course, a bit low.'

Newspapers in Nepal had been splashing facts and gossip about the king: that he had taken to late-night online gambling to beat depression and insomnia. Wine and caviar consignments—along with choice dog food for the palace kennel—were stuck at customs warehouses in Kathmandu as royals no longer enjoyed immunity to import duties. Princess Prerana, Gyanendra's daughter, was getting the wrong end of the stick—the fist—from her commoner husband Raj Bahadur Singh. Her brother, Crown Prince Paras, had taken to lighting into his wife, Princess Himani.

'Who wouldn't be low?' Praveen continues. 'What he's going through now the royals in India went through more than 50 years ago.'

'Prachanda is really flying now, isn't he?' I ask Praveen.

'Hmm.' He's non-committal.

'The king won't give up, will he?'

'Hmm.'

'Well, Prachanda has good friends in India. He's hung around in India long enough during the revolution, in north Bengal, and around Delhi. Malviya Nagar, Noida...' I start to reel off some neighbourhoods in and near the capital.

'And Greater Kailash, where he...' Praveen giggles.

'Come,' says S, cutting into gossip. 'Let's get a drink.' The royals and we retire to the guest house, where a bunch of other royals, greater and lesser, are gathered, drinking cheap whisky and trading loud jokes.

Seeing my expression, S the diplomat drags me to a backroom along with Udit and introduces me to HH Surguja, a peer of Udit's and Praveen's.

'He's an old Congressman,' Udit allows. 'Doesn't drink. A Gandhian.' The buzz is that he's close to Mahendra Karma, Salwa Judum's visionary and hatchet man.

'So you're in the middle of it?' I ask the tall, gaunt, white-haired man dressed in a khadi kurta and pyjamas 'Surguja is a hot zone, isn't it?' It's just across the forested Daltonganj area in Jharkhand.

'Yes,' says T.S. Singh Deo, also called 'Baba Sahib' by his 'subjects'. He steeples his long fingers and gazes at me through thick glasses. 'There is trouble there.'

'Have they ever directly threatened you?'

'No.' He then launches into a long discourse on the

politics of feudalism—a point where Udit gruffly excuses himself and leaves with a promise to send in a supply of good whisky. 'There were so many states earlier. Now we have a democracy. I believe democracy is the best way ahead for India. Earlier you had a benevolent dictatorship or paternalistic system, now you have democracy.'

'So why is there Naxalism?'

'Because there are gaps.'

The whisky arrives then. I take a glass still dewy from a wash, and raise my eyebrows at him.

He laughs. 'My needs are simple.' He signs a payment order for fencing work at the school and tells S the cheque will be ready the following day. S looks pleased and leaves with entreaties that I should talk to everybody I know on the Maoist trail about his company.

Seeing my look, HH Surguja smiles and shrugs. We settle into companionable silence. The tiny guest room has peeling paint, a noisy air conditioner, a rickety table. A small suitcase is placed in a corner, some articles of clothing and personal care neatly placed on a chair. I politely sip whisky; he politely sips water.

'The Naxals are very systematic, you know,' he resumes suddenly. 'They make plans; they target. They will first just arrive—no arms or anything. Some years ago I got reports from villagers that some people were asking questions. Who does what, what are the best routes to go from X to Y...They first do a reconnaissance. Then they move in deeper. Find out who owns what. Who owns guns, who, according to them, is exploiting people.'

The same everywhere. They quietly moved into Dandakaranya over 25 years ago, learnt local dialects, began to bond with the tribals, and slowly took over territory that the government never bothered with in the first place. Much later, after the DK 'liberated zone' was up and running, they moved into the forests of Surguja.

'And then,' I suggest, 'boom!'

'No, not boom,' HH Surguja corrects me, as I sense he

will, with a laugh. 'After they pinpoint the exploiter, they give a warning. Then they watch. Then they give another warning. Then they watch.'

'Then, boom,' I try again, eager to contribute to dialogue, the whiskey emboldening my casualness with this HH who is comfortable—as the other two are—with unroyal folk like me not bowing and scraping.

'Yes,' he agrees. 'Boom.'

We lapse again into companionable silence, nodding our heads in appreciation of Maoist modus operandi.

S comes in then, along with Udit—who rustles us out with a 'Maharaj, Sudeep, are you gentlemen going to talk all evening about these Naxal chaps or are you planning to join us for dinner too? The grub's not bad. School grub, but not bad.'

It isn't. A mish-mash of Anglo-Indian and Brown Sahib: tomato soup, bread, chicken in mayonnaise, boiled vegetables, and superb caramel custard.

Kunwars, Maharajkumars, Yuvrajs and HHs float about, satiated. Taken with drink and camaraderie, singing along with the school's music teacher who's been appointed bard for the evening.

S walks up, takes me aside. 'Don't forget to tell people about this security fencing stuff. You're travelling all over, aren't you, also meeting security chaps? Do you want a brochure? Here, keep a brochure. You must put in a word with the DGP here. I should have given you a brochure before your meeting.'

The brochure shows all kinds of surveillance equipment, regular barbed wire and razor wire.

I lose my temper. 'I'm not bloody pimping for you,' I snarl. 'Go sell the damned stuff yourself. Ask the Naxals if they want some. They have camps, too. And the money.'

'Take it easy, boss,' S knows he has crossed numerous lines. 'You've just had a good dinner, no?'

'It's a fucking war out there, damn you.' I can't stop myself cursing.

'Yeah,' he agrees, dismissing my naïveté with a shrug. 'The more trouble there is, the better it is for my business.'

'Good night,' he says in farewell, as a former prince offers to reach me to my hotel, but not before smartly reversing into a car, calmly going forward into a hedge and then reversing into another car. 'Good luck.'

3 0

I finally get through to M in September after several weeks. We were initially to meet at the Cricket Club of India at his suggestion, but he got busy that day, 11 July 2006. Seven bombs went off in commuter trains, Mumbai's lifeline, at various places during rush hour. I had caught the mayhem on live television at the Cricket Club's first-floor bar-lounge, as for over an hour, choked mobile phone networks refused to accept or deliver any more calls or text messages. The explosions, apparently the work of homegrown Islamic militants supported by Pakistan's Inter Services Intelligence, left 190 dead, and 700 wounded by blast force and shrapnel.

Since 1993, when Muslim underworld kingpins triggered serial blasts across Mumbai, in retaliation for Hindu extremists tearing down the Babri mosque in Ayodhya and the subsequent anti-Muslim riots in Mumbai, the city, along with the rest of the country, had simply accepted violence as a way of life. Deny something can explode till it does.

This time I meet M in his second-floor office. It's like a tomb, cut off from the romance of granite walls, enchanting gargoyles, busy pigeons and saplings sprouting from tiled roofs: the Police Headquarter of Maharashtra is housed in a glorious nineteenth-century structure that once housed sailors. It's a short walk from the Gateway of India. To get into the building takes surprisingly less rigour for a state besieged by all manner of threats. The protocol is simple. At the 'In' gate, all you are required to do is scribble a name, a vague address, the name—even initials will do—of the person to be visited, the time of visit and some sort of signature. No ID check, no checking of bags. And I'm carrying a tape recorder, spare batteries, a mobile phone—all potential explosive devices. A wave in to the grand main reception area, where I'm tensely waved to the desk to make way for a police burra sahib making stately progress down the ornate staircase. Six or so police personnel stiffen in respect, and two in the porch come to attention and work a parade ground manoeuvre with their rifles. After a cursory query about the person I am to meet and some more vague scribbling, I'm waved in.

The room is sparsely decorated, like the lean M. It's as if he wants to travel light; he knows too much and doesn't want additional baggage. His table is piled with files, on either side of a tiny cleared workspace covered in glass. A couple of telephones and mobile phones on the desk, a shredder nearby.

'You've been busy,' I venture, trying to get back for the 45 minutes I'd had to wait as M's boss called an unscheduled meeting. 'Thanks for taking the time.'

'Yes, yes. Coffee? Okay, so tell me...Maoists...Naxalites...' M leans back. 'You know, when I was in college, they had a saying: If you're below 25 and not a leftist there must be something wrong with you. And if you're above 25 and a leftist there must be something wrong with you.'

That's a good one, I tell him. I had heard it many times before from self-deprecatory lapsed leftists from the 1960s and 1970s, and those who would shrug at their current careers as top executives, bureaucrats or editors.

'Let me tell you, I was there, you know, in Chandrapur, more than ten years ago. Between then and now they must have spent 100 crore on development in that small area. And the problem is still there. It's even worse now. Where has all the money gone? What has the money done?'

You tell me.

'Yes, yes. Nothing. The bloody money has just disappeared. What did you expect?' We sip unsweetened milky coffee. M then starts to mark Maoist geography in the districts. 'Chandrapur is partly with them. Gadhchiroli is totally with them, Bhandara, partly. Gondiya...gone.'

M is describing the four districts of the extreme eastern part of Maharashtra. The state's Human Development Report of 2002 describes the area as having large forest cover, tribal population and 'high levels of landlessness'. Census and other indicators consistently score the four districts lowest in terms of availability of pucca housing, drinking water and toilets. Illiteracy and school dropout rates are among the highest in the state.

Landlessness and low standards of living—the highest percentage of families living the below the poverty line in the state—is true also of the remaining part of the Vidarbha region—the districts of Wardha, Nagpur, Buldhana, Akola, Amravati, Washim and Yavatmal—an area the size of some European countries. The first four districts comprise the state's current Naxal belt. The second lot, with the exception of Nagpur, is now better known as the state's suicide belt—and high on the list of potential Naxal threat, according to security officials and analysts.

I bring up the reports of farmer suicides.

'A CM of Maharashtra went to these areas for the first time in 30 years,' M is livid-cold. 'What the bloody hell do you expect? You expect things to change overnight?'

Do these guys get it, I ask. Do they see what non-development and knee-jerk policies are doing? Do they see they are handing over Vidarbha to the Naxals on a platter, and the next to go will be Marathwada—the eight districts of Aurangabad, Jalna, Parbhani, Hingoli, Nanded, Osmanabad, Beed and Latur—as backward and dirt poor as the contiguous areas of Andhra Pradesh? In fact, if you look at HDR parameters, next in line will be everything north of Nashik, a short drive from Mumbai. Look at the forest cover and concentration of tribals. That forms a link with the poor tribal areas of southern Gujarat and...

'Yes, yes, I know all that,' M sounds tired. 'But who is going to tell these politicians?'

'Well, if guys like you can't bell the cat, who will?'

'Who gave you the idea politicians listen to intelligent...

intelligence people unless it has to do with their personal survival?' M carries on, without a trace of reaction to his unintended double-entendre. 'The obvious answer is to plan medium- and long-term development of these places. But they don't care, *na*? These chaps are only interested in power— have I saved my seat for another day, have I made a *koti* [crore] or not? These chaps use a simple equation. Money is there for development, but there can be no development in Naxal areas because those chaps won't let you in, so why waste all that money? Let's make some kotis. This is a rich state, no? Why to worry?'

'Are you saying the CM of this state, who's into his second stint at the job, who's seen a spurt in Naxalite violence and the greatest burst of farmer suicides in recent times, doesn't care about how all this will provide fodder to extremists of all kinds?'

'They understand Mumbai and Pune and the sugarcane belt. That's where the real money is. Finished!'

M is as close to angry as I have seen him. 'None of them give a damn about the Naxals or anything. *Arrey baba*, they don't even *understand* the problem, how will they do anything about it? You talk about Islamic terrorism, they sit up...'

'Yeah,' I agree. 'More sexy, immediate.'

'...You talk about Naxalites and they go to sleep.'

'Even the state home minister?'

'He understands. But he's weak. No spine.'

'You mean, he won't allow strong action.'

'No. He has no idea of what policing means in these areas. Our police fight with old weapons, little training in terrorism or jungle warfare, and they have no ideological drive like these chaps.'

In this, M is on the same line of agreement as Pankaj Gupta, a portly, no-nonsense senior policeman heading anti-Naxal operations in Maharashtra. Gupta has no illusions about what present-day Maoists are out to do. 'They are out to grab power. People still believe they are starry-eyed, out to correct social imbalances, socio-economic imbalances. That's one part. They have moved ahead. They have merged the underground movement with public movement. They are out to seize power.'

So, what's the solution?

M recites the now increasingly articulated anti-Naxal mantra. 'In the medium- and long-term you have to develop these areas. There is no option.'

The army is training your boys in jungle warfare and counter-terrorism, right? The same as in other Naxal-affected states?

'Yes, the first batches are now graduating and being deployed.'

Maharashtra's director general of police P.S. Pasricha had this past June announced the setting up of anti-Naxal forces on the lines of Andhra's Greyhound, for which the police had received clearance. The India Reserve police would also set up two bases in the state, in Gondiya and Aurangabad districts—the second location as clear an admission as any that the myth of Naxal threat being limited only to the state's far east, a thousand kilometres from Mumbai, now lies shattered.

'But these are small batches,' M adds. 'It will take a while to build up momentum, at least a few years. The idea is to train forces and gradually build up momentum in Maharashtra and all across the country. You will then have the ability to eliminate them totally. It's a bit long-term.'

'What about short-term solutions?'

'Kill them. Just finish them. Whatever you can.'

But the Naxals aren't about to give up. And with so much leakage, where's the guarantee medium- and long-term development solutions are going to work—instead, would the mishandling of development programmes breed more resentment against the state? And if your boys are to be better trained and deployed in the long-term, what's to guarantee the Naxalites won't increase their cadre or skills?

'They already are,' M sighs. 'When I was there, the dalams, their armed squads, had eight people. These days they have twenty. And we're supposed to be on top of the problem.

How will the problem go away if they don't develop the damn place? There are 300 armed cadre in those four districts. They are recruiting. We're giving them all the excuses to recruit. These chaps are going to spread, you watch. They will spread into other areas of Vidarbha and areas of Marathwada. And I can see it happening.'

M goes quiet; so I change tack, ask him if the Salwa Judum will work in Maharashtra and if the state is at all thinking along those lines.

'It's dangerous. It won't work,' he echoes Bengal's Majumder. 'We want nothing to do with it. We want to engage the Naxalites directly, not put people against their own kind. It gets messy. We're fighting a war, and it's a dirty war, but there are limits. You can't do something to alienate people and create more problems.' M goes quiet again, and starts to fidget with his mobile phone.

A few minutes more, I request him: we'll carry on with the conversation later. Can I meet some surrendered Naxalites in Maharashtra?

'It's all bullshit,' M explodes, which for him is blazing eyes and cold tone. 'You think you can buy all these chaps off? Why should they surrender and where will they live? In the same place, where the government won't care? And will their former comrades let them live?'

He sees my raised eyebrows. 'There are a few here and there, but the numbers are all bullshit. The state gets and spends so much money to fight Naxalites—some numbers need to be shown, that's all.'

I would be reminded of M's outburst in January 2007, when Chief Minister Raman Singh would be accused of doing exactly this in Chhattisgarh by an MLA of his own party. The MLA, Mahesh Baghel from Keshkal, would allege that the surrender by 79 Maoists in early December 2006 was just show. He would claim that many were farmers, 'most of them are BJP cadres and I personally know them'. Another BJP politician, Lok Sabha MP from Kanker, Sohan Potai, would also speak out against the surrender.

'I keep saying this,' M continues, jabbing a forefinger on the Formica-topped table. 'All you need is development.'

'We'll meet again.' M says and straightens up. 'We'll talk more. Now, if you will excuse me.'

He presses the buzzer. I thank him for the coffee and his time, and get up to leave. M rubs his forehead with forefinger and thumb.

'You know, I haven't seen a single minister who is not corrupt, MLA who is not corrupt. There is corruption everywhere...everywhere. Sometimes I wish I could take a gun and just...'

He looks up. 'These Naxal chaps, they break the law, for which I will fight them and kill them. But they are fighting for the right things. Isn't it?'

31

K.P.S. Gill didn't have time for me in Raipur—or so claimed a factotum with the Chhattisgarh Police—but here in Delhi he can squeeze in a few minutes even though '*sa'ab*' is very busy. There is a framed image of Swami Vivekanand in the tiny waiting room of his residence in Talkatora Road. 'Strength is Life,' is the message from the iconic swami. 'Weakness is Death.' A gentler, more inclusive explanation followed the original, an elaboration that framed image I see here has no need for: 'Strength is felicity, life eternal, immortal; weakness is constant strain and misery: weakness is death.'

I'll wait. Gill is a legend: self-created, result-oriented, media-hyped—among the first of a breed of policeman-celebrities. He took care—still does, past 70—to show fearlessness. In Punjab during the late 1980s, he took a simple, brutal line against Khalistani separatists. No territory can be ceded, physically and psychologically; governance must be seen to return to the state at any cost. So, among other initiatives, he launched Operation Night Domination, travelling in convoy to the heart of terrorist strongholds. Short of standing in the blood-soaked fields of Punjab and daring terrorists to shoot him, the display of state-machismo mocked terrorists.

Few counted the bodies in kill-or-be-killed. As trouble wound down, courtesy of a combination of Gill's strategy and terrorist overkill that extended to outright intimidation, thuggery and arbitrariness, this man, with savage logic, offered terrorists a way out. Stay in, and your life is forfeit. Or go back to your village, and if you can survive the resurgent tradition of vendetta of the Punjab village, your life is yours to keep. The state will drop charges against you. That was as far as rehabilitation went: no money, just a chance to live and rebuild lives.

'Sa'ab will see you now,' Gill's personal assistant says after a 45-minute wait. 'Sorry, he takes a little time to get ready in the morning. And he's busy these days.'

When I walk into the darkened drawing room, Gill is either taking a call, or placing one. The talk on the phone is about hockey, not terrorism. In measured Hindi he explains how the Indian Hockey Federation, of which he is president, must change the approach of play of India's demoralized hockey team which has a string of poor performances behind it. Over the past year, media sniping has escalated to high pitch, calling for Gill's scalp on a platter for contributing to the ruin.

'Right now, the style of play is too defensive. We must play a more attacking game,' Gill says. 'If you keep shooting at the goal, the chances of scoring a goal are higher. If you are defensive, how will you win?' He switches to English for emphasis. 'More shots on goal means more scoring opportunities.'

After a lengthy discussion on the need for faster, world-class AstroTurf pitches across India, he puts down the mobile phone on a small table—five more machines are stacked on a wooden rack usually used to keep envelopes. He slowly turns his head towards me, fixes me with a stare, and grunts. It's a signal for me to begin.

'How're things in Chhattisgarh?'

'I've been there just a few months,' he tells me. 'It's too early to form an opinion.'

'Surely you've been tracking the situation for a while. Do you have the time? How long is your assignment for?'

He looks surprised but decides to answer. 'My contract is for one year, with one month's notice from either side.' If not renewed, it will end in April 2007. I remind him of it; there isn't that much time. What is his sense of things?

'Human beings are fighting human beings. In this situation, you can't be too doctrinaire, too dogmatic. You can't move too quickly in human situations. There are complex issues, complex situations.'

I ask about the Punjab situation he dealt with earlier, and Assam before that—how does that compare with what he faces in Chhattisgarh? He unhesitatingly differentiates the past from the present. 'Terrorism and movements are very different. Terrorism has a single-point agenda.' But in both, people need to be won over, he stresses.

I voice concern about the way things are being approached in Chhattisgarh, with the Salwa Judum. If indeed a person in his position sees Maoism as a movement and not as terrorism, then why is the approach so drastic?

I don't get a straight answer, or maybe it's as straight a one as he can give. 'Political parties look at their self-interest first. It's all about the political aspect. The election in Andhra Pradesh is a good example of how much impact Naxalism has had on politics.'

And Chhattisgarh?

'After a while all movements become extortionist. I can say that in Chhattisgarh they are committed to seriously dealing with the issue.'

Why did it take them so long to wake up to it? What does it take for a state, or administration, to wake up to something? Body count? A series of big attacks? Egg in the face? The momentum of Maoism has been building up for several years now.

Gill's answer is simple. 'It's very difficult to estimate the threshold in this. There is no method.'

Pay in blood and learn from it. Only, the state acts as if it has nothing to lose. Maoists, like they have everything to lose.

'How will you bring them around? Do you advocate a surrender, compensation and rehabilitation policy? Or do you still swear by your approach in Punjab?'

'Compensation is not a good policy. People want to talk to you when they are weakened, not when they are strong. I still don't know why they are talking to ULFA.'

Gill's suggestion: ULFA is weak; bulldoze it.

I had heard a similar suggestion from an angry D, when I brought it up with him, only he used the example of Bodo militants, a majority of whom had formally given up on arms and a movement to create an ethnic Bodoland out of huge chunks of Assam and North Bengal in 2005, and contested elections as allies of the ruling Congress in Assam. 'The Bodos came home when they were beaten to shit. The ULFA will come home because it is now near about beaten to shit, okay? Everywhere in the world terrorists, revolutionaries, whatever, only talk to you when they have been already beaten on the ground.' Gill is talking the same talk.

My inference from all this: the Maoists are still strong. They don't want to talk yet. They don't need to talk yet, despite being acutely aware of the gears of state grinding into motion against them, and some pretty stunning losses they themselves freely acknowledge in great detail—of course, they play up every death as martyrdom, to do less would be suicidal. So, 21 September 2006 would be hailed with much exclamation: 'Hail the third foundation day of CPI (Maoist)!'

'In less than two years, over 500 comrades of the party (over 300 in the past ten months) became martyrs,' I read in a declaration. 'Politburo member Comrade Shamsher Singh Seri; Comrade Saketh Rajan, secretary of the Karnataka state committee; Comrade Naemuddin (Ravi), secretary of Uttar Bihar-Uttar Pradesh-Uttarakhand Special Area Committee;

Comrade Mohan, secretary of Andhra Pradesh state committee; Comrade Ravi alias Sridhar, Andhra Pradesh state committee member; Comrade Yodanna, member of NTSZC [North Telengana Special Zonal Committee]; Comrade Mangthu, a member of DKSZC [Dandakaranya Special Zonal Committee] and (military commission) member; several members of regional, zonal/divisional/district, sub-zone and area party committees, brave commanders and fighters of the companies and platoons, LGS [local guerilla squads], LOS [local organization squads], people's militia units of the PLGA, leaders and activists of revolutionary mass organizations, and members of the revolutionary masses had laid down their lives fighting heroically with the state's forces and the reactionary forces.'

The acceptance of state response was equally deadpan, more post-mortem of a situation than breastbeating, an indication of a realistic organization: 'The Centre and...state governments have established a joint task force under the Joint Operation Command (JOC) to suppress the people's war and have fully engaged their repressive machinery against the Party...these forces are being equipped with sophisticated weapons, explosives, launchers, mine-proof vehicles, unmanned aerial vehicles, etc. The enemy intelligence network is being expanded from the countryside into the cities, from the state capitals to Delhi...

'...the informer network is being expanded in a planned manner and covert assets are being sent within the Party and the movement in order to eliminate the leadership and sabotage the movement. In the past two years two PB (Politburo) members of the party, comrades Barunda and Vijayda, were arrested, a CC (Central Committee) member, secretary of West Bengal state committee, comrade Tapas was arrested along with other state committee members...'

The Maoists don't perceive themselves to be weaker than they clinically are. They are learning all the time. And the angry have all the time in the world.

I take away another inference from the interaction with Gill: he seems to be learning a thing or two from the Maoists; as he says, without a trace of irony, 'Today's Naxals are much too violent for me.'

—

Some time later, I'll hear Gill again, at what is called the 'Summit of the Powerless'. It's theme: Two Indias, One Future.

The statistics of deprivation have been coming in at such a trot, it's numbing. A thousand dead from suicide in Vidarbha this past year; 2000 dead in India's grain depot of Punjab a year earlier. Counting over a decade, 1,50,000 farmers dead by their own hand across India's south, west and north. Nearly two every hour.

'In 1969, 70 per cent of agricultural credit came from private moneylenders,' activist Mihir Shah tells an auditorium full of students, activists, researchers, lawyers and a smattering of media and corporate elite at Delhi's Jamia Millia University, the venue of the summit. Then came the nationalization of banks, says Shah, signed by a belligerent Indira Gandhi eager to cut the feet from fat cats of industry who presumed to bankroll her political demise. A key effect, besides general consternation and onset of decades of sloth and institutional corruption endemic to this day, was that private moneylending dropped to 30 per cent of the total by 1990. So, some good came of the bad, the trodden got some breathing room through an aspect of enforced socialism. Now, says Shah, who runs the NGO Samaj Pragati Sahayog, private money-lending is back up, at 50 per cent, and driving rampant usury.

This is doom, as he sees it. 'Agriculture is seen as a no-hope sector.' Unless credit goes hand in hand with reform of rural governance, pushing better seeds, reducing the practice of monoculture, and reforming water policy—to alleviate the lives of two-thirds of India's people who live in dry land areas—rural India could go kaput.

The audience applauds as the session ends and, before the next begins, an audio-visual reminds us of the summit's theme: two boys, one fair and the other dark, the fair one visibly—

stereotypically—comfortable and the other visibly—stereotypically—ragged, are joined at the feet with rope. Together they win a three-legged race. India and Bharat go into the shining future.

Over two days, the agenda will be on broad topics that are finally forcing their way into the nation's urban, policy and media mind spaces. Farmer suicides, reservations, equal opportunity in education, the state as protector or alienator, the Naxals, the powerless in the city. It's a good thing the President, Abdul Kalam, has been to inaugurate this summit. At least it puts official conscience on record.

This summit, the first of its kind, is organized by *Tehelka*, an alternative weekly paper—now a magazine—that, in its launch incarnation five years back, was a website that ran a sting to expose corruption in defence deals. This summit, on 20 and 21 November of 2006, begins as another one, also in Delhi, also organized by a media organization, closes: The *Hindustan Times* Leadership Initiative. The latter is a platform for the high and mighty to discuss India's place in the sun in a luxury hotel.

This year, Prachanda visited the *Hindustan Times* (HT) summit and was treated as royalty. For all practical purposes, he was the new power centre of Nepal, fresh from formalizing a peace deal with the government and negotiating for the (CPN) 83 seats in the interim legislature of 330 members. At the *HT* summit Prachanda also smoothly declared that Nepal's Maoists had no links with India's Maoists. This would soon bring a cold rebuttal from the CPI (Maoist) leadership, delivered by the ubiquitous Azad, hinting at a Maoist sell-out to the establishment in Nepal: 'There can be no genuine democracy in any country without the capture of state power by the proletariat.'

The joint declaration of August 2006 by Nepal's and India's Maoists—in November, already a lifetime ago—would seem hollow.

Another comment in the Maoist Web-space about Nepal's 'new democracy' would be far more caustic: '...And this is the model that these people recommend to the Indian Maoist revolutionaries and all the Maoist revolutionaries in the semi-feudal and semi-colonial countries in the twenty-first century. This is the road to "paradise on earth"? The path to hell is paved with good intentions!'

Nepal's Maoists would offer a face-saver, through central committee leader and CPN (Maoist) Politburo member Chandra Prasad Gajurel, recently released from Indian prisons after being arrested in 2003 from Chennai airport while trying to travel on a fake passport to London—a major centre for overseas Nepali financial and PR support to the rebels. Gajurel would say: 'As far as the ground situation in Nepal is concerned, we understand it better than they do.'

Gajurel, who goes by the *nom de guerre* of Comrade Gaurav, seemed to have forgotten the time in 2001 when he was one of two 'fraternal guests'—the other was from the Communist Party of Turkey (Maoist)—at the People's War Group-led Congress in the wilds of central India, with the flag of the People's Guerilla Army, a hammer and sickle with the outline of a rifle running though it, festooned everywhere. He had read out a 'fraternal message' then: '...The process of learning from each other is an unfolding process. We are very hopeful to gain more from each other's experiences which we have learnt at the expense of the blood of our comrades.'

Another time, another place. The business of revolution, as any other business, is dynamic.

The *Tehelka* show is vastly more dressed down than the *Hindustan Times* event, but it too scores a coup of sorts, and not just for its own series of spats. It has on marquee VV representing Other India, the urban guerilla Kavita Krishnan's boss Dipankar Bhattacharya, and 'super cop' Gill. But that is for the next day. For now, I listen to more of the agriculture horror show. So does VV. He is across the aisle with his wife, watching the reiteration of his faith: nearly everything that is said and displayed shows up 'Shining India' as shining half truth, or less.

320

VV and I greet each other warmly; I joke about him being still out of jail and about Prachanda turning establishment. Behind me sits Medha Patkar, discreet for now; she will soon make her point, railing against Special Economic Zones, calling these 'Special Exploitation Zones' and declaring in a voice hoarse with shouting, 'If the government did what it should be doing in the proper way people like me would not need to shout so much. You agree to address issues and I will stop shouting.' To her right and front is a strong Dalit-brigade.

'Agriculture extension has collapsed. Why are mostly cotton farmers committing suicide? According to WTO the import duty on cotton can be raised to 90 per cent to protect farmers but the duty is at only 10 per cent.' This is not Mihir Shah, but Digvijay Singh, two-term Congress chief minister of Madhya Pradesh, voted out after ten years, in 2003, even after pushing for grassroots development.

Digvijay is known, too, for commissioning the first UNDP-backed Human Development Report in India. He did it for Madhya Pradesh in 1995. A classmate of mine from college, Suraj Kumar, and Delhi chief minister Sheila Dikshit's son Sandeep, now a member of Parliament, helped put that report together. Of course, that and the subsequent reports fashionably commissioned by Maharashtra, Karnataka, West Bengal, Andhra Pradesh and Chhattisgarh made no mention of Naxal inroads, perhaps to better embalm truth in fancy documentation. To be sure, Digvijay Singh has a conscience insofar as any politician has a conscience, but during his seven-year tenure as head of undivided Madhya Pradesh, the current territory of Chhattisgarh saw steady Maoist build-up and abdication by the state that the current administration of Chhattisgarh is grappling with.

'Farmers pay a compound rate of interest...there is massive depletion of groundwater,' Singh says.

I think of B, who is away in Nepal on a soul-searching trip with Maoist cadre and several leaders still shell-shocked with the onrush of peace. He would have loved this; the irony of the former chief minister of Madhya Pradesh talking as he is.

The panel that Digvijay is part of is an interesting mix. There's Kishor Tiwari, the chronicler of suicides in Vidarbha; D. Raja, secretary of the Communist Party of India; PepsiCo India CEO Rajiv Bakshi; the strident pro-organic warhorse Vandana Shiva; Sukhbir Singh Badal, an influential politician from Punjab; and scientist-technocrat Pushp Bhargav.

Kishor Tiwari, who runs the Vidarbha Janandolan Samiti, speaks in low-key. He doesn't need to raise his voice when his ammunition is so potent. 'The government of Maharashtra has withdrawn the advance bonus system for cotton farmers,' he says softly. 'Support prices have been reduced by Rs 500 to 700 at a time of crop failure and low prices. There is distress sale of cotton...

'There have been 1,280 suicides this year. A report by the government itself, dated 18 June 2006, says that out of 17 lakh families in Vidarbha, 15 lakh are in deep distress—potentially, five lakh people can commit suicide at any time...

'All the while, the government of Maharashtra was pushing Bt seeds through its venture with Monsanto...'

There is hardly any applause when he finishes. It seems right: How do you applaud the telling of death and the destruction of futures?

The Maoists, typically, don't mince any words about accountability in Maharashtra, especially when it is to do with Monsanto and those associated with it. CPI (Maoist) propaganda is clinical: 'In 2004, up to 80 per cent cotton growers harvested Bt, genetically modified seeds produced by Monsanto. When actor Nana Patekar, the brand ambassador of Monsanto, toured this region last year to promote Bt, his public meetings had a huge impact. Farmers went for Bt in a big way. The seeds, with prices ranging above Rs 1,600 a packet (compared to the normal hybrid variety of Rs 450 a packet) have demonstrated no sustainability in the parched environment of Vidarbha. This year, the fungal infection of Lal Rog struck the fields...Monsanto's claim that a test application would involve minimum pesticides and maximum yield has proved fatal...Meanwhile, while the cotton farmers have been destroyed even further, Monsanto and film actor Nana Patekar have made a small fortune. Both should be treated as criminals and lynched by the masses. It is they who should be forced to pay the farmers' debts.'

The CPI's Raja is up next, qualifying his stand, insisting that farmer suicides will form a key point of discussion when the Left parties gather for their strategy meeting as a run-up to the Parliament's winter session in December.

'Interest rates should be lowered to 4 per cent,' Raja says. 'But this has not been done. Why is the government saying it wants FDI in banking for infusion of capital in small private banks? Why not infuse funds in agricultural banks and public sector banks as well?'

'Is the guy going to keep asking questions or is he going to provide some answers as well?' mutters a voice behind me. Our knot of listeners breaks into short, stifled laughter.

Raja makes up for it then, sticking his neck out a mile, though few will hold him to it. 'We have been saying, "Don't be afraid of isolation; nobody can dare isolate India. India will have to impose Quantitative Restrictions on Imports. The European Community gives $76 billion in subsidies to its farmers, the US up to $72 billion, whereas India is going on $9 billion....Even UPA chairman Sonia Gandhi said at a Left-UPA meeting [that] crops and credit is there in the CMP [Common Minimum Programme], but it has not been implemented.'

'Good morning India.' The same voice behind me grumbles. I turn around to look. It's a wisp of a girl. Her look tells me to back off.

Raja looks at his watch; he is running behind schedule for the Left coordination meeting; his party, the CPI (M), and others meet regularly to formulate stances to pass on to the UPA. 'Farmer suicides,' he looks up. 'I can call it a national shame.'

The hall breaks into applause. And then the moment is gone.

'Hope the guy remembers to carry his angst into the meeting,' I tell my old friend Premila Nazareth, seated next to me. She works on projects for the World Bank in Delhi.

'Since when did you become a Naxal?' she teases.

'I'm not. This thing is going to explode, you watch.'

Our sideshow is derailed by a spectacular spat between Rajiv Bakshi of PepsiCo and the high-pitched Vandana Shiva. Bakshi, to his credit, has showed up—the only transnational, or multinational, company represented on the panel in any session—and is talking about his company's policy, developed from the late 1980s, when in return for permission to do business in India, import capital goods and repatriate profit, it undertook to export foodstuff to make the project 'foreign exchange neutral'. Over time and with relaxation of restrictions, this naturally grew to sourcing farm produce for its own food operations in India and elsewhere—a corporate-farmer model that many in the private sector and policy world argue is an important way to guarantee livelihood for many of India's farmers.

Bakshi talks of how Pepsi is successfully partnering contract-farming ventures for tomato, potato, barley and chilli. 'We're contract farming for potatoes in Maharashtra,' he says, ending his brief speech with a very corporate, 'We want to create islands of excellence.'

This Shiva greets with a snort of derision and outright attack, accusing Pepsi and similar companies of pushing for high-cost imports for farming inputs, holding farmers to ransom, and mocks the 'Pepsi for Peace' campaign in Punjab. Bakshi is red-faced, and sits sullenly through the rest of the session that is a long litany of the imposition of Bt crops and genetically modified seeds—forcing farmers to shop for seeds from MNCs every year instead of being able to set aside seeds as they could from non-GM stock. And how high-cost fertilizer is being forced on them too, driving them ever closer to the edge.

Pushp Bhargav, the molecular biologist, is scathing. 'We are very unfortunate to have a nexus between MNCs, the government and the bureaucracy,' he says. 'Thirty-five per cent of the seeds and agrochemicals business in India is in the hands of MNCs. I was in Bangalore to attend a seminar organized by the government. There, MNCs made a statement that in 3 to 5 years, 100 per cent of the business will be MNC. They had the courage to make that statement in a government sponsored meeting...Ninety per cent of a farmer's input cost is debt, pesticide, seeds, diesel, tractor...The MNCs are pushing next generation terminator seeds—you can't save seeds from these crops, you have to buy each time...'

'These guys are scare mongering,' Premila says.

'Because it's scary,' I tell her. 'Take Vandana Shiva. She's very shrill, but she has a point.' I tell her how even folks like well-known trade economist Jagdish Bhagwati, university professor at New York's Columbia University, root for her. 'He says people like her give voice to the voiceless.'

'Hmm.'

'What connects urban India and rural India is the food chain,' Shiva has calmed down a bit in conclusion; Bakshi is still sullenly staring at the speakers' table, arms tightly folded. But at least nobody has left.

Later in the day, at the session on continuing—even increasing—reservation for low-caste students in educational institutions and offices as affirmative action, the high-casters and low-casters nearly come to blows in the audience, while Dailt leaders on stage preach fire, brimstone and violence if they are walked over any longer.

But nobody leaves the auditorium, even after a near-brawl.

These are good signs, such as they are.

'You know, a strange thing happened to me.' I tell Nandita Das over tea during a break the next day.

'What? Don't tell me.' She looks a bit wary. We don't know each other. She is a famous art house film star. I'm just another guy who walks up to her to talk.

'Saw one of your early movies.'

'Oh *god*!' she quickly looks around. 'Which one?'

'*Lal Salaam*. Saw it in Chhattisgarh, in the forest. Pretty apt.'

She looks embarrassed. 'That was a long time ago.'

Then she moves away to sit at a table and begins a long conversation on her mobile phone.

It *has* been a while since that 2002 movie with the tagline, 'Revolution is always written in blood'. And Nandita Das has moved on since to celebrity status, acclaimed for passionate, offbeat roles in Indian and overseas productions. *Lal Salaam* has moved on, too. Without fuss, beyond headlines, it has grown bigger over the years. In some ways, it has become a recruitment film for the masses.

Like *Blazing Trail*, made in the early 2000s. Using a grainy stock footage of the Vietnam war to dramatic effect, *Blazing Trail* opens with American B-52 bombers raining death and destruction to the anthemic Bob Dylan track '*How many roads must a man walk down before you can call him a man?...*' Later, there are clips of a series of protests in Andhra and West Bengal. The narrator in pronounced Bengali accent tracks the evolution of the movement with exclamatory flourish, as a Pablo Neruda poem about the Spainish civil war scrolls up:

> *...and from every dead child a rifle with eyes,*
> *and from every crime bullets are born*
> *which will one day find*
> *the bull's eye of your hearts...*
> *...Come and see the blood in the streets...*

Along with *Blazing Trail*, *Lal Salaam* is today standard indoctrination and propaganda fare, living on in 'burnt' CDs and MPEG files long after it disappeared, except as filmography and in some alternative bookstores in metropolises.

As far as the movie goes, personally, I believe Das should only be embarrassed about the opening scene, which purports to be of a bunch of tribals spontaneously dancing around a fire. It looks like a concoction of flashy, improbable Bombay-style choreography. That, and the fact that every now and then, Naxals in olive green and fierce moustaches break into rousing song about how they whack oppressors into submission and liberate the world. Their leader, the Das-character Rupi's eventual guru-at-arms Rajayya, is played by one of Mumbai's best known theatre actor-directors, Makrand Deshpaande.

The rest of the movie is true-to-life. Corrupt forest officials who intimidate and rape—twice over, in case of the character Das plays—and who, in collusion with the local police, beats up the brother-of-Nandita character so savagely for asking for wages after a day's hard labour, that he goes off to become a Naxal. Das' character does too. In the end, she takes revenge by shooting her rapist, and then chooses the life of an itinerant Naxal in the jungle over a secure life with her childhood sweetheart, now a doctor who returns to his home village in search of his love, and a cause: to care for his people.

I can understand why police officials in Orissa are concerned about finding copies of *Lal Salaam* among Maoist propaganda in the state. On 23 September 2006 they arrested six Kui tribals from Gajapati district, charging them with sedition. The tribals, part of a Maoist cultural troupe, had with them copies of *Lal Salaam*, along with propaganda booklets, tributes to Charu Mazumdar, and exhortations against corporate ingress into Kalinganagar.

Feelings run deep in these parts. Till as recently as 2004, when it struck the state government to act and withdraw several such cases, by its own admission there were nearly 11,500 cases registered against tribals for offences with regard to taking produce from the forest—their home—worth not more than a hundred rupees. In several cases, the 'stolen' produce amounted to less than ten-rupees' value. Ready leads for forest officials, police and local government to harass tribals. And make them angry.

It's like revisiting the plot of *Lal Salaam*. The film has the power to ignite feelings as it records a time and space that, unfortunately for India, remains deeply relevant.

It's what Sumanto Banerjee, chronicler of early Naxalism, reminds the audience as the session on Naxalism/Maoism begins.

'Let me demystify it for those who don't know Naxalism, or Maoism as it has also come to be called. It's not an ethno-linguistic movement. It's different from any other movement in India,' Banerjee explains in his clipped manner, and then takes a dig at the state. 'When one is deaf the other person has to shout. When the state is suffering from atrophy of the senses, one has to shout. And in extreme cases, take up arms.'

This is broad daylight in Delhi. All is well. In Hyderabad or Raipur, he would likely be marked or in jail for uttering this. Delhi, thus far, is more softly-softly. Less than two weeks earlier, at the India Social Forum in Delhi, little-known, seemingly radical-Left organizations had rubbished the 'jholawalas'—a name derisively given by right-wingers to socialists fond of carrying ethnic bags—at the Forum, a localized clone of the World Social Forum. Calling it a 'farce' containing nothing but 'idle discourses and movements', the Disha Students Organization, Naujawan Bharat Sabha and the Hundred Flower Marxist Study Circle argued that the Forum, and similar gatherings, 'do not integrate various mass struggles'. In Hyderabad or Raipur, they too would have been marked or jailed.

The dais is diverse, as with all sessions—the true joy of this 'summit'. There is Naveen Jindal, young billionaire businessman, fiercely patriotic, a member of the Standing Committee of Home Affairs—and head of the steel and metals conglomerate that has bid for huge projects in Chhattisgarh and Orissa, both of which are held up on account of the Maoists' and people's protests. VV is by him. Then Dilip Simeon, former Naxal, and historian. And finally, at the end of the arc, K.P.S. Gill. All others are watchful as Sumanto outlines the session. Gill has his head lowered; it looks like he's taking a nap.

Jindal, for all his savoir-faire, sounds sanctimonious. 'Government responses are lacking, missing,' he admits. 'Government doesn't trust citizens and citizens don't trust government. But is this the right way? That's why cowards commit suicide. Right living is more difficult than ending a life.'

He finally finds his groove. 'Can it always be "if you don't agree with me I'm going to shoot you"?'

VV fixes him with a beady stare. Gill, unmoving, still has his eyes shut.

'Misguided youth,' Jindal offers. 'We have to talk to them. Start a dialogue.'

Jindal finishes. Next up is VV, looking even smaller than when I'd met him in Hyderabad. He's in a crumpled blue shirt worn over gray trousers, and a pair of simple black shoes.

I hear an echo of our conversation in Hyderabad from several months earlier. His speech is passionate, as always. It's deeply romantic. It's also deeply doctrinaire—but that realization is the next stage. For the moment, the poet has the audience rapt. Gill twitches about.

'What the state does is violence. What we are doing is counter-violence,' VV thunders in radical justification.

'Where do you get food? From the people. Where do you get weapons? From the very hands of the ruling classes.' There is a smattering of applause. A female voice shouts, 'Yes!'

He talks about rocket launchers made on the 'footpaths of Vijaywada and Chennai'. Made with basic materials. And for the physics of it, VV says, Tech Madhu and others took recourse to the lessons of space-scientist and nuclear-arms-loving President Kalam; 'a text by him', says VV, led them down the last mile through a suggestion: '"For more details, see the website——."'

The auditorium dissolves in laughter and applause.

'Violence is a non-issue,' VV then says, too smoothly for me. 'Inequality is violence. This society itself is violence.'

'We represent the aspirations of the people of India,' he wraps up. 'In today's context I think the revolutionaries are playing a patriotic role.'

Gill, of course, will have none of it. He starts off by eloquently rubbishing politicians, deriding them for having 'no time and understanding for the grassroots' and for living 'in their own self-constructs of India'.

That out of the way, he rubbishes Naxalism. 'Why has it

collapsed again and again?' he asks conversationally, pointing to weaknesses within Naxalism. This, of course, is the exact opposite of what the Naxals—and numerous security officials and analysts—say: that Naxalism in one form or another keeps resurfacing, because of bad governance.

'Never since '71 there has been a threat to the Naxals as the Salwa Judum,' Gill pronounces. This is astonishing, as the think tank of which he is president is on record saying how dangerous a move like the Salwa Judum can be, how dangerous forced relocation can be.

By the time he comes around to 'India needs a creed that is for India,' Gill has lost the audience.

Dilip Simeon, the peacemaker, speaks next, of the 'politics of virtuous murder, whether by the Government of India or others.'

He too has lost the audience, though what he says makes supreme sense. 'Policies are based on the notion of superior knowledge,' he aims this at the panel at large and at VV in particular—at the self-righteousness that decides for angry Maoists that there is no alternative, chooses for the dogmatic which class enemy to kill and whom to let live. 'You need minimum demands and maximum unity,' Simeon pleads. 'You have to make it easier for people to come with you.'

He turns to VV. 'Glorification of violence is not a socialist ethic.' VV looks straight ahead at a point above the audience.

Sumanto concludes the session with a pointer to developments in Nepal, official rapprochement between the government and the Maoists, from just two days earlier. 'We need to create a space for dialogue of the powerful and the powerless.' No contest: moderates, as always, will need to suggest the bridge, walk it with the interchangeably angry and passionate, the weakened and the dominant.

The session breaks up and everyone leaves the stage. I wave at Gill, who doesn't wave back. I walk up to VV, who smilingly asks me, 'How was it?'

'Not bad,' I say neutrally.

Then a crowd of loud students mobs him. Many reach out

and shake his hand. He wanted an audience. He has it. Democracy, with all its ills, allows him this public space. I hope he realizes the irony that dogma and undemocratic institutions have no space for others, tolerate no dissent. Mao didn't. The bloom of a Hundred Flowers turned into deepest tragedy. Maybe when the Maoists talk about New India, they really need to talk about gentler Maoism—possibly an oxymoron—as their compatriots have done for Nepal's fragile peace.

Two Indias. One future. The future of one is being written by aspiration. The future of another in blood—suspended aspiration. The state has all the power at its disposal. The Maoists, all the anger. Both won't hesitate to kill, as they haven't in the past.

I think of the long-ago poem by VV in Telugu that Sumanto had earlier compiled—the context and the movement has moved so quickly, so urgently, from then; the context will have evolved into something unrecognizable now as it attempts to travel from the jungle to the farm to the city; as the species of empty prosperity and the species of overblown rage scrabble for their piece of bleeding, festering sanctuary:

The truth that the worker's sweat will never utter,
The truth that his empty stomach will never utter,
The truth that his tears will never utter,
The truth that his toiling fists will never utter—
Can a drop of ink from a poet's pen
Ever express it?

The future is a very disturbing place.

BOOK V

...The 9th Unity Congress [of CPI (Maoist)] affirmed the general line of the new democratic revolution with agrarian revolution as its axis and protracted people's war as the path of the Indian revolution that had first come into the agenda with the Naxalbari upsurge...It set several new tasks for the party with the main focus on establishment of base areas as the immediate, basic and central task before the entire party. It also resolved to advance the people's war throughout the country...and wage a broad-based militant mass movement against the neo-liberal policies of globalization, liberalization, privatization pursued by the reactionary ruling classes under the dictates of imperialism...

The Congress also passed a number of political resolutions on numerous current events like the world people's struggles to support nationality struggles; against Indian expansionism, on [the] post-Khairlanji Dalit upsurge and against caste oppression, against Hindu fascism, against SEZs and displacement, etc...

...Rise up as a tide to smash Imperialism and all its running dogs! Advance the revolutionary war throughout the world!! The Unity Congress-9th of the CPI (Maoist) finally called on the people of India to

come forward in large numbers to support the ongoing people's war in the country and the embryonic power emerging, to build a truly democratic society built on justice, equality, free from the chains of imperialism and semi-feudal bondage.

—Ganapathy, General Secretary, CPI (Maoist),
19 February 2007

32

Sometimes, the future can be lunatic.

Things have been taking a bizarre turn in Jharkhand. In the third week of February 2007, the state's health minister, Bhanu Pratap Shahi, told the Ranchi correspondent of *Hindustan Times* of a novel method of combating Maoism, beginning with Palamau district, a Red zone in the northwest of the state.

'I have already instructed doctors in Palamau to launch a vasectomy campaign...The Health Department will solve at least half of the extremist problem...other government agencies can take care of the rest.' To put it beyond reasonable doubt, the minister clarified, 'One vasectomy in a Naxalite dominated village means that many potential comrades less...when you have too many mouths to feed and too little food to eat, you may turn into a Naxalite. All I want is to minimize the number of mouths.'

Shahi's chief minister, Madhu Koda, at the head of a UPA-supported government in the state, just months into toppling a BJP-led government the previous September, added to the surrealism. On 24 February, he received an official certificate from the *Limca Book of Records*, India's version of the *Guinness*, for becoming the first independent legislator to become a chief minister; he formed a government with just four other MLAs. At a function in the capital, Ranchi, he beamed, bedecked in garlands of marigold.

Through the unintended hilarity of these moments, I was struck by another bizarre twist, from a month earlier.

It was yet another example of divisions and in-fighting,

this time among the Maoists, though the 'comrades' have long denied it. Twenty-sixth January, India's Republic Day, is traditionally celebrated with the raising of both red and black flags in Maoist-dominated areas, along with assorted revolutionary symbolism. On Republic Day, 2007, in West Bengal's Belpahari and Charakpahari areas, the Maoists constructed two new martyr's columns covered in bright red paint and hoisted party flags, right under the nose of the CRPF. But to the west, in Jharkhand, there was the sight of a band of camouflage-uniform-clad masked men standing in front of the Indian flag in the jungles of Kuba. They fired four shots into the air to honour the flag. Then, along with a bunch of curious children, they shouted '*Bharat Mata ki Jai*', Long Live Mother India. Then, they sang the national anthem.

They were of a group that calls itself Jharkhand Prastuti Committee (JPC), yet another breakaway, a brand new one, from CPI (Maoist). The 'zonal commander', Rampati, there with a group of 70 rebels, announced to assembled villagers that CPI (Maoist) were traitors, that they believed the Indian tricolour was a symbol of false independence from British rule. But JPC believed it to be the true symbol. 'You don't any longer have to fear *videshi* extremists,' Rampati announced. 'We will get rid of them in Jharkhand.'

Videshi. Foreign. A reference to Maoists from Andhra Pradesh and Bihar. Evidently, Jharkhand would now have its own brand of Maoist rebels, patriotic to the core, looking after the needs of the people of Jharkhand.

For good measure, Rampati also rubbished Tritiya Prastuti Committee (TPC), the other breakaway that had been under sustained CPI (Maoist) attacks since the summer of 2006, by saying that TPC too was unpatriotic. In Dadighagar village, Rampati's colleague, 'sub-zonal commander' Shravan, also known as Vikas, was preaching similar sentiments to a gathering at the local school.

If this is not later proved to be an elaborate charade concocted by suddenly awakened anti-Naxal operatives in the state intelligence bureau, this twisted tale of 'patriotic' Maoists and 'unpatriotic' Maoists could spell trouble for revolutionaries in north and central Jharkhand. Meanwhile, the state could turn the pressure on with strikes every now and then, play sides, and watch revolution fall apart. If this ever came to pass, and even if it didn't, for people caught in the middle, the nightmare of bloody turf war would continue for a long time.

—

'You see,' T tells me, wiping his face with a dirty multicoloured towel, standing in pyjamas, track-suit top and woollen cap, cleaning one ear with a forefinger laden with a heavy gold ring, 'the problem is all these peoples have come from outside.'

'Outside?' I'm at an audience at the financier's house in Hazaribagh district. He has just seen off two men keen on buying a second-hand motorcycle, saying the price they quote, Rs 25,000, is too low. Not a rupee under 30,000, they are told. They leave, dejected. T is furious. '*Koi bhi madarchod aa jata hai apney aap ko raja samajhkay.*' Any motherfucker just shows up thinking he's a king.

'Outside, you know. Andhra, here and there,' he resumes our conversation in a mix of Hindi and English, settling into a plastic chair in the vehicle-strewn driveway. The sun is gentle. Hazaribagh too was gentle once, a small town by the forest. Today's madness of choked traffic, open sewers and nuked roads, promoted by helter-skelter growth—despite a couple of recent terms as the constituency of a former finance minister of India—is away from the relative quiet of this gated compound.

'In the old days it was clear: People's War and MCC. First they fight. Then they unite. But the territories are same, *na*? All these years you manage things your way, suddenly your business partner comes and says, "*Arrey baba*, we are one party only. Let us share." But *how* you can share? The business is same, cut is same, money is same, *na*? You have contacts and networks over so many years. How *you* will feel,' he jabs a finger at me, 'if someone asks for *your* share?'

'Not nice,' I say weakly.

'Ek-*jack*-lee! Naturally-*na*?'

T isn't the only one to talk about this. I've heard it in Patna, Ranchi and Jamshedpur. Some rumbling in the ranks, cracks in the Maoist conglomerate. Resentment from being dictated to; demands for a share in the Maoist parallel economy, parallel to India's other subterranean economy—the 'black' economy—that thrives beyond the eyes of the taxman. All this, in addition to coping with greater state response against rebels.

Any which way, enough reason for CPI (Maoist) to hold a 'Unity Congress', billed as the '9th Unity Congress', in the jungles of Jharkhand at the end of January, a meet designed to dispel notions of cracks, and throw the gauntlet down yet again to the central and state governments. For greater dissemination, neatly printed press releases in English and Hindi were hand delivered and faxed to the media across India on 19 February, signed by the Maoist supremo, Ganapathy.

'How do you know so much?' I ask T, totally taken in with this larger than life person.

'What is Hazaribagh? It's a Naxal district or no? Forests all around or no?'

'Yes.'

'How can financier survive here without knowing some things?'

'Okay.'

'Ek-*jack*-lee!'

'So they are fighting...'

'Naturally. It's natural.' T strokes his huge belly.

'But how do *you* survive?'

'I have to survive with everyone,' T switches completely to Hindi, explaining the other side of his business: he is also the area's premier collector. If someone defaults on payments for a vehicle—motorcycle, car, van, jeep, or tractor—his toughs go out and 'collect' the goods from all across Hazaribagh district, from town to jungle, and the adjacent Maoist-infested districts of Chatra and Latehar. It's impossible without a compact with the Maoists, the same as any business person who needs to work in such areas. 'I had to survive with one. Now I have to survive with two, three, as many as there are. It's a headache. But the *mama*s are still number one.'

'Mama? I thought they are called *dada* [elder brother].'

'Here, we call them mama [maternal uncle].' Ironically, in many parts of the country a policeman is called a mama.

T's path was made clearer a year ago. Demands on his time and money from the Maoists lessened after the night a man showed up at his home, saying he needed to 'borrow' a vehicle, as his young son was unwell and had to be taken to hospital. On urging from his staff, T gave him a van.

'He turned out to be R—, a big leader of the Maoists here.' T hasn't had any trouble since.

'There,' he says, 'the brother has come. He works for me sometimes. Lives in Chatra. Goes for party meeting-*weeting*. Another brother is the security guard of a judge. Like this only, *bas*.'

He turns to the newly arrived man. '*Kya yeh tumko* CID *lagta hai? Nahin na?*' He points at my frayed jeans, backpack and eagerly clutched notebook and pen as evidence that I'm not from Jharkhand's Crime Investigation Department (CID is often colloquialized to include a state's Intelligence Bureau, even India's).

The brother talks of yet another faction, not directly of the Maoists but supported by them, an amorphous organization called Jharkhand Tiger Liberation Force. He says there is some '*taal-mel*' between the two, some understanding.

'How do you get by?' I ask him.

'I'm for everybody. They are all the same to me. But one has to be careful these days. Police is active. Murder-*oorder*. Arrest-*warrest*.'

Just days ago a sub-zonal commander of CPI (Maoist), Bhagirath Mahato, was arrested, along with Meena Devi, a key member of Nari Mukti Sangh, a women's front organization, in the Hazaribagh area. The capture was helped by government-sponsored village defence committees.

'*Sabkey liye* danger.' T says.

I tell T what I heard in Patna from a Maoist conduit, that the Maoists in Bihar are trying to change and stem any public resentment against them. I'd been told that *jan adalat*s or people's courts—the notorious Maoist system of justice in the villages—are not any more handing out sentences for amputating limbs. That they now pronounce capital punishment only in extreme cases of perceived wrongdoing. That landlords—even those known to be sympathizers of the once rabid, now somnolent Ranvir Sena, the upper-caste 'army'— are being allowed to return to their home villages. If they petition the local Maoist leadership, they are sometimes given an acre or two of land to sell off for family exigencies like a marriage or raising dowry for a daughter.

'Is anything like that happening here?' I ask.

'It's all about adjusting,' T says vaguely. 'We all have to adjust in this *duniya*.'

'Take him,' T regally orders his multiple-Maoist-minion, flashing gold rings to wave me away. 'And tell him what he wants to know. *Sabsey bhent karao*.' Present him to everyone.

There's a last bit of advice for me. 'Catch hold of a root and it will take you where you want to go, make you meet who you want to meet.'

'That's what I've been trying to do,' I reply. 'But I can't always talk and write about who I have met, or where I met them, how I got there and what they told me.'

'*How* you can?' T agrees with a grin, his belly shaking with silent laughter. 'They could die also, *na*? And you. Maybe, *na*?'

—

Death comes in strange ways in these parts. It could come as it did in the third week of June 2006 to five CPI (Maoist) 'deserters'. On 20 June, Ritesh, a zonal commander, Jitendra Das or Prabhat—Dawn—an area commander, sub-zonal commanders Kalu Turi and Kishori Ghanju, who also went by the names of Birodhi—Rebel—and Nandkishore Sahu all walked out with 30 other comrades and joined the breakaway Tritiya Prastuti Committee. Literally, Third Preparation Committee, but more Third Way. Among other things, they complained about CPI (Maoist) leaders being caste-led by the dominant Yadav community, and how lower castes—Turi, Ghanju, Oraon, Badai, Bhokta and several other backward castes—are given the go by.

The word went out from CPI (Maoist) bosses almost immediately: finish the upstarts. If need be, move a few mobile units from the Saranda forests in the state's deep south, near the border with Orissa, 200 or so, and base them in Tritiya Prastuti strongholds till the situation can be brought under control.

Just weeks ago, a TPC sympathizer's house had been dynamited in Leslieganj. On 9 February, just days back, two TPC members were shot dead.

CPI (Maoist)—former MCC cadre—protecting their revolution is a key reason, of course. But there's also the other: both groups, CPI (Maoist) and Tritiya Prastuti, would now compete to squeeze transporters and contractors for bread, butter and sometimes—for the crooked ones—jam.

There is a story told in local police and media circles about a former senior cop in Hazaribagh, V, now posted elsewhere in Jharkhand. V 'turned' a CPI (Maoist) fellow in the know of things, Umesh Ojha, and the two entered into a compact. Umesh knew a cache of Maoist money secreted in the region's forests, estimated at up to eight crores, Rs 80 million. An operation was duly launched and the money recovered.

Ojha had one condition, though. Could he please have a little of it—say, half a million rupees, as a gesture of goodwill? Nobody need know. He would still continue to be with the Maoists, and also act as informant for the police.

V, says nearly everyone I asked about the incident, had other ideas. He wanted the loot for himself. So he 'encountered'

Ojha and kept the money for himself, but for the little that he had to give some others in the know who had to be kept quiet.

The grapevine post-mortem of the incident reeks of missed opportunity. Locally, it is felt that V could have kept a little for himself—people, especially in crunch postings, need to feather nests every now and then—but should on no account have bumped off Ojha. Because then it would have been win-win for police, state and infiltrator. And the Maoists would have continued to receive jolts, at least until they wizened up to Ojha, to his parallel game and his dipping into the till of parallel economy.

But V the police officer went overboard. This much greed isn't good, people would gravely tell me.

33

Kiriburu could be on another planet, if it were not for what comes out of the land that binds it to the country: iron ore. Steel Authority of India Limited (SAIL), the government-run steel corporation, has its captive mines spread over a massive hill: Kiriburu Iron Ore Mines, and its cousin, up the hill, Meghahatuburu Iron Ore Mines. They are smack in the middle of some of the densest forests in India, the Saranda, straddling southwestern Jharkhand and northern Orissa.

A large part of India's steel backbone was built by ore from these mines. Twenty-odd kilometres away, in Noamundi, near the edge of Saranda, Tata Steel, in the headlines after its takeover of European steel giant Corus, has its mines. These supply the company's steel mills in Jamshedpur. The roads from Kiriburu to Jamshedpur past Bara Jamda, Noamundi and Chaibasa are churned up with thousands of ore-trucks a day. In reality, there are no roads any more except as surprising bits of tar: it's a wave of muddy, dirty tracks rutted so deep that a journey of 160 kilometres takes between seven and eight tortuous hours. The landscape is awash in dust, leached earth and ore, turning green to red.

Iron ore is only one of the riches here. Any ore and mineral map of Jharkhand shows in these parts, and in West Singhbhum, Saraikela-Kharsawan and East Singhbhum districts—the last two directly across West Bengal's Maoist zones—a profusion of manganese, limestone, graphite, steatite, apatite, quartzite, asbestos, lead, zinc, copper, some gold.

To the northwest of Kiriburu, also in the Saranda forests, also known for its mines, is Gua. Something happened here in 1980. This was at a time when Jharkhand was still part of Bihar, and supplied the state—indeed, much of the country's eastern region—with iron ore, manganese and coal, and electricity through thermal and hydroelectric projects. In turn, it got minimal development funds based on a time-honoured assumption: tribals lived there, and tribals, after all, live simply, they need little.

Driven to desperation, the area's displaced tribals, organized by a tribal rights and right-to-statehood organization called Jharkhand Mukti Morcha, started a campaign of going back to the forests to claim what had been theirs for as long as anyone cared to remember. They had also had enough of exploitation by the well-established threesome of contractors, officials and moneylenders. The state's response was to send a large team of Bihar Military Police, which did what security forces often do: intimidate, arrest, take food at will. To protest this, an estimated 3,000 tribals gathered in Gua town for a march. Local authorities intervened, and convinced the tribals to call off the march; the compromise was that they would address a meeting at the market square and disperse.

As that happened, on 8 September 1980, the police showed up and dragged the speakers away. There was an altercation, and the police fired. The tribals fought back with bows and arrows. Three tribals and four policemen died—human rights activists put the figure of tribal dead at 100, the discrepancy on account of the authorities playing down the incident. Both lots took their wounded to the Gua Mines Hospital, where the tribals were all made to deposit their bows and arrows before the hospital took their injured comrades in. All of a sudden,

Bihar Military Police personnel opened fire on the now unarmed tribals. Eight died.

The police then went on a rampage in the villages, in much the same way that they are today accused of doing in Chhattisgarh: threats, looting, destruction, molestation, rape, occasional murder. The tribals escaped to take shelter in the Saranda forests, in places too thick and deep even for forest officials.

Saranda is one of the biggest forest zones of the Maoists outside Dandakaranya. Jharkhand offers several such zones, pockets that total nearly 24,000 square kilometres—in the northwest and north, along the borders with Chhattisgarh, Uttar Pradesh and Bihar; and in the east, along the border with West Bengal. But Saranda is special; it is arguably the least penetrated by security forces. It's a place for the Maoists to gather, lick their wounds, regroup and launch attacks from.

—

I reach Kiriburu on 25 February 2007, and realize it is a big day here. The Thirty-fourth Inter-Mines Games are on at Kiriburu Stadium. The level of excitement about such an event is understandable in this little town far above the plains of Jharkhand, with surprising patches of pine in the middle of lush evergreen. It has the feel of a small cantonment town in the hills of Himachal Pradesh or Uttarakhand: ambushing clouds, snaking roads, a row of tiny, soot-blackened tea-and-snacks and grocery stores, a single branch of a state-run bank. Here, but for cable television there's little by way of twenty-first century entertainment or even connection with the bigger, 'happening' world. Newspapers arrive late, and the communications network often goes on the blink, as it has today—only local calls work, routed through the exchange.

Worker-teams have come from several mines in the area, including from Gua and Chiria, and the Tata mines at Noamundi. It's barely lunch, and KIOL—Kiriburu Iron Ore Mines Ltd—is at first place, with sister-mine Meghahatuburu's

MIOL team in third. The Tata team too has saved pride: they are running second. Jharkhand's minister for welfare, Joba Majhi, a tribal politician, like the chief minister himself—indeed, like all chief ministers in Jharkhand's short and chequered history as a state—has just been over to inaugurate the games.

Unlike most ministers in Jharkhand's new cabinet, 'Joba Madam', as she is respectfully called, is not known to make statements against the Maoists. In the 1980s, her husband, tribal leader Devendra Majhi, along with another leader, Mora Munda, led a series of major movements in Saranda to prevent the illegal felling of trees—the hardy sal and prized teak, among others.

Those were militant times. The fire from Gua had spread. Tribal people wanted their land back. The Gua incident was only one of many skirmishes between tribal protestors and police. Those days, the movement received the full backing of the Jharkhand Mukti Morcha—literally, Jharkhand Freedom Movement—and its leader, 'Guruji'—Shibu Soren. (As I visit, Soren is in jail, disgraced, forced to resign from his post as Union cabinet minister in the UPA government on account of his conviction by a trial court in Jharkhand for the murder of his personal assistant 13 years earlier.) Some who participated in the early movement say it was almost natural, as resentment peaked through the 1980s and 1990s, for its leaders to search out other bands of disaffected, but those who had the firepower that the tribals and their leaders lacked. Enter, the Maoists—the Maoist Communist Centre.

So many things have changed. MCC is merged into CPI (Maoist). Both Majhi and Munda have passed on. And Majhi's widow Joba is today an MLA in a bizarre manner: she is formally allied to the United Goans Democratic Party, as she used the party's two-leaf symbol to contest and win the last elections in Jharkhand. The link with Goa, though, may not be quite as tenuous. Already, there have been anti-eviction protests by several thousand tribals in the Manoharpur Block of Gumla district against a major Goan iron ore mining and exporting company seeking to prospect beyond its tiny home state.

There is also another, perhaps more equivocal change since the early days of tribal protest. Tribal right over forest land, for which so many across India have fought for decades and lost their livelihoods and lives, is close to being enacted into law: The Scheduled Tribes and other Traditional Forest Dwellers (Recognition of Forest Rights) Bill 2006. According to Bharat Jan Andolan, an NGO, the bill has the potential to ensure better lives for at least 15 million people across the country and take into account 1.25 million acres of forest land. However, there are still many controversies over this bill. What of the tribals and forest dwellers—from central and peninsular India, in particular—who have already been evicted, leaving contractors and traders in their place? What of the traditional land deserted as a result of persecution by forest officials, contractors and police, or the fear of Maoists? The rightful owners are now dispersed across Indian cities as daily wage labourers, household help and, in extreme cases, trafficked into prostitution. What if people claim false identities to grab their land? Some analysts say these problems will persist as long as there isn't a clearly defined larger policy to empower indigenous people to protect forests from industry and bureaucracy.

This, then, looks more like change as status quo. There are estimates that only ten per cent of those the Bill is intended for will really benefit. The issue of tribal rights will churn large parts of India for several years.

The other status quo is that the Maoists have stayed on in the Saranda forests.

Over the years, they expanded their dominion, moving rapidly since 2001. Now, few forest guards are found inside Saranda. In several places, forest guard posts have been destroyed by the Maoists, as have forest rest houses. There's still an old MCC slogan in Hindi on a remaining wall in the small, destroyed forest guard building in Karampada hamlet. This is deep inside the forest, not far from the spot where the

346

Maoists blew up a mine-proof vehicle in early June 2006, killing a dozen CRPF men. '*Van Vibhaag ko maar bhagao, jangal par janta ka adhikaar kaayam karo,*' the slogan screams. Beat up and throw out the forest department, establish the rights of the people over the jungle.

On another wall nearby, a more recent slogan: '*Gaon-gaon aur ilakay-ilakay mein krantikari kisan kameti, lal rakshak dal, jan militia dal gathan tej karo.*' Speed up the formation of revolutionary peasants' committees, Red protection bands and people's militias in village after village.

This call to arms seems worlds removed from the sort of hilarious—yet at once earnest and chilling—outpourings on Maoist-friendly websites, like one that reached my mail service just days before I reached Kiriburu:

> *...Along this tortuous thorny road,*
> *Epic fight against the haves.*
> *Spare not Dengists, centrist toads,*
> *Ever lay them in their graves.*

Both sorts of messages, though, imply death to the enemy. And Kiriburu, the jump-off into the forest, is at the centre of the battle. There's a CRPF battalion posted here in a heavily fortified camp. The 132nd Battalion, trying to contain Maoists with four smaller camps in the jungle, and three more on the way. Troopers returning from patrol and those going on one pass each other through a tangle of athletes heading back for lunch from the stadium to Kiriburu's community centre. In the zone, this is normal.

—

'You know, my grandmother used to ask us, "*Diku kua dasi?*" In our language, the language of the Ho tribes, it means, "Will you work for outsiders?"' Vijay Melgandi is being generous. 'Diku' may have come to mean that, but it's closer to 'intruder'.

The Bah Parab, a major spring festival of the Ho tribes, is underway. There has been much drinking through the day.

There is now dancing at Meghahatuburu's Children of God School for children of tribal daily wagers at the mines.

'Look at us now,' says Vijay, a labour leader affiliated to a BJP-controlled union. I look. A line of children, young girls and boys, women and men, dance around a flagpole reserved for raising the Indian flag twice a year, on Republic Day and Independence Day. This is 'civilization', so they have all traded in their traditional short sari and dhoti for skirts and blouses, salwar-kameez, and T-shirts and jeans.

It's just after dusk. The dance, with changes in rhythm provided by medium-sized drums slung from the neck, moves snakelike, front and back, the head of the line taking the tail in a wavy, perfectly synchronized clockwise movement around the empty flagpole.

There are no smiles. No laughter. It's a sad, forlorn dance, so unlike what it should be: a spring in the step because there is spring in the air and parts of the surrounding forest are alight with flame of the forest. The dance is more remembered cultural DNA, something to be cherished at any cost in a place that is both home and not-home.

'We are rootless,' Melgandi says. A few others seated near him sigh. 'We work for the diku.' He wipes a tear. 'Many of our kind are diku in our own lands.'

34

Babloo is skittish. He drinks heavily. He has a road to finish.

It's just six kilometres, beyond the steep descent from the gigantic crater of Kiriburu mines, so vast that from where Babloo and I are, snarling two-storey-tall dumper trucks look like gently crawling Mechano toys. Ore dust covers everything like rusty lava flow. Clouds are drifting in, and Babloo says it looks like rain, but it looks to me the landscape will never be rid of the red, there is so much to wash away.

The mines are a little distance away from Kiriburu town, and accessible through a hilltop road that winds between

Jharkhand and Orissa; posters praising Jharkhand's chief minister Madhu Koda are soon followed by posters praising his Orissa counterpart Naveen Patnaik. Where Babloo and his friends drink every evening—a small, abandoned asbestos-roof workers' home with its backyard littered with empty bottles of beer and hard liquor—is by the border of Orissa. Jharkhand provides water; Orissa the electricity. The liquor for the den comes from Jharkhand; the snacks to go with it from the old man's shop across the lane in Orissa. It's the way life is in these borderlands. Residents, Maoists and security forces criss-cross them at their will, and peril.

Today is groundbreaking day in Karampada. The road Babloo and his partners have contracted to finish is working its way back to the base of Kiriburu's ore hill.

'Have you done the deal yet?' I ask him.

'No, not yet. But I wish I had. I wish they had come to me earlier. Then I wouldn't have this tension.'

'How much can you pay?'

'First, it's not how much I can pay, but how much they ask for. Then we negotiate.'

'How much do you think they will ask for? Five per cent? Ten? Fifteeen?'

'Look, the road is going to cost Rs 24.59 lakh per kilometre. I get paid only after some of the work is done. We're just four-five friends who have pooled in our life's savings to win the tender, get the contract. This is our first project. How much do you think I can pay them? I'll just tell them we're just young people who want to make a living, why kill us? Let us live, let us share what we can, so we can share more. Simple.' Babloo looks deflated after this burst of expression. He wipes his perspiring face, and the handkerchief comes away ore red. 'Let's see what happens.'

'Do you think we'll meet them today?' I'm eager to see the negotiations with Maoists, were they to take place.

'Maybe not. There are too many CRPF here today.'

There would be even more in a few days.

True to their new mantra of 'mobile war' articulated in 2004 and now in the process of being implemented, Maoist cadres shot dead Lok Sabha MP Sunil Mahato, legislator for East Singhbhum district's Jamshedpur constituency, and three others as they watched a football match at Baguria on 4 March. A few days later, West Bengal's CPI (Maoist) state secretary Somen—lending credence to a police theory that a cross-border mobile group, a Medinipur-based squad, carried out the hit—told a TV channel how they had targeted Mahato as far back as 2003, but had only now found the opportunity to kill him. Mahato's fault: making anti-Naxal noises and, according to Somen, threatening to foist the concept of Salwa Judum on to Jharkhand by raising a tribal militia in the state.

There was further—bizarre, in keeping with the state's recent tradition—speculation. The media quoted Shankar Hembrom, an associate of Mahato's and president of the vigilante group Nagarik Suraksha Samiti, as saying that Mahato had suggested at a meeting of the group on 22 February that they initiate a desperate measure: poison the food that villagers offer to the Maoists. That gem reached the Maoists, and the axe fell.

Mahato's killing caused panic in Jharkhand and consternation in Parliament. There were renewed calls for pumping the state full of forces, and much criticism about Jharkhand's lackadaisical approach to security issues. (Senior police officials of other states openly laughed when they spoke to me, somewhat exaggeratedly, of the 'Jharkhand system' of increasing police posts—just establishing one and telling political leadership it was done, irrespective of whether the police post was required at the place or not.)

But the clamour over Mahato's killing would soon be overtaken by two major incidents, which, ironically, would bury in public memory the astounding reality of a legislator to Parliament killed by rebels.

One would take place in West Bengal on 14 March, when the situation in Nandigram, brewing dangerously since January, spiralled out of control. CPI (M) partymen and a thousand policemen attacked villagers who were protesting the intention of the state to hand over 10,000 acres of their land to Indonesia's Salim Group to operate a Special Economic Zone. Police would fire to quell the protestors. According to the police, 11 villagers died; district authorities mentioned 14; senior CPI (M) leaders in the state claimed ten. Locals claimed dozens dead and several hundred injured. A senior leader of the Revolutionary Socialist Party, a constituent of West Bengal's Left Front government, put the figure at 50 dead. Locals spoke of several bodies being taken away and buried, adding to both rumour and body count.

In the following week, the state government dealt with appeasing a shaky left coalition cringing from headlines that blared, 'Enemy of the People' and 'Executioners of the Poor', and threats by coalition partners to walk out of the state government. CPI (M)'s habitual arrogance was dented in Parliament as it came under severe verbal attack. Even then, there was no back-pedalling by the party's leader Prakash Karat; and spokesperson Sitaram Yechury disingenuously hinted at Maoist triggers in Nandigram, without once acknowledging the sledgehammer policy of his comrades in West Bengal. But the party had to relent, a stunned chief minister Buddhadeb Bhattacharjee forced to apologize and withdraw the state's plans of going ahead with SEZs.

The Union Ministry of Commerce, too, quietly announced, on 21 March, an amendment to its earlier SEZ policy: 'The developer [of Special Economic Zones] shall make adequate provision for rehabilitation of the displaced persons as per the relief and rehabilitation policy of the State government.' By the end of March, concern for a Nandigram-type had flared up and spread westwards; the government of Maharashtra held back clearance for Reliance Industries' mammoth SEZ across Mumbai.

As ever, it took violence or death for the state and central governments to wake up.

The second incident to overshadow Mahato's killing took place in Dantewada just a day after the mowing down of protestors in Nandigram.

Early in the morning on 15 March, close to 400 Maoist rebels and militia converged on the police post at Rani Bodli, near Kutru, and attacked a large group of the Chhattisgarh Armed Force and Special Police Officers of the Salwa Judum after first sealing off exit routes. Fifty-four at the post, mostly SJ, died after a firefight—out of ammunition, completely overwhelmed.

The governments of Chhattisgarh and India vowed revenge. There was even angry talk of calling in the air force and bombing Maoist strongholds.

The Maoists crowed about the 'heroic' assault, and promised more such strikes if SJ wasn't withdrawn—or if it were introduced to newer areas. Meanwhile, they also sent a formal appeal to SJ, asking SPOs and others how long they would continue to fight their brothers and sisters—and how much longer it would take for them to see that the government had pitted tribal against tribal. A message also went out to Naga troops—and another lot of recent imports from the North-East, troops from Mizoram—to 'disobey orders' and return home.

The promised escalation, the promised 'mobile war', the promised lateral expansion, had arrived.

—

But all this is some weeks away while Babloo and I drive into one of the greenest places I've ever seen. The dense, evergreen Saranda forest.

A track of red earth winds through it. Babloo is right about CRPF. One trooper ducks and disappears to our left, a flash of camouflage fabric becoming part of the jungle. Another walks towards a clump of trees and becomes them. A third sits on a log on the opposite side of the track—I see him only because he moves, and only then do I see a fourth, positioned by his side to the back. I wave out. They wave back, smiling.

'They seem to be resting. Or waiting for something.'

'Maybe they have heard about some movement. I talked

to ——' here Babloo mentions my host, who made a call on his mobile phone in front of me, only to be told a Maoist unit has moved on north towards 'CKP', short for Chakradharpur, for a patrol, so Babloo may have to wait a few days more to learn how much he should 'donate' to the Maoists.

Every few minutes after this, Babloo presses the horn of his motorbike in a steady beep-beep-beep. After the fourth time, I ask him the reason. 'We have been told to press the horn when we enter the jungle. It lets them know we are here.'

The CRPF, of course, have no such instructions—or the inclination. In June 2006, a dozen of them were blown up in their mine-proof vehicle when an IED exploded under it. 'Here, this is where it happened.' Babloo points at a huge crater in the track, as we swerve past it. It's been cleaned up a bit. But there are still bits and pieces of twisted black metal lying around the sides of the track. CRPF now walk, and keep off the tracks completely. The jungle is safer that way for them, such as it is.

Babloo and I later meet another motley bunch of troopers; their home, it turns out, is Etawah, Uttar Pradesh. I tease one of them about drinking water from a plastic litre-bottle of Mirinda.

'It's not a joke,' he says, AK-47 gripped loosely in his left hand as he takes another sip. Five of his mates crowd around, curious to know who we are, and seem satisfied with our identities of contractor and writer. Two clutch AK-47s. The third, a sleek variant in matte black, which he says is an AKM; it's lighter. The fourth holds an INSAS rifle, the fifth a small mortar and square slung bag of shells. All swear by the AK-47 and its dependability. So do the Maoists, like rebels and insurgents the world over.

'This soft drink bottle is lighter,' the first trooper tells me. 'The bottles we are issued can weigh up to three kilos with water. And it's mostly the weight of the bottle. This,' he waves the plastic bottle, 'is lighter and carries more water.' I tell them the Maoists appear to be equipped more practically. They live in the same jungle, but often carry water bottles of the sort schoolchildren use: easy to procure, easy to carry.

It acts as a trigger for woes. They first complain about the extra weight they carry—18 kilos, of which half is breastplate and back armour. One takes out a breastplate from a vest he wears over the uniform to show me the slightly concave metal. I heft it.

'You better put it back,' I hurriedly open the Velcro strap of the vest, and make a mess of re-inserting the plate. They all laugh in low pitch.

'The plates used to be much heavier, almost double the weight,' says the one carrying the AKM. 'Imagine, we have to run from the enemy, or chase the enemy, wearing all this.' I ask if he has heard of Kevlar, that these make bulletproof vests derived from composite materials for several of the world's armies and paramilitary. He tells me he has never heard of it. They fight with what they are given. Another says Kevlar vests are reserved for those who go to Kashmir—a friend in the army would tell me the same thing. 'At least we have better *banduk* now.'

He then breaks into a string of curses in Hindi, and freely accuses the Chhattisgarh police of corruption and inefficiency. His companions join in. One had been posted to guard former home minister L.K. Advani; another to guard Maninder Singh Bitta, a Congress functionary known as much for his sycophancy to party leadership as for having survived a bombing in Delhi. Both politicians are described in the vilest terms. Politicians in general seem to upset them—'they have fun, we die.'

'We get paid Rs 4,000 a month to do this, while *madarchod poltishun-log* do *aish* in Delhi. Why should we guard them? Their lives are in danger because of what *they* do.' AKM lets off another string of curses while his colleagues smile. 'What have we done to be here? It's only because of all these *madarchod* leader-*log* who make mistakes.'

Babloo watches us goggle-eyed. I wave farewell. They melt away.

Babloo is nervous as we reach Karampada. A dozen labourers, drawn from Karampada and other villages, have

354

arrived. A 25-metre stretch is already churned up with picks, with crushed stone lying by to be poured. But Babloo instructs the foreman to go a little slow on the work. It wouldn't do, Babloo tells him, to move too quickly and then find he can't strike the deal with the Maoists. He won't be able to afford the loss of time and money and the project will have to be abandoned. He tells his foreman to send word to nearby villages for people to not be too eager to show up for work till a deal is struck.

He is edgy, and we still have a distance to travel to Thalkobad, several kilometres deeper into jungle. So I ask him to tea at Uncle-ji's small hut. Babloo has one helping of tea, a potato *pakora* and a *jalebi*. Then another. He manages a tiny smile. It's all the succour he will have till he drinks himself to sleep.

We carry on to Thalkobad. Babloo has no business there except to ferry me. I've asked to be taken there, based on a tip that a group of Maoists are around the area. Still uptight about not having done his deal, Babloo agrees to take me there in the hope that he too might come by a Maoist.

Beyond Karampada it is strictly no-man's-land. The jungle envelops us. Streams peer at us every now and then. The only noise is from the motorbike, and the beeping of the horn, a desperate, tinny sound.

I ask him to stop at a tiny bit of red ribbon hanging from a shrub by the track. There's another, about 50 metres further on. I take a photograph, fascinated. Then something I heard from a chat with locals comes back to me. It's how the Maoists sometimes tag a place to provide visual reference for a mined zone, set up an ambush between a field of fire from A to B. I tell Babloo this as I photograph the bits of ribbon, touch these to reassure myself that the tiny flags to mark death and destruction are the same as what I've seen little girls, especially in rural India and the slums of urban India, plait their hair with. He isn't amused with my what-is-decoration-for-one-is-death-for-the-other explanation, and furtively glances all around.

There's nobody there. Just the jungle, beautiful as ever, live camouflage; Babloo's dust-caked bike; and the smell of our fear.

35

Photography was born for this.

Jharkhand is blessed with tree-shapes to make a perfect picture, drive nature photographers wild with rapture. Thalkobad has several. Bare branches that make for zen black-and-white portraits. Flames of the forest that set fire to a frame. Flowering mango. Dignified sal.

A brook cuts through the clearing that has new paddy on either side, light green on surrounding emerald. A few huts, fewer people. A mother hen walks her brood by the water. A new-born calf prances on a barren field.

It is good to be careful with framing, though, or the broken school building, roof and walls in horrific jigsaw, blown up the previous year by Maoists to deny sanctuary to CRPF troopers, will intrude. At times, it seems like a conspiracy to deny education. So often across the country's Maoist zones, troops take shelter in school buildings, sometimes the only structures made of brick and concrete and big enough to house a group, and fortify these. The Maoists attack and destroy these. In the end, what the two forces of 'good' really end up doing is destroying for the truly needy a chance at basic education.

The Maoists blew up the school building after an initial attempt to explode it with buried mines—CRPF would recover a dozen mines planted around the building—with troopers inside failed. Someone had leaked information to the forces.

'No school any more for the children, then,' I tell Sargia Hunhaga.

'What else is there?' says the grizzled tribal farmer, squinting against the sharp sun, taking a break from helping some young boys tie togoi bark on stripped branches to fence off the young paddy. Not that it will stop the elephants that call Saranda home, but villagers still try; it will at least keep away deer and sambhar. 'Most of the people of the village have gone away to look for jobs in the mines, in the cities. Only we are left.'

He sweeps his arm to take in the dozen people by him, scattered homes of Thalkobad, slapped on with layers of mud, neatly painted over with earth colours of rust and ochre, topped with a broad stripe of white and thatch from the forest that once housed more than 300 people. These days, there are a few dozen.

It's the same story in many hamlets and villages in Saranda. Last June, CRPF went on an aggressive sweep in several parts after Maoists blew up their colleagues. Typically, villagers were easy meat for CRPF anger. The Saranda Shramik Swavalambhi Sahkarita Samiti, a provider of unskilled labour for the mines, recorded several hundred villagers, mostly men, arriving at its offices in Meghahatuburu with stories of beatings by CRPF men keen to drag confessions from them of alliance with the Maoists, of leads as to how the attack had been set up. Few of these villagers had returned, opting instead to take up low-paying jobs at the mines.

'At least the police leave you alone, with the school building gone,' I try to pacifiy Hunhaga. 'There is nowhere for them to take shelter, is there?'

'They don't leave anyone alone. But yes, they come much less after the bombings. They don't stay long. They are afraid.'

'And the dadas? Mamas?'

'Da. We call them "da" here.' He mentions a shortened suffix for dada, older brother, typically used in eastern India. 'Barko-da *kal aye thhey*,' he says. Barko-da was here yesterday.

'Who is he?'

'Leader *hain*.'

'What did he want?'

'*Thoda baat kiya. Thoda khuraak liya. Unka chhota khuraak se to hota nahin, na?*' Talked a little. Took a little food and provisions—but they don't have small appetites.

Two teenage boys continue to strip togoi bark and knot it into restraining rope as others gather around us, a collection of pre-teen snot-nosed boys and girls.

I haven't heard of Barko-da. But there are several 'da's in these jungles, in various capacities, leading four armed groups that together are estimated to number between 250 and 300. They come and go, drift in and out of control and memories: Bikas-da, Ramchandra-da, Xavier-da, Rajesh-da, Anmol-da, and Birbal-da, or Birbal Munda, named after Mughal emperor Akbar's famed court wit and counsel, a key member of the Saranda sub-zonal committee and the South Chhotanagpur Regional Committee.

They rule here, and will, as long they are able. Forest guards, traditional exploiters, have long been chased away from these parts, the forest 'rest house' over a small rise too destroyed by Maoists, denying officers and troops pre-cast shelter, and keeping out wildlife enthusiasts who decades ago made Saranda a cult destination. Maoist-da rules Old Man Hunhaga's life as he does young Babloo's.

'How long will this paddy last you?'

'Six months,' Hunhaga says. 'There is also some maize. We don't sell, this is our food.'

'What will you do when the food is over? Can you go into the forest?'

Hunhaga looks at me suspiciously. 'Are you sure you are not with the forest department? This village has its own forest, Block 19. It's ours. We don't need to go into the revenue forest.' He smiles to cover discomfort.

He knows he must go into the revenue forest. He knows I know he must. There's no other way to survive here. He and others of this village and other villages will have to go in deeper to collect meaningful volumes of tendu leaves, sial leaves that are larger than the utilitarian sal leaf and more prized, some kusum flower, some dori. They will hand these over to agents cleared by Government-da and Maoist-da. The few rupees they earn will be traded for provisions and things for the hut, purchased after a day's walk through the jungle to the nearest village market.

'It's the way it has been since we remember. It will always be this way.'

'Do you feel more protected by the Maoists? At least they seem to trouble you less. They seem to keep even the police away. The dadas say all they want is food, shelter and information.'

Hunhaga is mute.

'Well, there's the mango,' I lamely suggest a cause to celebrate. 'Look at that tree. Just a few more months, May-June is not too far. Looks like it will fruit well this year.'

'If they want,' Hunhaga says, pointing a finger at the overcast sky. Then he looks at me, and smiles hugely. The children smile with him, and bring back the sun.

'Yes, you must come and share with us. The mango will be good this year.'

EPILOGUE

The cast of characters has changed somewhat since I started work on *Red Sun* in early 2006 and since the book was first published about two years later. And yet, much remains the same, to little surprise.

When I began my travel and research, K.P.S. Gill was on the ascendant in Chhattisgarh as the soon-to-be appointed security advisor who could do no wrong. His one-year term ended in April 2007. It wasn't renewed. The state doesn't now have an anti-terror guru-in-residence. B.K.S. Ray, the bureaucrat-poet, was moved from his post as additional chief secretary (home). Om Prakash Rathor, the state's director general of police, died of a cardiac arrest in May 2007 at the Academy of Administration in Raipur (which Ray himself ran) while attending a function to mark 'Anti-Terrorism Day'. Lesser bureaucrats and policemen have been shuffled around in the roulette of administration.

Among the Maoists, some have come above ground, some have been arrested, some killed.

While in the long-term scheme of things all this constitutes a mere shuffle across the chessboard of red and grey, there have also been some dramatic shifts. Few developments, of course, can match the immensity of change in Nepal through 2008. These changes hold great relevance for the Indian situation in several ways and throw up at least two key questions: Are India's Maoists in a position to 'do a Nepal'? Is Nepal's peacemaking formula a possible template for India?

Prachanda, the Fierce One, is now prime minister of Nepal, and a major mover in the Constituent Assembly elected in the spring of 2008 to provide the impoverished, war-ravaged country a new constitution and future. It's been a journey from being a leader of a rag-tag band of rebels to firebrand supremo of the Communist Party of Nepal (Maoist) to ruler of the country. All in a dozen years, since the first shots were fired in 1996 in a remote hamlet in western Nepal. Gyanendra is no longer king, stripped of every power and all pomp. Statues of former kings and prime ministers lie toppled in Kathmandu and elsewhere in the once-kingdom.

But no one is sure if there has been a resolution. The Maoists having to accommodate institutionalized democracy in their plans; the political parties as divided and clueless as before; the old social and ideological divisions and bitterness still strong beneath the surface...The times are strangely, worryingly uncertain in Nepal.

The greatest lesson for India at this time is that even if peace is achieved in the near future—almost impossible, of course—it would take several years for emotions to cool and deep differences to be reconciled.

On a visit to Kathmandu in late 2007, I caught a show of *Awaaz* (Voice), a movie that claimed to be the 'first Nepali-language movie based on the great people's struggle that changed the course of history'. This was at Biswojyoti, a dilapidated, betel-stained place just beyond Durbar Marg, close to the grounds where over 200,000 Maoist supporters once gathered in post-conflict celebration. Tickets for the prime 'balcony' seats cost 30 Nepali rupees, half-price on account of it being a weekday morning. The show sold out. The place was full of workers with their families, even children. Couples discreetly held hands.

The kitschy, overly-loud movie, with relatively unknown stars, unabashedly played out the Maoist saga of fighting for a trodden people. Corrupt police harassed villagers, a low-caste lady was denied water from the village well, landlords brutalized landless peasantry. There were a number of other such delights of Nepal that are also all too common in India. Gradually, the plot moved to teachers and intellectuals converting to the cause of revolution and taking on the state. More state repression—torture, rape and killings—followed. My taxi driver, Nabin Khadgi, cried. I heard sniffles all around. When a man hung upside down and beaten in a police station managed to break free and escape, the audience applauded. When a captured and raped female Maoist escaped and with karate kicks first incapacitated her tormentor and then killed him, some in the audience stood up in excitement and whistled. Policemen were dying all over the place, and the applause was louder than gunfire. The film ended with enacted scenes and real footage from Jan Andolan II, with the actors playing revolutionaries among protesters on the streets. It implied the Maoists' major role in triggering the movie and the movement—and that is true enough.

There is today a Truth and Reconciliation Commission in Nepal. 'But it is far too early for it to be effective,' a top United Nations official told me. 'Nepal needs to emerge more fully from the conflict.'

Who killed how many and in what grotesque way? Who tortured whom? How many were 'disappeared' (to use a chilling verb form used by Nepal's human rights groups and media to refer to those gone missing, especially after civil war escalated from 2001)? What manner of compensation—legal, financial and emotional—can and should be provided to shattered families and orphaned children, the living victims of a war that has claimed at least 13,000 lives?

An example of the churn came in December 2007, when all that Kathmandu's media could talk about was a tip-off by the National Human Rights Commission (NHRC) about the remains found on the slopes of Shivapuri National Park of forty-nine Maoists who were allegedly 'disappeared' in 2003 by the Royal Nepal Army. Were they burnt there? Or buried? Burnt *and* buried, most probably. There had long been a buzz that these forty-nine were tortured and killed in the headquarters of the crack Bhairabnath Battalion situated on Lazimpat, Embassy Row, a route that runs all the way north to Shivapuri where many of Kathmandu's wealthy maintain weekend homes.

Public credence was fuelled, after reports of the remains found in the national park, because to get to the area would necessitate cutting through the grounds of the army's Command and Staff College. When media persons showed up in the area, they were threatened by a belligerent lieutenant colonel. 'What incident are you talking about?' he shouted. 'You will face severe consequences if you don't go back.' It all added up to morbid mystery.

I headed up towards Shivapuri with Nabin one morning in his wheezing red Maruti-Suzuki sub-compact. At the first check post, we were asked our purpose and destination. 'Body, body,' Nabin blurted out. After we'd shown our IDs, we were, amazingly, waved through. The pine-fringed road—fringed too with razor wire—wound upwards through administrative and residential blocks, past a helipad, and then the road simply disappeared into track, still 3 kilometres from where a local villager said NHRC staff and volunteers were digging around. Nabin and I ditched the tired car and walked.

It was a walk through picture postcard country. We were surrounded by the kind of intense beauty that can make the casual visitor forget the brutal realities of Nepal's long civil war. I was reminded of something that the well-known media person and rights activist Kanak Dixit had told me. In 2003, even as a Maoist negotiation team discussed peace with government officials in the seventh month of a rare ceasefire, news broke of the army killing seventeen Maoists in Doramba village in eastern Nepal. Human rights activists later exhumed the bodies of victims killed point-blank by the army after being made to dig the ditch they would be buried in. Dixit, who was part of the team, told me that he had had to coin a new word in Nepali—*shabodhkhanan*—to explain 'exhumation'.

By the time Nabin and I reached the exhumation site in Shivapuri, now cordoned off with rope and restricted-area signs, NHRC team members in blue and white jackets were tagging the day's collection—sacks full of mud and bits of burnt wood. A lady who had been poking around with a trowel under a mound of stones emerged with some black fragments and earth and asked a male colleague: '*Asthi chha koyla chha?*' I didn't need Nabin's ready translation to figure it out: Is this bone or coal?

An official told me the remains would be shipped to a forensic lab in India. It would take months to get a report, he said. Closure will take several years.

While such reminders of the worst of the civil war keep surfacing in the newly peaceful Nepal, rumbles have already begun within the Maoist hierarchy. The party controls a third of Nepal's Constituent Assembly and, besides the premiership, the key portfolios of finance and home. The queries are as to where the revolution is now headed, in its mainstream format, with former political enemies as allies in government, soldiers of the People's Liberation Army still not reintegrated and the Young Communists League still as belligerent as before. Communist hardliners are pushing Prachanda to the wall, accusing him of selling out the revolution, and the majority of Nepal's population remains suspicious of Maoist intention.

(As I write this in early 2009, Prachanda has been threatening for weeks now to resign and bring Maoist cadre back into the streets. The dispute is over integrating former Maoist soldiers into the Nepal army, a move that the Maoists' main political adversary, the Nepali Congress, is firmly opposed to. Prachanda, already wearied of hardliner reaction, has no alternative but to make dangerous noises, always holding out the spectre of more conflict to a nation deathly tired of it.)

During my visit to Nepal in 2007, I had shared similar, early concerns with Baburam Bhattarai, Prachanda's deputy during the revolution and finance minister in the new dispensation. He had smiled, and then launched into a mini lecture. We were at his home in Kathmandu and had just been served Pepsi cola. 'Revolution doesn't move in a straight line,' he said, his tone that of a teacher. 'There are some people who will abandon the goal of revolution. There will be temporary gains and setbacks, but ultimately the goal...You factor in practical politics and power balances on the arc towards the goal. We are trying to make a balance of this—what we call strategic firmness and tactical flexibility. That's all.'

When I expressed surprise he brushed it away with realpolitik: 'It's to balance both sides. We tell our revolutionary friends, "See, we haven't abandoned the revolution; we have our army, our weapons..." And the other side [politicians and civil society] also has doubts.' He paused to sip cola. 'You see, both sides have doubts.'

To their cadre the Maoists insist they will do whatever it takes to retain the edge. 'The war hasn't ended,' Bhattarai said. 'But the form of war has changed.'

Nepal's Maoists will have to live by this credo of doublespeak in the foreseeable future.

—

The relative primacy of the Maoists in Nepal does not mean India's Maoists will soon attain it. That country was at a dead end politically and economically, allowing left-wing extremism to leapfrog ahead. In India, there is considerable forward socio-economic and political movement. India's Maoists acknowledge their task is made more difficult precisely on account of India's growth.

But Maoist leaders and cadre—tellingly—see no reason to give up their chosen path even at the cost of their destruction.

In August 2007 Mumbai Police captured two senior-level Maoists, Shridhar Srinivasan aka Vishnu, and Vernon Gonsalves aka Vikram, from the suburb of Govandi. Gonsalves, a longtime member of the movement, had at one time run the state committee for Maoists. Srinivasan was key in planning strategy, and is a top member of the CPI (Maoist) Politburo. Official Maoist reaction openly admitted to the duo's association, and pointed to the resolution adopted at the 9th Congress of the party earlier in the year: that it would stress ever more on bringing revolution to urban areas. Srinivasan and Gonsalves had only been doing what the party believes in. In a way, in the month that India's benchmark Bombay Stock Exchange index began its climb to a giddy 19000 points, the war within had come home as visibly as wealth.

Through 2008 it has been more of the same in Chhattisgarh, too. Salwa Judum is in full play. Mizo paramilitary troops were brought in to take over from their Naga compatriots. Tribals as collateral damage is still fair game on both sides (though unlike the administration the Maoists, for what it is worth, do offer apologies and explanations).

In May, a three-year-old child and a twenty-two-year-old lady who lived in the Cherpal Salwa Judum camp in the Bijapur area of Dantewada were killed by CRPF troopers. Their families, according to human rights activists who visited them, were threatened with 'consequences' should they seek legal help. In June, another team visited Nendra village and saw nearly a dozen houses burnt by Salwa Judum toughs; according to the villagers this was done to punish them for submitting potentially damaging testimonies—damaging for the administration—to a visiting team from the National Human Rights Commission.

Protesters have generally been threatened and forced to lie low. Himanshu Kumar has been repeatedly asked by the state government why the permission to operate his NGO, Vanvasi Chetna Ashram, in Dantewada should not be revoked. In conversations with me since the publication of this book, he has often mentioned an apprehension of being killed in a state-sponsored attack or even a Maoist-sponsored one. As always, Himanshu continues to be in the middle. Over July and August 2008 he invited the ire of both the state and the Maoists for trying to resettle several dozen villagers from Salwa Judum camps. The administration was upset because such a move would, in theory, offer the Maoists more fodder for recruitment and support; local Maoist leaders were incensed because they saw this as an attempt at forcing normalcy and blunting the revolution.

Such bizarre and dangerous byplay is not limited to the forests. It is nearing two years since Binayak Sen, vice president of the People's Union for Civil Liberties (PUCL) in Chhattisgarh, long disliked by the authorities for his human rights work and criticism of bad policies, was put in jail in the state's capital.

Sen's is quite a story, and I got a glimpse into it during a visit to Raipur in July 2008 with filmmaker Sudhir Mishra and Binayak's younger brother, Dipankar. Mishra wanted Binayak's permission to make a movie that would involve a telling of his life; Dipankar was there simply as grieving observer.

Raipur Central Jail, Binayak's new home, was decorated with patriotic bells and whistles. A bust of Subhash Chandra Bose painted in Bollywood silver rested in front of the arched entrance. On either side of it were similarly adorned busts of Gandhi and Vivekananda. Inside, the reception area was a jumble of registers, framed prints of gods, a dusty close-circuit TV screen, nervous supplicants and guards who looked bored and self-important by turn. There was also a marble plaque with the names of freedom fighters incarcerated in Raipur jail by the British.

For decades a doctor to the rural poor, public health specialist and human rights activist, Binayak is a declared public enemy for the government of Chhattisgarh.

'People tell me I may be safer in jail,' Binayak spoke softly. 'Outside, anything can happen.'

An emphatic bullet; an engineered mob; death by bureaucracy.

The crowded deputy jailor's room was abuzz. New prisoners were checked off in a bulky register as they shouted out their names, addresses, caste, crime and punishment—in that order. In a corner, on a bench, lay some home remedies that Binayak's elder daughter Pranhita had brought from their tiny flat in the Katora Talao area, now a transit camp in the battle for Binayak. There was also a plastic bag containing cereal, a couple of packets of biscuits, half a dozen bananas. And a small photo album with colour prints of the prize-giving ceremony of the 2008 Thomas Mann prize for Global Health and Human Rights. Pranhita, her younger sister Aparajita and their mother Ilina had travelled to the United States to receive the award on Binayak's behalf.

Binayak looked at the photos. Then he turned to Pranhita and wordlessly stroked her hair. She clutched both his frail hands in hers. She was visiting Raipur for a few days from Mumbai, where she is a student of media. Binayak could meet her for a few minutes. A political prisoner, he lives in a cell among those charged with murder and other crimes. The prisoners respect him, protect him, prevent isolation and temper despair. That day, I saw one prisoner hold an umbrella for Binayak as he walked in the rain from his cell, several hundred metres away.

Dipankar, an oil industry executive in Brussels, was angry, teary, voluble and mute in turn. A large man dressed in executive leisurewear, he clutched his brother's arm. The diminutive Binayak, shrunken in a faded blue khadi kurta and white pyjamas, calmed him, as he had Pranhita.

Binayak helped to publicize the 'Malik-Makbuja' scam, by which tribals have for years been cheated of valuable timber on their land by colluding traders and politicians. He blew the lid off Salwa Judum through several reports and a telling documentary. As the state fought back with an overkill of fire and fear, Binayak suggested that the game was to help business. He named the Tata, Essar and Jindal enterprises, among others, all with the ability to reach far, wide and all the way to the top. The government, he charged, hadn't safeguarded the interests of tribals and forest dwellers before trading their future for Rs 170 billion in memoranda signed with businesses from home and abroad for mining iron ore and diamond and setting up steel and power plants.

In a way, what Binayak did was similar to what Medha Patkar tried for those displaced by the Sardar Sarovar project, or what Aruna Roy did to empower the poor and powerless with the right to information. Only, there wasn't a state of 'civil' war on Patkar's and Roy's patch. In May 2007 Chhattisgarh police, pressured by political masters in deep sulk, arrested Binayak for interacting with Narayan Sanyal, an ailing and elderly Maoist leader in Raipur jail. Permission for such interaction had been sought in writing by Binayak in his capacity as both doctor and human rights activist and had been granted, also in writing, by a deputy inspector general of police. The charge sheet accused Binayak, a highly-regarded graduate of Vellore's Christian Medical College, of not being a doctor, besides ferrying communication for Maoists. Both charges have since been disproved in local courts.

No dice. And no bail. As I write this, perhaps emboldened by the repeat electoral victory of the Raman Singh-led BJP in Chhattisgarh's assembly elections in December 2008, fresh charge-sheets have been presented against Binayak.

Binayak is severally hit by provisions in India's Penal Code. Among these, a Section 121 charge censures against 'Waging or attempting to wage war, or abetting waging of war, against the Government of India.' It carries a maximum penalty of death. A bit of a big hammer for exposing wrongs. Very Cultural Revolution.

For nearly two years now, Binayak's lawyers, Ilina, other family and well-wishers have visited corridors of substantial power in Raipur, Delhi and elsewhere, pleading his case. Nobel laureates have written letters to Chief Minister Raman Singh and Prime Minister Manmohan Singh. Several of Binayak's fellow doctors from India and abroad have petitioned his case to lawmakers and the public at large. The effect: zero.

In this season of paranoia and ham-handed application of official antibiotics, it may be too much to expect a fraught national security apparatus to melt its heart for an injustice. Or a BJP-led state government to bend to suggestions of 'snafu' from a Congress-led central government. And so, the tragic circus continues. In several court hearings since Binayak's incarceration, the case for the prosecution has proved hollow, and some witnesses for the prosecution have turned hostile— this in Chhattisgarh! Senior administration officials admit that higher courts could, ultimately, dismiss the case against Binayak on points of law, but that lower courts, closer to imperatives that drive the politics of Chhattisgarh, would be less moved. Sudhir Mishra, Dipankar and I heard this with some dread but no surprise. Director general of police Vishwaranjan offered us time, coffee, a short discussion on poetry and commiseration that, at least, Ilina Sen was not jailed too, as she had suffered enough. Besides, he said, who would look after the children?

(Vishwaranjan's qualification seemed a bit woolly and even revealing to me, as he should, on the face of it, have little sympathy for an alleged Maoist sympathizer. In late August of 2007 the helicopter in which he was travelling to Dantewada, where thirteen policemen had been killed just days earlier, was fired upon. Nothing happened to the chopper or its occupants, but Dandakaranya's Maoists had made their point: it's still their turf.)

The simple truth of Binayak's continuing imprisonment could well be that the political masters of Chhattisgarh have either not been provided or have not come up with a face-saving strategy for withdrawal—the same as in the case of Salwa Judum, which is now little else than a PR noose around the state's neck. There are officials who admit in private that, left to themselves, they would have intensified the watch over Binayak to ascertain links with Maoists, not arrested him in a massive fit of pique. Similar enlightenment sprung bail on 6 August 2008 for Ajay TG, a video documentarist, arrested in May 2008 for alleged links with the Maoists. The fact that the state refrained from manufacturing evidence against Ajay is being seen as a glimmer of good sense. (The administration did try its hand at getting Ajay to certify PUCL a Maoist front. Ajay declined.)

Thus far, the only thing that could trigger Binayak's freedom is political give-and-take. An indication was provided during my visit to Raipur: if Binayak is to be released, it may help to first lower the temperature around him, cool the rights-rhetoric. And, by all means, keep grovelling. Until then, in him the Chhattisgarh government has what it surely did not wish to create: a cause célèbre who is providing even greater exposition of the state's failures as a prisoner than he had done as a free man.

—

Chhattisgarh, and those battling Maoism, are desperate to out civil rights activists as enemies of the state. While such a case can be made against some activists—the Maoists have, after all, adopted the route of front organizations in their multi-level approach—the eagerness to prove the state response in Chhattisgarh as righteous is deeply disturbing.

I have personally experienced this.

In mid-2008, I was invited to be part of an academic advisory group of a forensics and criminology institute run by the Ministry of Home Affairs in New Delhi. I agreed, as the person heading the institute, an officer of the rank of inspector general of police, had earlier formed part of anti-Naxal operations at the ministry, and with this interaction I hoped to understand better the state's view of the rebellion. In the matter of a few weeks, the real reason for the group—a collection of academicians, retired judges, serving mid-level bureaucrats and me—was made clear: an 'independent' study as to the benefits and flaws of Salwa Judum. Basically, we were to arrive at various camps run by Salwa Judum and ask: 'Were you forced by Salwa Judum to come here? Or did you come here of your own accord, frightened of the Maoists?' All along, of course, we would be provided close security by the state and Salwa Judum, to ensure both the safety of our lives—imagine the negotiating conundrum if the Maoists captured a police officer of the rank of inspector general—and 'freedom of expression' in the camps.

I acquiesced, frankly, out of great curiosity as to how such a group would progress. All along, I had made my views on Salwa Judum, as expressed in *Red Sun* and in articles and interactions since, abundantly clear. To me, all evidence suggests that a legitimate grouse of a section of the tribal population of Chhattisgarh protesting Maoist heavy-handedness had been used by the state administration to support and fund a cynical, deadly and socially destructive mechanism to counter rebellion, with little regard to human life and rights. Perhaps the study group needed a token dissident in me. But I had nothing to lose, and only insight to gain.

The funds for the study were routed through the political science department of Delhi University. A professor of the department—part of the study group—was designated leader. We gathered in Raipur on 2 October 2008. Most arrived from Delhi; I travelled from Goa, my present home. At a briefing the same evening, we were told that we didn't have much time for the study—that some of the group had to return to Delhi in time for Durga Puja and Dussehra celebrations! A helicopter already under charter to the Chhattisgarh government—primarily for operations in Bastar and Dantewada, I learnt—would be available from the following day for two days. This would enable us to make quick forays into admittedly inaccessible terrain deep inside Dantewada.

On the morning of 3 October, three of us piled into the civilian Bell Jet Ranger III owned by Dhillon Aviation and leased to the Chhattisgarh government through an intermediary, Mesco Aviation. We took off from the police barracks helipad in the heart of Raipur. (The remainder of the team would join us in Dantewada town the same evening after driving south from Raipur.) There was a refuelling stop in Jagdalpur, the district headquarters of Bastar, and then a forty-five-minute hop to Dornapal, following the marker of the wild and beautiful Sabari river.

However, upon landing at the disused, collapsed stadium that now acted as a helipad, ringed by the festering, baking slums that pass for Salwa Judum resettlement, the senior police officer decided the Dornapal camp was 'too old' for our purpose. After a quick lunch of vegetables and rotis at the offices of a CRPF deputy commandant, we flew the short, twenty-minute hop to Jagargunda, deep in the jungles to the west.

This area, for all practical purposes, is Maoist territory. Chhattisgarh Police are yet to forget an incident from 2007 when on 29 August a police party led by a crack officer, Hemant Singh, was lured into the jungle between Dornapal and Jagargunda. At a place called Tarmetla, he and a dozen police personnel were ambushed and killed. Singh lives on as a colour photograph on the wall of the police mess in Dantewada, now named after him, a constant reminder of a conflict seemingly without end.

Jagargunda, now a broken village, is completely cut-off by the Maoists. Weapons and food supplies for both paramilitary and Salwa Judum camps have either to be trucked in every three months with heavily armed convoys, or choppered in. As we landed, the senior police officer admonished a guard for saluting him—a potential giveaway for Maoist sharp-shooters on any of the hillsides that overlooked the landing zone. Just weeks earlier, the same helicopter had had a bullet shot through its rotor. The Austrian pilot had taped a sheet of plastic on the small hole and managed to take off.

Our interview with those in the Salwa Judum camp, ringed by barbed wire and razor wire and guarded on every side by guard posts, was farcical.

We stopped near some mud huts after walking down a narrow strip of road in grand procession. The camp housed nearly 3,000 people from several villages and hamlets in the area, among them Milanpalli, Kunder, Tarlagada and Kudmer. It seemed the entire camp, children included, were with us.

'*Kisne laya tumko?*' the police officer barked at the crowd in Hindi. A bureaucrat accompanying us, a tribal lady, hadn't the Muria dialect these people spoke. A Salwa Judum recruit was translating back and forth in broken Hindi. '*Maobadi ke dar se aya ki Salwa Judum wale laya? Theek-theek batao, darne ki koi baat nahin.*' Who—or what—brought you? Your fear of Maoists, or did Salwa Judum bring you? Tell us correctly, don't be afraid.

It seemed an unlikely place for straight answers, surrounded as we were by several hundred people and heavily armed paramilitary and armed SPOs—Special Police Officers.

Finally, Uika Massa, a husk of a lady, answered: 'Ramesh and Munna brought us here.'

Who were Ramesh and Munna? She waved around vaguely. Nobody was able to tell. The senior police officer looked furious, and was not too pleased with my suggestion of what-did-you-expect.

Markam Massa, another resident, formerly a village elder of Kunder, only 4 kilometres or so away, could offer us little more than insight into their previous lives: an average of 6 acres of holding and farmland, some cattle and goats. The once-upon-a-usual. Every four months or so, he said, some villagers now made the trek to the abandoned hamlet under heavy protection to perform puja to the deities of the village. That protection didn't always work, he said. Just the day before, a villager was 'taken away' by the Maoists.

'This is a joke,' I finally grumbled to the police officer. 'How can you expect to conduct a proper interview in a few minutes with so many people? How can we expect any answers with senior officers, SPOs and weapons around?'

I tried to walk out of the camp into the village of Jagargunda, where I was told there had once been a State Bank of India branch. That I had to see. But I was prevented by my companions, armed guards and a Salwa Judum tough, a former Maoist called Rajura Mandavi. Carrying an AK-47, he smilingly told me how, in his previous avatar as a Naxal, he had helped mine the roads and tracks in the area. These days, he occasionally helped security forces to tag and clear those mines.

So, 'interviews' over, we walked over to the CRPF camp, had tea with the troops, were shown how they had planted a kitchen garden by the perimeter to supplement rations, and then took off in a tight spiral—to avoid overflying Maoist positions. Total time spent in Jagargunda, inclusive of everything: one hour and fifteen minutes. By 4.30 p.m. the same day, we had arrived at Dantewada. The following day, we drove to Kasoli, a village an hour's drive north, for more desultory interaction and, later that afternoon, flew to Jagdalpur, our overnight base before a journey back to Raipur and our homes.

In a few weeks, along with others I received an email from the Delhi University professor leading this 'study', saying there was very little time for the report to be compiled, that he had already begun to write it, and could we send 'bullet points' for him to add 'if required'. A telephonic row with him followed, during which I raged about how this study was being forced and was grossly inadequate. Weren't we supposed to submit full reports that would individually be published without biased intervention? The Chhattisgarh elections were due in just a few weeks, I remarked—suggesting clearly, of course, that the report could be used as a Salwa Judum white-wash by anyone who cared and was that the reason for the hurry?

I put my dissent on record in an email and sent it off to the professor of political science and the police officer.

I haven't heard from them since.

—

Daily, horrors unfold across the country, and in nine cases out of ten there will be no justice. Extreme inequality, oppression and bad governance ensure that there remain enough reasons—ammunition—from the Maoist point of view to do battle.

Karnataka's administration has over the past year been forced to upgrade its anti-Naxal forces and support systems across the hilly, forested north and central parts of the state. Security officials confirm the spread of Maoist rebellion into newer parts of Orissa and Madhya Pradesh. There have been attacks on police posts, announcement of de-facto ministries by CPI (Maoist), raids on factories to protest governments signing memoranda with corporations for mining and power.

To combat them, the state provides two questionable examples. One is Chhattisgarh's Salwa Judum, a strategy to divert attention from failures of governance and socio-economic development that no electoral victory—allegedly aided by vote-buying—can hide. The other example is that of Andhra Pradesh, where Maoists are on the defensive on account of a largely successful, ruthless policing strategy. But this vacuum of enforced peace is still not filled with development beyond the half-baked urban bling of Greater Hyderabad, leaving vast swathes vulnerable to recurring disaffection.

Meanwhile, the prime minister, at a meeting in New Delhi of directors general of police from across India in November 2008, reiterated the point he had made two and a half years previously, one that had created such a flutter in urban India: Maoism and its manifestations are the country's most challenging internal security threat.

That pretty much answered the question on several minds: are the Maoists in a last-gap phase or are they even more powerful now?

'It's do or die,' a key Maoist sympathizer told me last year in New Delhi during a conversation in which he spoke passionately of 'social reconstruction'. Of rebuilding. Whatever the polemic, the statement is born of the abysmal state of affairs in India beyond the space taken for granted by the middle and ruling classes.

In late December 2008, Rahul Sharma, superintendent of police in Dantewada, said in an interview with Kumkum Dasgupta of the *Hindustan Times*, in a chilling echo of my conversation with him two months earlier: 'The Naxals say they have 40 per cent of the district under [their] control. We control the other 40, and there is fierce fighting for the rest.' Given the propensity of our present political and social system to create great anger and resentment, in some years this may well be true of much of the country.

Or perhaps someone will heed the message implicit in the other thing that the police chief of Dantewada told *Hindustan Times*, voicing a sentiment common to nearly all police officials—and certainly his predecessor P.K. Das—engaged in combating rebels: 'I can fight the Naxals but not Naxalism. That has to be done only through development.'

ACKNOWLEDGEMENTS

My deepest gratitude to:

Dr Nandini Sundar, Professor, Department of Sociology, Delhi School of Economics, and Dr Ajai Sahni, Executive Director, Institute for Conflict Management, for encouragement and help.

Reema Barooah, Himanshu Kumar, Shailesh Singh, Mohit Satyanand and Premila Nazareth for their kindness and hospitality.

Gita Roka for help with Nepali translations.

Dr V. Anantha Nageswaran, head of investment research (Asia-Pacific and Middle East) with Bank Julius Baer, Singapore, and Bhaskar Goswami for their critical review of the manuscript and for correcting errors.

Several people who appear in this book as single alphabets in capital letters (revealing their identities any more would have jeopardized their positions and, in several cases, their lives).

Ravi Singh, my editor at Penguin, with whom I first discussed the idea and approach for this book, for appropriate mix of empathy and clinical appraisal.

Hindustan Times and *Rolling Stone—India*. After the release of the hardcover edition of *Red Sun*, I undertook some travels which I used for a number of articles and essays in these publications. Parts of some are included in the paperback volume.

And finally, Mario Mascarenhas, who had this well-known, but always welcome, advice: if you upset people on both sides, you're probably doing the right thing.

APPENDIX

EXCERPTS FROM THE 'URBAN PERSPECTIVE
PLAN' 2004 OF CPI (MAOIST)

(The text has not been edited for style, consistency and grammar for reasons of authenticity. Where necessary, parenthetical explanations are provided to clarify time, a term, title or acronym.)

OUR WORK IN URBAN AREAS

INTRODUCTION

Urbanisation Pattern

The old hierarchy of four mega cities located in different regions of the country is...giving way to urban corridors and clusters of new investment located mostly in the southern and western parts of the country.

With the exception of the Delhi region and adjacent areas in Haryana, Punjab, Rajasthan and Uttar Pradesh, much of the north, the east and the centre of the country have been bypassed. This vast area covering the eastern half of UP and stretching across Bihar, West Bengal, the North-Eastern states, Orissa, Madhya Pradesh and the eastern part of Maharashtra is remaining as an area of urban backwardness, with old industrial bases and high unemployment. These areas are thus the main sources of cheap migrant labour for the large metropolitan cities.

The above inequalities are being encouraged by the policies of the government. In the earlier period under industrial licensing there were some small attempts at bringing about balanced industrial development and this led to some projects being set up in relatively backward areas like the central India minerals belt. Now under the liberalisation policies investment is not regulated and goes to the areas promising the greatest profits. Thus the main investment is centred in and around a few areas of growing urban concentration.

De-industrialisation of major cities

Over the years most major cities have seen a decline in manufacturing activity as compared to business activity in banking, finance, and other service sectors. This process started first with the largest cities, with the close down of many of Kolkata's jute mills and other industries from the late sixties [1960s]. This process however became very generalised from the early eighties [1980s] with the decline of the textile mills in Mumbai, Ahmedabad, Chennai, and other centres. Lakhs of blue-collar jobs were destroyed without the setting up of any new industries within the city. Since the last twenty years now, hardly any new industry has been located within the major old cities. New industrialisation is normally taking place on the outskirts of the main city, or in the nearby towns and cities. This is combined by an increase of white-collar jobs in the field of services, with investment normally going into these areas.

This process has led to a change in the class composition of most cities, particularly the metropolitan cities.

Since this factor is very important for our organisational perspective, plans, and tasks at the city level, all the respective committees should conduct city level class analysis regarding the situation and trend in their areas.

Changes in the Workforce

With closures of industries and the accompanying loss of jobs, many workers are forced to take up casual work or earn on their own through hawking, plying rickshaws, running roadside tea stalls and food joints, etc. At the same time new youth entering the work force do not get regular jobs immediately (unemployment rate is the highest in the 15 to 24 age group) and are forced to take casual employment or also run some small trade. This trend is increasing in recent years in the urban areas. At the same time more and more women are being employed in jobs but at much lower wage rates. This trend which had started since the early eighties in most cities has further accelerated since the liberalisation policies [in the 1990s].

The percentage of urban males in regular work has dropped and the percentage of self-employed and casual labourers has gone up. At the same time the percentage of women in regular work has gone up, though this does not affect the total size of the working class so much because women compose only 17% of the total urban workforce.

This then means a change in the composition of the working people. Firstly there has been an increase in the proportion of the semi-proletariat (i.e. self-employed); secondly there has been an increase in the proportion of women workers being paid very low wages; and thirdly there has been an increase in the casual labour force.

Besides the above given changes, another change has been the shift of jobs from the larger factories of the organised sector to the small workshops and industries. In recent years the percentage of workers in the organised sector as compared to the total workforce has fallen from 8.5% in 1991 to 7.1% in 1997 to 6.9% in 1999-2000. As the workers are divided into smaller units their potential for unionisation also reduces.

All the above changes in the workforce have been presented here at the all-India level. These changes have significant consequences for our planning at the city and area levels. We should conduct local class analysis and plan accordingly.

Division or Segmentation of Cities

Cities and towns in India, basing on the colonial pattern, have always had a rich British section and a poorer Indian section. This separation however reduced to some extent in the process of growth of the metropolitan cities. Thus it became quite common to have slums adjoining posh high-rise buildings, and hawkers and vendors occupying space right next to the offices of multinationals in the heart of the central business district. Periodically drives would be taken up to demolish slums or evict hawkers, but they would most often manage to struggle and maintain their space within the centre of the city.

This process of dividing or segmenting the city is done through various measures. These measures extend from the old measures of slum demolition and hawker eviction to new forms like closure of 'polluting' factories, banning of protests in central areas, law changes encouraging privatisation and localisation of urban finance and urban facilities, regulations encouraging concentration of development in the richer zones, etc.

The role of the state is most prominent. Bureaucrats and urban planners operating under direct instructions from the World Bank, Asian Development Bank, and other imperialist institutions have formulated laws, regulations, policies and master plans, which have given up even the earlier pretence of the slogans of equity and alleviating of urban poverty. Now the basic thrust of the plans are on 'efficiency' and 'clean and green' cities, which means basically providing sanitized five star enclaves with the best infrastructure and communication facilities for the offices, houses, and entertainment facilities of the corporate managers and elites, while pushing the urban poor along with their 'unclean' slums and 'polluting' industries to the borders of the city. The basic thrust of the National Capital Plan for Delhi and the 1993 Mega-City programme for the other 5 top cities mentioned above basically has this objective. The High Courts and Supreme Court, aided by anti-people so-called environmentalists, have also played a very active role in this process giving numerous court rulings to speed up this process in the name of 'public interest' litigation.

POLICY AND GUIDELINES

Strategic Approach in Urban Work

Role of Urban Work within the Political Strategy

...Being the centres of concentration of the industrial proletariat, urban areas play an important part within the political strategy of the New Democratic Revolution. Urban work thus means, firstly, forming the closest possible links with the working class, and, through the class struggle, establishing the party as a proletarian vanguard; further, it means the mobilisation and unification of all other sections under proletarian leadership in the struggle to achieve the tasks of the revolution.

Role of Urban Work within the Military Strategy

...It is clear that the armed struggle and the movement in the rural areas will play the primary role, and the work in the cities will play a secondary role, complementary to the rural work. However, while giving first priority to the rural work, we must also give due importance to the urban struggle. Without a strong urban revolutionary movement, the ongoing people's war faces difficulties; further, without the participation of the urban masses it is impossible to achieve countrywide victory. As Com. Mao says, 'the final objective of the revolution is the capture of the cities, the enemy's main bases, and this objective cannot be achieved without adequate work in the cities.' (Mao, *Selected Works*, Vol. II, p. 317)

Long-term Approach

The cities and big industrial centres are the strongholds of reaction where the enemy is the most powerful. In these places the police, army, other state organs, and other forces of counter-revolution are concentrated and are in a dominant position from which they can suppress the people's forces.

In such a situation, where the enemy is much stronger, we cannot have a short-term approach of direct confrontation in order to achieve 'quick results'. Rather, we should have a long-term approach.

As Com. Mao, while outlining the tasks of the Party in the urban and other white areas dominated by the reactionaries, explained, 'the Communist Party must not be impetuous and adventurist in its propaganda and organizational work...it must have well-selected cadres working underground, must accumulate strength and bide its time there. In leading the people in struggle against the enemy, the Party must adopt the tactics of...waging struggles on just grounds, to our advantage, and with restraint, and making use of such open forms of activity as are permitted by law, decree and social custom; empty clamour and reckless action can never lead to success.' (Mao, *Selected Works*, Vol. II, p. 318)

Main Objectives of Our Urban Work

Work in the cities and towns involves a number of tasks. All these tasks can however be combined under three broad heads or objectives. They are as follows:

1. *Mobilise and organise the basic masses and build the Party on that basis:* This is the main activity of the Party. It is the Party's task to organise the working class, as well as other classes and sections like the semi-proletariat, students, middle class employees, intellectuals, etc. It also has the task of dealing with

the problems of special social groups like women, dalits, and religious minorities and mobilising them for the revolutionary movement. It is on this basis that the masses are politicized and the advanced sections consolidated into the Party.

2. *Build the United Front:* This involves the task of unifying the working class, building worker-peasant solidarity and alliance, uniting with other classes in the cities, building the fronts against globalisation, against Hindu fascism, against repression, etc. This is a very important aspect of the work of the Party in the city.

3. *Military Tasks:* While the main military tasks are performed by the PGA [People's Guerilla Army] and PLA [People's Liberation Army] in the countryside, the urban movement too performs tasks complementary to the rural armed struggle. These involve the sending of cadre to the countryside, infiltration of enemy ranks, organising in key industries, sabotage actions in coordination with the rural armed struggle, logistical support, etc.

Of the above three, the first task of organising the basic masses is fundamental and primary. Without widely mobilising the masses it is not possible to perform any of the other tasks such as building of UF [United Front] and performing the military tasks.

Mass Mobilisation and Party Building

We need to build the broadest mass base by building various types of mass organisations, such as, open revolutionary mass organisations, legal democratic organisations, secret mass organisations, cover organisations, etc. Depending upon the situation one or other type of organisation becomes primary for that period. But keeping in mind long term approach, we need to build several types of mass organisations simultaneously...As the Indian political situation is uneven, we need to explore right combination of various types of mass organisations. While there is no possibility to form open revolutionary mass organisations in AP [Andhra Pradesh], there are several states in which still such possibility still exists.

Correctly coordinating between illegal and legal structures, we should have an approach of step by step raising the forms of struggle and preparing the masses to stand up against the might of the state.

Types of Mass Organisations

[There are] three types of mass organisations: 1) Secret revolutionary mass organisations, 2) Open and semi-open revolutionary mass organisations, and 3) Open legal mass organisations, which are not directly linked to the Party. Urban work within the third type of organisations can further be subdivided into three broad categories: a) Fractional work, b) Party-formed cover organisations, and c) Legal democratic organisations.

Secret Revolutionary Mass Oganisations

In our party such mass organisations were not formed as a plan. They emerged in and around the struggle areas when the open revolutionary mass organisations were forced to go underground under severe repression. Later they were consciously formed even in areas with relatively less repression. Today with the imposition of an All-India ban...mass organisations in many more areas will be built underground. Many of these organisations are principally functioning in urban areas. Though such secret organisations may be formed in any section of the masses, we have so far, in the urban areas, mainly set them up among the youth, students, and workers.

It is the task of the secret units and committees to plan the forms and methods of propagating the Party line, the dissemination of Party propaganda, and the formulation and propagation of the revolutionary standpoint on various issues of the day—particularly the issues affecting the section which they are organising. These can be done through secret posters, voices, pamphlets, cassettes, booklets, and other forms of propaganda; it can be done through personal contact by the organisation members; it can be done through planned dramatic actions like attacks on imperialist, comprador, and other ruling class targets, etc. Through sustained and effective propaganda, and planned actions, the secret revolutionary mass organisation must aim to reach a position where it influences, guides and even determines the actions and decisions of the non-Party organisations and the masses in its field of operation.

...The secret organisation performs its revolutionary role by giving calls and conducting propaganda to guide and push the open organisations in the correct direction. However this too should be avoided in areas where the field of fractional or cover work is too small or where the open revolutionary propaganda may lead to exposure that we are doing such work in that area. If it is necessary for the secret organisation members to actively work within the open organisation, they will work as ordinary open members of the organisation, while taking special care to safeguard their political identity. It is better to avoid combining of the tasks of the secret organisation activist and open organisation leader; wherever possible different comrades should be assigned these separate tasks.

Open Revolutionary Mass Organisations

These are the open and semi-open mass organisations, which openly propagate the politics of New Democratic Revolution and prepare the people for armed struggle. These organisations make use of the available legal opportunities to carry on revolutionary propaganda and agitation openly and try to mobilise anti-imperialist, anti-feudal forces as widely as possible.

Our Party has formed and run such open revolutionary mass organisations since the seventies, particularly in the period following the lifting of the Emergency in 1977. These open organisations were then the main organs of mass mobilisation both in the rural and urban areas. They were the banners under which thousands and lakhs were mobilised, particularly in the struggle areas of AP and Bihar. These mobilizations reached their peak in the 'open' periods upto 1986 and during 1991 in AP. They played the role of attracting the broad masses towards the revolution. However with the onset of repression most of these organisations were denied any legal opportunities and were forced to go underground. Direct bans were imposed in AP and Bihar, whereas serious restrictions and surveillance were placed on the organisations in other states. Thus the scope of such organisations has drastically reduced with the rise in repression on our Party throughout the country. Today only very small open bodies exist in some cities.

As is clear from experience, this form of organisation can only be used when the ruling classes, due to various reasons cannot or do not bring repression. This being the case there is limited scope for this type of organisation in the urban areas.

...We should expose only a small section of our forces and make sure that the majority of our cadre remain hidden from enemy surveillance. We should on no account indulge in small demonstrations where all our activists are easily identified and even videofilmed for easy targeting in future.

Fractional Work

Work of this nature can be carried out in various types of organisations. The best organisations are those which are more oriented to struggle, like trade unions, slum and other locality based organisations, youth organisations, unemployed organisations, students' associations and unions, women's organisations, commuter associations, etc. Besides there are also other organisations which are welfare oriented, community based or are self-help organizations— like workers' cooperatives, cultural organisations, sports clubs and gymnasiums, libraries, bhajan mandals, non-governmental welfare organisations, women's welfare organisations, caste based and nationality based welfare organisations, minorities' bodies, etc. There are also many organisations, which emerge on a particular issue, for a particular period, or for a particular festival, etc.

Once we have decided to do fractional work within an organisation we should strive to achieve a leading position in it. This means we should be in a position to influence and guide the decisions of the organisation. If it is necessary to takeover office bearers' posts in order to achieve this influence, then we should make attempts to do so.

Whether we take up office bearers' posts or not, the important point in fractional work is the skilful exposure of the reactionaries and reformists leading or participating within these organisations. This exposure is essential to draw the masses away from their influence. This must however be done without exposing ourselves to the enemy. The forms of exposure will thus differ depending upon the concrete situation. In vast areas where risk of direct exposure of our fractional work activists is low, we can use propaganda by the secret revolutionary mass organisation or even direct calls by the Party. In smaller areas like a single factory or slum we may have to mainly or only use word-of-mouth propaganda. Sometimes we can create artificial banners like 'angry workers', 'concerned slum dwellers', etc. for doing our propaganda. Very often we may have to use a combination of various methods. Whatever be the method it should be applied carefully, skilfully, and consistently.

The crucial point is to achieve the correct balance of making the fullest use of the legal opportunities without crossing the boundaries set by social customs, habits, existing forms of struggle, etc. Our speech and actions should suit the normal functioning of the activists and masses in the particular area. This will of course vary from situation to situation. While it may not be abnormal to resort to gherao among many sections of industrial workers, we may have to restrict to black badges and dharnas for bank employees; while militant anti-dowry and anti-caste struggles may be normal in some areas and states, social norms in other states or areas may be such that they would draw immediate suspicion if we tried to engage in such struggles through cover organisations. We would probably have to restrict ourselves to propaganda in such situations. Thus we should plan our activities, and our issues and forms of struggle according to the concrete situation of the class struggle, so that our Party identity is not quickly suspected and exposed. We should of course not reduce ourselves to mere tails of the masses. We should be skilful enough to remain one step ahead of the masses, without getting exposed.

Party-formed Cover Mass Organisations

It sometimes becomes necessary for us to directly form mass organisations under cover without disclosing their link with the Party. Mostly, such a need arises due to the absence of any other suitable mass organisation within which we can do fractional work. An example is the case of unorganised workers, where the established trade unions have a limited presence and we often have no option but to set up our own trade union organisation to take up the unorganised workers' demands. This however is not the only area where we may form cover organisations. In fact, cover organisations can be of as many varied types as the organisations for fractional work we have mentioned in the earlier section. They can range from trade union type struggle organisations to welfare type organisations to issue-based organisations, etc.

We should be careful (especially in repression areas) not to attract the attention of the state by far exceeding the socially acceptable limits of militancy for that area. For example if the normal weapons used in the area are knives and swords we should not resort to firearms, or we should not normally resort to annihilations in a new area where there has not been any history of such actions.

We have had some experience of building cover organisations now since the last few years. We have committed various mistakes...leading to the quick exposure of our forces in many areas.

Legal Democratic Organisations

These are the organisations formed on an explicit political basis with some or all aspects of an anti-imperialist, anti-feudal programme, and with a programme of action and forms of struggle that broadly fall within a legal framework. Some such organisations may be those catering to a particular section like trade unions, student bodies, women's fronts, caste abolition organisations, nationality organisations, writers' associations, lawyers' organisations, teachers' associations, cultural bodies, etc. Others may be formed with issue-oriented programmes focussing on particular core questions like contract labour system, unemployment and job losses, caste atrocities, communalism, imperialist culture, violence on women, saffronisation of education, corruption, regional backwardness and statehood, etc.

...Actually the legal democratic organisations serve as important means to the Party's attempts at the political mobilisation of the urban masses. This is because repression normally prevents the open revolutionary mass organisations from functioning. The legal democratic movement is thus the arena where the masses can participate in thousands and lakhs and gain political experience. It thus has a very important role in the revolution, complementary to the armed struggle in the countryside. Revolutionaries in other countries, particularly the Philippines, have participated within and utilised the legal democratic movement very effectively.

...As long as the organisation adheres to the principles of legal democratic functioning, and as long as it has a broad enough base of support, it will be difficult for the state to close it down.

Organising at the Place of Residence

In slums and other poor localities there are already numerous traditional organisations in existence. Constantly living in precarious conditions, the urban poor naturally come together to help each other and unite within organisations to fight for their rights, to secure better living conditions, to solve problems among themselves and to better organise their social and cultural activities. The common types of traditional organisations are slum-dwellers' organisations, basti or chawl committees, mahila mandals, youth clubs, sports clubs, cultural bodies, committees for various festivals like Ganesh festival, Durga puja, Ambedkar Jayanti, etc. There are also some organisations that are peculiar to certain regions, cities, and areas.

Since such organisations offer the best cover we should try to make the best use of these traditional organisations and mainly work from within them. Even if there is a need to form new legal organisations, we should normally give them the forms already existing among the masses.

Struggle issues are a regular feature of locality work, particularly slum work. Fights for basic amenities like water, electricity, toilets and sewerage, against corruption and exploitation of ration shop owners, adulterators and black marketeers, against slumlords, goonda gangs and other lumpens, and against demolitions are some of the regular issues. We should organise the struggles on these issues through the local committees and the slum-dweller organisations. As women and unemployed youth play a leading role in most of these struggles, the mahila mandals and youth clubs should also be involved and struggles can even be led under their banners.

A problem peculiar to slum work is the problem of imperialist funded NGOs. They are today in existence in almost all the slums of the main cities of the country. We should educate the slum masses and particularly the activists about the sinister role of such organisations and the agencies financing them. We should particularly expose them when they stand in the path of the people's struggles. However if such organisations come forward for struggles we can have issue-based unity with them. In situations of repression we can also work within them.

We should consolidate the activists emerging from the struggle first into basti activist groups and then into Party candidate cells and full cells. The basti activist groups, the Party cells and the basti Party committees are the cores for planning and leading all the activities and struggles in the bastis, for political propaganda and education, and for recruiting new members into the Party.

The situation of the urban poor in the slums and poor localities is worsening continuously. The slum population of India today stands at 4.1 crores [41 million], spread in 607 towns. The largest mega city, Mumbai, has 49% of its population in the slums. Our Party has so far paid limited attention to the organising of this section. Other revolutionary parties, particularly the Peru Communist Party (PCP) have been particularly successful in this respect. In fact the shanty towns of Lima have been the strongholds of the revolutionaries for a long period. We too should work at creating such strongholds in India's major cities.

Activist Groups

The secret activist group is a crucial unit in the Party-building and recruitment process. It is the preliminary organisational form for consolidation of the most active and sincere elements emerging from the class struggle. It is the unit through which the activities of its members are given political direction, through which they receive ideological and political education, through which their life decisions are politicised, and through which they are chosen to become members of the Party.

The activist group may be formed at the workplace—factory, mine, industrial estate, shift, department, section, office, branch, or any other level which is a unit for organising; it may be formed at the place of residence—the slum, chawl, street, society, or any other level which is a unit for organising; it may be formed in schools, colleges, or other institutions; and where the organising is based on a particular section, the activist group can be formed at the level suitable for that section.

While leading the group in the above responsibilities, it is the task of the PM [Party Member] in charge to conduct the ideological and political education of the group. While classes and joint study should be conducted, great importance should also be given to other more flexible methods like informal discussion, films, individual reading, etc. As the group develops, where feasible, there should be collective discussion on personal and family problems and this should be used to help the members to take political decisions in their personal life.

Through the above process some or all or even none of the activist group members may develop to become candidate members and members of the Party. This will lead to the formation of a cell in the same area where the activist group had been operating. Once such a cell has been formed, the activist group should be dissolved or reconstituted without exposing the cell-formation to the non-PMs...Thus the activist group is a transitory form of organisation.

Political Education

Mass organisational education should use open forms of mass education for all topics permissible without attracting the attention of the state. We should try to adopt and adapt all locally prevalent forms used by the ruling classes and other classes. These can be like libraries, street corner reading posts and other such means which can be used to disseminate progressive literature among other general books; lecture series during festivals, debate competitions, elocution competitions, etc. where our comrades express progressive views; public speaking courses, personality development courses, etc. with political topics included in the syllabus; mass organisation training camps, and the like. The level of political education possible through such methods will of course be very low, but it is very essential to be conducted on a regular basis to keep up a political atmosphere among even the more backward sections within the mass organisation. For the more advanced sections we have of course to use different forums and methods—e.g. the activist group.

Party Structure

The essential principle forming the basis of our Party structure, particularly in the urban area, is political centralisation combined with organisational decentralisation. This means that all PMs and all bodies, particularly at the lower level, should have solid ideological-political foundations, so that they are able to independently find their bearings and take the correct organisational decisions according to the political line of the Party. This is particularly important in the urban areas because of the technical difficulties of maintaining close and constant links between the secret higher bodies and those at the lower levels engaged in direct open work.

This is also important because urban work often demands immediate and quick responses to the events of the day. With rapid advances in electronic communication and media, delays of days and sometimes even hours in politically reacting to major events can hinder the impact that our Party can have on the urban movement. This thus depends on the strength of the bodies that form the foundation of our urban Party structure—the cells and the lower level committees—as well as on the Party fractions that link the Party with the mass organisations.

Party Cell

The urban Party cell can be formed on the basis of unit of production— for workers this could be factory, shop, department, section, shift, production line, industrial estate, etc. For students and middle class employees it could be the college, school, institution, office, etc. The cell can also be formed on geographical basis (i.e. the place of residence)—this would be the slum, chawl, street, society, etc. Wherever the number of PMs in a particular unit (e.g. factory) is less than three they can be combined with adjoining units to form a cell. However this should not be done indiscriminately in the urban areas as this would lead to unnecessary exposure. Where the work is integrated a common cell may be formed. In other cases it is better to wait for further recruitment before formation of a cell.

The cell is the body leading all other organisational units within its sphere of responsibility. It performs its basic tasks under the leadership of the next higher committee. The basic tasks of the urban cell include organising the masses, politicising them, educating the advanced elements and recruiting them into the party, and preparing its members and other activists to go to the countryside to work for the success of the agrarian revolution.

The cell should develop its own secret network of shelters and meeting places. As far as possible meetings should not be held in the areas where the members do their political work among the masses. Generally cell members should not be transferred from cell to cell as this would lead to unnecessary exposure.

Where there are at least three PRs functioning in an area and are known to each other, a Professional Revolutionary Cell (PRC) may be formed...The main function of the PRC is to provide the political training and development to the PR, which would not be possible within the time constraints and other limitations of a part timer cell. Longer political education programmes, collective study and debate, and other similar activities can be conducted through the PRC. Thus it can play a positive role in rapidly developing the future Party leadership.

Layers

Layers refers to the various levels in the urban Party organisation like city committee, area committees, factory/basti/college committees, cells, candidate cells, as well as the links to the mass organisations like activist groups and fractions. Due to greater enemy threat in the urban areas it is always necessary to maintain a number of layers from the lowest to the highest levels, and it is important to work through these layers without bypassing them.

The core question for functioning through layers is to see that each layer is trained and developed to independently perform the functions at the particular level. This requires the close guidance and follow-up of the next higher level. The guidance should be directed to developing the independent capabilities of the comrades at that level as well as the team functioning of the committee.

United Front

The urban areas are the centres for struggle by various classes, under the leadership of several organisations representing them. It is essential that we unite with such struggling organisations and build up broad struggles against the ruling classes Thus a significant part of the party's work in the urban areas concerns joint front activity. This includes the formation of various tactical united fronts, as well as building the worker peasant alliance, which is the basis of the strategic united front. This extends from the task of building basic working class unity, to solidarity with the peasantry, to unity with the other revolutionary classes like the semi-proletariat and petty bourgeoisie, right up to maintaining relations and even joint activity with national bourgeois and even ruling class organisations. Let us look at the main forms of such united front activity:

Working Class Unity

Joint trade union fronts are important for increasing the fighting strength of the working class. These joint fronts may be issue-based or based on a minimum political understanding and programme. They may be organised at various levels—industry, area, city, region, all-India, and international...The legal democratic working class joint front organisations can play a very useful role in achieving this long term objective.

Industry-based Unity

Due to the multiplicity of unions in India, in most industries there is very low possibility of achieving the 'one industry, one union' principle. In such a situation we should work for or support the next best option of forming co-ordination committees of the unions within a particular industry. We should try to draw all the unions with significant membership into such bodies. Such unity can start on issue basis and can later advance to a more permanent minimum understanding.

Similarly it is necessary to unite the various factory level unions within a particular company. Such unity can start at the co-ordination committee level or be formed as a federation.

In the present globalisation scenario where the production in one country is easily transferred across international borders, international workers' unity is also very important and necessary. Such unity is today very weak. We should however support initiatives for building the international unity of workers within a single multinational or within a particular industry. Even where it is not possible to give the unity an organisational form we should push for solidarity struggles and strikes and do propaganda in this regard.

Issue-based Unity

Our approach in such joint fronts is to build the broadest possible struggling unity of all organisations that have a minimum common stand on the issue. At the same time there should be no compromise on basic principles. Very often joint front bodies tend to become ineffective top heavy bodies, or forums for endless debate. Our approach should be to see that the joint front builds the broadest possible unity of the masses and is not merely the joint front of a few leaders. The attempt should be to take the masses forward in militant struggle and politicise them in the process.

Area-based Unity

This unity can be for an industrial area, town/city, region, state, all-India etc. Unity in a particular industrial area or locality may be restricted to only putting up a common front against problems faced by the workers of the area like goondas, transport, sanitation, water, etc. However area unity at higher levels is normally based on some minimum political understanding. It is the unity of like-minded unions and other bodies, who agree to struggle together to achieve a common set of demands or issues or stand by common political goals. This is thus the most common type of legal democratic workers' organisation.

Workers' Platforms

Another form of uniting the working class on a political basis is to directly form legal democratic workers' organisations as forums or platforms with a minimum workers' programme. Such platforms do not principally attempt to unite the unions, but target the worker activists of various unions and attempt to rally them politically. Such bodies use meetings, demonstrations, talks, seminars, cultural programmes and various means of propaganda to draw the advanced sections from among the workers on a political basis. They should also mobilise for agitations and struggles on political and other issues. The aim should be to draw the widest possible non-Party forces who can be united around the programme.

Worker-Peasant Alliance

The revolutionary workers' organisation has a particularly important role to play. It has to take on the main responsibility of propaganda and agitation regarding the agrarian war. Constant and continuous propaganda regarding the progress of the rural movement, the victories achieved, and the repression it faces, and the need for solidarity of the workers with this movement should be an essential part of the work of this organisation. Since the organisation has to normally function secretly it will not be possible to organise open solidarity demonstrations by the workers. However the revolutionary organisation activists can use the method of secret shock actions for propaganda purposes to highlight issues concerning the agrarian struggle.

...We should however not organise open demonstrations in support of our movement if we expect the mobilisation to be low, as it will only result in the exposure of our forces. We should in fact plan such actions in order to mobilise non-Party forces in large numbers. Another type of programme which can be taken up through the legal democratic organisations is large joint mobilisations of workers and peasants on common issues like WTO, state repression, etc.

Unity of the Urban Exploited Classes

Besides the working class, the other exploited classes and sections of the urban areas include the semi-proletariat, the urban poor concentrated in the slums, the students, teachers, employees, and other sections of the middle classes, etc. The Party sends its cadre to organise and lead the mass organisations of all these classes. This however is not the only way by which the working class and its Party unites and provides leadership to all these classes. Solidarity struggles and united front activity are the important means by which the working class inspires and leads all other classes in struggle.

The other medium through which the urban united front is built is through joint fronts on various issues concerning the general mass of the urban population, like price rise, corruption, closure of a key industry or many industries, or various urban problems like water shortage, commuter problems, sanitation issues, etc. Such issues unite all classes but mainly involve the exploited sections.

Unity with the Semi-Proletariat

The semi-proletariat, living in extremely poor conditions, is the urban class with the greatest potential for unity with the proletariat. In recent years the new economic policies have led to a steep rise in their numbers. Many workers are being thrown into the ranks of the semi-proletariat and many rural migrants who come in search of jobs end up in petty trades or in doing sundry odd jobs. Because of their dispersed nature they are not as well organised as the proletariat. It is therefore the task of Party to organise this class and build about its close unity with the industrial workers.

White-collar Employees

In the globalisation period the ruling classes have launched a concentrated propaganda attack against this section as an overpaid, underworked section whose salaries and numbers should be reduced. Thus some sections are being forced to agree to very meagre rises in salary and cuts in earlier allowances. They have also been the target of various privatisation and VRS [Voluntary Retirement Scheme] schemes. Though they have been struggling continuously they often do not receive the sympathy and support of other sections. Our workers' unions, legal democratic and secret workers' organisations, and sometimes even the Party should make it a point to express solidarity in various ways with the struggles of the bank employees, teachers, journalists, etc.

Other Sections of the Petty Bourgeoisie

Some section or the other of the petty bourgeoisie is often in struggle. The students come out in agitations, the lawyers resort to strikes, the shopkeepers also have their protests and bandhs. When these struggles take a militant turn they face the attacks of the state. The working class should be alive to the struggles of these sections. We should, through the trade unions, legal democratic organisations and even the Party, express solidarity. Where possible we should not restrict ourselves merely to statements of support. During major struggles and repression we should make all attempts to mobilise the workers in large numbers to come out on the streets in support. Where there is sufficient support we should attempt to widen the scope of the issue and involve as many sections as possible in support.

Among the urban petty bourgeiosie students and youth constitute important category. They react to the events and historically from the anti-British movement they played a significant role. In the wake of Naxalbari their role is exemplary. Our party has good experience in organising them. While working in urban areas, we must pay necessary attention to organise them.

There is need to empahsise the necessity of uniting with intellectuals. We need to allot sufficient cadre to work among them and some special effort be put in to unite and organise them.

Relations with the National Bourgeoisie

Due to the vacillating and exploitative nature of the national bourgeoisie, its wide participation in the strategic united front generally takes place only at later stages in the revolution. However there is scope in the urban areas, for supporting or uniting with various sections of the national bourgeoisie in tactical united fronts.

These can be on various issues like reduction of taxes, cut in electricity rates, anti small industry policies and court decisions, protest against entry of multinationals and foreign goods, exploitation of ancillary producers by big industry, etc. Our support can take the form of propaganda or even extend to militant mobilising of workers on the issue.

Another mode of unity could be through joint front bodies with national bourgeois organisations. Mostly such unity will be issue-based like preventing relocation or closure of industries, opposing anti small industry laws and tax increases, etc. However as the anti-globalisation and anti-WTO movement picks up we will have to try our best to draw the more progressive sections and organisations of the national bourgeoisie into the movement.

The ceaseless attacks of the imperialists and their Indian agents are daily pushing the national bourgeoisie into more conflict with the ruling classes. Thus today the practical possibilities of unity from below are growing. These possibilities are greater in cities with a stronger national bourgeois presence like the Delhi belt, the Coimbatore-Erode belt in Tamil Nadu, Surat in Gujarat, etc.

Front Against Repression

[An] excellent form of building broad fighting unity against repression is to take up particular cases of brutal state repression and immediately mobilise all sections of the masses in militant struggle. Police firings, lock up deaths, rape by security forces, are some of the examples that can be used to rouse the masses into open battle. There have been many instances like the Rameeza Bee case and others, where such incidents proved to be the turning points for building not only militant struggle but also much broader democratic movements. In some cases where the above methods lead to broad movements we can work with others for the formation of organisations of a more long term nature with a broad anti-fascist repression programme.

United Front Against Hindu Fascist Forces

An important call of the Ninth Congress is to build a broad UF of all secular forces and persecuted religious minorities such as Muslims, Christians, and Sikhs against the Hindu fascist forces. Since a large proportion of the minorities are urbanised and since the attacks of the Hindu fascists are as yet mostly concentrated in the cities, this UF has basically been the responsibility of the urban organisation. This task has appeared in our documents now from many years, but very little has as yet been done. One of the explanations for this failure is the weakness of our urban organisations, but the other more important reason is our neglect of work among the minorities.

The above UF cannot be built merely by uniting some secular individuals on the basis of a political programme. In order to be effective it has to involve the masses, particularly the masses from the minorities. This therefore means that we must have substantial grassroots work among the minorities, particularly the Muslim masses who are the most numerous and the worst victims of the Hindu fascists' atrocities. However due to extreme ghettoisation in almost all Indian cities, this is only possible if we take a conscious decision to shift out at least some forces from Hindu dominated areas and base them in the slums and localities inhabited by the Muslim poor. This would be the first step to building any united front.

The line of action for building anti-globalisation fronts should...rely primarily on the working class, while rallying around all other sections in the struggles against the imperialist policies.

Other classes and sections of importance we should try to draw into the anti-globalisation front are the peasants' organisations and the farmers' bodies, slum bodies, students' organisations, intellectuals, writers and cultural activists, pro-people environmental groups, teachers and other middle class employees' associations' etc. The scope of the antiglobalisation movement is so large that it includes practically all classes who are part of the strategic UF. While the separate organisations formed by these sections against various aspects of globalisation objectively form part of the movement, we should nevertheless try to draw all such organisations into common united struggle on a common anti-imperialist programme.

Reactionaries like Swadeshi Jagran Manch, revisionists like CPI, CPI (M) and foreign funded NGOs are some of the forces involved in anti-globalisation movement. These forces are linked to the ruling classes or part of them. We must keep away from the reactionaries in any joint front. With regard to the revisionists who are part of ruling classes, we ourselves should not invite them into any joint front, but if they are part of a front called by others, we need to keep away because of their presence. The revisionists and foreign funded NGOs may participate to some extent but there is always danger of them attempting to sabotage the movement at higher levels of struggles. We must be alert to this danger.

MILITARY TASKS

As explained earlier, the urban movement plays a secondary and complementary role in the military strategy of the revolution. While the main military tasks are performed by the PGA and PLA in the countryside, the urban organisation too performs tasks complementary to the rural armed struggle. Due to the spread of urbanisation, the growth of a number of mega cities, and the sharper division of the cities into rich and poor sections, the possibility and importance of urban military operations increases. These however yet remain second to the rural military tasks. The varied military tasks performed in the urban areas relate to, 1) the defence of the urban movement, 2) help by the urban organisation to the rural armed struggle, and 3) direct military operations conducted under central direction. These thus form the main categories of military tasks and forms of organisation in the urban areas.

Defence of the Urban Movement

The nature of urban work being primarily legal and defensive, the military tasks directly related to the urban movement are basically defensive in nature and will remain that way till the final period of the [r]evolution. However even a defensive urban movement requires the military type organisation of the armed defence of the urban masses against the peoples' enemies. These enemies are of various types—goonda gangs acting in the service of the ruling classes, Hindu fascist organisations and their militias, vigilante gangs specifically organised by the state to attack activists and sympathisers of our movement, state forces themselves, etc. Without standing up to such forces it would not be possible for an organisation to survive and develop. While we cannot and should not, at this stage, organise for armed offensive confrontation with the state, we should definitely build such defence organisations as are suited to the concrete situation.

Open Self Defence Teams

Wherever necessary the legal organisations should organise self defence against the local enemies. Examples of such self-defence teams are union self defence against lumpen strike breakers, basti self defence teams against goonda gangs, mahila organisation self defence teams against eve-teasers and molesters, mohalla all-community self defence during communal riot situations, mass self defence against slum demolition, etc. Open self defence teams should be organised in such a way as to mobilise sizeable sections of the masses in this task, particularly motivating the youth to participate in large numbers. When such defence is organised systematically involving the broad masses, it greatly strengthens the legal organisation, gives confidence to the rank and file and the local leadership, and releases the creative energies of the masses. If such activity grows in an area it gives rise to new creative forms of militant mass fighting. Conversely, it demoralises and paralyses the enemy, and prevents him from using his old forms of repression.

Often such open self defence is organised on a temporary basis for a particular situation or period. However wherever possible we should plan and attempt to give this mass self defence a permanent form and structure, allocating specific responsibilities, and linking with the mass organisational committees. Such bodies can run *vyayamshalas*, martial arts centres, sports clubs, etc.

Secret Self Defence Squads

Secret squads are necessary to supplement the open defence teams, or where, due to repression, it is not possible to form such teams. They too are formed with the broad objective of defending the urban mass movement. One significant form of activity is to participate along with the masses and give them the confidence to undertake militant mass action. Other tasks are to secretly hit particular targets who are obstacles in the advance of the mass movement.

The secret squads require proper military training, and military and political education. The extent and depth of the training will depend on the facilities available, but we must make the best efforts to ensure that the squads are properly trained and armed. The arms used will depend on the situation in the area. As far as possible arms which are not normally used in the area should not be employed.

Due attention should be paid to the discipline of such squads. Selection of members should not be merely on the basis of military abilities, but should consider the political level and discipline of the comrades. All squad members maintain their jobs or other responsibilities and only combine for the purpose of training or actions. They disperse again immediately after that.

The squads should function under direct and strict party control, with each squad functioning under a responsible Party comrade. As far as possible no two squads should be combined for performing an action. The knowledge of existence of such squads too should be as restricted as possible. Each squad is a separate entity and there should not be any separate line of command within the self defence squads. All State committees should periodically review the activities of such formations and give guidelines to the committees immediately responsible for them.

Urban Militia

At this stage of the revolution all the open and secret organs of people's defence will maintain a separate identity and the Party will be the only body coordinating their activities. Today there is no scope for bringing together all or many of the self defence teams and squads under a single organisational mechanism to form a militia. This may be possible during certain periods of upsurge when significant sections of the urban population are ready to take up arms either against the fascist militias or against the state. At such times the Party should take immediate initiative to launch urban militia without exposing all its forces. The concrete organisational form of such an urban militia would however depend on the particular situation and the specific forces operating at that time.

Local Intelligence

Intelligence is a much-neglected function in our Party. Very often we suffer severe losses, or lose good opportunities due to the absence of proper intelligence. In the urban areas intelligence is also very necessary to protect and preserve the urban Party as well as the mass movement. Thus the task of information collection and analysis should be taken up from the beginning itself and responsibility should be allocated accordingly. As the organisation grows this task and responsibility should exist at all levels and should be integrated into the functioning of the organisation.

The objectives of our intelligence work should be to learn about and study the tactics and plans of the enemy forces in the area, to study the activities of informers, to prevent infiltration into the organisation, etc. The methods and structure, particularly at the lower levels, should be as simple as possible and should utilise to the maximum the forces available to us from among the masses.

Help to the Rural Armed Struggle

There are numerous ways through which the urban movement can assist the rural armed struggle and particularly, the base areas and the guerilla zones. Some involve direct and immediate help in terms of materials and personnel; others involve the long-term preparation for the decisive battles in the later stages of the peoples' war.

Work in Key Industries

Some industries like transport, communications, power, oil and natural gas, defence production, etc. can play a crucial role in the peoples' war. Disruption of production in these industries has an immediate impact on the enemy's ability to fight the war. If struggles in such industries are coordinated with developments in the peoples' war they can provide direct assistance to the PGA/PLA. Party led units within such industries can also perform industrial sabotage actions, which would provide effective assistance during certain points in the war. It is thus the responsibility of the urban organisation to establish a presence and influence in such key industries.

The key industries have normally been in the public sector. Now however with the policy of privatisation, many of the old units are being privatised and new units are being set up directly in the private sector. Thus some of these industries, like the electricity boards and telecommunications department, are experiencing many militant struggles in opposition to the privatisation policies and there has been a significant revival of the trade unions. In the context of the general upswing of the workers' movement, the workers of other key industries too are resorting to struggle. We can therefore make use of this situation to try and influence the workers in these industries.

Infiltration into the Enemy Camp

It is very important to penetrate into the military, para-military forces, police, and higher levels of the administrative machinery of the state. It is necessary to obtain information regarding the enemy, to build support for the revolution within these organs, and even to incite revolt when the time is ripe. Other types of technical help are also possible.

The cities are the strongholds of the enemy and have a large concentration of enemy forces. It is therefore from the cities that attention must be given to this task. Such work can be done by following up contacts obtained from the civilian sphere, or by directly allocating comrades to penetrate the enemy ranks. Whatever be the method, the work is of a very special type which requires a high degree of political reliability, skill and patience. Such work should be without the knowledge of the lower level committees and the details of the work should only remain with the comrades directly responsible.

Associated with this task is the need for a plan to work in the cantonment towns spread out throughout the country. Such work even among the civilian population of these towns can give us valuable information and openings for penetration in the enemy ranks.

Sending Cadre to the Rural Areas and the PGA/PLA

A steady supply of urban cadre is necessary to fulfill the needs of the rural movement and the people's war. This is necessary for providing working class leadership, as well as technical skills to the people's war.

To fulfill the need of recruitment from workers in large numbers and sending them to rural areas, we need to work in the unorganized sector where overwhelming percentage of working class is there. While we need to work in key industries which is organised sector for the strategic reasons, we must mobilise and organise millions of workers who are in the unorganised segment. The working conditions are horrendous in this sector and militant struggles are bound to come up here. Most of the working class has live connections with backward rural pockets, in some of which already armed struggles are going on. If we work patiently we can get good recruitment whom we can send to the areas of armed struggle zones.

Logistical Support to the Armed Struggle

The enemy gets all its logistics support from the urban areas. The People's Army however relies as far as possible on the rural areas and the rural masses. However for certain crucial things there is need for support from the urban areas. Depending on its strength, the urban organisation should make all efforts to provide such support.

Supplies or contacts for supplies of certain types are only available in the urban areas. Examples of such supplies are arms and ammunitions, spare parts, certain types of medical supplies, etc. Helping the People's Army to establish the supply lines in this regard is a task that the urban organisation can perform. However once such a supply line is established it is best maintained by the rural organisation. As the needs of the base areas and guerilla zones grow there will be even a need to establish a separate supply and transport wing in this regard.

Medical networks of sympathetic doctors and use of hospital facilities to treat PGA/PLA fighters are also necessary in the urban areas. This is necessary for certain cases which cannot be treated with the facilities available in the guerilla zone areas. Here too the urban Party should always be on the lookout for sources and contacts to set up such a network in various cities. Once a network has been established however it should be separated from the Party bodies leading the urban mass work.

Technical help in the form of repairs and maintenance of fighting, communication and other equipment of the PGA/PLA is another area where the urban organisation has to provide assistance. This is best done by preparing comrades with technical, electrical, electronic and other skills to go and take up such responsibilities in the countryside. It can also be done be sending city comrades to conduct training courses for the PGA/PLA. In some cases where necessary the repair of some equipment can be done in the urban areas. Providing the contacts to help set up a network for production of certain items in the urban areas is also another area of necessary help.

Development of new technologies for the People's War is another crucial area. With the daily advance of technology, there are numerous new devices that could be adapted in the service of the people's war. Since the large metropolitan centres are the points where such technologies or the information regarding such technologies are obtained, it would be the responsibility of all comrades in such areas to be ever alert to any opportunity in this regard. Proposals and devices obtained or developed should be sent to the higher committees for consideration and implementation. Since it would in the future be necessary to set up separate research and development wings in this regard, it would be the task of the urban organisation to develop suitable comrades for such work.

Urban Military Operations under Central Direction

Though the countryside is the main area of operations of the People's Army, there are certain military objectives that need to be performed through operations in the urban areas. This even requires the setting up of permanent structures of the PGA/PLA in the cities and towns.

City Action Teams

These action teams are small secret teams of disciplined and trained soldiers of the PGA/PLA who are permanently based in the cities or towns to hit at important, selected, enemy targets. Such targets may be annihilation of individuals of military importance or sabotage actions like the blowing up of ammunition depots, destroying communications networks, damaging oil installations, etc. These action teams which form part of the main force of the PGA/PLA, perform these actions under the guidance and orders of their respective command. Thus these teams should have no connection whatsoever with the local urban Party structure. The selection of targets and timing of operations too would be based on the overall political and military needs of the people's war. However the secret team should have some broad understanding of the schedules and plans of the programmes of the open mass organisations. This could where possible help prevent problems due to clashing between the open and secret plans.

Details regarding the role, tasks, training and education of the city action teams should be undertaken by the Central Military Commission (CMC).

Central Intelligence

Since the enemy is centred in the big cities, it is very important that our Party develops a network to obtain and analyse political and military intelligence at higher levels. Besides human intelligence, we can make use of the Internet and other modern electronic means for gathering information by entering the enemy's networks. For this it is necessary to allocate separate responsibility. Urban Party organisation may provide contacts and individuals for this work. However once they are assigned to this work they do not maintain any links with the local organisation. Such networks are led and directed by the highest bodies of the Party.

Cyber Warfare

We should, to the extent possible, make use of computers and the Internet...to further the military objectives of the revolution. Though we are today quite distant from this possibility, we should have the perspective of setting up units with the task of damaging the military and other important networks of the enemy. The possibility of setting up such a structure however depends primarily on the development of the urban mass movement and the ability of the urban Party organisation to draw in and consolidate comrades with the required skills for such work.

REFERENCES

GENERAL

Amnesty International Report 2005; *amnesty.org*
Asian Development Bank, *adb.org*
awtw.org—A World to Win
Blazing Trail, CPI (ML) People's War
'CPI (M) Calls for Land Reforms,' *People's Democracy*, weekly organ of the Communist Party of India (Marxist), Vol XXIX, No. 35, 28 August 2005
cpimlnd.org—Communist Part of India (ML) New Democracy
cpiml.org—Communist Party of India (ML) Liberation
cpnm.org—Communist Party of Nepal (Maoist)
'Counterinsurgency Warfare—The Use and Abuse of Military Force,' Virendra Singh Jafa, *Faultlines, Vol 3*, Bulwark Books & The Institute of Conflict Management, November 1999
The Dancing Democracy, Prakash A. Raj, Rupa & Co, 2006
Deng Xiaoping and the Making of Modern China, Richard Evans, Penguin, 1995
Dreaming with BRICs: The Path to 2050, Goldman Sachs, 2003
Dust on the Road, Mahasweta Devi, Seagull Books, 2000
Business India Intelligence, Economist Intelligence Unit, Vol XIII No.7, 2006
Empowring the Poor—Community-based Environmental and Financial Management in Adilabad District; Emmanuel D'Silva, Urmila Pingle, Mark Poffenberger, Community Forest International, 2004
'Forms and sites of Untouchability: An Overview,' Grassroots, October

2006; Exceprts from *Untouchability in Rural India*, Ghanshyam Shah, Harsh Mander, Sukhadeo Thorat, Satish Deshpande, Amita Baviskar, Sage Publications

http://ambedkar.net

Human Development Report, Chhattisgarh, 2005

Human Development Report, Madhya Pradesh, 2002

Human Development Report, Maharashtra, 2002

'India's Nowhere Revolution: Riddles, Mysteries and Enigmas,' Ajay K. Mehra, *Mainstream*, Vol. XLIV, No. 34, 12 August 2006

In the Midst of Santals, Dhanpati Nag, Subarnarekha, 1987

krishnasenonline.org

Liberation, July 1971-January 1972. Selected Works of Charu Mazumdar, Marxists Internet Archive (2006)

Lok Sabha Questions, Lok Sabha Secretariat

'Manipur Protests—Rethinking the Armed Forces Special Powers Act,' K.R. Jawahar, *Sapra India Bulletin*, September 2004

Mao, the Guerilla Who Became a God, Time Inc, 1996

Maoist Revolution—Internet News Group

http://naxalrevolution.blogspot.com

http://naxalwatch.blogspot.com

Ministry of Home Affairs, Government of India (Annual Reports 2002-03; 2003-04; 2004-05; 2005-06; 2006-07); *http://mha.gov.in*

Ministry of Finance, Government of India (Economic Survey 2005-06; 2006-07)

Ministry of Finance, Government of Chhattisgarh (Economic Survey 2005-06)

Monarch vs Democracy, Baburam Bhattarai, Samkaleen Teesari Duniya, 2005

Naxalism—The Retreat of Civil Governnance, Ajai Sahni, *Faultlines*, Vol 5, Bulwark Books & The Institute of Conflict Management, May 2000

'Nepal's New Alliance: The Mainstream Parties and the Maoists,' International Crisis Group, *Asia Report N°106*, 28 November 2005

On the Paris Commune—Speeches, Documents and Atricles, K. Marx, F. Engels, Progress Publishers, 1976

'Peasant Movements in Contemporary India: Emerging Forms of Domination and Resistance,' Debal K. Singharoy, *Economic and Political Weekly*, 24 December 2005

Peoples War—Internet News Group

The Naxalites and their Ideology, Rabindra Ray, Oxford University Press, (Second Edition) 2002

'The Naxalite Movement in India,' Sumanto Banerjee, *Asia Media*

Rajya Sabha Questions, Rajya Sabha Secretariat

Sahas Gatha, P. Varavara Rao, Vani Prakashan, 2005

Smarana, C. Vanaja

Situation Assessment Survey of Farmers, Report No. 497/(59/33/5); Report No. 498/(59/33/1); Report No. 496/(59/33/3). National Sample Survey Organisation, Ministry of Statistics and Programme Implementation, Government of India, 2005

satp.org—South Asia Terrorism Portal

The Collected Works of Charu Mazumdar, Deshabrati Prakashani, [publishing house of the Undivided C.P.I. (M-L)], Charu Mazumdar Reference Archive, January, 2005

The Truth Unites—Essays in Tribute to Samar Sen, (Ed.) Ashok Mitra, Subarnarekha, 1985

'The Question of 'Going Too Far', Report on an investigation of the peasant movement in Hunan (*Selected Works of Mao Tse-tung*, The Maoist Documentation Project)

transparency.org—Transparency International

'Tryst with Destiny,' *The Argumentative Indian—Writings on Indian History, Culture and Identity*, Amartya Sen, Allen Lane, 2005

United Nations Development Fund, *undp.org*

Unicef, *unicef.org*

United Nations Population Fund, *unfpa.org*

Where The State Makes War On Its Own People: A report on violation of people's rights during the Salwa Judum campaign in Dantewada, Chattisgarh, People's Union for Civil Liberties; People's Union for Democractic Rights; Association for the Protection of Democratic Rights; Indian Association of People's Lawyers, April 2006.

World Food Programme, *wfp.org*

MEDIA

Aaj-Kaal

Aaj Tak

Amukh

Ananda Bazar Patrika

The Asian Age

Asia Media
Bartaman
CNN-IBN; *ibnlive.com*
Dainik Bhaskar
Deccan Chronicle
Deccan Herald
Down to Earth
DNA-Daily News & Analysis
Economic and Political Weekly
The Financial Express
Fortune
Frontline
Gomantak Times
Headlines Today
Himal Khabarpatrika
Himal South Asia
The Himalayan Times
The Hindu; *hinduonline.com*
Hindustan
Hindustan Times; *hindustantimes.com*
India Abroad News Service
ifj-asia.org
India Today; *indiatoday.com*
kantipuronline.com
The Kathmandu Post
Liberation—CPI (ML) Liberation monthly
ML Update—CPI (ML) Liberation weekly
Mumbai Mirror
NDTV
Nepali Times
The New York Times
Outlook
People's Democracy—CPI (Marxist)
People's March; *peoplesmarch.com* (server blocked);
http://peoplesmarch.googlepages.com
Prabhat Khabar
Press Trust of India
rediff.com
Reuters
The Statesman
Tehelka